Hard Times

STUDS TERKEL

HARD TIMES

An Oral History

of the Great Depression

PANTHEON BOOKS

A Division of Random House, New York

FOR
my wife, my son and my editor

NOTE

This being a book about Time as well as *a* time; for some the bell has tolled. Heroes and dragons of a long-gone day were old men, some vigorous, some weary, when I last saw them. Some have died.

See, I never heard that word "depression" before.
They would all just say hard times to me. It still is.

> Roger, a fourteen-year-old
> Appalachian boy, living in
> Chicago

A Depression might be interesting today. It could
really be something. To be on the bum, and have
nobody say: "Look, I'll give you $10,000 if you'd
just come back and go to school." We have a choice
today. What would it be like if we had no choice?

> Tom, 20

This I remember. Some people put this out of their
minds and forget it. I don't want to forget it. I don't
want it to take the best of me, but I want to be there
because it happened. This is the truth, you know.
History.

> Cesar Chavez

They loved us who had passed away.
They forgot all our errors. Our names were mixed.
    The story was long.
The young people danced. They brought down new
boughs for the flame. They said, Go on with the
story now. What happened next?
    For us there was silence. . . .

> Genevieve Taggard, 1940

ACKNOWLEDGMENTS

FRIENDS, acquaintances and, in astonishing number, strangers were gracious in offering suggestions. Without their hunches and tips, this work may not have been possible. Among these casual scouts: Richard Lamparski, Robert Cromie, Herman Kogan, Mike Royko, Lew Frank, Jr., Lucy Fairbank, Robert Sherrill, Phyllis Jackson, James Patton, Clifford and Virginia Durr, John Dierkes, Lou Gilbert, Phil McMartin, Sanka Bristow, Harry Bouras, King Solomon, Brendan McMahon, Earl Doty, Lou Abraham, Elizabeth Cooper, Jesse Prosten and Leon Beverly.

As in a previous work, *Division Street: America,* it was Cathy Zmuda, who did more than transcribe the hundreds of thousands of spoken words onto pages. She offered gratuitous editorial comments and thus provided me with a perspective that might otherwise have been missing.

My colleagues at radio station WFMT, notably Norm Pellegrini, Ray Nordstrand and Lois Baum, were remarkably understanding and ingenious during my leaves of absence. My daily programs, re-broadcasts, had an air of contemporaneity, thanks to them. My gratitude, too, to Jim Unrath for beyond-the-call-of-duty chores as my companion and chauffeur, during a memorable trip through Arkansas.

Especially am I grateful to my editor, André Schiffrin, whose idea this was. His insistence and quiet encouragement are evident in all these pages. And to his perceptive associates, Verne Moberg and Linda Faulhaber, for their bright-eyed look at what was becoming burdensome matter—a salute.

Contents

A Personal Memoir
(*and parenthetical comment*)

BOOK ONE

THE MARCH

THE SONG

SGT. PEPPER'S LONELY HEARTS CLUB BAND

HARD TRAVELIN'

THE BIG MONEY

MAN AND BOY

GOD BLESS' THE CHILD

BONNIE LABORING BOY

THREE STRIKES

BOOK TWO

OLD FAMILIES

BOOK THREE

CONCERNING THE NEW DEAL

BOOK FOUR

MERELY PASSING THROUGH

THREE O'CLOCK IN THE MORNING

A CABLE

BOOK FIVE

THE FINE AND LIVELY ARTS

PUBLIC SERVANT—THE CITY

EVICTIONS, ARRESTS AND OTHER RUNNING SORES

HONOR AND HUMILIATION

STRIVE AND SUCCEED

EPILOGUE

Hard Times

A Personal Memoir

(and parenthetical comment)

THIS IS *a memory book, rather than one of hard fact and precise statistic. In recalling an epoch, some thirty, forty years ago, my colleagues experienced pain, in some instances; exhilaration, in others. Often it was a fusing of both. A hesitancy, at first, was followed by a flow of memories: long-ago hurts and small triumphs. Honors and humiliations. There was laughter, too.*

Are they telling the truth? The question is as academic as the day Pilate asked it, his philosophy not quite washing out his guilt. It's the question Pa Joad asked of Preacher Casy, when the ragged man, in a transient camp, poured out his California agony.

"Pa said, 'S'pose he's tellin' the truth—that fella?' The preacher answered, 'He's tellin' the truth, awright. The truth for him. He wasn't makin' nothin' up.' 'How about us?' Tom demanded. 'Is that the truth for us?' 'I don' know,' said Casy."[1]

I suspect the preacher spoke for the people in this book, too. In their rememberings are their truths. The precise fact or the precise date is of small consequence. This is not a lawyer's brief nor an annotated sociological treatise. It is simply an attempt to get the story of the holocaust known as the Great Depression from an improvised battalion of survivors.

That there are some who were untouched or, indeed, did rather well

[1] John Steinbeck, *The Grapes of Wrath* (New York, Viking Press, 1939), p. 261.

isn't exactly news. This has been true of all disasters. The great many were wounded, in one manner or another. It left upon them an "invisible scar," as Caroline Bird put it.[2] *To those who have chosen to reveal it in this work, my gratitude. And to those hundred or so others, in scattered parts of this land, whose life-fragments I did not include, my apologies as well as my profound appreciation: they have enriched my own sense of this neglected time.*

There are young people in this book, too. They did not experience the Great Depression. In many instances, they are bewildered, wholly ignorant of it. It is no sign of their immaturity, but of ours. It's time they knew. And it's time we knew, too—what it did to us. And, thus, to them.

I myself don't remember the bleak October day, 1929. Nor do I recall with anything like a camera eye the events that shaped the Thirties. Rather, a blur of images comes to mind. Faces, voices and, occasionally, a rueful remembrance or a delightful flash. Or the astonishing innocence of a time past. Yet a feeling persists. . . .

Even now, when on the highway, seeing in faint neon, VACANCY, outside a modest motel, I am reminded of my mother's enterprise, The Wells-Grand. I ask myself, with unreasonable anxiety, perhaps, "Will it survive? Will this place be here next year?"

Fear of losing things, of property, is one legacy of the Thirties, as a young colleague pointed out. An elderly civil servant in Washington buys a piece of land as often as she can afford. "If it comes again, I'll have something to live off." She remembers the rotten bananas, near the wharves of New Orleans: her daily fare.

That, thanks to technology, things today can make things, in abundance, is a point psychically difficult for Depression survivors to understand. And thus, in severe cases, they will fight, even kill, to protect their things (read: property). Many of the young fail to diagnose this illness because of their innocence concerning the Great Depression. Its occasional invocation, for scolding purposes, tells them little of its truth.

In the mid-Twenties, all fifty rooms of The Wells-Grand were occupied. There was often a waiting list. Our guests were men of varied

[2] Caroline Bird, *The Invisible Scar* (New York, David McKay Co., 1965).

skills and some sense of permanence. The only transients were the wayward couple who couldn't afford a more de luxe rendezvous. Mysteriously, there was always room at the inn, even for sinners. Ours were the winking Gospels.

On Saturdays, most of our guests paid their weekly rent. On those evenings, I walked at a certain pace to the deposit window of the neighborhood bank. All the guests, with the exception of a few retired boomers and an ancient coppersmith (made idle by the Volstead Act), had steady jobs. It was a euphoric time.

The weekly magazines, *Judge* and *Life* (pre-Luce), were exciting with with George Jean Nathan and Pare Lorentz critiques and Jefferson Machamer girls. *Liberty* carried sports pieces by Westbrook Pegler—the most memorable, a tribute to Battling Siki, the childlike, noble savage destroyed by civilization. *Literary Digest* was still around and solvent, having not yet forecast Alf Landon's triumph some years later. On the high school debating team, we resolved that the United States should or should not grant independence to the Philippines, should or should not join the World Court, should or should not recognize the Soviet Union. We took either side. It was a casual time.

Perhaps it was the best of times. Or was it the worst? Scott Nearing inveighed against dollar diplomacy. Bob La Follette and George Norris took to the hustings as well as the Senate floor in Horatio-like stands against the Big Money. Yet two faces appear and reappear in my mind's eye: Vice Presidents Charles G. Dawes and Charles Curtis; the first, of the responsible banker's jaw, clamped determinedly to an underslung pipe; the other, a genial ex-jockey, of the Throttlebottom look. There was an innocence, perhaps. But it was not quite Eden's.

As for the Crash itself, there is nothing I personally remember, other than the gradual, at first, hardly noticeable, diminishing in the roster of our guests. It was as though they were carted away, unprotesting and unseen, unlike Edward Albee's grandma. At the entrance, we posted a placard: VACANCY.

The presence of our remaining guests was felt more and more, daily, in the lobby. Hitherto, we had seen them only evenings and on weekends. The decks of cards were wearing out more quickly. The black and red squares of the checkerboard were becoming indistinguishable. Cribbage pegs were being more frequently lost. . . . Tempers were getting shorter. Sudden fights broke out for seemingly unaccountable reasons.

The suddenly-idle hands blamed themselves, rather than society. True, there were hunger marches and protestations to City Hall and Washington, but the millions experienced a private kind of shame when the pink slip came. No matter that others suffered the same fate, the inner voice whispered, "I'm a failure."

True, there was a sharing among many of the dispossessed, but, at close quarters, frustration became, at times, violence, and violence turned inward. Thus, sons and fathers fell away, one from the other. And the mother, seeking work, said nothing. Outside forces, except to the more articulate and political rebels, were in some vague way responsible, but not really. It was a personal guilt.

We were carrying the regulars on the books, but the fate of others was daily debated as my mother, my brother and I scanned the more and more indecipherable ledger. At times, the issue was joined, with a great deal of heat, as my brother and I sought to convince our mother that somehow we and our guests shall overcome. In reply, her finger pointed to the undeniable scrawl: the debts were mounting.

With more frequency, we visited our landlord. (We had signed a long-term lease in happier days.) He was a turn-of-the-century man, who had no telephone and signed all his documents longhand. His was a bold and flowing penmanship. There was no mistaking the terms. His adjustments, in view of this strange turn of events, were eminently fair. A man of absolute certainties, who had voted the straight ticket from McKinley to Hoover, he seemed more at sea than I had imagined possible. I was astonished by his sudden fumbling, his bewilderment.

A highly respected Wall Street financier recalled: "The Street had general confusion. They didn't understand it any more than anybody else. They thought something would be announced." (My emphasis.) In 1930, Andrew Mellon, Secretary of Treasury, predicted, ". . . during the coming year the country will make steady progress." A speculator remembers, with awe, "Men like Pierpont Morgan and John Rockefeller lost immense amounts of money. Nobody was immune."

Carey McWilliams suggests a study of the Washington hearings dealing with the cause of the Depression: "They make the finest comic reading. The leading industrialists and bankers testified. They hadn't the foggiest notion. . . ."

As for our guests, who now half-occupied the hotel, many proffered relief checks as rent rather than the accustomed cash. It was no longer a high-spirited Saturday night moment.

There was less talk of the girls in the Orleans street cribs and a marked increase in daily drinking. There was, interestingly enough, an upswing in playing the horses: half dollar bets, six bits; a more desperate examination of *The Racing Form. Bert E. Collyer's Eye,* and a scratch sheet, passed from hand to hand. While lost blacks played the numbers, lost whites played the nags.

Of my three years at the University of Chicago Law School, little need be said. I remember hardly anything, other than the presence of one black in my class, an African prince, whose land was a British—or was it a French?—possession. Only one case do I remember: it concerned statutory rape. The fault lay not in the professors, who were good and learned men, but in my studied somnolence. Why, I don't know. Even to this day. Was it a feeling, without my being aware, at the time, of the irrelevance of standard procedure to the circumstances of the day? Or is this a rationalization, ex post facto, of a lazy student? It was a hard case all around.

Yet those years, '31 to '34, at the University, did lead to an education of sorts. On my way from The Wells-Grand to the campus, I traveled through the Black Belt. Was it to escape Torts and Real Property that I sought out the blues? I don't know.

I do know that in those gallimaufry shops I discovered treasures: "race records," they were called by men with dollar signs for eyes. The artists, Big Bill, Memphis Minnie, Tampa Red, Big Maceo, among those I remember, informed me there was more to the stuff of life—and Battling Siki and Senegal, for that matter—than even Westbrook Pegler imagined. Or my professors.

Survival. The marrow of the black man's blues, then and now, has been poverty. Though the articulated theme, the lyric, is often woman, fickle or constant, or the prowess of John the Conqueror, its felt truth is his "low-down" condition. "The Negro was born in depression," murmurs the elderly black. "If you can tell me the difference between the depression today and the Depression of 1932 for the black man, I'd like to know."

It accounts for the bite of his laughter, as he recalls those "hard times": "Why did these big wheels kill themselves? He couldn't stand bringing home beans to his woman, instead of steak and capon. It was a rarity to hear a Negro kill himself over money. There are so few who had any."

And yet, even during the Great Depression, when the white man was "lowdown," the black was below whatever that was. This hard fact was constantly sung around, about, under, and over in his blues.

> I'm just like Job's turkey,
> I can't do nothing but gobble,
> I'm so poor, baby,
> I have to lean against the fence to gabble.
> Yeah, now, baby, I believe I'll change town,
> Lord, I'm so low down, baby,
> I declare I'm looking up at down.
>
> The men in the mine, baby,
> They all looking down at me. . . .
>
> —Big Bill Broonzy

Here the images blur and time turns somersaults. It is the year of Repeal. A classmate and I appear at suddenly-legal taverns. A ritual, in the spirit of the day, comes into play: the house "pops" for every third beer.[3] It was so in all the taverns we visited. Today, it is a custom more honored in the breach than in the observance.

None I know was more rewarded by the triumph of the Wets than the coppersmith, old Heinicke. He had been the lobby elder, ill, hard of hearing, grown weary with life. Suddenly, his services were in desperate demand by any number of breweries. The shortage of skilled coppersmiths was in direct ratio to the unslaked thirst for beer.

As a result of the six-day week he was putting in, the unexpected harvest of money and, most significantly, the delight in his skills, he was transformed, Faustlike, into a younger man. His newly purchased, super-heterodyne radio set, in a baroque cabinet that occupied half his room, was heard loud and clear in all fifty quarters. Ascribe it to his exhilaration as much as to his deafness.

As for the others, political argument, often bitter, often hilarious, replaced desuetude. Aside from F.D.R.'s fireside chats, on Sundays a new voice dominated the lobby. It was Father Charles E. Coughlin, coming through the box radio, high on a wooden pedestal. There were

---

[3] It was "on the house."

8

those who muttered, "Turn the Roman off." But it was Matthew Mc-
Graw, our gaunt, bespectacled, fiery-eyed night clerk (his resemblance
to Father Coughlin was remarkable) who insisted the voice be heard.

Matt was something of an intellectual. Before the Crash, he had been
a master carpenter. He was constantly quoting from books, weeklies
and monthly radical journals. He inveighed against the moneyed interests, against the privileged, against monopoly. He quoted Debs, Dar-
row, Paine. . . . Somewhere between October, 1929, and November,
1934 (when the Union for Social Justice was formed), something had
happened to Matthew McGraw. A forgotten man, his cup of wormwood
had flowed over.

A printer remembers his father swinging from Bob La Follette, Wiscon-
sin's progressive Senator, to Father Coughlin. The hurt, frustrated man,
hearing of the powerful, alien East, sought an answer. So did the gentle,
soft-spoken salesman, who hardly questioned anything. "He has the
right idea," his daughter remembers him saying of the priest from Royal
Oak. The salesman had voted for Roosevelt.

As for my mother, most of her tight-fisted savings were lost with the
collapse of Samuel Insull's empire. My errands to the bank were for nothing, it seemed. It was a particularly bitter blow for her. She had previously out-jousted a neighborhood banker. R. L. Chisholm insisted on
the soundness of his institution—named, by some ironic God, The Re-
liance State Bank. Despite his oath on his mother's grave and his expressed admiration for *my* mother's thrift, she withdrew her several
thousand. His bank closed the following day. Yet, the utilities magnate
took her, a fact for which she forgave neither him nor herself.[4]

It was 1936. Having long abandoned any thoughts of following the
law, I joined the Illinois Writers' Project. I was a member of the radio
division. We wrote scripts inspired by paintings at the Art Institute.
They were broadcast over WGN, the Chicago *Tribune*'s station.
Colonel McCormick, the publisher, was quite proud of these contributions to the city's culture. Though the front page of his paper invariably featured a cartoon of a loony, subversive professor in cap and
gown, or a WPA boondoggler leaning on his shovel, he saw no incon-

[4] Subsequently, during Insull's trial in Chicago, "Little Orphan Annie," the
comic strip, was featuring the ordeal of Daddy Warbucks, the indomitable red-
head's benefactor. He, too, was being crucified by alien forces.

sistency in programming the Great Artists series, with credits: ". . . under the auspices of the Works Progress Administration, Harry Hopkins, Director." I am told he listened to them regularly, with a great deal of pleasure.

By chance, I became a gangster in radio soap operas, among them, "Ma Perkins," "Betty and Bob" and "First Nighter." The jobs were fairly frequent, but tenure was lacking. Cause of dismissal: Electrocution, life imprisonment, or being shot to death.

As the fervor of unionism spread, with an assist by the Wagner Act, the American Federation of Radio Artists was formed. There was hardly any dissent among the performers. There were, of course, obstinate executives, who played Canute, but the waves rolled over them. The climate, in this instance, was salubrious.

Not so, with other professional unions. The Newspaper Guild, for example. Perhaps my most vivid single memory—certainly my most traumatic—of the Thirties, with which I bring these impressions to a close, concerns this battle in Chicago. The Hearst morning newspaper, the *Herald-Examiner,* was suffering a long and critical strike. Outside the building, journalists picketed. The Hearst delivery trucks were manned by a hard lot; some I remembered as alumni of my high school; some with syndicate friendships. They were employed in a dual capacity: as delivery men and as terrorists. Whenever the situation presented itself, they'd slug a journalist-picket.

I see a tableau: a pale, bloodied reporter lying on the pavement as colleagues and passersby stare in horror. In the middle of the street stands a squat heavyweight, an auto jack in his grasp. His arms and legs are spread-eagled. He appears to be challenging all comers. Yet, I see, quite unblurred, the terror in his eyes.

The rest is history, which I leave to those whose less-flawed memories and reflections comprise this book.

BOOK ONE

The March

Jim Sheridan

It is a large hotel: a halfway house for its hundreds of guests, who are convalescing from nervous breakdowns. The benches near the entrance—and the lobby—are overflowing with the elderly and the young, engaged in highly animated conversations. On this summer's evening, it was certainly the most alive area in the neighborhood.

He is sixty-three years old.

THE SOLDIERS were walking the streets, the fellas who had fought for democracy in Germany. They thought they should get the bonus right then and there because they needed the money. A fella by the name of Waters, I think, got up the idea of these ex-soldiers would go to Washington, make the kind of trip the hoboes made with Coxey in 1898,[1] they would be able to get the government to come through.

D. C. Webb organized a group from Bughouse Square to go on this bonus march. Not having been in the army—I was too young for World War I and too old for World War II (laughs)—I was wondering if I would be a legitimate marcher. But the ten or fifteen other fellas were

[1] In 1894, Jacob S. Coxey led a march of unemployed into Washington. It failed in its purpose. The small size of the group led to the coinage of the derogatory phrase, "Coxey's Army."

all soldiers, and they thought it would be O.K. for me to go. Webb said, "Come along, you're a pretty good bum." (Laughs.)

We went down to the railyards and grabbed a freight train. Our first stop was in Peru, Indiana. We jungled up there for a little while, and then we bummed the town, so to speak. Go to different grocers and give them a tale of woe. They would give us sausage or bread or meat or canned goods. Then we'd go back to the railroad yards, the jungle, where we'd build a little fire and we'd cook it up in these cans. We'd sit around the fire and eat. . . .

Peru was the first division point outside of Chicago on the C & O.[2] We'd stop off and rest and scrounge up something to eat. We'd generally be told by the conductors the train was made up and ready to go out. Some of these fellas had come with their families. Can you imagine women and children riding boxcars?

The conductor'd want to find out how many guys were in the yard, so he would know how many empty boxcars to put onto the train. Of course, the railroad companies didn't know this, but these conductors, out of their sympathy, would put two or three empty boxcars in the train, so these bonus marchers could crawl into them and ride comfortable into Washington. Even the railroad detectives were very generous.

Sometimes there'd be fifty, sixty people in a boxcar. We'd just be sprawled out on the floor. The toilet . . . you had to hold it till you got a division point. (Laughs.) That's generally a hundred miles. You didn't carry food with you. You had to bum the town. It was beggary on a grand scale.

In one town, D. C. Webb got up on the bandstand and made a speech. We passed the hat, even, among the local citizenry. The money was used to buy cigarettes for the boys. Townspeople, they were very sympathetic.

There was none of this hatred you see now when strange people come to town, or strangers come to a neighborhood. They resent it, I don't know why. That's one of the things about the Depression. There was more camaraderie than there is now. Even more comradeship than the Commies could even dream about. That was one of the feelings that America lost. People had different ideas, they disagreed with one another. But there was a fine feeling among them. You were in trouble . . . damn it, if they could help ya, they would help ya.

[2] Chesapeake and Ohio Railway.

14

One incident stuck in my memory. We had reached a place in Virginia. It was a very hot day. In this jungle, there was a man, a very tall man. He had his wife with him and several small children. We invited them over to have something to eat with us, and they refused. Then I brought something over to them in an old pie plate. They still refused. It was the husband who told me that he didn't care for anything to eat. But see, the baby was crying from hunger.

Finally, me and some others went down to bum the center of the town. I remember going into a drugstore and bumming a baby bottle with a nipple. Now, can you imagine a guy bumming a baby bottle with a nipple? It took me a few guts to work it up. I explained the circumstances. Then I went and bummed the milk.

When I got back to the jungle camp, it was kinda dark. I first reported in to Captain Webb and then he kidded me about the baby bottle. "Christ," I said, "that baby there's gotta eat." And he said, "This afternoon you got pretty much of a rebuff." "Well," I said, "I'm gonna try again." So I went over and addressed myself to his wife. And I told her: here is the baby bottle. We had even warmed up the milk. But she looked at her husband, and her husband said he didn't want it.

What could I do about it, but just feel blue? I didn't look upon it as charity. It seemed to me that here was a fella's pride getting the best of him.

The tragedy came when the train was going through Virginia.

We had to go through these mountain countries. The smoke from the stacks of the engines, and the soot, would be flying back through the tunnels and would be coming into the boxcars. So in order to avoid getting choked, we'd close the boxcars and hold handkerchiefs over our noses. There was quite a discussion about this. What would happen to the little infant? We was afraid it would smother. The mother was holding the baby, but the baby seemed very still. The mother screamed. We didn't know what the scream was about. After we reached Washington, we found out that the baby had died going through the tunnels.

When the baby died, a feeling of sadness came over those in the boxcar. It seemed that they had lost one of their own.

When we got to Washington, there was quite a few ex-servicemen there before us. There was no arrangements for housing. Most of the men that had wives and children were living in Hooverville. This was across the Potomac River—what was known as Anacostia Flats. They had set up housing there, made of cardboard and of all kinds. I don't know how they managed to get their food. Most other contingents was along Pennsylvania Avenue.

They were tearing down a lot of buildings along that street, where they were going to do some renewal, build some federal buildings. A lot of ex-servicemen just sort of turned them into barracks. They just sorta bunked there. Garages that were vacant, they took over. Had no respect for private property. They didn't even ask permission of the owners. They didn't even know who the hell the owners was.

They had come to petition Hoover, to give them the bonus before it was due. And Hoover refused this. He told them they couldn't get it because it would make the country go broke. They would hold midnight vigils around the White House and march around the White House in shifts.

The question was now: How were they going to get them out of Washington? They were ordered out four or five times, and they refused. The police chief was called to send them out, but he[3] refused. I also heard that the marine commander, who was called to bring out the marines, also refused. Finally, the one they did get to shove these bedraggled ex-servicemen out of Washington was none other than the great MacArthur.

The picture I'll always remember . . . here is MacArthur coming down Pennsylvania Avenue. And, believe me, ladies and gentlemen, he came on a white horse. He was riding a white horse. Behind him were tanks, troops of the regular army.

This was really a riot that wasn't a riot, in a way. When these ex-soldiers wouldn't move, they'd poke them with their bayonets, and hit them on the head with the butt of a rifle. First, they had a hell of a time getting them out of the buildings they were in. Like a sit-in.

They managed to get them out. A big colored soldier, about six feet tall, had a big American flag he was carrying. He was one of the bonus marchers. He turned to one of the soldiers who was pushing him along, saying: "Get along there, you big black bastard." That was it. He turned and said, "Don't try to push me. I fought for this flag. I fought for this flag in France and I'm gonna fight for it here on Pennsylvania Avenue." The soldier hit him on the side of the legs with the bayonet. I think he was injured. But I don't know if he was sent to the hospital.

This was the beginning of a riot, in a way. These soldiers were pushing

[3] General Pelham D. Glassford.

these people. They didn't want to move, but they were pushing them anyway.

As night fell, they crossed the Potomac. They were given orders to get out of Anacostia Flats, and they refused. The soldiers set those shanties on fire. They were practically smoked out. I saw it from a distance. I could see the pandemonium. The fires were something like the fires you see nowadays that are started in these ghettoes. But they weren't started by the people that live there.

The soldiers threw tear gas at them and vomiting gas. It was one assignment they reluctantly took on. They were younger than the marchers. It was like sons attacking their fathers. The next day the newspapers deplored the fact and so forth, but they realized the necessity of getting these men off. Because they were causing a health hazard to the city. MacArthur was looked upon as a hero.[4]

And so the bonus marchers straggled back to the various places they came from. And without their bonus.

POSTSCRIPT: *"After the Bonus March, I bummed my way to New York. I couldn't get on relief there because I wasn't a resident. So I resorted to one of the oldest professions—that is, begging. I became a professional panhandler. I had quite a few steady clients. One of them was Heywood Broun. Every time I put the bite on him, he'd say, "For Chrissake, don't you know any other guy in the city beside me?"* (*Laughs.*)

A. Everette McIntyre

Federal Trade Commissioner.

ON A PARTICULAR MORNING—I believe this was on the twenty-sixth or twenty-seventh of June, 1932—the police blocked the avenue and turned the marchers back. The bonus men had undertaken to march around the White House. The President didn't like that. A lot of other people didn't

---

[4] He was aided by General George Patton and Major Dwight Eisenhower. "Thank God," said President Hoover, "we still have a government that knows how to deal with a mob."

like it, either, because they were clogging up Pennsylvania Avenue, in the busy part of the day.

About five thousand of the bonus marchers and their families were camping in some of the demolished buildings. The police encircled them. There was some brick-throwing. A couple of the police retaliated by firing. A bonus man was killed and another seriously wounded.

During lunch time, the following day, I heard some army commands. To my right, down by the ellipse toward the monument, military units were being formed. It looked like trouble. We didn't have long to wait.

A squadron of cavalry was in front of this army column. Then, some staff cars, and four trucks with baby tanks on them, stopped near this camp. They let the ramps down and the baby tanks rolled out into the street. When the army appeared, the bonus people, who were in these old buildings, started beating on tin pans and shouted: "Here come our buddies." They expected the army to be in sympathy with them.

One of these staff cars unloaded—not very far from where I was standing—and out of it came MacArthur, Chief of Staff. He had a youngish major as an aide. His name was Dwight Eisenhower. With their hands on their hips, they surveyed the situation.

The 12th Infantry was in full battle dress. Each had a gas mask and his belt was full of tear gas bombs. They were given a "right face," which caused them to face the camp. They fixed their bayonets and also fixed the gas masks over their faces. At orders, they brought their bayonets at thrust and moved in. The bayonets were used to jab people, to make them move.

Soon, almost everybody disappeared from view, because tear gas bombs exploded. The entire block was covered by tear gas. Flames were coming up, where the soldiers had set fire to the buildings to drive these people out. The infantry was apparently under orders to drive this group toward the bridges, across the Potomac. Through the whole afternoon, they took one camp after another.

My colleagues and I decided that the army would assault the camp in Anacostia Flats, across the river. There were about twenty thousand to forty thousand bonus people there. We went on the roof of a building and watched what occurred there that evening. It happened after dark.

The 12th Infantry did march across the bridge, in full battle dress as before. This was quite a sight. We could see the fires. Soon, all the occupants of that camp were driven into the Maryland Woods, into the night.

The next day, I read accounts of some of the people who had been jabbed with bayonets. Some had been injured seriously. People who had raised their arms had their arms cut by some sabres. Others were hit by the flat of the sword. In some instances, ears were cut off. . . .

Edward C. Schalk

A veteran of World War I.

WHEN THE ARMY came out, what else could they do? They just walked off, like good Spartans would do.

I remember when they come back from Washington. They landed over here on State Street. They had sort of a reunion. It was nice weather, summertime. And all kinds of people came to visit 'em. They had a flag spread out, and everyone was throwin' money in—quarter, half a dollar. Showin' that they were welcomin' 'em back and were all for 'em. They had quite a time. After that, where they went, nobody knows.

The Song

Once in khaki suits,
Gee, we looked swell,
Full of that Yankee Doodle-de-dum.
Half a million boots went sloggin' through Hell,
I was the kid with the drum.
Say, don't you remember, they called me Al—
It was Al all the time.
Say, don't you remember I'm your pal—
Brother, can you spare a dime.[1]

E. Y. (Yip) Harburg

Song lyricist and writer of light verse. Among the works in which his lyrics were sung are: Finian's Rainbow, The Bloomer Girl, Jamaica, The Wizard of Oz *and* Earl Carroll's Vanities.

[1] "Brother, Can You Spare a Dime?" words by E. Y. Harburg, music by Jay Gorney. Copyright 1932 by Harms, Inc. Used by permission of Warner Bros.–Seven Arts Music. All rights reserved.

I NEVER LIKED the idea of living on scallions in a left bank garret. I like writing in comfort. So I went into business, a classmate and I. I thought I'd retire in a year or two. And a thing called Collapse, bango! socked everything out. 1929. All I had left was a pencil.

Luckily, I had a friend named Ira Gershwin, and he said to me, "You've got your pencil. Get your rhyming dictionary and go to work." I did. There was nothing else to do. I was doing light verse at the time, writing a poem here and there for ten bucks a crack. It was an era when kids at college were interested in light verse and ballads and sonnets. This is the early Thirties.

I was relieved when the Crash came. I was released. Being in business was something I detested. When I found that I could sell a song or a poem, I became me, I became alive. Other people didn't see it that way. They were throwing themselves out of windows.

Someone who lost money found that his life was gone. When I lost my possessions, I found my creativity. I felt I was being born for the first time. So for me the world became beautiful.

With the Crash, I realized that the greatest fantasy of all was business. The only realistic way of making a living was versifying. Living off your imagination.

We thought American business was the Rock of Gibraltar. We were the prosperous nation, and nothing could stop us now. A brownstone house was forever. You gave it to your kids and they put marble fronts on it. There was a feeling of continuity. If you made it, it was there forever. Suddenly the big dream exploded. The impact was unbelievable.

I was walking along the street at that time, and you'd see the bread lines. The biggest one in New York City was owned by William Randolph Hearst. He had a big truck with several people on it, and big cauldrons of hot soup, bread. Fellows with burlap on their shoes were lined up all around Columbus Circle, and went for blocks and blocks around the park, waiting.

There was a skit in one of the first shows I did, *Americana*. This was 1930. In the sketch, Mrs. Ogden Reid of the *Herald Tribune* was very jealous of Hearst's beautiful bread line. It was bigger than her bread line. It was a satiric, volatile show. We needed a song for it.

On stage, we had men in old soldiers' uniforms, dilapidated, waiting around. And then into the song. We had to have a title. And how do you do a song so it isn't maudlin? Not to say: my wife is sick, I've got six children, the Crash put me out of business, hand me a dime. I hate songs of that kind. I hate songs that are on the nose. I don't like songs that describe a historic moment pitifully.

The prevailing greeting at that time, on every block you passed, by some poor guy coming up, was: "Can you spare a dime?" Or: "Can you spare something for a cup of coffee?" . . . "Brother, Can You Spare a Dime?" finally hit on every block, on every street. I thought that could be a beautiful title. If I could only work it out by telling people, through the song, it isn't just a man asking for a dime.

This is the man who says: I built the railroads. I built that tower. I fought your wars. I was the kid with the drum. Why the hell should I be standing in line now? What happened to all this wealth I created?

I think that's what made the song. Of course, together with the idea and meaning, a song must have poetry. It must have the phrase that rings a bell. The art of song writing is a craft. Yet, "Brother, Can You Spare a Dime?" opens up a political question. Why should this man be penniless at any time in his life, due to some fantastic thing called a Depression or sickness or whatever it is that makes him so insecure?

In the song the man is really saying: I made an investment in this country. Where the hell are my dividends? Is it a dividend to say: "Can you spare a dime?" What the hell is wrong? Let's examine this thing. It's more than just a bit of pathos. It doesn't reduce him to a beggar. It makes him a dignified human, asking questions—and a bit outraged, too, as he should be.

Everybody picked the song up in '30 and '31. Bands were playing it and records were made. When Roosevelt was a candidate for President, the Republicans got pretty worried about it. Some of the network radio people were told to lay low on the song. In some cases, they tried to ban it from the air. But it was too late. The song had already done its damage.

Sgt. Pepper's Lonely Hearts Club Band

It was twenty years ago today,
Sgt. Pepper taught the band to play
They've been going in and out of style
But they're guaranteed to raise a smile.
            —John Lennon and Paul McCartney[1]

Lily, Roy and Bucky

Lily is eighteen. Her brother, Roy, is sixteen. Bucky is seventeen. They are of lower middle-class families.

LILY: My grandmother'd tell us things about the Depression. You can read about it, too. What they tell us is different than what you read.
ROY: They're always tellin' us that we should be glad we got food and all that, 'cause back in the Thirties they used to tell us people were starving and got no jobs and all that stuff.
LILY: The food lines they told us about.

Roy: Yeah, you had to stay in line and wait for food.

Lily: And everything. You got when it was there. If it wasn't, then you made without it. She said there was a lot of waiting.

Bucky: I never had a Depression, so it don't bother me really.

Roy: From what you hear, you'd hate to live in that time.

Bucky: Well, I ain't livin' in that time.

Roy: We really don't know what it would be like. It seems like a long time ago.

Lily: There's a time I remember bein' hungry. Livin' away from home. I didn't have anybody to depend on. (Indicates the others.) But they didn't leave home. They stay home where it's at.

Roy: Like little things when you're home: where's the butter? There's no butter, you go out and buy it. But like them people: where's the butter? No butter, you gotta wait till you get the butter.

Lily: Maybe it was margarine.

Roy: Now you just walk into your house and sit down, turn on the TV, walk out into the kitchen, get a glass of milk or somethin', watch a football game, baseball game for a few hours. They couldn't do that. If they were hungry and there was nothin' there, they'd just have to wait.

Bucky: When my parents talk: you should be glad and happy that we got all this now. The clothes you're wearin', the food we eat and all that stuff.

Lily: They used to tell us about this one silver dollar that they had. Whenever they ran out, it was this silver dollar they used to take down to the little shop on the corner and get a dollar's worth of food. They'd give the silver dollar. The guy'd hold it for 'em and when they got a dollar of currency, they could take it in and get their silver dollar back.

I think we'd hurt more now if we had a Depression. You don't see how they'd make it if it happened to 'em again. Because they take a lot of things for granted. I mean, you see 'em now and they have everything. You can't imagine how they would act if they didn't have it. If they would even remember what they did. 'Cause they're past it now. They already done it, and they figure they're over it. If we fell now, I think everybody would take it a lot harder.

Everybody'd step on each other. They'd just walk all over and kill each other. They got more than they ever need that they'd just step on anybody to keep it. They got cars, they got houses, they got this and that. It's more than they need, but they *think* they need it, so they want to keep it. Human life isn't as important as what they got.

Diane

A twenty-seven-year-old journalist.

EVERY TIME I've encountered the Depression, it has been used as a barrier and a club. It's been a counter-communication. Older people use it to explain to me that I can't understand *anything:* I didn't live through the Depression. They never say to me: We can't understand you because we didn't live through the leisure society. All attempts at communication are totally blocked. All of a sudden there's a generation gap. It's a frightening thing.

What they're saying is: For twenty years I've starved and I've worked hard. You must fight. It's very Calvinistic. Work, suffer, have twenty lashes a day, and you can have a bowl of bean soup.

I've never understood a society of want. We don't have a society of want—not on a general level. We have a society of total surplus: unwanted goods and unwanted people.

The society I was raised in . . . you got into a car and you were driven to a high school, where you didn't do a lot of work and you got A's. I thought white gloves was the total protection. It was the ultimate armor.

To me, the Depression is old newsreels and the term, "soup line," and *Grapes of Wrath* with Henry Fonda looking sincere and downcast. I can identify with the Industrial Revolution sooner than I can with the Depression, because that was an instance of men being thrown out of work by things beyond their control.

I never could understand why the Depression occurred. Perhaps that's why I've not been as sympathetic as I'm expected to be. You're supposed to admire them because they've been in the "Flaring Twenties" —is that what it was called?[2]—where they danced a lot and drank gin in automobiles, hail F. Scott Fitzgerald! The connection is not made economically, but socially.

2 "The Roaring Twenties."

25

It runs from the morally errant generation of the Twenties, with the too-short skirts and the bathtub gin, the rise of the stock market and bad poetry. It's all confused in my mind. Prohibition comes in somewhere. I'm not quite certain whether it preceded or came after the Depression. And then there's Al Capone and people on film in wonderfully wide-shouldered suits, with machine guns, gunning down other people. It's an incredible, historical jungle. It's cinematically very mixed up, terribly fluid.

Andy, 19

WHEN I WAS at Cornell, a documentary film group showed *The River,* the Pare Lorentz thing, a fantastic movie.[3] So much of it is this sentimental, renaissance-type feeling, which they got out of the TVA, which I'm sure sprung up out of the Depression, sort of regeneration and so on. The poem that Lorentz wrote, with all the names of the rivers, so, so derivative, but sort of nice when you listen to it—the great thing about the river.

And people were *laughing,* all through the movie. Laughing at all the corny lines. I was so horrified. It sort of hurt me. I said to the faculty guy, "What's the matter with these people?" He said, "It doesn't mean anything to them." So, I suppose that's the way it goes. . . .

Michael, 19

WHAT DOES the Depression mean to me? I don't know. I'm not depressed. I can pot out any time I want. A Depression is to me when I

---

[3] It was produced under the auspices of the Farm Security Administration (FSA) in the late Thirties. (See C. B. Baldwin in the sequence "Concerning the New Deal.")

can't sit down on my chaise lounge and have a beer and this boob tube right in my face.

Tad, 20

IT'S SOMETHING that has been filtered through by my parents. I didn't know much about it, and they don't mind my not knowing much about it. They control the source of information—sort of like the high priest: you can't approach the altar too closely, or you'll be struck dead. This purple heart in their background has become a justification for their present affluence. If we got the idea they didn't have it so bad, they'd have less psychological control over us. That's why they don't approve of the hippies. These people are saying: our parents told us it was this way. Now we're doin' it, and it's not so bad. Our parents don't like that. They want to keep it a secret. They try to control the information that filters down to us. They're screwed up and they don't want people to find out about it.

They say, "You have it soft now." The point is, *they* have it soft now. They sort of feel guilty about it. If they make other people feel guilty about it, it won't be so noticeable in their own instance.

Nancy, 21

MONEY is one of my father's big values. He wishes he was a millionaire. I don't think of money in that way. I think of it as a sideline, as something you have to have. But I don't think day and night about it. . . .

Marshall and Steve

Marshall is twenty-three. Steve is twenty-one. They had both attended college. One edits a syndicated service for underground newspapers. The other manages a coffeehouse.

MARSHALL: I never really thought much about the Depression until last year when I was at Resurrection City. I guess the first time there was a march of the poor, soldiers cleared the people off and there was a lot of fighting. The Depression is something I don't think about. I guess I should. It's been no part of my experience.

STEVE: It means something very personal to me. My mother graduated high school when she was young and had a chance to go to college. But she had to go to work, her parents were starving. Her life since has been one unremitting struggle to make do. I think of dreams people had, they were forced to give up in order to stay in American society. To make a buck. Like my mother did. Crushed hope.

It gets across to me that there were a great many Americans who were ashamed of the Depression. I remember the McCarthy period. People were recanting what they had done during the Depression. And publicly proving they were ashamed of what they had done.

MARSHALL: The Depression is an embarrassing thing. It is a shame to the system: the American Way that seemed so successful. All of a sudden, things broke down and didn't work. It's a difficult thing to understand today. To imagine this system, all of a sudden—for reasons having to do with paper, money, abstract things—breaking down.

In a lot of young people's minds today, it's proof of the irrationality of this kind of economic system. After all, there were all those factories, and all those people who wanted to work. There was the equipment. Yet nothing was being worked. Today, if we had great storehouses of grain, if they wouldn't be opened up immediately to feed people who are starving, people would take guns and see that they were opened up. People are not imprisoned by the idea that you don't have a right to food. Why should people starve to death when there is food?

STEVE: Many times, young people are told idealism is fine for youth, but there comes a point when one must face up to the realities of existence. That lesson was learned during the Depression. At least by my parents. They were forced to give up their idealism, forced to face the hard realities of making a buck to stay alive. This lesson was so hard learned, they felt it necessary to transmit it to us. These experiences have come to me second hand. I see its effects.

I repudiate it. I have repudiated the kind of life my parents were forced into. I repudiate the lessons that they seem to have learned.

MARSHALL: The issue between the generations is what is known as value. The value of the dollar. What it means to your generation is blood, sweat and tears . . . what you had to do to make a buck.

When a group of young people burnt money at the stock exchange and threw the bills down from the balcony, it caused pandemonium. There was a scramble for the dollar bills on the floor of the exchange. They were trying to say something about the value of money. A Vietnamese person can be burned with napalm. Animals are slaughtered. But a dollar is sacred. A dollar is not to be burned. In fact, it's a federal crime. This worship of the dollar is inherently an alienated idea. The people who killed themselves in 1929 were victims of it.

STEVE: Our quality of life, character and tone since the Thirties has been determined by the Depression: the buck is almighty. Which side are you on? Most people—and that includes the young—would choose the buck.

Can you re-create—at least in your imaginations—the tone of the Great Depression?

MARSHALL: Fear. It unsettled the securities, apparently false securities that people had. People haven't felt unfearful since. Fear of Communists, fear of people living in sin, fear of the hippies—fear, fear, fear. I think people learned it from the Depression.

Money brings security, that was the idea. But it turned out to be just the opposite. If you have a great big house, that meant you had to be fearful again: somebody might rob you. If you had a great big store, you had to be fearful now that there's gonna be a riot—and everything in your store would be stolen. See, money brings more fear than security.

STEVE: Fear is an emotion people don't talk about. But it's one they reflect in their lives. My parents have managed to overcome a good deal of it. When I resisted the draft, they were with me every step of the way. But at the beginning, when I was joining the demonstrations, they were afraid my father would lose his job. Fear was so obvious you could taste it. That you were going to do something which might wreck your chance of achieving the economic success they never had. I can't imagine that fear without the Depression. It shaped their lives and consciences.

I got the feeling it was a time of utter chaos, in which there were no road signs. The moral and social guideposts had been wiped out. Why wasn't there more violence in that period? What shape did that violence take? What happened? Was it government pump-priming or was it the Second World War that pulled us out of the Depression? I don't know enough of this period from the cold, printed page.

POSTSCRIPT: *Marshall committed suicide, November 1, 1969.*

Hard Travelin'

I've been doin' some hard travelin',
I thought you knowd
I've been doin' some hard ramblin'
Away down the road. . . .

. . . I've been layin' in a hard rock jail,
I thought you knowd
I've been laid out ninety days
Way down the road.
The darned old judge, he said to me,
It's ninety days for vagrancy,
And I've been doin' some hard travelin', Lord.
                                        —Woody Guthrie[1]

Ed Paulsen

From 1926 on, when he was fourteen, he, himself, knocked around and
about the states—"I rode the freights" across the land. "I always went

[1] Words and Music by Woody Guthrie TRO–© Copyright 1959, 1963 by Ludlow Music, Inc. New York, N.Y. Used by permission.

back to my home in South Dakota. My sister and her husband had a little farm. It was a retreat. I played semi-pro baseball up there at one time. You know who I faced? Satchell Paige. He was pitching for Bismarck. I worked punching cattle, $10 a month. I was never satisfied to stay there. I was always taking a pop at L.A. or San Francisco.

"Everybody talks of the Crash of '29. In small towns out West, we didn't know there was a Crash. What did the stock market mean to us? Not a dang thing. If you were in Cut Bank, Montana, who owned stock? The farmer was a ping-pong ball in a very tough game.

"I finished high school in 1930, and I walked out into this thing. . . ." He picked apples in Washington, "hustled sheets" in Los Angeles, and worked on road gangs all along the coast. "It got tougher. We didn't know how to make out in the city. It was terrifying. There were great queues of guys in soup lines. We didn't know how to join a soup line. We—my two brothers and I—didn't see ourselves that way. We had middle-class ideas without a middle-class income. (Laughs.)

"We ended up in San Francisco in 1931. I tried to get a job on the docks. I was a big husky athlete, but there just wasn't any work. Already by that time, if you were looking for a job at a Standard Oil Service Station, you had to have a college degree. It was that kind of market. . . ."

I'D GET UP at five in the morning and head for the waterfront. Outside the Spreckles Sugar Refinery, outside the gates, there would be a thousand men. You know dang well there's only three or four jobs. The guy would come out with two little Pinkerton cops: "I need two guys for the bull gang. Two guys to go into the hole." A thousand men would fight like a pack of Alaskan dogs to get through there. Only four of us would get through. I was too young a punk.

So you'd drift up to Skid Row. There'd be thousands of men there. Guys on baskets, making weird speeches, phony theories on economics. About eleven-thirty, the real leaders would take over. They'd say: O.K., we're going to City Hall. The Mayor was Angelo Rossi, a dapper little guy. He wore expensive boots and a tight vest. We'd shout around the steps. Finally, he'd come out and tell us nothing.

I remember the demands: We demand work, we demand shelter for our families, we demand groceries, this kind of thing. . . . Half the guys up there making the demands were Negroes. Now there wasn't a big black colony in San Francisco in those days. But they were pretty cagey, the leaders—they always kept a mixture of black and white.

I remember as a kid how courageous this seemed to me, the demands, because you knew that society wasn't going to give it to you. They'd demand that they open up unrented houses and give decent shelters for their families.[2] But you just knew society wasn't yielding. There was nothing coming.

This parade would be four blocks long, curb to curb. Nobody had a dime. There were guys on the corner trying to sell apples to this moneyless wonder. (Laughs.)

The guys'd start to yell and there come some horses. They used to have cops on horseback in those days. Then there'd be some fighting. Finally it got to killing. I think they killed three people there that day, besides the wounded. It really got rough because the guys had brought a bunch of marbles and threw them on the street, and the horses were slipping and sliding around. This made the cops mad and they got rough.

There'd be this kind of futile struggle, because somehow you never expected to win. We had a built-in losing complex. That's the way those crowds felt. A lot of them would drift back into the Sally.[3] By now it's one o'clock, and everybody's hungry. We were a gentle crowd. These were fathers, eighty percent of them. They had held jobs and didn't want to kick society to pieces. They just wanted to go to work and they just couldn't understand. There was a mysterious thing. You watched the papers, you listened to rumors, you'd get word somebody's gonna build a building.

So the next morning you get up at five o'clock and you dash over there. You got a big tip. There's three thousand men there, carpenters, cement men, guys who knew machinery and everything else. These fellas always had faith that the job was gonna mature, somehow. More and more men were after fewer and fewer jobs. So San Francisco just ground to a halt. Nothing was moving.

We were always trying to get to sea, but I didn't have any ticket. Oh, I made that waterfront a thousand times. There used to be those great old liners that sailed out to Hawaii. You could hear the band play "Aloha Away," and all the guys were standing there with tears in their

---

[2] "Thirteen public aid families squatted in a vacant building . . . they defied the police to evict them. Most were victims of a recent fire. The others decided to abandon their sub-standard housing in favor of the three-story building. . . . 'Man, we're going to stake out those apartments just like the early settlers when they took it away from the Indians,' announced Mrs. Pearl Moore, a Tenants' Union representative." (Chicago *Daily News*, February 21, 1969).

[3] The Salvation Army.

eyes. As though you had somebody going some place. And you didn't know a damn soul. (Laughs.)

We weren't greatly agitated in terms of society. Ours was a bewilderment, not an anger. Not a sense of being particularly put upon. We weren't talking revolution; we were talking jobs.

We'd grown up in small-town high schools. There wasn't much expression, in the press, of the intelligentsia. It was just a tough world, and you had been born into it. I had no great sense of fervor until I went to L.A. and ran into Upton Sinclair in 1934. If I were picking a time when I began to say, "What the hell's this all about?" it came when I wandered into a meeting one day where Upton Sinclair was talking.[4] This was the winter of '33, '34. There was this little pink-and-white guy up there speaking, the least likely guy ever to be a radical you ever saw. You automatically think of pince-nez glasses and a shock of white hair. His audience was made up mostly of working stiffs.

He pointed out the great piles of oranges, the piles of lumber laying there idle. . . . They'd put up a rick of oranges and apples, put gasoline over it and set fire to them. Vegetables were being destroyed and everything. Everybody who cried so much later about federal programs destroying little pigs . . . they should have seen what industry was doing at this time. To keep the price up.

Sinclair's idea was to relate the unemployed to the resources not being used. This appealed to me tremendously. It made sense to have this food eaten up by hungry people. I got a job singing with the quartet that was campaigning with him.

If I had to pick one constant enemy during this time, it was the American Legion. They were made up of home guard types. They were the most vicious enemies of this drifting, reckless, hungry crowd of people. Every place I went, Hoovervilles—they were raided. This bunch of Legionnaires with those damn caps on. Guys with baseball bats, driving them out of the jungles around the railroad grounds. Even in the little towns I lived in. I had a war with those guys by the time I was in high school. They were always the bane of my existence.

They were the Main Streeters. They were doing all right. Merchants, storekeepers, landowners. They had a fix that was just awful to live with. They were hard on the little candidate for Governor. They'd come to his meetings with baseball bats and clubs and break it up. Once,

---

[4] He was candidate for Governor of California. EPIC was his symbol and credo: End Poverty in California.

when we sang in the Valley, they attacked us and beat the hell out of us. We barely got out of there.

During the Sinclair campaign, I was going to the library, picking up books I'd never read before, books that never crossed my track. You'd go down to look for work in the morning, and then you'd give up at eleven o'clock and drift into that library. I got my education there, really.

By this time, Roosevelt was President. There was the NRA . . . mystical things were going on we didn't understand at all. People were talking price-fixing and what have you. Very, very weird world. It didn't mean a damn to us. There were three brothers of us, we got a freight and went down to Portland. They'd started to work on the Bonneville Dam. Beautiful sight down that river. On a decent day, if you set on top of a boxcar, it was beautiful. . . .

We drifted down to the jungle. We go into a beanery, 'cause there was no train out till eleven that night. In comes a Mexican whore and a colored whore. They order a hamburger. The proprietor says, "I don't serve niggers. Get that dame out of here." The Mexican girl comes back and orders two hamburgers. The guy grumbles, fries up a couple. The colored girl walks in. This guy goes under the counter and comes up with a sap.[5] He lashes out at the girl's head, bong! Jeez, I think he's killed her. She groans and staggers back off this stool. He cuts around the corner in a wild rage. I put my foot out and trip him. He just went ass over Tecumseh. The girls get out in time. He'd a killed that girl, I believe. We lam out of there, too. We grab the midnight freight and get off at Phoenix. It's a hostile town, so we beat it.

We make an orange freight. We rode in the reefer.[6] Clear to Kansas City. It goes like a bat out of hell, a rough ride. We broke through the wire netting and ate the oranges. We got vitamins like mad. (Laughs.) But your mouth gets burnt by that acid juice and your teeth get so damn sore from that ride. By the time we got off at K.C., I could hardly close my mouth.

We catch a train into Kansas City, Kansas, that night. At the stops, colored people were gettin' on the trains and throwin' off coal. You could see people gatherin' the coal. You could see the railroad dicks were gettin' tough.

[5] A blackjack.
[6] The refrigerator car.

Hal and I are ridin' on the top of the boxcar, it's a fairly nice night. All of a sudden, there's a railroad dick with a flashlight that reaches a thousand miles. Bam! Bam! He starts shooting. We hear the bullets hitting the cars, bam! like that. I throw my hands up and start walking towards that light. Hal's behind me. The guy says, "Get off." I said, "Christ, I can't." This thing's rollin' fifty miles an hour or more. He says, "Jump." I says, "I can't." He says, "Turn around and march ahead." He marches us over the top. There's a gondola, about eight feet down. He says, "Jump." So I jumped and landed in wet sand, up to my knees.

We come to a little town in Nebraska, Beatrice. It's morning. I'm chilled to the bone. We crawl into a railroad sandbox, almost frozen to death. We dry out, get warmed up, and make the train again. We pull into Omaha. It's night. All of a sudden, the train is surrounded by deputies, with pistols. The guy says, "Get in those trucks." I said, "What for? We haven't done anything." He said, "You're not going to jail. You're going to the Transient Camp."

They drive us up to an old army warehouse. They check you in, take off your clothes, run them through a de-louser, and you take a bath. It's midnight. We come out, and here's a spread with scrambled eggs, bacon, bread, coffee and toast. We ate a great meal. It was wonderful. We go upstairs to bed. Here's a double-decker, sheets, toothbrush, towels, everything. I sat down on this damn bed, I can't tell you, full of wonderment. We thought we'd gone to heaven. Hal's a young punk, he's seventeen. He said, "What the hell kind of a place is this?" I said, "I don't know, but it's sure somethin' different."

The next morning, they called us up to a social worker. By this time, there's a thousand guys in there. They're playing baseball, some guys are washing down walls—bums, bindlestiffs, cynical rough guys who've been on the road for years. It's kind of like a playhouse. It's unbelievable.

Through a social worker, he is assigned to a job with the National Youth Administration, at "a little cold-water college" in Aberdeen, South Dakota. "And then the good life began for me.

"Before Roosevelt, the Federal Government hardly touched your life. Outside of the postmaster, there was little local representation. Now people you knew were appointed to government jobs. Joe Blow or some guy from the corner.

"It came right down to Main Street. Half of them loved it, half of them hated it. There was the immediacy of its effect on you. In Aberdeen, Main Street was against it. But they were delighted to have those green relief checks cashed in their cash registers. They'd have been out of business had it not been for them. It was a split thing. They were cursing Roosevelt for the intrusion into their lives. At the same time, they were living off it. Main Street still has this fix."

The NYA was my salvation. I could just as easily have been in Sing Sing as with the UN.[7] Just every bit a chance. Hell, yes. Everybody was a criminal. You stole, you cheated through. You were getting by, survival. Stole clothes off lines, stole milk off back porches, you stole bread. I remember going through Tucumcari, New Mexico, on a freight. We made a brief stop. There was a grocery store, a supermarket kind of thing for those days. I beat it off the train and came back with rolls and crackers. This guy is standing in the window shaking his fist at you.

It wasn't a big thing, but it created a coyote mentality. You were a predator. You had to be. The coyote is crafty. He can be fantastically courageous and a coward at the same time. He'll run, but when he's cornered, he'll fight. I grew up where they were hated, 'cause they'd kill sheep. They'll kill a calf, get in the chicken pen. They're mean. But how else does a coyote stay alive? He's not as powerful as a wolf. He has a small body. He's in such bad condition, a dog can run him down. He's not like a fox. A coyote is nature's victim as well as man's. We were coyotes in the Thirties, the jobless.

No, I don't see the Depression as an ennobling experience. Survivors are still ridin' with the ghost—the ghost of those days when things came hard.

[7] He has an administrative job with UNICEF.

Pauline Kael

Film critic, The New Yorker.

THE FIRST VIOLENCE I had ever seen was along the Embarcadero. The anger of the men. I never saw it again until recently in Philadelphia— between cops and little Negro kids.

Angry men were yelling. They had weapons and were angry at other men. I was in a car with my father. I had seen passive bread lines. But this was different. Girls don't usually see this, particularly if you're a bookish girl from a bookish family.

It may have been a prelude to the San Francisco General Strike. I'm not sure. That was almost like a blackout. It had a sense of paralysis.

The kids with lots of money had actually been moved to the peninsula out of harm's way. The rich people thought there was going to be a revolution, and they moved out of town.

My neighbors were angry with my mother, because she fed hungry men at the back door. They said it would bring others, and then what would she do? She said, "I'll feed them till the food runs out." It wasn't until years later, I realized the fear people had of these men. We didn't have it in our house.

I understand why these neighbors were afraid. They had lived with domestic violence all their lives. They were beaten up by their husbands every Saturday night. You could hear them screaming. So their fear of men was generalized. I'm sure my father never hit my mother. Ours was a nonviolent family, so we weren't particularly scared of these strange men.

Frank Czerwonka

"I'm a garbage man. Work for the city. I have a steady income, twice a month. My wife has an independent income—me.

"I mean, there's a conditioning here by the Depression. I'm what I call a security cat. I don't like the job I have, but I don't dare switch. 'Cause I got too much whiskers on it, seniority.

"I won't hang around with failures. When you hang around with successful people, it rubs off on ya. When you hang around with failures, it may rub off on ya, too. So I'm a snob, so do me somethin'."

WHEN MY FATHER DIED, my mother involved herself in speak-easies, blinds and beer flats. Married a couple of times.

In 1928, I started working. And I got laid off a week before the Depression. I had everything I wanted. I didn't want much. My life's ambition was to be a bum, and I failed at that. (Laughs.)

In 1930, my stepfather had this flat, where we had a speak-easy going. People from a small syndicate moved in the next flat. In our neighborhood, we wouldn't drink moonshine, just refined alcohol. My stepfather would peddle the moonshine on the South Side.

These moonshiners, they got the gas company men to tap the main with a three-inch pipe. Using company tools to steal their own gas. The gas company men, I mean, they take money, too. They tapped the gas main pipe and ran it up to the second floor and put a burner on it. Put a hundred-gallon still on it, going twenty-four hours a day. Just time off to put a new batch in.

There was cooperation in the neighborhood. Like this friend of mine, his father ran a joint. He got a job with the utility company to repair meters. Things got rough in the neighborhood. So everybody was cheatin' on gas, electricity, everything they could. A lot of people had their meters taken out. So he'd rig up jumpers on the meters in the whole neighborhood. He warned 'em: if they see anybody climbin' up a pole to put a meter on, let him know. The electric company came around, put a meter on it. So he climbed the pole and put a jumper[8] on the meter.

The whole neighborhood would cooperate . . . ?

Yeah, to beat the utility. And there's the bit about the case workers, too. The case worker was the enemy. They'd see case workers snoopin' around—they'd know 'em by sight—they'd pass the word around. If they

[8] "A jumper is a way of puttin' a wire on it so the current goes around the meter instead of through it and doesn't rotate the wheels. The current is goin' all the time, but not registerin'."

were havin' parties or they were eatin' or the old man was moonlighting somewhere to pick up a few bucks, they'd cover up for each other.

The syndicate boys had barrels of mash all over the place. One day my stepfather gets drunk—he was goofy that way. He liked to get arguments goin' and get pounded up. So they asked my mother if it's all right to kill him. She said: "No, I haven't got insurance on him."

Our speak-easy had a candy-store front. That was the come-on. The fuzz wasn't botherin' us. They were just shakin' down the syndicate. They were tryin' to get money from them because it was a big operation. They'd take out two truckloads of this moonshine. In five-gallon cans that were always a quart short. Even the one-gallon cans were about four ounces short. They never gave you a full measure. That was the standard practice in them days. They were gyppers.

Did you pay off the syndicate?

No, we bought through their channels. We bought alcohol. This moonshine was obviously for the South Side trade, the colored. The syndicate got a big place cheap to cook, about eight rooms. They used to get knocked off every so often, but not too often. Because the police captain was taken care of. They didn't believe in payin' off the men on the beat. They'd give him a drink and that was it. Because it would run into many expenses otherwise. 'Cause if one got something, he'd tell everybody else, and they'd all be in on it. This way, they'd pay the captain off and he wouldn't come around.

We'd been raided a couple of times, but they never could find the booze. My mother had a clever gimmick. She'd drive a nail in the wall, take a jug of booze and put a hat and coat on top of it. They never found it.

There was another candy-store front used by a woman. A cop started comin' around and gettin' friendly. She knew he was workin' up to a pinch. So she prepared a bottle for him. He talked her into sellin' it to him. He pinches her, takes her to court. He said: "I bought this half a dog of a booze. Half a pint." The woman said, "How do you know it's booze?" The cop takes a swig of it and spits it out. It was urine. Case dismissed.

When we had this place, the downtown Cadillac squad came in there —the open cars with sawed-off shotguns. They didn't want to drag us in. They wanted money. They wanted $40. My mother wasn't holding that day. So she had to wait for the customers to come in and borrow it from 'em. It took about three hours to pay these guys off.

Later on, in 1933, when Prohibition was lifted, alcohol dropped from $40 a gallon to $5. For a while $8 was the standard price, but $5 was the low point.

I wanted to get out of this. Get a job, more or less. I was goin' to work one day with seven cents and my lunch in my pocket. Believe it or not, I was waitin' for a streetcar. A truck was goin' out of town. Its tail gate was down. I jumped on it and was gone for six months. This was maybe '31. Still in Hoover's time. I went as far as the truck went. A freight train comes by.

I had my seven cents, but I ate my lunch. I bought a pack of Bull Durham, but I needed food. I found a jungle, ate somethin', and learned a few tricks from these 'boes.

Freight trains were amazing in them days. When a train would stop in a small town and the bums got off, the population tripled. So many ridin' the freight. Women even, and quite a few were tryin' to disguise themselves.

I ran into a couple of self-styled professors, safe blowers, skilled mechanics and all that. Quite a few boomers were traveling. These people usually had money. When they finished a job, they'd get paid, go on a bender and get rolled. They didn't like the farmer types. And there were quite a few farmers buried.

I'm talkin' about this big dam job out west, this big Hoover Dam. There was a lot of farmers in the concrete. They just shoved 'em in there. They didn't like 'em as job competition. Oh, there were some mean people travelin' around.

Old time hoboes had a circuit, like a preacher or a salesman. The towns knew 'em. They knew the good jails to spend the winter in. They would associate with each other, clannish. They wouldn't let outsiders in very much. A young boy, somebody they took a fancy to, they'd break him in. There was quite a bit of homosexual down there—wolves, punks and all that. I pushed one guy in the river. I don't know if he came up or not, 'cause I ran.

There was always Sally. While you listened to a sermon, they'd feed you a little something, and then you'd go on your way. The missions are pretty horrible because they pre-judge ya. I wanted a flop so I took it. Once in a while somebody would take a nose dive, profess religion.

41

They'd stick around a while just to have a roof. The first time they get enough money to get drunk, they did.

If you got lucky and got yourself a package of cigarettes, Camels was the bit, you put 'em in your socks and your Bull Durham was in your shirt pocket. So the ones that didn't have would mooch the Bull Durham instead of the Camels.

These kids amaze me today. I mean, they're smokin' and a bus comes, and they throw away the whole butt. I can't. I gotta clinch it. Put it in my pocket. Some days when I'm ridin' around in buses, I find the next day a half a dozen butts. I put 'em in the ash tray for when I run out of cigarettes.

The locals didn't care for the bums, they wouldn't take to 'em. There were always people bummin'. At back doors, tryin' to get a handout.

Did they know which doors to knock on?

No, this bit about the code that the old bums had broke down. If it was still being used, they weren't letting the newcomers know—the nouveau paupers.

Sometimes you'd sleep in a field, if the weather was nice. One time in North Dakota, all I had to cover myself was a road map underneath me and a road map on top of me. I woke up in the morning, there was frost on the road map. It didn't bother me, I slept. Now I'm paying the penalty. Arthritis.

Kitty McCulloch

"I'm seventy-one and I can still swim."

THERE WERE many beggars, who would come to your back door, and they would say they were hungry. I wouldn't give them money because I didn't have it. But I did take them in and put them in my kitchen and give them something to eat.

This one man came in—it was right before Christmas. My husband had a very nice suit, tailored. It was a black suit with a fine white pin-stripe in it. He put it to one side. I thought he didn't like the suit. I said to this man, "Your clothes are all ragged. I think I have a nice suit for you." So I gave him this suit.

The following Sunday my husband was to go to a wake. He said, "Where's my good suit?" And I said, "Well, Daddy, you never wore it. I—well, it's gone." He said, "Where is it gone to?" I said, "I gave it to a man who had such shabby clothes. Anyway, you got three other suits and he didn't have any. So I gave it to him." He said, "You're the limit, Mother."

One elderly man that had white whiskers and all, he came to my back door. He was pretty much of a philosopher. He was just charming. A man probably in his sixties. And he did look like St. Nicholas, I'll tell you that. I gave him a good, warm meal. He said, "Bring me a pencil and paper and I'll draw you a picture." So he sketched. And he was really good. He was an artist.

(Laughing.) A man came to my door, and I could smell liquor a little. He said, "You don't suppose you could have a couple of shirts you could give me, old shirts of your husband's?" I said, "Oh, I'm so very sorry, my husband hasn't anything but old shirts, really. That's all he has right now and he wears those." He said, "Lady, if I get some extra ones, I'll come back and give them to you." I said, "Go on, mind your own business."

And another one, I smelled liquor on *his* breath, too. He wanted to know if he could have a few pennies. I said, "Are you hungry?" He said, "I haven't had any food. I'd like some money to buy some food." I said, "I'll make you a nice sandwich." So I made him a sandwich with mayonnaise and chicken and lettuce, a double sandwich, put it in wax paper. He gave me a dirty look and he started down the alley. I watched him when he got, oh, two or three doors down, he threw it down the street.

Dawn, Kitty's Daughter

I REMEMBER that our apartment was marked. They had a mark, an actual chalk mark or something. You could see these marks on the bricks near the back porch. One mark signified: You could get something at this apartment, buddy, but you can't get anything up there. We'd be out

43

in the alley playing, and we'd hear comments from people: "Here's one." They wouldn't go to the neighbors upstairs, 'cause they didn't give them anything. But ours was marked. They'd come out from Chicago and they'd hit our apartment, and they knew they'd get something. Whatever the mark meant, some of them were like an X. They'd say, "You can't get money out of this place, but there's food here anyway." My mother was hospitable to people, it didn't matter who they were.

Louis Banks

From a bed at a Veteran's Hospital, he talks feverishly; the words pour out. . . .

"My family had a little old farm, cotton, McGehee, Arkansas. I came to Chicago, I was a little bitty boy, I used to prize-fight. When the big boys got through, they put us on there."

I GOT TO BE fourteen years old, I went to work on the Great Lakes at $41.50 a month. I thought: Someday I'm gonna be a great chef. Rough times, though. It was the year 1929. I would work from five in the morning till seven at night. Washing dishes, peeling potatoes, carrying heavy garbage. We would get to Detroit.

They was sleepin' on the docks and be drunk. Next day he'd be dead. I'd see 'em floatin' on the river where they would commit suicide because they didn't have anything. White guys and colored.

I'd get paid off, I'd draw $21 every two weeks and then comin' back I'd have to see where I was goin'. 'Cause I would get robbed. One fella named Scotty, he worked down there, he was firin' a boiler. He was tryin' to send some money home. He'd work so hard and sweat, the hot fire was cookin' his stomach. I felt sorry for him. They killed 'im and throwed 'im in the river, trying to get the $15 or $20 from him. They'd steal and kill each other for fifty cents.

1929 was pretty hard. I hoboed, I bummed, I begged for a nickel to get somethin' to eat. Go get a job, oh, at the foundry there. They didn't hire me because I didn't belong to the right kind of race. 'Nother time I went into Saginaw, it was two white fellas and myself made three. The fella there hired the two men and didn't hire me. I was back out on the streets. That hurt me pretty bad, the race part.

When I was hoboing, I would lay on the side of the tracks and wait until I could see the train comin'. I would always carry a bottle of water in my pocket and a piece of tape or rag to keep it from bustin' and put a piece of bread in my pocket, so I wouldn't starve on the way. I would ride all day and all night long in the hot sun.

I'd ride atop a boxcar and went to Los Angeles, four days and four nights. The Santa Fe, we'd go all the way with Santa Fe. I was goin' over the hump and I was so hungry and weak 'cause I was goin' into the d.t.'s, and I could see snakes draggin' through the smoke. I was sayin', "Lord, help me, Oh Lord, help me," until a white hobo named Callahan, he was a great big guy, looked like Jack Dempsey, and he got a scissors on me, took his legs and wrapped 'em around me. Otherwise, I was about to fall off the Flyer into a cornfield there. I was sick as a dog until I got into Long Beach, California.

Black and white, it didn't make any difference who you were, 'cause everybody was poor. All friendly, sleep in a jungle. We used to take a big pot and cook food, cabbage, meat and beans all together. We all set together, we made a tent. Twenty-five or thirty would be out on the side of the rail, white and colored. They didn't have no mothers or sisters, they didn't have no home, they were dirty, they had overalls on, they didn't have no food, they didn't have anything.

Sometimes we sent one hobo to walk, to see if there were any jobs open. He'd come back and say: Detroit, no jobs. He'd say: they're hirin' in New York City. So we went to New York City. Sometimes ten or fifteen of us would be on the train. And I'd hear one of 'em holler. He'd fall off, he'd get killed. He was tryin' to get off the train, he thought he was gettin' home there. He heard a sound. (Imitates train whistle, a low, long, mournful sound.)

And then I saw a railroad police, a white police. They call him Texas Slim. He shoots you off all trains. We come out of Lima, Ohio . . . Lima Slim, he would kill you if he catch you on any train. Sheep train or any kind of merchandise train. He would shoot you off, he wouldn't ask you to get off.

I was in chain gangs and been in jail all over the country. I was in a chain gang in Georgia. I had to pick cotton for four months, for just hoboin' on a train. Just for vag. They gave me thirty-five cents and a pair of overalls when I got out. Just took me off the train, the guard. 1930, during the Depression, in the summertime. Yes, sir, thirty-five cents, that's what they gave me.

I knocked on people's doors. They'd say, "What do you want? I'll call the police." And they'd put you in jail for vag. They'd make you milk cows, thirty or ninety days. Up in Wisconsin, they'd do the same thing. Alabama, they'd do the same thing. California, anywhere you'd go. Always in jail, and I never did nothin'.

A man had to be on the road. Had to leave his wife, had to leave his mother, leave his family just to try to get money to live on. But he think: my dear mother, tryin' to send her money, worryin' how she's starvin'.

The shame I was feeling. I walked out because I didn't have a job. I said, "I'm goin' out in the world and get me a job." And God help me, I couldn't get anything. I wouldn't let them see me dirty and ragged and I hadn't shaved. I wouldn't send 'em no picture.

I'd write: "Dear Mother, I'm doin' wonderful and wish you're all fine." That was in Los Angeles and I was sleeping under some steps and there was some paper over me. This is the slum part, Negroes lived down there. And my ma, she'd say, "Oh, my son is in Los Angeles, he's doin' pretty fair."

And I was with a bunch of hoboes, drinkin' canned heat. I wouldn't eat two or three days, 'cause I was too sick to eat. It's a wonder I didn't die. But I believe in God.

I went to the hospital there in Los Angeles. They said, "Where do you live?" I'd say, "Travelers Aid, please send me home." Police says, "O.K., put him in jail." I'd get ninety days for vag. When I was hoboing I was in jail two-thirds of the time. Instead of sayin' five or ten days, they'd say sixty or ninety days. 'Cause that's free labor. Pick the fruit or pick the cotton, then they'd turn you loose.

I had fifteen or twenty jobs. Each job I would have it would be so hard. From six o'clock in the morning till seven o'clock at night. I was fixin' the meat, cookin', washin' dishes and cleaning up. Just like you throwed the ball at one end and run down and catch it on the other. You're jack of all trade, you're doin' it all. White chefs were gettin' $40 a week, but I was gettin' $21 for doin' what they were doin' and everything else. The poor people had it rough. The rich people was livin' off the poor.

'Cause I picked cotton down in Arkansas when I was a little bitty boy and I saw my dad, he was workin' all day long. $2 is what one day the

poor man would make. A piece of salt pork and a barrel of flour for us
and that was McGehee, Arkansas.

God knows, when he'd get that sack he would pick up maybe two,
three hundred pounds of cotton a day, gettin' snake bit and everything in
that hot sun. And all he had was a little house and a tub to keep the
water. 'Cause I went down there to see him in 1930. I got tired of hoboing and went down to see him and my daddy was all gray and didn't
have no bank account and no Blue Cross. He didn't have nothin', and he
worked himself to death. (Weeps.) And the white man, he would drive
a tractor in there. . . . It seems like yesterday to me, but it was 1930.

'33 in Chicago they had the World's Fair. A big hotel was hirin'
colored fellas as bellboys. The bellboys could make more money as a
white boy for the next ten or fifteen years. I worked as a bellhop on the
North Side at a hotel, lots of gangsters there. They don't have no colored
bellboys at no exclusive hotels now. I guess maybe in the small ones they
may have some.

Jobs were doing a little better after '35, after the World's Fair. You
could get dishwashin' jobs, little porter jobs.

Work on the WPA, earn $27.50. We just dig a ditch and cover it back
up. You thought you was rich. You could buy a suit of clothes. Before
that, you wanted money, you didn't have any. No clothes for the kids.
My little niece and my little kids had to have hand-down clothes.
Couldn't steal. If you did, you went to the penitentiary. You had to
shoot pool, walk all night and all day, the best you could make was $15.
I raised up all my kids during the Depression. Scuffled . . . a hard way
to go.

Did you find any kindness during the Depression?

No kindness. Except for Callahan, the hobo—only reason I'm alive is
'cause Callahan helped me on that train. And the hobo jungle. Everybody else was evil to each other. There was no friendships. Everybody
was worried and sad looking. It was pitiful.

When the war came, I was so glad when I got in the army. I knew I
was safe. I put a uniform on, and I said, "Now I'm safe." I had money
comin', I had food comin', and I had a lot of gang around me. I knew on
the streets or hoboing, I might be killed any time.

I'd rather be in the army than outside where I was so raggedy and
didn't have no jobs. I was glad to put on a United States Army uniform
and get some food. I didn't care about the rifle what scared me. In the

army, I wasn't gettin' killed on a train, I wasn't gonna starve. I felt proud to salute and look around and see all the good soldiers of the United States. I was a good soldier and got five battle stars. I'd rather be in the army now than see another Depression.

POSTSCRIPT: *On recovery, he will return to his job as a washroom attendant in one of Chicago's leading hotels.*

"When I was hoboin' through the Dakatos and Montana, down there by General Custer's Last Stand, Little Big Horn, I wrote my name down, yes, sir. For the memories, just for the note, so it will always be there. Yes, sir."

Emma Tiller

At the time, she lived and worked in western Texas as a cook.

WHEN TRAMPS and hoboes would come to their door for food, the southern white people would drive them away. But if a Negro come, they will feed him. They'll even give them money. They'll ask them: Do you smoke, do you dip snuff? Yes, ma'am, yes, ma'am. They was always nice in a nasty way to Negroes. But their own color, they wouldn't do *that* for 'em.

They would hire Negroes for these type jobs where they wouldn't hire whites. They wouldn't hire a white woman to do housework, because they were afraid she'd take her husband.

When the Negro woman would say, "Miz So-and-So, we got some cold food in the kitchen left from lunch. Why don't you give it to 'im?" she'll say, "Oh, no, don't give 'im nothin'. He'll be back tomorrow with a gang of 'em. He ought to get a job and work."

The Negro woman who worked for the white woman would take food and wrap it in newspapers. Sometimes we would hurry down the alley and holler at 'im: "Hey, mister, come here!" And we'd say, "Come back by after a while and I'll put some food in a bag, and I'll sit down aside the garbage can so they won't see it." Then he'd get food, and we'd swipe a bar of soap and a face razor or somethin', stick it in there for 'im. Negroes would always feed these tramps.

48

Sometimes we would see them on the railroad tracks pickin' up stuff, and we would tell 'em: "Come to our house." They would come by and we would give 'em an old shirt or a pair of pants or some old shoes. We would always give 'em food.

Many times I have gone in my house and taken my husband's old shoes—some of 'em he needed hisself, but that other man was in worser shape than he was. Regardless of whether it was Negro or white, we would give to 'em.

We would gather stuff out in the field, pull our corn, roastin' ears, and put 'em in a cloth bag, because a paper bag would tear. When they get hungry, they can stop and build a fire and roast this corn. We did that ourselves, we loved it like that. And give them salt and stuff we figured would last 'em until he gets to the next place.

They would sit and talk and tell us their hard luck story. Whether it was true or not, we never questioned it. It's very important you learn people as people are. Anybody can go around and write a book about a person, but that book doesn't always tell you that person really. At that particular moment when you are talkin' to that person, maybe that's how that person were. Tomorrow they can be different people. It's very important to see people as people and not try to see them through a book. Experience and age give you this. There's an awful lot of people that has outstanding educations, but when it comes down to common sense, especially about people, they really don't know. . . .

Peggy Terry and Her Mother, Mary Owsley

It is a crowded apartment in Uptown.[9] Young people from the neighborhood wander in and out, casually. The flow of visitors is constant; occasionally, a small, raggedy-clothed boy shuffles in, stares, vanishes. Peggy Terry is known in these parts as a spokesman for the poor southern whites. . . . "Hillbillies are up here for a few years and they get their guts kicked out and they realize their white skin doesn't mean what they always thought it meant."

[9] A Chicago area in which many of the southern white émigrés live; furnished flats in most instances.

HARD TIMES

Mrs. Owsley is the first to tell her story.

Kentucky-born, she married an Oklahoma boy "when he came back from World War I. He was so restless and disturbed from the war, we just drifted back and forth." It was a constant shifting from Oklahoma to Kentucky and back again; three, four times the route. "He saw the tragedies of war so vividly that he was discontented everywhere." From 1929 to 1936, they lived in Oklahoma.

THERE WAS thousands of people out of work in Oklahoma City. They set up a soup line, and the food was clean and it was delicious. Many, many people, colored and white, I didn't see any difference, 'cause there was just as many white people out of work than were colored. Lost everything they had accumulated from their young days. And these are facts. I remember several families had to leave in covered wagons. To Californy, I guess.

See, the oil boom come in '29. People come from every direction in there. A coupla years later, they was livin' in everything from pup tents, houses built out of cardboard boxes and old pieces of metal that they'd pick up—anything that they could find to put somethin' together to put a wall around 'em to protect 'em from the public.

I knew one family there in Oklahoma City, a man and a woman and seven children lived in a hole in the ground. You'd be surprised how nice it was, how nice they kept it. They had chairs and tables and beds back in that hole. And they had the dirt all braced up there, just like a cave.

"Oh, the dust storms, they were terrible. You could wash and hang clothes on a line, and if you happened to be away from the house and couldn't get those clothes in before that storm got there, you'd never wash that out. Oil was in that sand. It'd color them the most awful color you ever saw. It just ruined them. They was just never fit to use, actually. I had to use 'em, understand, but they wasn't very presentable. Before my husband was laid off, we lived in a good home. It wasn't a brick house, but it wouldn't have made any difference. These storms, when they would hit, you had to clean house from the attic to ground. Everything was covered in sand. Red sand, just full of oil.

The majority of people were hit and hit hard. They were mentally disturbed you're bound to know, 'cause they didn't know when the end of all this was comin'. There was a lot of suicides that I know of. From nothin' else but just they couldn't see any hope for a better tomorrow. I

50

absolutely know some who did. Part of 'em were farmers and part of 'em were businessmen, even. They went flat broke and they committed suicide on the strength of it, nothing else.

A lot of times one family would have some food. They would divide. And everyone would share. Even the people that were quite well to do, they was ashamed. 'Cause they was eatin', and other people wasn't.

My husband was very bitter. That's just puttin' it mild. He was an intelligent man. He couldn't see why as wealthy a country as this is, that there was any sense in so many people starving to death, when so much of it, wheat and everything else, was being poured into the ocean. There's many excuses, but he looked for a reason. And he found one.

My husband went to Washington. To march with that group that went to Washington . . . the bonus boys.

He was a machine gunner in the war. He'd say them damn Germans gassed him in Germany. And he come home and his own Government stooges gassed him and run him off the country up there with the water hose, half drownded him. Oh, yes *sir,* yes sir, he was a hell-raiser (laughs —a sudden sigh). I think I've run my race.

PEGGY TERRY'S STORY:

I first noticed the difference when we'd come home from school in the evening. My mother'd send us to the soup line. And we were never allowed to cuss. If you happened to be one of the first ones in line, you didn't get anything but water that was on top. So we'd ask the guy that was ladling out the soup into the buckets—everybody had to bring their own bucket to get the soup—he'd dip the greasy, watery stuff off the top. So we'd ask him to please dip down to get some meat and potatoes from the bottom of the kettle. But he wouldn't do it. So we learned to cuss. We'd say: "Dip down, God damn it."

Then we'd go across the street. One place had bread, large loaves of bread. Down the road just a little piece was a big shed, and they gave milk. My sister and me would take two buckets each. And that's what we lived off for the longest time.

I can remember one time, the only thing in the house to eat was mustard. My sister and I put so much mustard on biscuits that we got sick. And we can't stand mustard till today.

There was only one family around that ate good. Mr. Barr worked at the ice plant. Whenever Mrs. Barr could, she'd feed the kids. But she couldn't feed 'em *all*. They had a big tree that had fruit on it. She'd let us pick those. Sometimes we'd pick and eat 'em until we were sick.

Her two daughters got to go to Norman for their college. When they'd talk about all the good things they had at the college, she'd kind of hush 'em up because there was always poor kids that didn't have anything to eat. I remember she always felt bad because people in the neighborhood were hungry. But there was a feeling of together. . . .

When they had food to give to people, you'd get a notice and you'd go down. So Daddy went down that day and he took my sister and me. They were giving away potatoes and things like that. But they had a truck of oranges parked in the alley. Somebody asked them who the oranges were for, and they wouldn't tell 'em. So they said, well, we're gonna take those oranges. And they did. My dad was one of the ones that got up on the truck. They called the police, and the police chased us all away. But we got the oranges.

It's different today. People are made to feel ashamed now if they don't have anything. Back then, I'm not sure how the rich felt. I think the rich were as contemptuous of the poor then as they are now. But among the people that I knew, we all had an understanding that it wasn't our fault. It was something that had happened to the machinery. Most people blamed Hoover, and they cussed him up one side and down the other—it was all his fault. I'm not saying he's blameless, but I'm not saying either it was all his fault. Our system doesn't run by just one man, and it doesn't fall by just one man, either.

You don't recall at any time feeling a sense of shame?

I remember it was fun. It was fun going to the soup line. 'Cause we all went down the road, and we laughed and we played. The only thing we felt is that we were hungry and we were going to get food. Nobody made us feel ashamed. There just wasn't any of that.

Today you're made to feel that it's your own fault. If you're poor, it's only because you're lazy and you're ignorant, and you don't try to help yourself. You're made to feel that if you get a check from Welfare that the bank at Fort Knox is gonna go broke.

Even after the soup line, there wasn't anything. The WPA came, and I married. My husband worked on the WPA. This was back in Paducah, Kentucky. We were just kids. I was fifteen, and he was sixteen. My husband was digging ditches. They were putting in a water main. Parts of the city, even at that late date, 1937, didn't have city water.

My husband and me just started traveling around, for about three years. It was a very nice time, because when you're poor and you stay in one spot, trouble just seems to catch up with you. But when you're moving from town to town, you don't stay there long enough for trouble to catch up with you. It's really a good life, if you're poor and you can manage to move around.

I was pregnant when we first started hitchhiking, and people were really very nice to us. Sometimes they would feed us. I remember one time we slept in a haystack, and the lady of the house came out and found us and she said, "This is really very bad for you because you're going to have a baby. You need a lot of milk." So she took us up to the house.

She had a lot of rugs hanging on the clothesline because she was doing her house cleaning. We told her we'd beat the rugs for her giving us the food. She said, no, she didn't expect that. She just wanted to feed us. We said, no, we couldn't take it unless we worked for it. And she let us beat her rugs. I think she had a million rugs, and we cleaned them. Then we went in and she had a beautiful table, full of all kind of food and milk. When we left, she filled a gallon bucket full of milk and we took it with us.

You don't find that now. I think maybe if you did that now, you'd get arrested. Somebody'd call the police. The atmosphere since the end of the Second War—it seems like the minute the war ended, the propaganda started. In making people hate each other.

I remember one night, we walked for a long time, and we were so tired and hungry, and a wagon came along. There was a Negro family going into town. Of course, they're not allowed to stop and eat in restaurants, so they'd cook their own food and brought it with 'em. They had the back of the wagon filled with hay. We asked them if we could lay down and sleep in the wagon, and they said yes. We woke up, and it was morning, and she invited us to eat with 'em. She had this box, and she had chicken and biscuits and sweet potatoes and everything in there. It was just really wonderful.

I didn't like black people. In fact, I hated 'em. If they just shipped 'em all out, I don't think it woulda bothered me.

She recalls her feelings of white superiority, her discoveries. "If I really knew what changed me . . . I don't know. I've thought about it and thought about it. You don't go anywhere, because you always see your-

self as something you're not. As long as you can say I'm better than they are, then there's somebody below you can kick. But once you get over that, you see that you're not any better off than they are. In fact, you're worse off 'cause you're believin' a lie. And it was right there, in front of us. In the cotton field, chopping cotton, and right over in the next field, there's these black people—Alabama, Texas, Kentucky. Never once did it occur to me that we had anything in common.

"After I was up here for a while and I saw how poor white people were treated, poor white southerners, they were treated just as badly as black people are. I think maybe that just crystallized the whole thing."

I didn't feel any identification with the Mexicans, either. My husband and me were migrant workers. We went down in the valley of Texas, which is very beautiful. We picked oranges and lemons and grapefruits, limes in the Rio Grande Valley.

We got a nickel a bushel for citrus fruits. On the grapefruits you had to ring them. You hold a ring in your hand that's about like that (she draws a circle with her hands), and it has a little thing that slips down over your thumb. You climb the tree and you put that ring around the grapefruit. If the grapefruit slips through, you can't pick it. And any grapefruit that's in your box—you can work real hard, especially if you want to make enough to buy food that day—you'll pick some that aren't big enough. Then when you carry your box up and they check it, they throw out all the ones that go through the ring.

I remember this one little boy in particular. He was really a beautiful child. Every day when we'd start our lunch, we'd sit under the trees and eat. And these peppers grew wild. I saw him sitting there, and every once in a while he'd reach over and get a pepper and pop it in his mouth. With his food, whatever he was eating. I thought they looked pretty good. So I reached over and popped it in my mouth, and, oh, it was like liquid fire. He was rolling in the grass laughing. He thought it was so funny —that white people couldn't eat peppers like they could. And he was tearing open grapefruits for me to suck the juice, because my mouth was all cooked from the pepper. He used to run and ask if he could help me. Sometimes he'd help me fill my boxes of grapefruits, 'cause he felt sorry for me, 'cause I got burned on the peppers. (Laughs.)

But that was a little boy. I felt all right toward him. But the men and the women, they were just spics and they should be sent back to Mexico.

I remember I was very irritated because there were very few gringos in this little Texas town, where we lived. Hardly anybody spoke English.

When you tried to talk to the Mexicans, they couldn't understand English. It never occurred to us that we should learn to speak Spanish. It's really hard to talk about a time like that, 'cause it seems like a different person. When I remember those times, it's like looking into a world where another person is doing those things.

This may sound impossible, but if there's one thing that started me thinking, it was President Roosevelt's cuff links. I read in the paper how many pairs of cuff links he had. It told that some of them were rubies and precious stones—these were his cuff links. And I'll never forget, I was setting on an old tire out in the front yard and we were poor and hungry. I was sitting out there in the hot sun, there weren't any trees. And I was wondering why it is that one man could have all those cuff links when we couldn't even have enough to eat. When we lived on gravy and biscuits. That's the first time I remember ever wondering why.

And when my father finally got his bonus, he bought a secondhand car for us to come back to Kentucky in. My dad said to us kids: "All of you get in the car. I want to take you and show you something." On the way over there, he'd talk about how life had been rough for us, and he said: "If you think it's been rough for us, I want you to see people that really had it rough." This was in Oklahoma City, and he took us to one of the Hoovervilles, and that was the most incredible thing.

Here were all these people living in old, rusted-out car bodies. I mean that was their home. There were people living in shacks made of orange crates. One family with a whole lot of kids were living in a piano box. This wasn't just a little section, this was maybe ten-miles wide and ten-miles long. People living in whatever they could junk together.

And when I read *Grapes of Wrath*—she bought that for me (indicates young girl seated across the room)—that was like reliving my life. Particularly the part where they lived in this Government camp. Because when we were picking fruit in Texas, we lived in a Government place like that. They came around, and they helped the women make mattresses. See, we didn't have anything. And they showed us how to sew and make dresses. And every Saturday night, we'd have a dance. And when I was reading *Grapes of Wrath* this was just like my life. I was never so proud of poor people before, as I was after I read that book.

I think that's the worst thing that our system does to people, is to take away their pride. It prevents them from being a human being. And wondering why the Harlem and why the Detroit. They're talking about troops and law and order. You get law and order in this country when people are allowed to be decent human beings. Every time I hear another building's on fire, I say: oh, boy, baby, hit 'em again. (Laughs.)

I don't think people were put on earth to suffer. I think that's a lot of nonsense. I think we are the highest development on the earth, and I think we were put here to live and be happy and to enjoy everything that's here. I don't think it's right for a handful of people to get ahold of all the things that make living a joy instead of a sorrow. You wake up in the morning, and it consciously hits you—it's just like a big hand that takes your heart and squeezes it—because you don't know what that day is going to bring: hunger or you don't know.

POSTSCRIPT: (*A sudden flash of memory by Peggy Terry, as I was about to leave.*) *"It was the Christmas of '35, just before my dad got his bonus. We didn't get anything for Christmas. I mean nothing. Not an orange, not an apple—nothing. I just felt so bad. I went to the church, to the children's program and I stole a Christmas package. It was this pretty box and it had a big red ribbon on it. I stole it off the piano, and I took it home with me. I told my mother my Sunday school teacher had given me a Christmas present. When I opened it, it was a beautiful long scarf made out of velvet—a cover for a piano. My mother knew my Sunday school teacher didn't give me that. 'Cause we were living in one room, in a little shack in what they called Gander Flat. (Laughs.) For a child—I mean, they teach you about Santa Claus and they teach you all that stuff—and then for a child to have to go to church and steal a present . . . and then it turned out to be something so fantastic, a piano scarf. Children shouldn't have to go around stealing. There's enough to give all of them everything they want, any time they want it. I say that's what we're gonna have."*

Kiko Konagamitsu

He is a Japanese-American (Nisei), *living in a Midwestern city.*

MY FATHER had a farm in southern California. I remember the *Grapes of Wrath* kind of people. They used to work for us, pick crops. It amazed me. They'd say, "Let the Jap boy count it." They'd come in from the fields, and I'd tally up the totals for the day. I'd weigh them on the scale.

I didn't feel I was qualified. I was just a little kid. But I could count. They would honor my counting. It was a tremendous trust. It seems the less affluent you are, the more you are able to trust people, the more you are able to give others.

My father had many old-type Oriental feelings about things. If one of his friends had trouble and couldn't afford to have anyone working for him, my father would ask me to go over. I remember once feeling badly. I had worked all day for this man, cleaning lettuce, stacking vegetables. He didn't pay me. My father gave me a real tongue-lashing: "You're not expected to get paid. He didn't ask you to go. *I* asked you to go."

The communal spirit of the Nisei is less today than it was in the Depression. The second-generation Japanese has become the most so-called American.

Someone laughingly told: Maybe the war—and the internment camp[10]—was good for us. How else could we have gotten out of California? There were hundreds of Nisei Ph.D.'s working on the family's farm or fruit stands. Their parents would live in shacks so their sons and daughters could go to college. (Laughs.)

Thousands of us—after Pearl Harbor—were assembled at the Santa Anita race track. We were assigned to camps or contracted out to farmers. My brother and I signed up to pick sugar beets for a farmer in Idaho. Here we worked on a sugar beet farm, but we couldn't get any sugar coupons. I didn't know the taste of sugar. (Laughs.)

Country Joe McDonald

A rock musician, he's a member of "Country Joe And The Fish." He is twenty-six.

I USED TO ask my father what he did. He never said much, except he rode around in freight trains and couldn't find work, and at one point he went up to Alaska and worked and was hungry. He hardly talked about it at all, as a matter of fact.

---

[10] Thousands of Japanese families living on the West Coast were interned in relocation camps, during World War II. These structures are still standing.

Could you imagine what a Depression would be like?

No. But there've been times like when the band was first formed. We spent about two years on a below-poverty level. We had incomes of about anywhere from $5 to $25 a week. We managed to make it all right, though it got to be a real drag in the second year. We really started to get a craving for good food. We were surrounded by an affluent society. I just can't imagine a whole country living like that.

It's a long ways from me. I remember Woody Guthrie records, where he talked about this big cloud of dust coming along and they losing all their homes. They actually had houses that a bulldozer could just knock over. (Laughs.) I can't imagine bulldozing my parents' house down there in Berkeley. You'd have a hard time knocking down a stucco house. Maybe it's impossible to relive that period.

I travel around and talk to some of the Mexican migrant workers. In a way, they seem closer to each other than most well-off middle-class people. Their impoverished condition somehow made them very real people. It's hard to be phony when you haven't got anything. I mean when you're really down and out. I think the Depression had some kind of human qualities with it that we lack now.

Cesar Chavez

Like so many who have worked from early childhood, particularly in the open country, he appears older than his forty-one years. His manner is diffident, his voice soft.

He is president of the United Farm Workers of America (UFWA). It is, unlike craft and industrial unions, a quite new labor fraternity. In contrast to these others, agricultural workers—those who "follow the crops"—had been excluded from many of the benefits that came along with the New Deal.

OH, I REMEMBER having to move out of our house. My father had brought in a team of horses and wagon. We had always lived in that house, and we couldn't understand why we were moving out. When we got to the other house, it was a worse house, a poor house. That must have been around 1934. I was about six years old.

It's known as the North Gila Valley, about fifty miles north of Yuma. My dad was being turned out of his small plot of land. He had inherited this from his father, who had homesteaded it. I saw my two, three other uncles also moving out. And for the same reason. The bank had foreclosed on the loan.

If the local bank approved, the Government would guarantee the loan and small farmers like my father would continue in business. It so happened the president of the bank was the guy who most wanted our land. We were surrounded by him: he owned all the land around us. Of course, he wouldn't pass the loan.

One morning a giant tractor came in, like we had never seen before. My daddy used to do all his work with horses. So this huge tractor came in and began to knock down this corral, this small corral where my father kept his horses. We didn't understand why. In the matter of a week, the whole face of the land was changed. Ditches were dug, and it was different. I didn't like it as much.

We all of us climbed into an old Chevy that my dad had. And then we were in California, and migratory workers. There were five kids—a small family by those standards. It must have been around '36. I was about eight. Well, it was a strange life. We had been poor, but we knew every night there was a bed *there,* and that *this* was our room. There was a kitchen. It was sort of a settled life, and we had chickens and hogs, eggs and all those things. But that all of a sudden changed. When you're small, you can't figure these things out. You know something's not right and you don't like it, but you don't question it and you don't let that get you down. You sort of just continue to move.

But this had quite an impact on my father. He had been used to owning the land and all of a sudden there was no more land. What I heard . . . what I made out of conversations between my mother and my father—things like, we'll work this season and then we'll get enough money and we'll go and buy a piece of land in Arizona. Things like that. Became like a habit. He never gave up hope that some day he would come back and get a little piece of land.

I can understand very, very well this feeling. These conversations were sort of melancholy. I guess my brothers and my sisters could also see this very sad look on my father's face.

That piece of land he wanted . . . ?

No, never. It never happened. He stopped talking about that some years ago. The drive for land, it's a very powerful drive.

When we moved to California, we would work after school. Sometimes we wouldn't go. "Following the crops," we missed much school. Trying to get enough money to stay alive the following winter, the whole family picking apricots, walnuts, prunes. We were pretty new, we had never been migratory workers. We were taken advantage of quite a bit by the labor contractor and the crew pusher.[11] In some pretty silly ways. (Laughs.)

Sometimes we can't help but laugh about it. We trusted everybody that came around. You're traveling in California with all your belongings in your car: it's obvious. Those days we didn't have a trailer. This is bait for the labor contractor. Anywhere we stopped, there was a labor contractor offering all kinds of jobs and good wages, and we were always deceived by them and we always went. Trust them.

Coming into San Jose, not finding—being lied to, that there was work. We had no money at all, and had to live on the outskirts of town under a bridge and dry creek. That wasn't really unbearable. What was unbearable was so many families living just a quarter of a mile. And you know how kids are. They'd bring in those things that really hurt us quite a bit. Most of those kids were middle-class families.

We got hooked on a real scheme once. We were going by Fresno on our way to Delano. We stopped at some service station and this labor contractor saw the car. He offered a lot of money. We went. We worked the first week: the grapes were pretty bad and we couldn't make much. We all stayed off from school in order to make some money. Saturday we were to be paid and we didn't get paid. He came and said the winery hadn't paid him. We'd have money next week. He gave us $10. My dad took the $10 and went to the store and bought $10 worth of groceries. So we worked another week and in the middle of the second week, my father was asking him for his last week's pay, and he had the same excuse. This went on and we'd get $5 or $10 or $7 a week for about four weeks. For the whole family.

So one morning my father made the resolution no more work. If he

[11] "That's a man who specializes in contracting human beings to do cheap labor."

doesn't pay us, we won't work. We got in a car and went over to see him. The house was empty. He had left. The winery said they had paid him and they showed us where they had paid him. This man had taken it.

Labor strikes were everywhere. We were one of the strikingest families, I guess. My dad didn't like the conditions, and he began to agitate. Some families would follow, and we'd go elsewhere. Sometimes we'd come back. We couldn't find a job elsewhere, so we'd come back. Sort of beg for a job. Employers would know and they would make it very humiliating. . . .

Did these strikes ever win?

Never.

We were among these families who always honored somebody else's grievance. Somebody would have a personal grievance with the employer. He'd say I'm not gonna work for this man. Even though we were working, we'd honor it. We felt we had to. So we'd walk out, too. Because we were prepared to honor those things, we caused many of the things ourselves. If we were picking at a piece rate and we knew they were cheating on the weight, we wouldn't stand for it. So we'd lose the job, and we'd go elsewhere. There were other families like that.

Sometimes when you had to come back, the contractor knew this . . . ?

They knew it, and they rubbed it in quite well. Sort of shameful to come back. We were trapped. We'd have to do it for a few days to get enough money to get enough gas.

One of the experiences I had. We went through Indio, California. Along the highway there were signs in most of the small restaurants that said "White Trade Only." My dad read English, but he didn't really know the meaning. He went in to get some coffee—a pot that he had, to get some coffee for my mother. He asked us not to come in, but we followed him anyway. And this young waitress said, "We don't serve Mexicans here. Get out of here." I was there, and I saw it and heard it. She paid no more attention. I'm sure for the rest of her life she never thought of it again. But every time we thought of it, it hurt us. So we got back in the car and we had a difficult time trying—in fact, we never got the coffee. These are sort of unimportant, but they're . . . you remember 'em very well.

61

One time there was a little diner across the tracks in Brawley. We used to shine shoes after school. Saturday was a good day. We used to shine shoes for three cents, two cents. Hamburgers were then, as I remember, seven cents. There was this little diner all the way across town. The moment we stepped across the tracks, the police stopped us. They would let us go there, to what we called "the American town," the Anglo town, with a shoe shine box. We went to this little place and we walked in.

There was this young waitress again. With either her boyfriend or someone close, because they were involved in conversation. And there was this familiar sign again, but we paid no attention to it. She looked up at us and she sort of—it wasn't what she said, it was just a gesture. A sort of gesture of total rejection. Her hand, you know, and the way she turned her face away from us. She said: "Wattaya want?" So we told her we'd like to buy two hamburgers. She sort of laughed, a sarcastic sort of laugh. And she said, "Oh, we don't sell to Mexicans. Why don't you go across to Mexican town, you can buy 'em over there." And then she turned around and continued her conversation.

She never knew how much she was hurting us. But it stayed with us.

We'd go to school two days sometimes, a week, two weeks, three weeks at most. This is when we were migrating. We'd come back to our winter base, and if we were lucky, we'd get in a good solid all of January, February, March, April, May. So we had five months out of a possible nine months. We started counting how many schools we'd been to and we counted thirty-seven. Elementary schools. From first to eighth grade. Thirty-seven. We never got a transfer. Friday we didn't tell the teacher or anything. We'd just go home. And they accepted this.

I remember one teacher—I wondered why she was asking so many questions. (In those days anybody asked questions, you became suspicious. Either a cop or a social worker.) She was a young teacher, and she just wanted to know why we were behind. One day she drove into the camp. That was quite an event, because we never had a teacher come over. Never. So it was, you know, a very meaningful day for us.

This I remember. Some people put this out of their minds and forget it. I don't. I don't want to forget it. I don't want it to take the best of me, but I want to be there because this is what happened. This is the truth, you know. History.

Fran

Fran is twenty-one. She's from Atlanta. Her family is considered affluent.

MY MOTHER HAD a really big family, she was one of seven kids. She brought me up, not on fairy tales, but on stories of the Depression. They feel almost like fairy tales to me because she used to tell bedtime stories about that kind of thing.

The things they teach you about the Depression in school are quite different from how it was: Well, you knew for some reason society didn't get along so well in those years. And then you found out that everybody worked very hard, and things somehow got better. People didn't talk about the fact that industries needed to make guns for World War II made that happen. "It just got better" 'cause people pitched in and worked. And 'cause Roosevelt was a nice guy, although some people thought he went too far. You never hear about the rough times.

A lot of young people feel angry about this kind of protectiveness. This particular kind is even more vicious somehow, because it's wanting you not to have to go through what is a very real experience, even though it is a very hard thing. Wanting to protect you from your own history, in a way.

Blackie Gold

A car dealer. He has a house in the suburbs.

WHATEVER I HAVE, I'm very thankful for. I've never brought up the Depression to my children. Never in my life. Why should I? What I had to do, what I had to do without, I never tell 'em what I went through, there's no reason for it. They don't have to know from bad times. All they know is the life they've had and the future that they're gonna have.

All I know is my children are well-behaved. If I say something to my daughters, it's "Yes, sir," "No, sir." I know where my kids are at all times. And I don't have no worries about them being a beatnik.

I've built my own home. I almost have no mortgage. I have a daughter who's graduating college, and my daughter did not have to work, for me to put her through college. At the age of sixteen, I gave her a car, that was her gift. She's graduating college now: I'll give her a new one.

We had to go out and beg for coal, buy bread that's two, three days old. My dad died when I was an infant. I went to an orphan home for fellas. Stood there till I was seventeen years old. I came out into the big wide world, and my mother who was trying to raise my six older brothers and sisters, couldn't afford another mouth to feed. So I enlisted in the Civilian Conservation Corps. The CCC. This was about 1937.

I was at CCC's for six months, I came home for fifteen days, looked around for work, and I couldn't make $30 a month, so I enlisted back in the CCC's and went to Michigan. I spent another six months there planting trees and building forests. And came out. But still no money to be made. So back in the CCC's again. From there I went to Boise, Idaho, and was attached to the forest rangers. Spent four and a half months fighting forest fires.

These big trees you see along the highways—all these big forests was all built by the CCC. We went along plain barren ground. There were no trees. We just dug trenches and kept planting trees. You could plant about a hundred an hour.

I really enjoyed it. I had three wonderful square meals a day. No matter what they put on the table, we ate and were glad to get it. Nobody ever turned down food. They sure made a man out of ya, because you learned that everybody here was equal. There was nobody better than another in the CCC's. We never had any race riots. Couple of colored guys there, they minded their business; we minded ours.

I came out of there, enlisted in the navy. I spent five and a half years in the United States Navy. It was the most wonderful experience I've ever had. Three wonderful meals a day and my taxes paid for. I had security.

I came up the hard way, was never in jail, never picked up and whatever I've done, I have myself to thank for. No matter how many people were on relief in those days, you never heard of any marches. The biggest stealing would be by a guy go by a fruit store and steal a potato. But you never heard of a guy breaking a window. In the Thirties, the crimes were a hundred percent less than they are now. If a guy wants to work, there's no reason for being poor. There's no reason for being dirty. Soap and water'll clean anybody. Anybody that's free and white in a wonderful country like these United States never had any wants, never.

In the days of the CCC's, if the fella wouldn't take a bath, we'd give 'im what we call a brushing. We'd take this fella, and we'd take a big scrub brush and we'd give 'em a bath, and we'd open up every pore, and these pores would get infected. That's all he needed was one bath. I imagine we gave a hundred of 'em. A guy'd come in, he'd stink, ten guys would get him in the shower, and we'd take a GI brush. If a guy come in, he wanted to look like a hillbilly—no reflection on the boys from the South—but if he wanted to look like the backwoods, we'd cut his hair off. Yeah, we'd keep him clean.

You know, in the CCC's or in the navy, you're sittin' amongst thirty guys in one room, and you're not gonna take that smell.

Did you have a committee that decided . . . ?

No, we'd just look at each other and we'd say, "Hey, look at this rat, he's dirty." Then we say, "O.K., he's ready for one. . . ." We'd tell him, "You got until today to take a bath." He'd say, "You're not gonna run my life." We'd say, "You got twenty-four hours." And if he didn't, I guarantee you we grabbed him. We never heard of a goatee. . . .

The guys pretty much conformed?

Absolutely, CCC or navy. I liked that very much. We didn't have to worry where our next three meals were coming from, what the hell. . . .

And in the orphan home . . . ?

Sure. And high school. We had a woodshop teacher, and he would tell you what to do. You give him any back talk, he'd pick up a ruler and crack across the rear end. You settled down. In those days, when I went to school, you said "Yes, sir" and "No, sir." You never gave 'em back talk. They had a parental school, Montefiore, that made a man out of you. You learn to keep yourself clean, I'll tell you that. Obedience. Today, they're giving kids cars when they're sixteen. Another thirty years from now, these kids graduating high school, one may be President, another may be up there buying a planet.

The Big Money

William Benton

During various phases of his life: United States Senator from Connecticut; Assistant Secretary of State; Vice President of the University of Chicago; publisher of Encyclopaedia Britannica; (a founder of the Committee for Economic Development . . . "We organized studies in three thousand American towns . . . planning for conversion to peace time production . . . born out of Depression experiences. . . .").

His ambition was to retire as a millionaire at the age of thirty-five. He did so, at thirty-six.

In 1929, he was the assistant general manager of Lord and Thomas, headed by Albert Lasker, "the most successful advertising agency man ever developed."

I LEFT CHICAGO in June of '29, just a few months before the Crash. Chester Bowles[1] and I started in business with seventeen hundred square feet, just the two of us and a couple of girls. July 15, 1929—this was the very day of the all-time peak on the stock market.

As I solicited business, my chart was kind of a cross. The left-hand line started at the top corner and ended in the bottom of the right-hand corner. That was the stock market index. The other line was Benton &

---

[1] At one time, Governor of Connecticut; later, American Ambassador to India.

66

Bowles. It started at the bottom left-hand corner and ended in the top right-hand corner. A cross. As the stock market plummeted into oblivion, Benton & Bowles went up into stardom. When I sold the agency in 1935, it was the single biggest office in the world. And the most profitable office.

My friend, Beardsley Ruml, was advocate of the theory: progress through catastrophe. In all catastrophes, there is the potential of benefit. I benefited out of the Depression. Others did, too. I suppose the people who sold red ink, red pencils and red crayons benefited.

I was only twenty-nine, and Bowles was only twenty-eight. When things are prosperous, big clients are not likely to listen to young men or to new ideas. In 1929, most of your Wall Street manipulators called it The New Era. They felt it was the start of a perpetual boom that would carry us on and on forever to new plateaus.

That year, the sales of Pepsodent were off fifty percent. Dentists talked about Pepsodent teeth. It was too abrasive, took the enamel off teeth, they said. None of the old-type advertising seemed to work. I was still in Chicago, with Lord and Thomas. Pepsodent was our account.

In May of 1929, I left my office in the new Palmolive Building[2] . . . we were its first tenants. I walked home to my apartment. It was a hot muggy night. All the windows were open, and I heard these colored voices leaping out into the street, from all the apartments. I turned around and walked back up the street. There were nineteen radios on and seventeen were tuned to "Amos and Andy." This is probably the first audience research survey in the history of radio broadcasting.

I went in to see Mr. Lasker the next morning and said we ought to buy "Amos and Andy" for Pepsodent right away. We bought them on the spot, and I went east to Benton & Bowles.

Pepsodent went on the air, and within a series of weeks it was the greatest sensation in the history of American show business. The only thing that's been more famous than "Amos and Andy" was Lindbergh's flight across the Atlantic. Pepsodent sales skyrocketed.

The Crash never hurt Pepsodent. Pepsodent sales doubled and quadrupled. It was sold to Lever Brothers at an enormous price, giving Lasker part of his great fortune. Benton & Bowles plunged into radio in a big way for our clients.

We didn't know the Depression was going on. Except that our clients'

[2] It is now the *Playboy* Building.

products were plummeting, and they were willing to talk to us about new ideas. They wouldn't have let us in the door if times were good. So the Depression benefited me. My income doubled every year. When I left Benton & Bowles, it must have been close to half a million dollars. That's the kind of money great motion picture stars weren't earning. That was 1935. The Depression just passed me right over. I'm not a good man to talk to about the Depression.

I had nothing to do with the creation of "Amos and Andy," just had the judgment to buy it. But I contributed enormously to the "Maxwell House Show Boat," which later became the Number One program in broadcasting. The show gave a quality of illusion to the radio audiences so perfectly that in its early weeks ten thousand and fifteen thousand people would come down to the docks in Memphis and Nashville, where we said the "Show Boat" was going to tie up.

"Show Boat" went on in 1933, really the bottom of the Depression. Maxwell House Coffee went up eighty-five percent within six months. And kept zooming. Thus, Maxwell House didn't know there was a Depression. The chain stores were selling coffee that was almost as good—the difference was indetectable—for a much lower price. But advertising so gave glamor and verve to Maxwell House that it made everybody think it was a whale of a lot better. It doubled and quadrupled in sales.

In "Show Boat" we did something nobody had ever done before. We cast two people in one role. We'd get a sexy singer, who might not be a good actress, then we'd get the sexiest actress we could find and we'd give her the speaking lines, softening the audience up, getting it warm and ready to melt. Then the girl would come in and sing.

People in the theater never thought of such an idea. Radio made it possible. It took new men coming into radio to think of new ideas. Hollywood fought it, Ziegfeld was no good at it. The advertising men made radio. We weren't inhibited. We didn't know you couldn't put two people in one part.

We went on to put out other shows like it. And they became big hits. "The Palmolive Beauty Box." I picked up an unknown member of the Metropolitan chorus, Gladys Swarthout, and we made her a big star. We put a $100-a-week gifted actress with her to speak the lines, while Gladys sang in that seductive voice of hers. They told me I couldn't use her because she was no soprano and the parts were too high. I just coolly said: rewrite the parts; write them lower. Nobody in opera would have thought of this. . . . We succeeded in radio because none of us knew any better.

These were the new techniques of the Depression. As their sales went off, the big advertisers looked around and said: Who are these new young men that have these new ideas that appeal to these new young people? We looked like college boys, and yet they paid us a great deal of money. This is why Chet Bowles and I escaped the Depression.

The type of men that largely dominated advertising, before the Depression, faded, the ones who played golf with their accounts. The Depression speeded up greatly the use of research in marketing. I developed new techniques, working for Lasker, which I took East with me. George Gallup brought in new standards. He once referred to me as his grandfather, because I pioneered in the advertising field . . . finding out what the consumers wanted.

The Maxwell House Coffee program was, to my eternal regret, the stimulus that changed the commercials. When we had Captain Andy drink coffee and smack his lips, you heard the coffee cups clinking and the coffee gurgling as it was poured. It put action and actors into commercials. That was a revolution, the full import of which we didn't suspect at the time. It inevitably led to the singing commercial and all the current excesses. As Bob Hutchins said, when he introduced me at a dinner in my honor at the University of Chicago—I invented things that I now apologize for.

I presumably lost $150,000 in the depression of 1937—on my one stock investment—because I did everything Lehman Brothers told me. I said, well, this is a fool's procedure . . . buying stock in other people's businesses. I'll have to buy my own company. I won't work at operating it, I'll just own it. I'll set the policies. I looked around and bought the Muzak Corporation. I never could have bought it except in a Depression. It was a busted, rundown company. That would be around '38.

Muzak was then only heard in hotels and restaurants in New York. It was only thought of as a substitute for live music. Jimmy Petrillo cursed it as the Number One enemy of musicians. I said to myself: This music ought to be in other places.

I went down to see the five salesmen—we only had five then. They said to me: "We have eighty percent of all the business you can get in New York. There isn't any other place to sell it." I said, "Why don't you put it in barber shops and doctors' offices?" "Oh, you can't put

Muzak in places like that!" I said: "Do you all five think that way?" There was a young man, who had only worked there six weeks, he said, "No, I think it's a good idea." I said, "Well, the other four of you guys had better quit and get some other jobs, and I'll make this young man the sales manager. We'll take Muzak into new areas."

Of course, this made a big wonderful business out of Muzak, now earning $2 million a year. And no extra money has ever gone into it. The Depression put me into it.

The first installation outside the customary public for music was a bank in New York. The manager said, "My people who work at night, it's very depressing in these electric-lit offices. They wanted a radio, but I didn't want them to have it. I told them I'd give them Muzak. Now it's all over the bank." There was a girl sitting as a receptionist in the personal loan department. That's where people would borrow money in small units and never come back unless they couldn't pay the installments. The girl said to me: "The music makes this place less gruesome."

I invented the phrase: "Music not to be listened to." That was my commercial phrase with which I sold Muzak. It was the first music deliberately created to which people were not supposed to listen. It was a new kind of background music. That's why my mother, who was a fine musician, held it in contempt. She wouldn't have it in her apartment. Anybody who knows anything about music holds Muzak in contempt.

I have a tin ear. That's why my ear was so good for radio. Most people in the United States have a tin ear like mine. A totally tin ear. I really like Rudy Vallee and Bing Crosby and the stars that were developed by radio.

I owned Muzak for twenty years and sold it for a profit of many millions . . . when I ran out of my first million and needed some more.

Muzak's habit-forming. The man who bought it from me gave me four installations for my homes and my offices. I always have it on. 'Cause I notice it when it's not on and don't notice it when it's on. That's how it's music not to be listened to. And that's how it's habit-forming.

Every businessman wants a product that is habit-forming. That's why cigarettes, Coca-Cola and coffee do so well. Even soap is habit-forming. Soaps were my biggest products when I was in the agency business.

I always thought—at Benton & Bowles—just six more months, three more, and it would all be behind me. But our business doubled every year. Every year, I would say: As soon as I get this new client, I won't be working like this. No intelligent man would put up with what I put up with, even to get a million dollars, if he could have foreseen the six years.

In the fall of '37, I became vice president of the University of Chicago. My day changed enormously, because I started to read and consort with economics professors, and to interest myself in educational broadcasting . . . to produce and guide the "University of Chicago Round Table." However, the habits of hard work were ingrained in me. I didn't lacerate myself in the same way. But I worked the long, hard week. My evenings, though, were different.

The Depression was very seriously affecting the University . . . great deficits run up by its expensive medical school and its clinics. Contributions were less.

When Mr. Walgreen withdrew his niece claiming she was being taught communism, almost every paper in this great city attacked, pilloried the University. The Depression added to the feeling about communism.

I called on Mr. Walgreen to talk to him about this. Nobody from the University had done this. The trustees were startled by Walgreen's charges—and offended. I went to a former client, who introduced me to Mr. Walgreen. I said: "Mr. Walgreen, these great institutions live off the beneficences of people like you. Why don't you help the University teach courses on American institutions, as you think they should be taught?" Hutchins gave me the idea. I said to him: "What can we do to fix things up with Mr. Walgreen?" He said, "Why it's easy. Get him to give some money to the University." The next day, after my talk, Mr. Hutchins went around and collected a half a million dollars from him. That fixed the Walgreen case up right away.

Do you feel the Depression has adversely affected people in the matter of installment buying?

The Encyclopaedia Britannica lives off installment buying, this is our whole business. We don't think about credit as a problem, particularly when we think about a Depression. With more men out of work, we'd have an easier time finding good salesmen. The more men out of work, the more applicants we have. By multiplying our salesmen, we'd have an offset to the fact that there are fewer people to whom to sell. Progress through catastrophe.

Arthur A. Robertson

His offices are on an upper floor of a New York skyscraper. On the walls are paintings and photographs. A portrait of President Johnson is inscribed "To my friend, a patriot who serves his country." Another, of Hubert Humphrey—"To my friend, Arthur Robertson, with all my good wishes." Also, a photograph of Dwight Eisenhower: "To my friend, Arthur Robertson." There are other mementoes of appreciation from Americans in high places.

He recounts his early days as a war correspondent, advertising man and engineer. "We built a section of the Sixth Avenue subway. I've had a peculiar kind of career. I'm an industrialist. I had been in Germany where I picked up a number of porcelain enamel plants. I had a hog's hair concession from the Russian government. I used to sell them to the outdoor advertising plants for brushes. With several associates, I bought a company nineteen years ago for $1,600,000. We're on the New York Stock Exchange now and recently turned down $200 million for it. I'm chairman of the board, I control the company, I built it.

"I thought seriously of retiring in 1928 when I was thirty. I had seven figures by the time I was twenty-four."

IN 1929, it was strictly a gambling casino with loaded dice. The few sharks taking advantage of the multitude of suckers. It was exchanging expensive dogs for expensive cats. There had been a recession in 1921. We came out of it about 1924. Then began the climb, the spurt, with no limit stakes. Frenzied finance that made Ponzi[3] look like an amateur. I saw shoeshine boys buying $50,000 worth of stock with $500 down. Everything was bought on hope.

Today, if you want to buy $100 worth of stock, you have to put up $80 and the broker will put up $20. In those days, you could put up

[3] A Boston financier of the Twenties. His "empire" crashed, many people were ruined. He went to prison.

$8 or $10. That was really responsible for the collapse. The slightest shake-up caused calamity because people didn't have the money required to cover the other $90 or so. There were not the controls you have today. They just sold you out: an unwilling seller to an unwilling buyer.

A cigar stock at the time was selling for $115 a share. The market collapsed. I got a call from the company president. Could I loan him $200 million? I refused, because at the time I had to protect my own fences, including those of my closest friends. His $115 stock dropped to $2 and he jumped out of the window of his Wall Street office.

There was a man who headed a company that had $17 million in cash. He was one of the leaders of his industry and controlled three or four situations that are today household words. When his stock began to drop, he began to protect it. When he came out of the second drop, the man was completely wiped out. He owed three banks a million dollars each.

The banks were in the same position he was, except that the government came to their aid and saved them. Suddenly they became holier than thou, and took over the businesses of the companies that owed them money. They discharged the experts, who had built the businesses, and put in their own men. I bought one of these companies from the banks. They sold it to me in order to stop their losses.

The worst day-to-day operators of businesses are bankers. They are great when it comes to scrutinizing a balance sheet. By training they're conservative, because they're loaning you other people's money. Consequently, they do not take the calculated risks operating businesses requires. They were losing so much money that they were tickled to get it off their backs. I recently sold it for $2 million. I bought it in 1933 for $33,000.

In the early Thirties, I was known as a scavenger. I used to buy broken-down businesses that banks took over. That was one of my best eras of prosperity. The whole period was characterized by men who were legends. When you talked about $1 million you were talking about loose change. Three or four of these men would get together, run up a stock to ridiculous prices and unload it on the unsuspecting public. The minute you heard of a man like Durant or Jesse Livermore buying stock, everybody followed. They knew it was going to go up. The only problem was to get out before they dumped it.

Durant owned General Motors twice and lost it twice . . . was worth way in excess of a billion dollars on paper, by present standards, four or five billion. He started his own automobile company, and it went under. When the Crash came, he caved in, like the rest of 'em. The last I heard of him I was told he ended up running a bowling alley. It was all on paper. Everybody in those days expected the sun to shine forever.

October 29, 1929, yeah. A frenzy. I must have gotten calls from a dozen and a half friends who were desperate. In each case, there was no sense in loaning them the money that they would give the broker. Tomorrow they'd be worse off than yesterday. Suicides, left and right, made a terrific impression on me, of course. People I knew. It was heartbreaking. One day you saw the prices at a hundred, the next day at $20, at $15.

On Wall Street, the people walked around like zombies. It was like *Death Takes A Holiday*. It was very dark. You saw people who yesterday rode around in Cadillacs lucky now to have carfare.

One of my friends said to me, "If things keep on as they are, we'll all have to go begging." I asked, "Who from?"

Many brokers did not lose money. They made fortunes on commissions while their customers went broke. The only brokers that got hurt badly were those that gambled on their own—or failed to sell out in time customers' accounts that were underwater. Of course, the brokerage business fell off badly, and practically all pulled in their belts, closed down offices and threw people out of work.

Banks used to get eighteen percent for call money—money with which to buy stock that paid perhaps one or two-percent dividends. They figured the price would continue to rise. Everybody was banking on it. I used to receive as much as twenty-two percent from brokers who borrowed from me. Twenty-two percent for money!

Men who built empires in utilities, would buy a small utility, add a big profit to it for themselves and sell it back to their own public company. That's how some like Samuel Insull became immensely wealthy. The thing that caused the Insull crash is the same that caused all these frenzied financiers to go broke. No matter how much they had, they'd pyramid it for more.

I had a great friend, John Hertz. At one time he owned ninety percent of the Yellow Cab stock. John also owned the Checker Cab. He also owned the Surface Line buses of Chicago. He was reputed to be worth $400 to $500 million. He asked me one day to join him on a yacht. There I met two men of such stature that I was in awe: Durant and Jesse Livermore.

We talked of all their holdings. Livermore said: "I own what I believe to be the controlling stock of IBM and Philip Morris." So I asked, "Why do you bother with anything else?" He answered, "I only understand stock. I can't bother with businesses." So I asked, "Do men of your kind put away $10 million where nobody can ever touch it?" He looked at me and answered, "Young man, what's the use of having ten million if you can't have big money?"

In 1934—after he went through two bankruptcies in succession—my accountant asked if I'd back Livermore. He was broke and wanted to make a comeback in the market. He always made a comeback and paid everybody off with interest. I agreed to do it. I put up $400,000. By 1939, we made enough money so that each of us could have $1,300,000 profit after taxes. Jesse was by this time in the late sixties, having gone through two bankruptcies. "Wouldn't it be wise to cash in?" I asked him. In those days, you could live like a king for $50,000 a year. He said he could just never get along on a pittance.

So I sold out, took my profits, and left Jesse on his own. He kept telling me he was going to make the killing of the century. Ben Smith, known as "Sell 'Em Short Ben," was in Europe and told him there was not going to be a war. Believing in Smith, Livermore went short on grain.[4] For every dollar he owned, plus everything he could pyramid.

When I arrived in Argentina, I learned that Germany invaded Poland. Poor Jesse was on the phone. "Art, you have to save me." I refused to do anything, being so far away. I knew it would be throwing good money after bad.

A couple of months later, I was back in New York, with Jesse waiting for me in my office. The poor fellow had lost everything he could lay his hands on. He asked for a $5,000 loan, which, of course, I gave him. Three days later, Jesse had gone to eat breakfast in the Sherry-Netherlands, went to the lavatory and shot himself. They found a note

---

[4] "Selling short is selling something you don't have and buying it back in order to cover it. You think a stock is not worth what it's selling for, say it's listed as $100. You sell a hundred shares of it, though you haven't got the stock. If you are right, and it goes down to $85, you buy it at that price, and deliver it to the fellow to whom you sold it for $100. You sell what you don't have." Obviously, if the stock rises in value, selling short is ruinous. . . . Ben Smith sold short during the Crash and made "a fortune."

made out to me for $5,000. This was the man who said, "What's the use having ten million if you can't have big money?" Jesse was one of the most brilliant minds in the trading world. He knew the crops of every area where grain grew. He was a great student, but always over-optimistic.

Did you sense the Crash coming in 1929?

I recognized it in May and saved myself a lot of money. I sold a good deal of my stocks in May. It was a case of becoming frightened. But, of course, I did not sell out completely, and finished with a very substantial loss.

In 1927 when I read Lindbergh was planning his memorable flight, I bought Wright Aeronautic stock. He was going to fly in a plane I heard was made by Wright. I lived in Milwaukee then. My office was about a mile from my home. When I left my house, I checked with my broker. By the time I reached my office, I had made sixty-five points. The idea of everything moving so fast was frightening. Everything you bought just seemed to have no ceiling.

People say we're getting a repetition of 1929. I don't see how it is possible. Today with SEC[5] controls and bank insurance, people know their savings are safe. If everybody believes, it's like believing in counterfeit money. Until it's caught, it serves its purpose.

In 1932 I came to New York to open an office in the Flatiron Building. Macfadden, the health faddist, created penny restaurants. There was a Negro chap I took a liking to that I had to deal with. He agreed to line up seventy-five people who needed to be fed. At six o'clock I would leave my office, I'd march seventy-five of 'em into the Macfadden restaurant and I'd feed 'em for seven cents apiece. I did this every day. It was just unbelievable, the bread lines. The only thing I could compare it with was Germany in 1922. It looked like there was no tomorrow.

I remember the Bank Holiday. I was one of the lucky ones. I had a smart brother-in-law, an attorney. One day he said to me, "I don't feel comfortable about the bank situation. I think we ought to have a lot of cash." About eight weeks before the bank closings, we decided to take every dollar out of the banks. We must have taken out close to a million dollars. In Clyde, Ohio, where I had a porcelain enamel plant, they used my signature for money. I used to come in every Saturday

[5] Securities and Exchange Commission.

and Sunday and deliver the cash. I would go around the department stores that I knew in Milwaukee and give them thirty-day IOU's of $1.05 for a dollar if they would give me cash.

In 1933, the night Jake Factor, "The Barber," was kidnapped, an associate of mine, his wife, and a niece from Wyoming were dancing in a night club. Each of us had $25,000 cash in our socks. We were leaving the following morning for Clyde, and I was supposed to bring in $100,000 to meet bills and the payroll. We were all dancing on $25,000 apiece. In the very place where Jake Factor was kidnapped for $100,000. The damn fools, they could have grabbed us and had the cash.

Jimmy McPartland

Jazz musician. A trumpet player, he was regarded by Bix Beiderbecke as his successor. He came East, out of Chicago, in the late Twenties, along with Benny Goodman, Bud Freeman, Gene Krupa, Eddie Condon.

So MANY GUYS were jumping out of windows, you know, because they lost their money. Goodness gracious, what for? We used to say to each other: Are they nuts? What is money? We were musicians, so what is money? That's nothing. The important thing is life and living and enjoying life. So these guys lose all their money, what the hell's the difference, we used to say, "You're still livin', aren't ya?" They can start all over again. I mean, this is what we used to think.

Actually, we didn't think about money. I personally didn't, because I always made it. For me, things have come so easy. I'm ashamed of myself. But money never bothered me. I'd give it away, if somebody needed money.

I remember the band was out of work. This was '28, '29, before the Crash. Bix was working with Paul Whiteman's band. We were out of work, six or eight weeks. We had no money left, and, man, I'm starvin' to death, no money to eat.

They'd invite you to a party, the social set, the money set. You'd play.

The best whiskey and everything like that—but no food. (Laughs.) Just all the liquor you could drink. We used to say: "You got a sandwich?"

So I got to this party on Park Avenue, we're invited: Benny Goodman and the guys. So who else is there, but the whole Whiteman band, Bix Beiderbecke and all those guys. So we're drinking and playing and jamming. Some big guy is the host. I get Bix on the side and I say, "Jesus, Bix, we aren't working. Can you lend me five bucks? I haven't eaten in two days." So God, he goes into his wallet, he had but two $100 bills and one fifty. He insisted I take the two $100 bills. I says, "No, I don't want that. All I want is $5, $10. I just want enough to buy some food." "Kid," he says, "you take this money and when you're working again, you pay me back."

Bix became ill and he left Whiteman, went home for a rest period, a dryout actually. I was working in the show *Sons of Guns,* and I'm making $275 a week, just in the show. In the daytime I'm working in the studios, $10 an hour. Making $300, $400 a week easy. So I got plenty of money and we used to meet at Plunkett's, a speak-easy. So I come in one day and Bix is there, flat broke and sick. He said to me, "Kid, you got any money?" I said, "Sure, you want some money?" I had about $175 in my pocket. The same thing happened. I gave him one fifty. I says, "Here." If I had more, I mean, he coulda had anything I had. He said he had a job, he'd pay me back. And don't you know, he died five or six days later, '32. He got pneumonia.

In the speak-easy, we knew some guys not doing so well. What the heck, you'd take out a $50 bill or ten, twenty, and slip it in their pocket and say, "Here, use it." When they get workin' again, they pay it back. And if they don't, so what? That was the feeling we used to have. I know Teagarden was that way, Bix was that way, and a lot of other guys.

It was during Prohibition. Between sets, we'd sneak into a speak-easy for a drink. One night we couldn't get in the speak. Jeez, the police were out. Some gangsters killed about three guys. They were pretty top-flight guys, so that was the end of that speak-easy. They used to make token raids once in a while. Everything was wide open. The police, I imagine, were in on it.

One night at the Park Central Hotel, somebody came in and said, "Somebody just got shot." It was Arnold Rothstein.[6] And we heard

[6] See Doc Graham in the sequence, "High Life," p. 201.

about the whole deal. Because we'd seen all these monkeys comin' in and out all the time. All the hoodlums in that era. They always liked us. Of course, we didn't bother with them. They'd come into the hotel, downstairs, in the basement. Dinner and dancing.

There were engagements in clubs and ballrooms throughout the country in the mid-Thirties, with various big bands and small combos. "We played nice places, the best hotels. There was dough. Some people didn't get jobs, but there was still plenty of money around. What would guys in the band talk about? Girls, mostly." (Laughs.) During this period, he was master of ceremonies at a Chicago jazz club, Three Deuces.

We had Billie Holiday in the show. She used to sing "Strange Fruit." Oh, beautiful. We got along great together, Billie and I. And I used to read in the back room sometimes to Art Tatum. He played intermission piano. 'Cause he couldn't see, you know. I used to bring books. He always talked about it: "Remember how you used to read to me, Jimmy?" He'd sit there and drink beer, and I'd read to him.

I never had this black and white feeling. Jesus, if you could sing or play, jeez, that was it. I never knew it was that bad till I went down to New Orleans in '34. Where we played, they had a gambling joint, Club Forest. They had a bunch of sheriffs around there because it could be held up. They even had a machine gun in an enclosed cage up above. They all carried guns.

One time, late at night, we were out drinking. There were three or four of these sheriffs. One of the guys said, "Hey there's that nigger son of a bitch. I'm gonna get him and blast his brains." They started towards him. He was really gonna shoot him. I pushed his hand away and I said, "Don't shoot him. I don't want to see you kill a guy." It was just a minor, simple little thing. I saved the guy's life just by pushin' this sheriff's hand away. They were gonna beat my brains out, the sheriffs. Oh, they started gettin' the pistol, one guy was gonna hit me. Another guy stopped them. Then I realized: Holy jeez, these guys are murder. They're gonna kill a guy for nothing. Just because— . . . wow, boy.

There was more camaraderie. It didn't make any difference if you were colored or white. If you were a good musician, that's all that counted. Now the colored guys say we can't play real jazz, soul music.

79

What the hell else we play with but our soul? Every guy's soul is not the same. Know what I mean? Miles Davis thinks I'm great—he likes me, and I like him. But so many others say: the white guy can't play. He hasn't got the soul. Who they kiddin'? There's nobody with a lock-up on soul. If I let myself go and play just the way I feel, that's my soul, isn't it? Whether it be white or black, you gotta play the way you want to.

The music of the Thirties *was* good. I don't mean you stand still. I haven't. But I must play the way I feel. If my style is any good, it will endure, Thirties or Sixties. Or Seventies.

I think everybody should have a job, and the Government should see that they get a job. That WPA deal, that was a darn good idea. I was one of the lucky guys that didn't need it, but this is what I believe. Everybody should work, but do what they want. I don't mean this as a communist thing, maybe it's socialism, I don't know. Like I'm a musician. Just pay me to do concerts for nothin'. Let people listen for nothing.

The Government should work something out so people have something to do. There are so many things to be done in these cities. You feel much better if you're workin' instead of gettin' a handout. You'll get self-respect, which is number one. Drama, dancing schools, musicians. . . . You could give guys like me jobs as teachers, to teach jazz. So you perpetuate what I've learned in my lifetime. You could give that to some younger person and let them carry on, make their own choice, but at least they'd have the background. It's like studying history. It's like being part of history. . . .

Sidney J. Weinberg

Senior partner, Goldman-Sachs Company, a leading investment house. He served during Roosevelt's first two Administrations as an industrial adviser.

OCTOBER 29, 1929—I remember that day very intimately. I stayed in the office a week without going home. The tape was running, I've forgotten how long that night. It must have been ten, eleven o'clock before we got the final reports. It was like a thunder clap. Everybody was stunned. Nobody knew what it was all about. The Street had general confusion. They didn't understand it any more than anybody else. They thought something would be announced.

Prominent people were making statements. John D. Rockefeller, Jr., announced on the steps of J. P. Morgan, I think, that he and his sons were buying common stock. Immediately, the market went down again. Pools combined to support the market, to no avail. The public got scared and sold. It was a very trying period for me. Our investment company went up to two, three hundred, and then went down to practically nothing. As all investment companies did.

Over-speculation was the cause, a reckless disregard of economics. There was a group ruthlessly selling short. You could sell anything and depress the market unduly. The more you depressed it, the more you created panic. Today we have protections against it. Call money went up—was it twenty percent?

No one was so sage that he saw this thing coming. You can be a Sunday morning quarterback. A lot of people have said afterwards, "I saw it coming, I sold all my securities." There's a credibility gap there. There are always some people who are conservative, who did sell out. I didn't know any of these.

I don't know anybody that jumped out of the window. But I know many who threatened to jump. They ended up in nursing homes and insane asylums and things like that. These were people who were trading in the market or in banking houses. They broke down physically, as well as financially.

Roosevelt saved the system. It's trite to say the system would have gone out the window. But certainly a lot of institutions would have changed. We were on the verge of something. You could have had a rebellion; you could have had a civil war.

The Street was against Roosevelt. Only me and Joe Kennedy, of those I know, were for Roosevelt in 1932. I was Assistant Treasurer of the Democratic National Committee. I did not support him after the first two terms. I had a great argument with him. I didn't think any man should serve any more than two terms. I was getting a little tired, too, of all the New Deal things. When I was asked to work with the War Production Board in 1940, he delayed initialing my employment paper. Later on, we had a rapprochement and were friendly again.

Confidence ended the Depression in 1934. We had a recession in 1937. People got a little too gay on the way up, and you had to have a little leveling off. The war had a great deal of stimulus in 1939.

A Depression could not happen again, not to the extent of the one in '29. Unless inflation went out of hand and values went beyond true worth. A deep stock market reaction could bring a Depression, yes. There would be immediate Government action, of course. A moratorium. But in panic, people sell regardless of worth. Today you've got twenty-odd million stockholders owning stock. At that time you had probably a million and a half. You could have a sharper decline now than you had in 1929.

Most of the net worth of people today is in values. They haven't got it in cash. In a panic, values go down regardless of worth. A house worth $30,000, the minute you have a panic, isn't worth anything. Everybody feels good because the stock they bought at fifty is now selling at eighty. So they have a good feeling. But it's all on paper.

Martin DeVries

PEOPLE WERE speculating. Now who are they gonna blame aside from themselves? It's their fault. See my point? If you gamble and make a mistake, why pick on somebody else? It's your fault, don't you see?

It's like many people on the bread lines. I certainly felt sorry for them. But many of them hadn't lived properly when they were making it. They hadn't saved anything. Many of them wouldn't have been in the shape they were in, if they had been living in a reasonable way. Way back in the '29s, people were wearing $20 silk shirts and throwing their money around like crazy. If they had been buying Arrow $2 shirts and putting the other eighteen in the bank, when the trouble came, they wouldn't have been in the condition they were in.

In 1929, I had a friend who speculated. He'd say, "What's good?" I'd say, "We're selling high-grade first mortgage bonds on Commonwealth Edison." "Oh, hell," he'd say, "five percent. I make ten percent on the stock market." He was buying on margin. He thought he was rich. Know what happened to him? He blew his brains out. The Government had nothing to do with that. It's people.

Most people today are living beyond their means. They don't give a damn. The Government'll take care of them. People today don't want to work. We had a nice colored woman that worked for us fifteen years. She had a grandson. We offered to pay him $2 an hour to take the paper off our bedroom wall. Nothing to it. One coat of paper. We'd provide the bucket and sponge and the ladder. Do you think he'd do it? No. We couldn't get anybody to do it. So I did it myself. Nothing to it.

Do you think the New Deal is responsible . . . ?

Certainly. This huge relief program they began. What do you think brings all the colored people to Chicago and New York?

So when I say F.D.R.—

—my blood begins to boil. The New Deal immediately attacked Wall Street. As far as the country was concerned, Wall Street was responsible for all the upheavals. They set up the Securities and Exchange Commission. That was all right. I know there were some evils. But these fellas Roosevelt put in the SEC were a bunch of young Harvard theorists. Except for old Joe Kennedy. He was a robber baron. These New Dealers felt they had a mission to perform. Roosevelt attacked people—with some reason. But without justice. All people on Wall Street are not crooks.

My friends and I often spoke about it. Especially after his hammy fireside chats. Here we were paying taxes and not asking for anything. Everybody else was asking for relief, for our money to help them out. . . . A certain amount of that is O.K., but when they strip you clean and still don't accomplish much, it's unfair.

They were do-gooders, trying to accomplish something. I give them credit for that. But they didn't listen to anybody who had any sense.

Hoover happened to be in a bad spot. The Depression came on, and there he was. If Jesus Christ had been there, he'd have had the same problem. It's too bad for poor old Herbie that he happened to be there. This was a world-wide Depression. It wasn't Hoover's fault. In 1932, a Chinaman or a monkey could have been elected against him, no question about it.

John Hersch

He is the senior partner in a large brokerage house in Chicago. From his LaSalle Street office, on this late afternoon we can see the crowds below, worrying toward buses and parking lots, heading home.

"It's been a fascinating business for me right from 1924 to 1968. I've been in it a long time, and I'm very proud of it. It's entirely different than it was in the Twenties. The canons of ethics are extremely strict. There are still bad episodes once in a while, but it's a big society."

His is an air of worldly-weariness.

I CAME into the business, out of the University of Chicago, about Christmas, 1924. I had about $3,000 in the stock market, which was all the money I had. On Black Friday—Thursday, was it?—that margin account went out of the window. I may have had about $62 left.

My wife had a colossal $125 a week job with a Shakespearean theater company. That night, she came home to our little apartment, and she said, "Guess what happened today?" I said, "What?" She said, "I quit." I was making about $60 a week and she was making $125. Two-thirds of our income and all of our savings disappeared that day.

I was a margin clerk. He's a man who keeps the figures on individual accounts, if they're carrying stocks on margin—that is, if they're carrying stocks without paying for them.

When the break started, you had a deluge of selling, from weakened margin accounts. We had to stay up all night figuring. We'd work till one o'clock and go to the LaSalle Hotel and get up about five and get some breakfast and continue figuring margin accounts. 'Cause everybody was in trouble. But everybody.

The guy I worked for was sitting in the wire room, watching the tape. The tape was something to see, because Radio Corporation, let's say, would be ninety-five on the tape . . . they'd flash you sixty on the floor. The floor was a madhouse. I said to him: "Are we solvent?" He says, "I won't know till about twelve tonight." He was half-serious. It was brutal.

The Crash—it didn't happen in one day. There were a great many warnings. The country was crazy. Everybody was in the stock market, whether he could afford it or not. Shoeshine boys and waiters and capitalists. . . . A great many holding company pyramids were unsound, really fictitious values. Mr. Insull was a case in point. It was a mad dream of get-rich-quick.

It wasn't only brokers involved in margin accounts. It was banks. They had a lot of stinking loans. The banks worked in as casual a way as the brokers did. And when they folded. . . .

I had a friend in Cincinnati who was young and attractive. He had a wife and children and he was insured for $100,000. Life was over as far as he was concerned. He took a dive, to take care of his wife and kids. There was a number who took the dive, to collect on insurance policies. It's unthinkable now, when you know how many people have been able to come back.

There were others that impress me. I kept hearing about town that their businesses were in trouble. But they never lowered their standard of living a bit. They lived like kings, right through the Depression. I've never been able to figure this out. I knew some people who maintained their Lake Shore Drive apartments and cars, and everybody knew they were in trouble. I never knew how they did it, and I didn't care particularly. My friends and I were all broke, and we had no pretensions.

You had no governmental control of margins, so people could buy on a shoestring. And when they began pulling the plug . . . you had a deluge of weakness. You also had short-selling and a lack of rules.[7] There were many cases of staid, reputable bankers making securities available on special deals—below the market price—for their friends. Anything went, and everything did go.

Today, there are very few bankers of any repute who have objected to the Securities Exchange Commission. They believe that the regulation in 1933 was a very, very sound thing for our business.

In '32 and '33, there was no securities business to speak of. We played a lot of bridge in the afternoons on LaSalle Street. There was nobody to call or see. It was so quiet, you could hear a certificate drop. (Laughs.) Nobody was making a living. A lot of them managed to eke out $40, $60 a week, but mostly we played bridge. (Laughs.)

[7] "Now under SEC rules, you can only sell if the stock goes up an eighth. You can't sell it on the downtake."

I found a certain obtuseness about what's going on in the country. Even after it happened. Of course, at the beginning of the New Deal, the capitalists embraced Franklin Roosevelt as a real savior of our system. The Chicago *Tribune* wrote laudatory articles about him. Editorials. As soon as things got a little better, the honeymoon was over. You know all those old stories about guys getting on the train at Lake Forest: they were always looking for one headline every morning, that black headline about F.D.R. These people. . . .

It took this guy with the long cigarette holder to do some planning about basic things—like the SEC and the WPA and even the lousy Blue Eagle. It put a new spirit in the country.

The Bank Holiday of 1933 brought a certain kind of joyous, devil-may-care mood. People were just gettin' along somehow. It was based on the theory: Good grief, it couldn't get much worse. They bartered things for things.

The Irish Players were in Chicago, and everybody took potatoes to get in. People were taking vegetables to the box office. And they had big audiences.

I'm not trying to detract from the fact that there was wholesale misery in the Depression, 'cause you knew there were people living under the Michigan Avenue Bridge. Gentlemen in old $200 suits were selling apples. There was plenty of misery. I never want to see another. . . .

I don't find that people remember the Depression or think about it. I don't find it coming up in conversations. I also discover that a great many people, even professors, who might have gotten $300 a month during the Depression—some of them are worth a hundred, a hundred fifty thousand bucks today. You've never seen so much money around in history as there is today. Never. It's happened in the last twenty-three years . . . the development of industry and the creation of equities in business.

Another remarkable thing about the Depression—it never resulted in revolution. I remember that out in Iowa some place, there was a fellow named Reno,[8] who led a small following. There were some trucks turned over, and sheriffs weren't allowed to foreclose. But when you consider what was going on in the country—the whole country was orderly: they just sat there and took it. In retrospect, it's amazing, just amazing. Either they were in shock, or they thought something would

[8] Milo Reno, leader of the Farm Holiday Association.

happen to turn it around. . . . My wife has often discussed this with me. She thinks it's astonishing, the lack of violent protest, especially in 1932 and 1933.

Anna Ramsey

JUST BEFORE the Crash my father, who was a barber, bought a building. We pinched. We didn't lose the building. He was a frugal man. I remember how he used to scrounge and scrape to make his mortgage payments. He borrowed money from a loan company very frequently. Oh, the tension in the house, when Pa used to scramble around trying to get enough money to pay that installment loan. That was the one degrading thing I remember.

It was a well-known loan company. I remember it as so dingy. I'm sure it wasn't. It was just the way I felt: there was something not quite right about it. I didn't feel shame. I felt resentment of conditions over which we had no control.

The worst thing I have to do every month is to pay my mortgage. I hate to think of all that interest being paid. If I had the money, I'd pay it all off. I just loathe it.

Dr. David J. Rossman

A psychiatrist. He had studied with Freud. His patients are upper middle class. He has been practicing since the Twenties.

MILLIONAIRES would come to me for treatment of anxiety attacks. In 1933, one of them said to me, "I'm here for treatment because I have lost all my money. All I have left is one house on Long Island which is worth $750,000. I don't know what I'd get for it if I tried to sell it."

He was a very aristocratic looking man. "I've always had a feeling of guilt about the money I've made."

I asked him, "Why do you feel guilty about it?" He said he was a floor trader and when he saw the market begin to fall, he would give it a big shove by selling short. At the end of the day, he had made $50–$75,000. This went on for a long time. He said, "I had always felt as if I had taken this money out of the mouths of orphans and widows."

He felt guilty after the walls caved in. He began to feel what it was like not to have any money. To give you an idea of the importance of this man: he was in a secret meeting at the J. P. Morgan bank, when they were trying to stop the decline. He had an appointment at five o'clock, and he said, "I won't be here today. But when I see you later, I'll have an important message for you."

If I had bought General Motors and Chrysler where it was in March, 1933, I could have been a multi-millionaire on the investment of $10,000. But that wasn't his message. He said, "We have decided to close the Bank of the United States because the President was truculent and insisted upon an enormously inflated price for his stock." This was a very small bank in New York. They decided to let him go to the wall. The bank failed.

This man told me to go to the bank and take all my money and get gold notes. They were yellowbacks that said on the back: Redeemable in demand at the U.S. Treasury for gold in bars. I got $10,000 in gold. I said, "What the hell am I going to do with this?" It was heavy as hell. In gold bullion. I put it in a safety deposit box. Two days later, I had to take it out because the President declared the possession of gold to be illegal. I gave it back to the bank, and they credited me with $10,000.

I learned about the crack in our economy long before the stock market crash of '29. I had a patient who was the biggest kitchen utensil distributor in America. He had a huge plant. He said: suddenly, without notice, his orders just stopped. May and June, 1929.

All of us believed a new era in finance dawned. How long was I in the stock market? From '26 to '29. I had doubled my money. I remember some of the stocks I bought. I bought Electric Bond and Share, for example. I bought it at $100 a share and sold it at $465.

That was the only way you could make any real money. Income was piddling. Physicians were the greatest amateur financiers in the world. The way in which doctors, some of my friends, became interested was they had patients in high finance. They told them which stocks to buy. They were heading for a fall.

I began to invest in 1926. At the time I was working for Veterans Administration, and I think every doctor there had his finger in some kind of stocks. Some did better than others. I was too timid. Until a couple of years later, when I got a tip to buy Montgomery Ward, and within ten days I'd made $1,000.

In May of 1929, I personally pulled out of the market. I took my money out of the house I was dealing with and entrusted it to a man who was the backer of one of the wealthiest men in the country. Thinking he was infallible. He began buying stocks. He bought me Johns-Manville, for example. It was selling at $112. He bought a hundred shares at a bargain, 105. I sold it at 50.

This man embezzled stocks in the spring of 1929, something like $3 million worth. He was in very deep trouble. He died of a coronary. There was no prosecution. He was a pawn. The man whose manager he was was worth about a hundred million. He was not injured in the Crash. He made vast fortunes in dealing with devaluating currencies in Europe. He passed tips along to his friends. A good many of them made $6–$8 million. $6 million is a lot of money. They were cashing in on the decline in European currency.

What was happening to humans . . . ?

Nothing much. You wouldn't know a Depression was going on. Except that people were complaining they didn't have any jobs. You could get the most wonderful kind of help for a pittance. People would work for next to nothing. That's when people were peddling apples and bread lines were forming all over the city. But on the whole—don't forget the highest unemployment was less than twenty percent.

Your patients, then, weren't really affected?

Not very much. They paid fairly reasonable fees. I just came across a bankbook that I had between 1931 and 1934, and, by God, I was in those days making $2,000 a month, which was a hell of a lot of money. Then in 1934, 1935, 1936, they began coming in droves, when things began to ease up. People were looking for help. All middle class. Money loosened up. At the outbreak of the war, all psychiatrists in New York were just simply drowned with work. I saw my first patient at seven in the morning and I worked till nine at night.

He dwells on the recession of 1937, his interest in the Spanish Civil War, the disappointment in Roosevelt's embargo on Spain, the fall of Barcelona. . . . A good many of his patients were liberals, some interested in Marxism as a solution; others were "the hard core of the big merchants."

Did you have contact with the lower . . . ?

The lower classes? No. Let's take the lower middle class, a contractor. He built me a ten-room stone house for $8,500. I would pay him five cents a square foot for knotty pine that would cost you $1.50 today. Same thing. No laborer that worked in my house got more than $5 a day. I asked the contractor what he got out of it. He said, "I ate for six months." It was catch as catch can. Undersell yourself, do good work, on the hope that you would be recommended to somebody else.

In those days everybody accepted his role, responsibility for his own fate. Everybody, more or less, blamed himself for his delinquency or lack of talent or bad luck. There was an acceptance that it was your own fault, your own indolence, your lack of ability. You took it and kept quiet.

A kind of shame about your own personal failure. I was wondering what the hell it was all about. I wasn't suffering.

An outstanding feature of the Depression was that there were very few disturbances. People mass-marching, there was some. People marched in Washington and Hoover promised everything was going to be all right. People hoped and people were bewildered.

Big business in 1930 and later in '32 came hat in hand, begging Roosevelt. They have never gotten over their humiliation, and they have never forgiven him for having the wits to do something about it. Priming the pump.

Now people think it's coming to them. The whole ethos has changed. There is a great deal more hatred and free-floating aggression all over the country. We have reached unprecedented prosperity. Everybody says: "Why not *me?*" The affluent society has made itself known to people . . . how the better half lives. It's put on television, you can see it. And everybody says, "Who the hell are they? What's the matter with me? My skin is black, so what?" You don't accept responsibility for your own fate. It's the other fellow who's to blame. It's terrible. It could tear our country apart.

Do you think there might be a revolution if the Depression came upon us again?

It would be an inchoate affair. It wouldn't be organized.

Today nobody is permitted to starve. Now they think it's coming to them. As a matter of fact, it was the government that brought this idea to the people, in the Thirties. The people didn't ask the government. They ask the question they can't answer themselves: Why am *I* the goat? Why *me?* They want pie in the sky. . . .

Man and Boy

Alonso Mosely, 20

He is a VISTA worker in the black community.

ALL I KNOW about the Depression is what I studied about it. People suffered and had to carry out food stamps. My parents mentioned it vaguely. I could get no information from them. . . .

Clifford Burke, 68

THE NEGRO was born in depression. It didn't mean too much to him, The Great American Depression, as you call it. There was no such thing. The best he could be is a janitor or a porter or shoeshine boy. It only became official when it hit the white man. If you can tell me the difference between the depression today and the Depression of 1932 for a black man, I'd like to know it. Now, it's worse, because of the prices. Know the rents they're payin' out here? I hate to tell ya.

He is a pensioner. Most of his days are spent as a volunteer with a community organization in the black ghetto on the West Side of the city.

We had one big advantage. Our wives, they could go to the store and get a bag of beans or a sack of flour and a piece of fat meat, and they could cook this. And we could eat it. Steak? A steak would kick in my stomach like a mule in a tin stable. Now you take the white fella, he couldn't do this. His wife would tell him: Look, if you can't do any better than this, I'm gonna leave you. I seen it happen. He couldn't stand bringing home beans instead of steak and capon. And he couldn't stand the idea of going on relief like a Negro.

You take a fella had a job paying him $60, and here I am making $25. If I go home taking beans to me wife, we'll eat it. It isn't exactly what we want, but we'll eat it. The white man that's been making big money, he's taking beans home, his wife'll say: Get out. (Laughs.)

Why did these big wheels kill themselves? They weren't able to live up to the standards they were accustomed to, and they got ashamed in front of their women. You see, you can tell anybody a lie, and he'll agree with you. But you start layin' down the facts of real life, he won't accept it. The American white man has been superior so long, he can't figure out why he should come down.

I remember a friend of mine, he didn't know he was a Negro. I mean he acted like he never knew it. He got tied downtown with some stock. He blew about twenty thousand. He came home and drank a bottle of poison. A bottle of iodine or something like that. It was a rarity to hear a Negro killing himself over a financial situation. He might have killed himself over some woman. Or getting in a fight. But when it came to the financial end of it, there were so few who had anything. (Laughs.)

I made out during that . . . *Great* Depression. (Laughs.) Worked as a teamster for a lumber yard. Forty cents an hour. Monday we'd have a little work. They'd say come back Friday. There wasn't no need to look for another job. The few people working, most all of them were white.

So I had another little hustle. I used to play pool pretty good. And I'd ride from poolroom to poolroom on this bicycle. I used to beat these guys, gamble what we had. I'd leave home with a dollar. First couple of games I could beat this guy, I'd put that money in my pocket. I'd take the rest of what I beat him out of and hustle the day on that. Sometimes I'd come home with a dollar and a half extra. That was a whole lot of money. Everybody was out trying to beat the other guy, so he could make it. It was pathetic.

I never applied for PWA or WPA, 'cause as long as I could hustle, there was no point in beating the other fellow out of a job, cuttin' some other guy out. . . .

God Bless' the Child

Them that's got shall get
Them that's not shall lose
So the Bible says,
And it still is news.
Mama may have, Papa may have,
But God bless' the child that's got his own. . . .

Yes, the strong gets more, while the weak ones fade
Empty pockets don't ever make the grade.
Mama may have, Papa may have,
But God bless' the child that's got his own. . . .

—Arthur Herzog, Jr. and Billie Holiday[1]

Jane Yoder

A house in Evanston. The green grass grows all around. "We're middle middle class. Not upper and not lower, either." Her husband is a junior executive in a large corporation. They have two sons: the elder, a lieutenant in the air force; the other, soon to be married, a graduate of Notre Dame.

[1] Copyright Edward B. Marks Music Corporation. Used by permission.

"I love the trees. This house represents his struggle and mine. We bought this house on a shoestring. I'm terribly afraid of debt. If I have one fear, it's the rich get richer when you buy on time. All these things that are hidden costs—like with this house, we had to buy it up quickly through a friend of my husband's father. So it was bought without the real estate commission.

"We've always paid our bills along the way. I have a real fear of being trapped into more than I need. I just turn away from it. Security to me is not what we have, but what we can do without. I don't want anything so badly that I can't wait for it. I think a second television set in our bedroom might be kind of nice. But I can dismiss it. We have one. How many can you watch?

"We got married in July of 1940. This cocktail table is an early decision in those days. And that end table. So my brothers come in, and they say, 'It's amazing. Same stuff is here, and you've added to it. By God, how did you do it?'"

Her father was a blacksmith in a small central Illinois mining town. There were seven children. The mines closed "early, about '28 or '30." The men, among them her father, went to other towns, seeking jobs.

DURING THE DEPRESSION, my father took a great deal of psychological abuse. Oh, tremendous. This brother-in-law that was superintendent of the mine . . . I look at these two men. . . . I really think my father had a marvelous mind. I wonder what he had the potential to become. . . .

He's like something out of Dostoevsky. My father was, I think, terribly intelligent. He learned to speak English, a couple of languages, and prided himself on not being like the rest in our neighborhood. He was constantly giving us things from either the paper or some fiction and being dramatic about it . . . "down with these people that didn't want to think." Just as proud of his kids . . . but he was schizophrenic. He could look at himself a little bit, and then just run like hell. Because what he saw was painful.

We were struggling, just desperate to be warm. No blankets, no coats. At this time I was in fourth grade. Katie[2] went to Chicago and bought an Indian blanket coat. I remember this incident of that Indian blanket coat. (Gasps.) Oh, because Katie came home with it and had it in her clothes closet for quite a while. And I didn't have a coat. I can remem-

[2] Her older sister.

ber putting on that coat in Sue Pond's house. I thought, oh, this is marvelous, gee. I took that coat home, and I waited till Sunday and wore it to church. And then everybody laughed. I looked horrid. Here was this black-haired kid, with a tendency to be overweight. My God, when I think of that. . . . But I wore that coat, laugh or not. And I can remember thinking: the hell with it. I don't care what . . . it doesn't mean a thing. Laugh hard, you'll get it out of your system. I was warm.

Before that I had one coat. It must have been a terrible lightweight coat or what, but I can remember being cold, just shivering. And came home, and nothing to do but go to bed, because if you went to bed, then you put the coat on the bed and you got warm.

The cold that I've known. I never had boots. I think when I got married, I had my first set of boots. In rainy weather, you just ran for it, you ran between the raindrops or whatever. This was luxuriating to have boots. You simply wore your old shoes if it was raining. Save the others. You always polished them and put shoe trees in them. You didn't have unlimited shoe trees, either. When the shoes are worn out, they're used around the house. And of the high heels, you cut the heels down and they're more comfortable.

We tell our boys: you have a black sweater, a white sweater, and a blue sweater. You can't wear ten sweaters at once, you can only wear one. What is this thing? . . . some of the people that I know have thirty blouses. Oh, my God, I have no desire to think where I'd hang them. For what? I can't even grasp it.

If we had a cold or we threw up, nobody ever took your temperature. We had no thermometer. But if you threw up and you were hot, my mother felt your head. She somehow felt that by bringing you oranges and bananas and these things you never had—there's nothing wrong with you, this is what she'd always say in Croatian; you'll be all right. Then she gave you all these good things. Oh, gee, you almost looked forward to the day you could throw up. I could remember dreaming about oranges and bananas, dreaming about them.

My oldest brother, terribly bright, wanted to go on to school to help pay those grocery bills that were back there. But my youngest brother, Frankie, didn't know. Oh, it just overwhelms me sometimes when I think of those two younger brothers, who would want to get some food and maybe go to the store. But they would see this $900 grocery bill, and they just couldn't do it.

We all laugh now, because Frankie is now down in New Mexico, and superintendent of two mines. And we all say, "Remember, Frankie?"

Frankie's *"To košta puno?"* That's "Did it cost a lot?" Everything that came into the house, he'd say, *"To košta puno?"*

Did it cost much? No matter what you brought in: bread and eggs and Karo syrup. Oh, Karo syrup was such a treat. I don't remember so much *my* going to the store and buying food. I must have been terribly proud and felt: I can't do it. How early we all stayed away from going to the store, because we sensed my father didn't have the money. So we stayed hungry. And we talked about it.

I can think of the WPA . . . my father immediately got employed in this WPA. This was a godsend. This was the greatest thing. It meant food, you know. Survival, just survival.

How stark it was for me to come into nurses' training and have the girls—one of them, Susan Stewart, lived across the hall from me, her father was a doctor—their impressions of the WPA. How it struck me. Before I could ever say that my father was employed in the WPA, discussions in the bull sessions in our rooms immediately was: these lazy people, the shovel leaners. I'd just sit there and listen to them. I'd look around and realize: sure, Susan Stewart was talking this way, but her father was a doctor, and her mother was a nurse. Well, how nice. They had respectable employment. In my family, there was no respectable employment. I thought, you don't know what it's like.

How can I defend him? I was never a person who could control this. It just had to come out or I think I'd just blow up. So I would say, "I wonder how much we know until we go through it. Just like the patients we take care of. None of them are in that hospital by choice." I would relate it in abstractions. I think it saved me from just blowing up.

I would come back after that and I'd just say: Gee, these are just two separate, separate worlds.

Tom Yoder, Jane's Son

He had entered the room during my conversation with his mother. His fiancée accompanied him.

IT SEEMS just absolutely—it's almost in a black humorous sense—funny to me. To realize that a hundred miles from Chicago, about forty years ago, my mother's brothers, whom I know well now, were out with little rifles, hunting for food to live on. And if they didn't find it, there were truly some empty stomachs. I mean, this is just too much. I don't think my generation can really comprehend what all this means. I've never gone to bed hungry—I wish I had. I haven't, and I probably never will.

Whenever I've griped about my home life, Mother's always said, "I hope you always have it so good." And I'm the kind of person that will say, "Look, what do you mean you hope I always have it so good? I intend when I'm forty to be making $25,000." But I understand what she means. I am grateful for what I have. But it's only human nature that we all want to go on and find something better.

Daisy Singer

A photographer.

I WAS SIX when the Crash came. Of classic, upper middle-class Jewish, you know, second-generation American. My father was sort of self-made.

He was something of a phony. He could always appear to be richer than he was. A lot of his friends were richer than he was, but he was the most flamboyant. He made what he had go a long way. Like he wasn't terribly intelligent, but he was fantastic at giving advice. People would come to him when they were contemplating suicide.

Headwaiters instantly knew he was someone to contend with. Like if he was on a transatlantic voyage, he would meet, at one time, Cardinal Spellman and, at another time, Al Capone. He was that kind of man.

We lived on Park Avenue before the Depression, like in eleven or fourteen rooms. One of those big apartments which are essentially very dreary. But they're what people hoped to achieve. After the Crash, we moved to Central Park West which wasn't such a terrible come-down. Except my grandparents moved in with us: keep up appearances and double in brass.

I remember vaguely family conferences, which took place behind closed doors. Like loans negotiated and things like that. The front would have to be maintained because I've learned that in business if people smell failure in you, you've had it.

I always had governesses. I had one I really loved when I was young, until I was seven. Then I had a succession of ones I loathed.

I remember going to the park with the one I really liked. There was a shanty town. Like a Hooverville. It was for me the palpable memory of the other side of the tracks. Ever since, when I encounter poverty, it is this memory . . . holding the hand of one's governess. For years, I felt exempt. I grew up feeling immune and exempt from circumstance. One of the things I suffered from was that I never felt adversity. I was confirmed in a sense of unreality. I never saw a real bread line. I saw it in the movies.

The outside world was so far from us, one didn't expect to encounter it. The doors were shut, as if there were some kind of contagion out there. I guess it was innocence, but I don't think of it as anything pretty at all: the less you experience, the better.

When my father was dying of cancer, he would hallucinate. Some of them were businessmen's hallucinations. He had an imaginary pocket with imaginary papers. He kept stashing them away. In a gesture that was familiar to him. Important papers. He always had a brief case or something and he had millions of papers. . . .

Robin Langston

He is a social worker by day, a jazz musician by night. He is forty-three years old. He lived in Hot Springs, Arkansas, until he was seventeen.

". . . there are so many places that would have been worse. Suppose I had come up, say in Mississippi . . . ?"

I KNEW the Depression had really hit when the electric lights went out. My parents could no longer pay the $1 electric bill. The kerosene lamps went up in the home. And in the business. My father had a restaurant. This did something to me, because it let me know that my father was not the greatest cat in the world. I always thought he was.

My father couldn't read or write. If an airplane wrote his name in the sky, he wouldn't be able to read it. But he had a thirst for knowledge. It was our task, my sister and I, to read to him. He was the type of cat who would keep the radio on all day, just to listen to the news.

I remember that kerosene lamp, because for Christmas, '30, around in there, I got a little book that pictured Lindbergh's flight. My mother was telling me how great Lindbergh was. She told me I would fly a plane like that. But she didn't tell me about my chances of flying. That was the point, you see. 'Cause they were trying to shield me.

My mother was a teacher. She never did teach, because my father never did want her to work. He was the person to wear the pants in the family. He wanted to be the strong one. I was exposed to a lot of books: Pushkin, Frederick Douglass, Raymond Moley, *Time* Magazine. No Booker T. Washington. He was anathema in my home.

My father taught us how to adjust to situations. We were fortunate compared to others. We always had food. Very little money, but there was so much spiritual guidance. I don't mean this Billy Graham type. I mean this thing that develops in a family where you anticipate the other's needs. I can kiss my father and not feel ashamed that I kissed a man. This is the type of thing we had going.

One time, my father and I tore a wall down to enlarge the business. I must have been around eight or nine. I could see blood coming from his hands, from using the crowbar, and I kissed his hand.

The restaurant was in the black community. But we made as much money off white people as we did off blacks. White people wanted to come in and get fried chicken. He had them fooled that there was something mystical about the batter he used. Another device he would use: they say that colored people like watermelon. Well, he raised the price of watermelon when white folks came in. All these survival techniques. . . .

I started washing dishes in the restaurant about five. My father didn't start me, I insisted. I'd get up on a Coca-Cola box to bend over the dish trough. My mother worked the cash register, and my sister was the waitress. It was a family type.

During the Depression, my father bought most things cash. The biggest thing we bought was a car and a refrigerator. I remember distinctly he paid on this in cash, because he didn't want to keep going back up to the store and taking this white man money and receipt book. My father did not like hat-in-hand situations.

My family always had a lot of white friends because there was always some food. A white friend would forget his supposedly superior attitude if there's food involved. They were going to get some of my father's mystical fried chicken.

There was a unique thing about this black community. It wasn't like Chicago. There were Caucasians in the community. The police chief lived right in the heart of it. I guess there must have been ten white families within fifty feet of us. I remember feeding snotty-nosed white kids. It was the Depression because no white and no blacks were working. The *whites* not working made it official. Father and Mother did that thing out of the goodness of their hearts.

I remember when times got so hard, this sheriff pawned a radio to my father for $10. He had come to the black man to get $10. He really needed the ten. He had some people out of town, he wanted to bring them there to eat some chicken. So he told my father he didn't have the money. Dad told him he had to have some collateral. So he brought the radio.

My father carried black people on the tab during the Depression. We had a basement in our home and people who would come there, down and out, my father let them live there as long as they would keep it up, work around the garden, keeping up the roses and things. This is how I learned to gamble and shoot dice, from these guys. We got in a couple of boxers there. One of them became a champ.

The schools were segregated. I doubt if we had one teacher who had a bachelor's degree. These were tremendous people, black people. One lady's been teaching there over fifty years. I doubt if she's finished tenth grade. You'd go to a sandbox, she'd show you how to make a pond in the sandbox by taking a mirror, putting it in the sand and letting the mirror shine through.

It might have been in eighth or ninth grade. It was in one of the English classes. We didn't have a library in the black school. We depended on what people who came in would give us. We were reading *Time* Magazine. There was an article on Raymond Moley on economics. We were supposed to get this article and make a report on it. I had to go to the white high school.

A frowsy Caucasian woman opened a crack in the door and threw the book on the floor. I tried to determine what's more important: this affront or getting Raymond Moley? My immediate thing was to get Raymond Moley. But my father always told me never to stoop. So I left the book on the floor. It hurt. I cried because I wanted the article so bad.

Hot Springs was a unique place. It was a health resort. It depended on rich people coming in. They came to the race track with their women. There was a sort of sophistication. A sort of *Encyclopaedia Britannica* attitude. It was cosmopolitan and yet semi-rural. A rurban area.

They had one mayor. It seemed like he stayed in office a million years. He would ride around in his carriage with two black ponies. He lived in the black ghetto. Only he was on top of the hill. He would visit all the gambling places in the community. White people came down and shot dice. They'd come down looking for women, too. The red-light district was always in the black area. The only white prostitutes you would find would be in the hotels. They would be the high-priced ones. They would go with the Negro bellhop. Say, if the bellhop caught a politician, maybe she made a couple of hundred bucks. She'd give him some money, plus she'd go to bed with him.

The church I knew was controlled by City Hall: "Every Christmas we'll get these niggers some turkeys. We'll send somebody from the white school board to talk to them. We might let one of you come to our church, sing." To keep us quiet like that. It was easy to control the black community in Hot Springs, because everything was geared toward money. "O.K., you don't give us any problems, we'll let your gambling houses stay. We'll let you play policy. We'll let the black racketeer who's in charge of everything, we'll let him get the nigger out of jail on Saturday night. You can fight and whip your woman on Saturday night, just don't bother us over here. We'll give you a break, a suspended thirty-day sentence. We'll let you go home and be a good boy."

We'd get the Chicago *Defender*. They had one edition for the North and another for the South. That's how we heard about the Scottsboro case. One of the people defending the boys came and spoke at the black church there. Oh yes, we knew about this case and this white woman, Ruby Something—

Ruby Bates.

This was during the time when a lot of young people wanted to get a job and venture out and go places, and they were afraid to hobo because they didn't want to get caught up in a Scottsboro case.

The *Defender* was read openly. It was brought down on a white railroad and thrown off a white boxcar. It was sold in the black community on the newsstands.

During the Depression, they had a transient bureau in my home town. Poor whites and poor blacks. This bureau would have them do work in the mountain area, say, cutting vines or shrubbery. This was in Roosevelt's time. They would go down and show people how to farm this no-good land. They would also give them a dole. I would see a line waiting to get beans. Boll weevils in them. It's almost an impossibility that some people lived through. Eating those beans and separating the bugs from the beans.

Roosevelt touched the temper of the black community. You did not look upon him as being white, black, blue or green. He was President Roosevelt. He had tremendous support through his wife. Yet the immediate image is "Great White Father."

The WPA and other projects introduced black people to handicrafts and trades. It gave Negroes a chance to have an office to work out of with a typewriter. It made us feel like there was something we could do in the scheme of things. I don't remember any serious black opposition to Roosevelt. When you see a blithe spirit, naturally you're attracted to it.

I think the powers-that-be missed the boat, during the Depression. There was a kind of integration of poverty. But even though everybody was poor, we still had this stiff-collar, white-shirted Puritanical Wilson thing going. So even though we were all in the same boat, I'm still white and you're still black, and so we don't need to get together. Things are going to get better for the white folks, and you black folks will have to . . .

Do you think a Depression of that depth could come again?

I think it could. But it would behoove the Federal Government not to let it come. Because you're dealing with a different breed of cat now. If they really want anarchy, let a Depression come now. My sixteen-year-old son is not the person I was when I was sixteen. He has manly responsibilities. And he doesn't want any shit. When I was sixteen, I wasn't afraid to die. But the kid, sixteen now, is not afraid to kill.

Dynamite Garland

In the old hotel, once elegant, where she is the most popular guest, from whom elderly widows and male pensioners ask advice and solace, her apartment flows over with paperbacks, art work, her own and others', oddments, indicative of varied and passing interests. . . .

She is an attractive forty-five-year-old waitress at an Italian-style restaurant in Chicago's Loop.

She comes from Cleveland, "a working-class family." Her father, before the Depression, had been a railroad man. "He's now seventy-eight and one of the roller skating experts in the country. He and my mother used to dance in marathons."

I REMEMBER all of a sudden we had to move. My father lost his job and we moved into a double-garage. The landlord didn't charge us rent for seven years. We had a coal stove, and we had to each take turns, the three of us kids, to warm our legs. It was awfully cold when you opened those garage doors. We would sleep with rugs and blankets over the top of us. Dress under the sheets.

In the morning, we'd get out and get some snow and put it on the stove and melt it and wash around our faces. Never the neck or anything. Put on our two pairs of socks on each hand and two pairs of socks on our feet, and long underwear and lace it up with Goodwill shoes. Off we'd walk, three, four miles to school.

My father had owned three or four homes. His father left them to him. He lost these one by one. One family couldn't pay the rent. They owned a bakery shop. They used to pay him off half in money, half in cookies. We lived on cracked cookies and those little bread things. So my father was pretty sharp in a way.

He always could get something to feed us kids. We lived about three months on candy cods, they're little chocolate square things. We had these melted in milk. And he had a part-time job in a Chinese restaurant. We lived on those fried noodles. I can't stand 'em today. He went to delivering Corn Flake samples. We lived on Corn Flake balls, Rice

Krispies, they used to come out of our ears. Can't eat 'em today either. Can't stand 'em. My mother used to make the bread, put it under a blanket to raise. Oh, that was tasty. I never tasted such good bread since.

Every Sunday we used to go house hunting. That was a recreation during the Depression. You'd get in the Model A with the family and go look at the houses. They were all for sale or rent. You'd go look and see where you could put this and where you could put that, and this is gonna be my room. I knew where I was gonna have my horse in the barn. My mother'd go down in the basement, saying, "Oh, this is well constructed. This is where we're gonna put the potato bin, this is where we're gonna put the onions." We knew just where everyone was gonna be. (Laughs.)

My mother was raised in a lace curtain Irish family and went to a finishing school. We had our napkin rings even during the Depression. My mother'd set up everything just so and so. I used to go to my girl friend's to eat. They used to have a pile of Italian food on the table. She'd come over to my place to eat, because she liked the way everything was set up.

Some of the kids seemed a little better off at the Catholic school. I used to spend most of my time under the desk, lookin' at the nun's black-top shoes. It seems I always was doin' somethin' to get punished. I was gonna bite her in the knee one time. (Laughs.) I wanted to be a nun. I was in awe of those lovely ladies. So I wound up bein' a strip dancer. (Laughs.)

They made you put your name on the collection envelope. All my mother could put in was two, three cents. Gold stars on the wall for scholastic achievements. I know doggone well I did better than some of 'em. They got a star and I never got one.

My mother always picked a school where the other children were far better off than we were. She would work at a cleaning store, managed the tuition and books. We could have gone to a free public school.

It was status with my mother. She used to walk around and my father used to call her "Queenie." She always had grandiose ideas.

My father did the best he could. He used to stuff in the mailboxes those little sheets, "Pink Sheets for Pale Purses." I think it was for a left-wingish organization. My father disagreed with whatever philosophy was on there. He got $3 a week for this.

'Cause he got a job in Akron, delivering carry-out food, we moved there. That was a dandy place: dirt, smoke, my mother scrubbing all the time. We lived right on the railroad tracks. They used to throw us watermelons and things like that. When the trains slowed down, he used to jump on and have us kids pick up the coal.

I was about fourteen when I joined the NYA.[3] I used to get $12.50 every two weeks. Making footlockers. I gave half to my mother. This was the first time I could buy some clothes. After I bought some nice clothes, I decided I didn't want to be a nun. (Laughs.)

My girl friend's father was in a new movement, Technocracy,[4] I used to wear a badge with her 'cause it was my girl friend. I remember the circular sort of thing on the badge.

I worked part-time in a bakery. I used to slide plastic papers under those nice chocolate eclairs. You'd be surprised how many times you picked 'em off the floor. Cockroaches runnin' all over the place. (Laughs.) Nobody got sick. You'd just kick 'em out of the way. They were big roaches, too.

I finished high school and got sort of engaged. I thought maybe if I got married I could eat hamburgers and hot dogs all night, have a ball, play the guitar and sing. I was singing with a hillbilly band and married the guitar player. Anything would be better than coming home and sleeping on the floor.

Trains along the Illinois Central tracks, just outside the hotel, are heard. "I miss those low train whistles. I'd like to take off like my grandfather did. He was a hobo, not a bum. He was an able-bodied seaman. He'd go maybe to China, bring back gifts, tell us fantastic stories. We didn't have a place for him, so he ensconced himself in the bathtub. He had a nice little pillow and bed right in the bathtub. He was an alcoholic. We used to hide all the silver, because he'd take it out and hock it to get a little mist. . . ."

Eleven months later, I had a baby. I was pregnant with another when war was declared. When we got married, my husband was making $14 a week. Seven of it went each week into the coat and suit we bought

[3] National Youth Administration.

[4] A movement popular in the early days of the Depression. It was based upon a price system measured in units of energy rather than dollars and cents. The society envisioned was to be run by engineers and scientists. Founded by Howard Scott, a young engineer, it was the subject of much discussion. With the election of Roosevelt, it fell out of public grace and memory.

for the marriage. From $14 a week, we jumped to $65 a week, working in a defense plant. It sort of went to my head. Wow! Boy, we were rich. First thing I did was to get me one of those red fur chubbies. I had to have a fur with that amount of money. Oooooh, those things looked awful. With my red hair, it looked like I was half orangutang. Then I had to get the shoes with the crisscross straps and balls hanging down, and the skirt with the fringe. Ick!

They say if you're raised poor, you'll know how to handle money. We were raised poor as church mice. But when I get it, I blow it. It's a personality thing. I don't regret any of it. But still. . . .

Slim Collier

A bartender.

"I was born in Waterloo. A great deal of Iowa, southern Iowa, particularly, didn't have electricity until the end of World War II. I was eleven years old before I lived in a house with running water. That was 1936.

"My people are Manx. The island between Scotland and Ireland. The first Collier came here in chains off a British warship. 1641. He was known as a white nigger. He was a political prisoner. He was sentenced to seventeen years for sedition. After ten years of servitude, he was granted a King's pardon. Nope, my people didn't come here on the Mayflower.

"Every Collier would go back to the Isle of Man to get himself a wife. My father broke the tradition. He married the daughter of a German immigrant living in the Dakotas. My mother was really a snot-nosed big sister. She was only fourteen years older than I was. . . ."

MY FATHER was sort of a fancy Dan. A very little man, five feet two. He was a tool-and-die maker in addition to being a farmer. The kind of man that would get up in the morning and put on a white shirt and tie, suit, camel hair coat, gloves, get in his late model Chrysler, drive from the farm into the city, park his car in the parking lot, get out, take off his coat, put his suit in the locker and put on those greasy overalls to be a tool-and-die maker. He had a lot of pretensions. When the Depression hit him, it hit hard.

He was the kind of man that would put a down payment on a place, get a second mortgage, put a down payment on another place. The Depression wiped out his houses. The anger and frustration he experienced colored my whole life. He was the kind of man, if somebody went broke he was pleased. Now it happened to him.

It was a 160-acre farm, primarily corn. My brother farms the same 160 acres today. He does it in an hour, two hours, with automation. But my father was a stubborn old cuss. I ran off because he wouldn't buy a tractor. I was fourteen in 1938, when I ran away from home. My last day's work that I did for the old man was taking logs out of the woods, with oxen. He bought a tractor in 1939. (Laughs.)

My father was laid off in the fall of '31 as a tool-and-die maker. He worked at the John Deere tractor plant. I was seven, and I just barely started school. All of a sudden, my father, who I saw only rarely, was around all the time. That was quite a shock. I suddenly became disciplined by him instead of my mother. The old woodshed was used extensively in those days.

Fear and worry was the one thing that identified the people. John Paul's was a furniture store in Westfield, near Waterloo—I suppose you'd call it a suburb today. It was sort of a village where roosters wake you up in the morning, where people kept cows and pigs. Parts of it had street lights, but it was rural enough to have farm animals. We kids would patronize the store, too, because it carried candy and a few school supplies.

I remember men congregating in the store. One man bragged how he had never been on welfare and wasn't going to be on welfare. Quite a few people there resented it, because most people in Westfield were on welfare.

This short temper was a characteristic of the time. Men who were willing to work couldn't find work. My father was the kind of man who had to be active. He'd invent work for himself. A child who was playing irritated him. It wasn't just my own father. They all got shook up.

My old man went back to work in '33, part-time. Nevertheless, he was earning cash money. That term, "cash money," impressed itself on my childhood. A dime was a weekly event. It brought me a bag of popcorn and a seat in the third row of the theater where I could see Bob Steele shoot off the Indians. On Saturday—buffalo nickel day, they called it. It provided conversation to my schoolmates for the rest of the week.

Cash was extremely rare. I remember having found a dollar and my father gravely taking charge of it and doling it out to me a dime at a time.

When he was hired back, we went to the 160 acres that the finance company had. Because he was able to make payments, they waived the foreclosure. They were so hard up for cash money themselves.

There was a family that experienced a farm foreclosure. It was the first of March when they were forced off, and all their household goods were sold. Even family pictures. They went for five cents, ten cents a piece. Quite a few of the kids were brought there by their parents, partly by morbid fascination, partly by sympathy, partly—well, there was something going on. In those days of no TV, no radio in some places, an event was an event.

It was a hilarious thing for us kids. We got together, there were lots of new kids. Games. . . . Gradually, I was aware, slightly, of the events. Overhearing the adults talk. The worry and the relief they expressed: it hadn't happened to them. The anticipation that it might . . . the fascination with catastrophe. I recall this undertone, horror, but also fascination. It dominated the conversation for weeks.

The dominant thing was this helpless despair and submission. There was anger and rebellion among a few but, by and large, that quiet desperation and submission.

The phrase, "Prosperity is just around the corner," was something we kids would repeat. But we didn't quite dig what prosperity meant. (Laughs.) Iowa is traditionally Republican. When my father was voting Democrat and announced it ahead of time—he voted for Roosevelt —it was something of a shock: "Collier is turning radical." (Laughs.) Well, Hoover got blamed for the Depression.

"When I quarreled with my father and left home, I worked as an itinerant farmer for $16 a month and found.[5] It was understood that a hired man went to church with the family. He didn't sit with 'em. The hired help all sat in the back row. Your hired men and hired girls would sit at the table and eat with the family. But in public you had certain amenities

---

[5] An archaic rural phrase: "That was your board. If you got sick, the farmer paid the doctor bill. The wife washed your clothes and saw you had a clean shirt on Sunday for church."

you had to observe. You held the door open and let every member of the family walk in before you came in. Oh yes, we had social classes in those days."

Among his other jobs: theater usher, bellhop, truck helper, coal loader. Finally at the age of seventeen, the army. Out of the entire company, only he and another had completed eighth grade; they were made medics.

In 1939, I went out an itinerant farm worker. I got a job cutting asparagus, fifteen cents an hour, as fast as you could move. I remember standing up once to rub my aching back, 'cause you worked in a crouch almost at a running pace, and the straw boss yelling: "See those men standing by the road? They're just waiting to get you fired. If I catch you straightening up once more, one of them will be working and you won't."

We'd gather at a certain site at four in the morning. And stand there waiting for the truck to come by, and they'd yell the terms off: fifteen cents an hour. If you wanted work, you'd come to these intersections in Waterloo. Men would be standing there, smoking and talking, bragging, joking as men talk when they get together and don't know each other. They'd decide: I'm not gonna work for fifteen cents an hour. After all, I got $2 cash money at home. The rest of us would pile on the truck, and a man would say: That's enough.

They were bringing people out of town to work in the country. The people in the country were getting up in arms, refusing to work at these wages. At that time, I didn't realize the exploitation, and the competitiveness of workers.

Was there talk of organizing?

Not in Iowa, not in that east central part. The people were too conservative. I was past forty years of age before I joined a union. I was conditioned—to join a labor union would take away your ability to stand on your own two feet. It would mean surrendering yourself. I probably picked up a great deal more of my father's arrogance than I realize. I was too arrogant to join a union. Hell, I'd work for less money just to be my own self.

To be a union man had some sort of shameful label to it. There was a man in our neighborhood, whose wife was a part-time prostitute. This was known. He smoked tailor-made cigarettes, as opposed to Bull Durham roll-your-owns. The man had very little respect. In the same way, being a union man wasn't quite respectable.

POSTSCRIPT: *"Back then, a woman by the time she was forty or fifty, was an old woman. When I was back in Iowa last September, some of these forty-five and fifty-year-old chicks are better lookin' than their twenty-year-old daughters. Labor-saving devices, cosmetics . . . and they're health conscious: vitamins. I have noticed a peculiar number of people my age wear dentures. We didn't get the right vitamins. We didn't get the minerals."*

Dorothe Bernstein

A waitress.

I WENT INTO an orphan home in 1933. I was about ten. I had clean clothes all the time, and we had plenty to eat. We'd go through the park when we walked to school. Railroad tracks came somewhere. The picture's like it was yesterday.

The men there waited for us to go through and hand them our lunches. If we had something the dietitian at the home would prepare that we didn't like. We'd give them the little brown paper bags.

Today I tell my daughters: be careful of people, especially a certain type that look a certain way. Then we didn't have any fear. You'd never think that if you walked by people, even strangers: gee, that person I got to be careful of. Nobody was really your enemy. These were guys who didn't have work. Who'd probably work if there was work. I don't know how they got where they were going or where they ended up. They were nice men. You would never think they would do you bodily harm. They weren't bums. These were hard luck guys.

On Fridays, we used to give 'em our lunch, all of us. They might be 125 of us going to school, carrying the same brown paper bag, with mashed sardine sandwiches and mayonnaise on it. This was thirty some years ago. I still don't eat a sardine. (Laughs.) Today when I serve a sardine in the restaurant, I hold my nose. Not with my fingers. Did you ever hold your breath through your nose, so you can't smell it? 'Cause I still see these sardine sandwiches with mayonnaise on them.

You hi'd them, and they hi'd you. That was it. If you asked me where they slept at night, I couldn't tell you. They knew we were friends, and we knew for some reason they were friends.

People talk about the good old times. These can't be the good old times when men wanted to work and couldn't work. When your kids wanted milk and you had to go scratch for it. I remember one girl friend I went to store with. She was real ashamed because they had food stamps. I remember how apologetic she was to me. It kind of embarrassed her. She said, "You want to wait outside?"

Louise was a Bohemian girl. Her mother had a grocery store that they lived behind. Louise used to do the books, and there was always owing. You never said to the people: "Do you have the money to pay me?" They would say, "Write it in the book." And you wrote it in the book, because this was their family food, and they had to have it. It wasn't that you were giving it away. Eventually, you'd be paid.

But there wasn't this impersonal—like the supermarkets. They'd say, "Hello, Dorothe, how's your sister?" And so forth. There's no such thing as books in the supermarket. You go in, you pay, you check out, and you don't even know what you're checking out. The faith people had in each other was different.

There are people out in the world today are ashamed to admit from whence they came. I met one at a PTA meeting. I went up nice and friendly and I said, "Aren't you La-da-da?" She looked at me. I said, "I'm Dorothe. Remember me?" Her eyebrow raised. I mean she was all dressed up to the hilt. She said, "You are completely mistaken. I don't know who you are." I bumped into this person five or six times since. She *is* who I thought she was. I let the subject drop. A lot of kids felt the stigma. While it wasn't your fault, they feel: I'd rather it's a closed door, those times.

I never knew any real millionaires who were diving out of windows. I would read it like it was fiction. Who had that kind of fantastic money? They would kill themselves because of loss of it? To me, it's easier and nicer to scratch a little bit and get up.

You know, when you get down so low that you can't get any lower, there's no place else to go but up. You do either one of two things: you either lay down and die, or you pull yourself up by your bootstraps and you start over.

Dawn, Kitty McCulloch's Daughter

THESE WERE the years I remember my dad, who was a white collar worker, being derisive of the strikers. And yet this man put in seventy-two hours, he worked so hard, and he couldn't see that it was necessary for people to strike. When the forty-hour week came through, boy, he really supported Roosevelt.

I can remember all the excitement. Politics was important. I remember that my folks used to get together with dear friends and listen on Sundays to Father Coughlin. It was a must that the kids keep quiet while this man was screaming over the radio. I don't really remember all the things he was saying, but I remember I hated him. I really don't know why, because I didn't know then. I know now. But isn't it funny, a child's reaction. . . . My father used to listen to him and think he was right: Coughlin's right. They would sit there and say he had the right idea. How important a part radio played in all our lives, all during the Depression.

Everything was important. If one man died, it was like a headline. Life was more important, it seemed to me. I remember a headline story of a young golfer—he had on metal shoes and was hit by lightning. Everybody in the neighborhood talked about it. It was very important that this *one* man died in such a freak accident. Now we hear traffic tolls, we hear Vietnam . . . life is just so, it's not precious now.

Phyllis Lorimer

"I was unaware of what was happening. I knew what happened to me. I did hear of people jumping out of windows. It didn't mean anything personally to me.

"I grew up in Greenwich, Connecticut, a lovely house. My family was extremely well off, but I always thought I was poor. All my cousins, everybody's father was a millionaire. My best friends had their own island. They each had their boat, and all had their jumping horses.

"My mother and father were divorced. My father was a successful motion picture producer in California. My mother took me out there. Came the Crash, and we all stayed."

WHEN IT HAPPENED, I was in a boarding school which I loved. At Glendora. It was the best boarding school in California at that time. A beautiful school in the middle of orange trees. I was about to be president of the student body and very proud of myself. Suddenly I couldn't get any pencils and went to the principal to find out why. She was embarrassed because we were old friends. She said, "I'm sorry, the bills just haven't been paid." She complimented me, saying, "Were there scholarships, you could have it." And, "I couldn't be sorrier."

I was mortified past belief. It was hard for the principal. I called my mother and said, "Come and pick me up." Which she did. I went back home which wasn't much of a home because we were living with a stepfather whom I detested.

It was rough on me, the Thirties. I wasn't aware of it being with everyone else. I thought it was just personal. I was in no way aware that it was a national thing. Having grown up in some affluence, I was suddenly in a small court in Hollywood with a stepfather who was drunk and ghastly.

My brother was still at Dartmouth, where he was fortunate enough not to know what was going on at home. Whatever money there was went to keep brother at Dartmouth. We were living on a form of relief. We had cans of tinned bully beef. And we had the gas turned off. My mother was an engaging lady who made everything a picnic. We cooked everything on an electric corn popper, so it was gay in certain aspects. (Laughs.) My mother had humor and charm, so I didn't know it was a desperate situation. When there wasn't any money, she'd buy me a china doll instead of a vegetable. (Laughs.) She was an eccentric, and everybody stared at her. I was the little brown mouse.

My father was still holding up his pride. He had been successful, and then things went. Two houses with everything in it. His own career had nothing to do with the Depression. He blew it. Lots of times bills weren't paid when there was no Depression.

I had come from this terribly wealthy family, with cousins who still had so much that, even during the Depression, they didn't lose it. Suddenly I had four great white horses. They were given to me by my cousins. I was a very good horse woman. (Laughs.) I rode at all the shows and steeplechases and all that. And went home to canned bully beef at night. (Laughs.)

My brother was socially oriented, a tremendous snob. While we were eating bully beef, he was living extremely well at Dartmouth. Nobody told him how bad things were. He lived magnificently, with a socialite friend, in a house with a manservant. He came back and found the truth, and the truth was ghastly.

He was five years older, a male, facing the fact that he had to go out and do it. It set for him a lifelong thing: he was never going to be caught in the same trap his parents were—never, ever going to be the failure his father was.

His first job was carrying rubber at the Firestone factory, and he got the white tennis clothes smelly and he violently hated the whole thing. He came home reeking of it and hating himself.

It was unbearable. He wouldn't tell the people with whom he played tennis on the weekends. He had an old Ford with no door, but if you held on, there was a door. When he would take me out in the car, I would be the one that held the door on. It was that kind of Ford.

He was going to get somewhere and he fixed himself a little black book: what he was going to do by such and such a date. And he did it— to make up for his parents' failures. He wished to be in color photography. He studied every night he came home from Firestone. Within a year, he was manager of the New York office of Technicolor. He had such determination. . . .

Now it was necessary for me to make some money because the stepfather was drunk all the time and the father was pretending it hadn't happened. Having gone to a proper lady's finishing school, I didn't know how to do anything. I spoke a little bad French, and I knew enough to stand up when an older person came into the room. As far as anything else was concerned, I was unequipped.

I heard there was a call for swimmers for a picture called *Footlight*

Parade. At Warner Brothers. The first big aquacade picture.[6] I went, terrified, tried out the high-diving thing and won. I couldn't have been more stunned. I truly think this is where I got a lifelong point of view: respect for those who *did,* no respect for those who *had* . . . just because their father had done something and they were sitting around.

I loved the chorus girls who worked. I hated the extras who sat around and were paid while we were endangering our lives. I had a ball. It was the first time I was better than anybody at something. I gained a self-respect which I'd never had.

In the midst of my suddenly getting $7.50 a day for risking my life daily on the high boards and stunt work, falling out of wagons, and no overtime, I discovered what a good union could mean. I had spent most of my childhood alone. Now I came to respect those who worked for each other and for others. I got a great respect for the Screen Actors' Guild, who were protecting us who were working under water for $7.50 a day.

It was the big thing in my life at that moment. I had been a brown wren in uniform in a lot of proper girls' schools. My mother was an exhibitionist, and I wanted just that nobody ever look at me. I just wanted to disappear. I was fond of my mother, who was of no world. She could have lived in any era. I never got from her what was going on. I did from my brother, because he was undone by it.

Always having felt slightly rejected by Westhampton society, Greenwich society, Great Neck society, I had the feeling we weren't "it," whatever "it" was. I was sure my relatives were "it." I knew my mother was a loon, wore fishnet and rode bicycles. We were odd.

All of a sudden I found another group with whom I belonged. The ex-Olympic stars who were diving and swimming and the chorus girls who worked like mad. Suddenly I didn't care about my brother's friends, the socially important. He kept saying, "When they ask what you're doing, don't say you're a chorus girl." I said, "I'm proud to be a chorus girl." That used to destroy him.

In Westhampton, Greenwich and Great Neck, my only knowledge of what people do about anything was to keep Polacks from moving in. I truly believed, as a child, the bridge across the canal from Southampton was to keep Jews out of the country club. (Laughs.) Suddenly I'm a wild labor enthusiast. I'm here with the chorus girls and the grips.

[6] Busby Berkeley's extravaganza, starring Ruby Keeler, Richard Powell and Toby Wing.

Bob Leary

A part-time cab driver, part-time student. During a tortuous ride through Manhattan's narrow streets, there was time for fragments of conversation. . . .

MY FATHER spent two years painting his father's house. He painted it twice. It gave him something to do. It prevented him from losing all his —well, I wouldn't say self-respect, because there were many, many people who were also out of work. He wasn't alone.

He belonged to the Steamfitters' Union. They were putting up the old Equitable Building at the time. But I guess they ran out of steam, just around '29.

He never forgot it. I guess it does do something to somebody to be out of work so long. It can affect your confidence in yourself. Not that it destroyed my father's self-confidence. But I could see how it affected his outlook on life, his reaction towards success. He was inordinately impressed by men who had made it in business. It's my feeling the Depression had something to do with this.

Bonnie Laboring Boy

I've worked in the Susquehanna yard
I've got one dollar a day
Toiling hard to make a living, boys,
I hardly think she pays.
They said they will raise our wages
If they do, I won't complain.
If they don't, I'll hoist my turkey[1]
And walk the road again.

—Traditional Folk Song

Larry Van Dusen

Fifty-five years old, he's been a labor union organizer most of his life.
"I was nineteen when I left home and never went back. Bummin' around
on the road—Colorado, Texas—hitchhiking, ridin' box cars . . . oh,
coming back home once in a while and finding the family on relief.
Checking out. . . ."

[1] A bindle: possessions wrapped in a handkerchief.

He was a social worker in Kansas City during the early Thirties; organized unemployed councils; participated in strikes; was arrested several times. . . .

I STILL PLAY a little game with myself, shaving. To get shaved before I'm picked up by the cops. Once I was picked up and I had a two-day beard on my face, and three days in a-hundred-degree weather in a Kansas City jail, I developed a terrific rash on the neck. It still comes back once in a while. So that's just a little gimmick you work . . . if they're gonna get you this time, you're gonna go to jail clean-shaven. When I want to entertain myself now, I still think: I'm gonna get shaved before the knock on the door.

The brutality in the jails, the treatment of the unemployed, especially Negroes—I remember this cursing crash of some new arrival. They were dragging a big Negro into a cell next to ours. The din and the hell-raising we made to try to get him medical attention. We assumed, because nobody came, and he was taken out pretty stiff the next morning, that he died in the cell.

In those days, Chicago was quite a place to be arrested in. They had a system of moving you from precinct station to precinct station, so that it might be two or three days before your lawyer could find out where you were at. It was rougher than I had been accustomed to in Kansas City. Police stations at the time had these gimmicks, like seats with electric shocks. We were kept six or eight to a cell. Arrests of this sort were common enough for people who were organizing.

Unemployed councils, in my opinion, laid the basis for much of the New Deal legislation. . . . They attracted people who subsequently became labor organizers, particularly in the CIO. They were youthful in character and in ideas. They were not hidebound as left-wing political parties were in that period, although Communists and Socialists took part. They sort of threw away the rule book and just organized people to get something to eat.

The unemployed council people out in St. Louis were responsible for the first strike I ever saw—a tiff[2] miners' strike in southern Missouri. The housing was primitive. It was a miserable existence—literally, dig-

[2] "Tiff is a material used in making paint, comparable to white lead. It was dug out of straight shafts, like little wells. The miners didn't own the land, of course. They were simply sinking these wells, getting the tiff out and selling it to big companies."

ging one out from the ground. They were trying to get better prices, so there was a strike. They tried to withhold their product from the market. I watched the meeting of the miners broken up by the local police and vigilantes.

Like most strikes of that period, it made more of a political than an economic point. There was a lot of publicity in the St. Louis *Post-Dispatch* and other papers. It pointed up the miserable conditions of the miners. It put into focus right on Park Avenue and Grosse Point and Winnetka . . . what was really going on. All the left-wing groups had a part in dramatizing it. And this reflected itself later in Roosevelt's New Deal measures.

One of the most common things—and it certainly happened to me—was this feeling of your father's failure. That somehow he hadn't beaten the rap. Sure things were tough, but why should I be the kid who had to put a piece of cardboard into the sole of my shoe to go to school? It was not a thing coupled with resentment against my father. It was simply this feeling of regret, that somehow he hadn't done better, that he hadn't gotten the breaks. Also a feeling of uneasiness about my father's rage against the way things are.

My father was very much of an individualist, as craftsmen usually are. He would get jobs he considered beneath his status during this period. Something would happen: he'd quarrel with the foreman, he'd have a fight with the boss. He was a carpenter. He couldn't be happy fixing a roadbed or driving a cab or something like that. He was a skilled tradesman and this whole thing had him beat. I think it bugged the family a lot.

Remember, too, the shock, the confusion, the hurt that many kids felt about their fathers not being able to provide for them. This reflected itself very often in bitter quarrels between father and son. I recall I had one. I was the oldest of six children. I think there was a special feeling between the father and the oldest son.

We had bitter arguments about new ideas. Was Roosevelt right in making relief available? Was the WPA a good idea? Did people have the right to occupy their farms and hold them by force? The old concept that there was something for everybody who worked in America went down the drain with the Great Depression. This created family strains. A lot of parents felt a sense of guilt, a feeling of shame that they had to be rescued by WPA and building a dam. A craftsman like my father felt pretty silly pouring concrete for a wall on the bluffs around the K.C.

railroad yards . . . when the nation needed houses and his craftsman-
ship could have been used. Men like him suffered indignity, working at
projects they considered to be alien to the American concept of productive labor.

My father led a rough life: he drank. During the Depression, he drank
more. There was more conflict in the home. A lot of fathers—mine,
among them—had a habit of taking off. They'd go to Chicago to look
for work. To Topeka. This left the family at home, waiting and hoping
that the old man would find something. And there was always the Saturday night ordeal as to whether or not the old man would get home with
his paycheck. Everything was sharpened and hurt more by the Depression.

Heaven would break out once in a while, and the old man would get
a week's work. I remember he'd come home at night, and he'd come
down the path through the trees. He always rode a bicycle. He'd stop and
sometimes say hello, or give me a hug. And that smell of fresh sawdust
on those carpenter overalls, and the fact that Dad was home, and there
was a week's wages—well, this is something you remember, too. That's
the good you remember.

And then there was always the bad part. That's when you'd see your
father coming home with the toolbox on his shoulder. Or carrying it.
That meant the job was over. The tools were home now, and we were
back on the treadmill again.

I remember coming back home, many years afterwards. Things were
better. It was after the Depression, after the war. To me, it was hardly
the same house. My father turned into an angel. They weren't wealthy,
but they were making it. They didn't have the acid and the recrimina-
tions and the bitterness that I had felt as a child.

I remember coming back that day. My mother had roast beef. It was
very good, and there was plenty of it. There was meat left over on the
table when we finished. During the Depression, one day a week, if we
were lucky enough, we got round steak. I was nineteen or twenty before
I knew there was any kind of steak except round steak. I can remember
all the kids sitting around, eyeing that meat, hands on forks, poised and
ready. Depending on which way my father started that meat: that decided who got the first choice. There was one piece of meat per kid, and
you were still hungry after the meal was over. I think of this very often
when I see my wife trying to force food down my children's throats.

I don't think most children escape this. The oldest son, like me—it had the effect of getting me out of the home earlier. It's not a question of disowning your family. Any great economic upheaval, I think, alters patterns. Children develop doubts about their parents. They leave home early, out of necessity. They must find jobs quicker and quicker. Different from the current generation.

It comes through clearly these days when old labor leaders like myself try to talk to young workers who come into the shop. You try to talk to them about what we've been through, when we were organizing a plant—the blacklist, how we'd go under other names . . . you tell them about the Memorial Day Massacre . . . you tell them about the troops in Flint and sit-down strikes and the revolution this represented in the auto industry. . . . Well, they listen, if they're polite. But it doesn't really touch them, these things. These things that mean so much to us.

The young worker comes into the plant very often having the same values as his parents. The parents were a Depression couple. But years have passed, fights have been won, and this couple now has a suburban home, a child or two to college or high school. So the youngster comes into a plant where the workers are much more middle-class than we were.

The Depression left a legacy of fear, but also a desire for acquisition —property, security. I now have twenty times more shirts than I need, because all during that time, shirts were something I never had.

Jose Yglesias

Author. Among his works are The Goodbye Land, In the Fist of the Revolution *and* An Orderly Life.

"Ybor City is a ward of Tampa. Spanish-speaking. I didn't learn English until I started public school."

It was built in the 1880s by Cuban cigar manufacturers, seeking a hot, damp climate and freedom from labor troubles. "Within two months, there were strikes. (Laughs.) Cigar makers are the most radical workers you could find. Wages were bitterly fought for. They had many, many strikes." There was no union recognition until the beginnings of World War II.

"People date their lives from various strikes in Tampa. When they

*refer to a scab, they say: 'It's no surprise he's trying to break this strike
since his mother did it in 1921.' In my home town, strikes were passionate affairs. Nobody considered it outrageous to make the life of a
strikebreaker totally miserable. It was a stigma never forgotten.*

*"Women beat up women scabs. Women worked in cigar factories
from the very beginning. Their pay was equal to that of the men. Oh
yes, the women were very militant."*

IN THE SUNLIT TOWN, the Depression came imperceptibly. The realiza-
tion came to me when Aunt Lila said there's no food in the house. My
aunt, who owned the house we lived in, would no longer charge rent.
It would be shameful to charge rent with $9 a week coming in.

The grocery man would come by and take a little order, which he
would bring the next day. When my mother would not order anything
because she owed, he'd insist: Why are you cutting down on the beans?

There was a certain difference between the Depression in my home
town than elsewhere. They weren't dark, satanic mills. The streets were
not like a city ghetto. There were poor homes, that hadn't been painted
in years. But it was out in the open. You played in the sunlight. I don't
remember real deprivation.

Ybor City was an island in the South. When an American got mad at
any Latin, he called him a Cuban nigger. This was one of the first feelings I remember: I want to be an American. You become ashamed of
the community. I was an ardent supporter of Henry Ford at the age of
twelve.

The strike of 1931 revolved around readers in the factory. The workers themselves used to pay twenty-five to fifty cents a week and would
hire a man to read to them during work. A cigar factory is one enormous
open area, with tables at which people work. A platform would be
erected, so that he'd look down at the cigar makers as he read to them
some four hours a day. He would read from newspapers and magazines
and a book would be read as a serial. The choice of the book was
democratically decided. Some of the readers were marvelous natural
actors. They wouldn't just read a book. They'd act out the scenes. Consequently, many cigar makers, who were illiterate, knew the novels of
Zola and Dickens and Cervantes and Tolstoy. And the works of the
anarchist, Kropotkin. Among the newspapers read were *The Daily
Worker* and the *Socialist Call*.

The factory owners decided to put an end to this, though it didn't cost
them a penny. Everyone went on strike when they arrived one morning

and found the lecture platform torn down. The strike was lost. Every strike in my home town was always lost. The readers never came back.

The Depression began in 1930, with seasonal unemployment. Factories would close down before Christmas, after having worked very hard to fill orders throughout late summer and fall. Only the cheaper grade cigars would be made. They cut off the more expensive type. Regalia.

My uncle was a foreman. He was ill-equipped for the job because he couldn't bear to fire anybody. He would discuss it with his wife: We have to cut off so many people. What am I going to do? My aunt would say: You can't fire him. They have twelve children. You'd hear a great deal of talk. You knew things were getting worse. No more apprentices were taken in. My sister was in the last batch.

The strike left a psychological scar on me. I was in junior high school and a member of the student patrol. I wore an arm band. During the strike, workers marched into the schools to close them down, bring the children out. The principal closed the gates, and had the student patrols guard them. If they come, what do I do? My mother was in the strike.

One member of the top strike committee was a woman. That day I stood patrol, she was taken off to jail. Her daughter was kept in the principal's office. I remember walking home from school, about a block behind her, trying to decide whether to tell her of my sympathies, to ask about her mother. I never got to say it. I used to feel bad about that. Years later, in New York, at a meeting for Loyalist Spain, I met her and told her.

Everybody gave ten percent of their pay for the Republic. It was wild. The total community was with Loyalist Spain. They used to send enormous amounts of things. It was totally organized. The song "No pasarán" that was taken to be Spanish was really by a Tampa cigar maker.

It was an extraordinarily radical strike. The cigar makers tried to march to City Hall with red flags, singing the old Italian anarchist song, "Avanti popolo," "Scarlet Banner." I thought it was Spanish because we used to sing "Avanca pueblo." You see, the bonus march made them feel the revolution was here.

It was a Latin town. Men didn't sit at home. They went to cafes, on street corners, at the Labor Temple, which they built themselves. It was very radical talk. The factory owners acted out of fright. The 1931 strike was openly radical. By then, there was a Communist Party in Ybor City. Leaflets would be distributed by people whom you knew.

(Laughs.) They'd come down the street in the car (whispers) with their headlights off. And then onto each porch. Everybody knew who it was. They'd say, "Oh, *cómo está,* Manuel." (Laughs.)

During the strike, the KKK would come into the Labor Temple with guns, and break up meetings. Very frequently, they were police in hoods. Though they were called the Citizens' Committee, everybody would call them Los Cuckoo Klan. (Laughs.) The picket lines would hold hands, and the KKK would beat them and cart them off.

The strike was a ghastly one. When the factories opened, they cut off many workers. There was one really hated manager, a Spaniard. They would say, "It takes a Spaniard to be that cruel to his fellow man." He stood at the top of the stairs. He'd hum "The Scarlet Banner": "You—you can come in." Then he'd hum "The Internationale": "You—you can come in." Then he'd turn his back on the others. They weren't hired. Nobody begged him, though.

When the strike was lost, the Tampa paper published a full page, in large type: the names of all the members of the strike committee. They were indicted for conspiracy and spent a year in jail. None of them got their jobs back.

The readers' strike lasted only a couple of weeks: *La huelga de los lectores.* I just don't know how they kept up their militancy. There were, of course, many little wildcat strikes. Cigar makers were just incredible. If they were given a leaf that would crumble: "Too dry—out!" When cigar makers walked out, they didn't just walk out at the end of a day. They'd walk out on the day the tobacco had been moistened, laid out. The manufacturer lost a few hundred dollars, in some cases, a thousand.

There were attempts to organize the CIO. I remember one of my older cousins going around in a very secretive manner. You'd think he was planning the assassination of the czar. He was trying to sign people up for the CIO. The AF of L International was very conservative and always considered as an enemy. They never gave the strike any support. It was considered the work of agitators.

People began to go off to New York to look for jobs. Almost all my family were in New York by 1937. You'd take that bus far to New York. There, we all stayed together. The only place people didn't sleep in was the kitchen. A bed was even in the foyer. People would show up from Tampa, and you'd put them up. We were the Puerto Rican immigrants of that time. In any cafeteria, in the kitchen, the busboys, the dishwashers, you were bound to find at least two from Ybor City.

Some would drift back as jobs would open up again in Tampa. Some went on the WPA. People would put off governmental aid as long as possible. Aunt Lila and her husband were the first in our family, and the last, to go on WPA. This was considered a terrible tragedy, because it was charity. You did not mention it to them.

That didn't mean you didn't accept another thing. There was no pay-day in any cigar factory that there wasn't a collection for anyone in trouble. If a father died, there was a collection for the funeral. When my father went to Havana for an operation, there was a collection. That was all right. You yourself didn't ask. Someone said: "Listen, so and so's in trouble." When Havana cigar makers would go on strike, it was a matter of honor: you sent money to them. It has to do with the Spanish-Cuban tradition.

Neighbors have always helped one another. The community has always been that way. There was a solidarity. There was just something very nice. . . .

People working in the cigar industry no longer have the intellectual horizons that my parents had, and my aunts and uncles. They were an extraordinarily cultivated people. It makes it very difficult for me today to read political analysts, even those of the New Left, who talk in a derogatory way of the "glorification" of the working class. The working class I knew was just great.

POSTSCRIPT: *"My family thought very highly of Roosevelt, except my grandfather. As a young man, he had known José Martí, the Cuban liberator. He'd say, 'We learned to eat stones and survived on it.' He'd say, 'Hoover was just a mean old skinflint and Roosevelt is just another Mussolini.' But the New Deal did become the basis of a new union drive. And people did find jobs. . . ."*

Evelyn Finn

She has worked as a seamstress. It was St. Louis in the early years of the Depression. . . .

YOU COULD UPSET the shop quite a bit. Even when there was no union. You'd get the girls on your side, one by one, until you had a majority. I

remember this one straw boss. He wanted us to speed up. In the morning, the girls'd be tired. He'd go through the shop: "Is everybody happy
today?" I'd say: "I'm not happy." He says, "What's the matter with
you?" I'd tell him: "I come here to fight."

Another girl sided with me. He fired us. "Troublemakers." He had the
nerve to say, "I'll write you a letter of recommendation." This poor
little thing, she was crying. I said, "I'd be ashamed to show anything
you'd write on paper. I wouldn't want anybody to know I worked for a
person like you." Lucky we got another job.

Sometime you'd have to fight for your moral support against your
boss. I've even lost jobs against *that*. I was still pretty young. I weighed
about 115 pounds, brown hair. I didn't notice my personality because I
had such fight in me. I used to tell 'em off.

He just kept after me, this one. Nagged me and nagged me to go out
with him. So all right, I said. Boy, he was so excited. We got in his car.
He said, "Where we going? Your house?" "No," I said, "we're goin' to
your house. For supper." You should've seen the look on his face.
(Laughs.) I knew his wife, a sweet little woman. I used to sew and fix
her clothes. I made him do just that. His wife was glad to see me.
(Laughs.) He never asked me again. And he was an old gray-haired
man with two grown sons.

One time I was on piecework. You get paid for the amount you do.
But the boss wanted us to ring the time clock. If you're a pieceworker
and you're very fast and very apt, which I was, you don't want him to
know this, that or the other. I refused to ring the clock. Did they have a
time with me! They didn't want to lose me. I was skilled.

"Why won't you *please* punch it?"

"You want me to work here?"

"Why, yes."

"Then don't bother me. If you stand when I come in in the morning,
you punch it. Watch me all day long. And when I get home, you punch
it again. O.K.?" (Laughs.)

They put up with it, even during the Depression. I had a gift in my
fingers. And I wasn't scared. (Laughs.)

One day I took out the whole shop. There never was a shop yet I
couldn't take out. This is when we had the union. I was the chairlady.
They didn't get us what we wanted. I think they were playin' sweet-
hearts with the boss. So we had a sit-in. I said to the girls: Just sit, don't
do nothin'. We sat and joked about a lot of things and had a lotta fun.

The boss was goin' crazy. The union officials came down. They went crazy, too. It was a hilarious day. They called us a bunch of Communists. The girls didn't know what it meant. I knew what it meant, but I wasn't. So, if that's the way they behave, I said, "Girls, it's a nice day. Let's all go for a walk." So we did, the whole shop. They got us what we wanted.

After all, I played a big part in organizin' our union in St. Louis. We used to go to the homes of people. It wears you out, but when you're young, you don't think about it. One day, this other girl and me, we're ringin' the bell, and somebody throwed buckets of water out on us. Everybody was not in favor of the union. They were just scared to death.

I don't remember ever bein' scared. Even if I didn't have a penny. And I was supporting a little girl. What can we lose? We haven't got that much to lose. But some people are just afraid of every little thing. What was there to be afraid of?

There were no colored girls in our shop. The one next door to us had four or five. They did very menial work. But they didn't work with white girls. Not in St. Louis. Now, three of us work together, these two colored girls and I. The rest of the shop can be dormant, but we've always got something going on in that corner. Not a dull moment. You wouldn't think we're doin' a thing, but we produce more than the rest of 'em. Even when we get mad about something, we laugh about it. When the boss nags us, we just laugh him to death.

I never made my work a drudgery. I always made it a hobby. I enjoy my work today like if I was sitting down reading a book.

Hank Oettinger

A linotype operator. Much of his spare time is devoted to writing "Letters to the Editor." "I like to throw barbs into my political opponents. I hang around bars in the Loop. I like arguments and I get into dillies. Even Birchers look toward my coming into the place. When I don't show up, they get worried: 'Where the hell ya been?'

"I go to work late in the afternoon, get through at midnight. See my friends at the taverns. Agitate. Get my sleep. I wake up, and it's nice

and warm and it's light. I go down and maybe have a couple of arguments before I go to work."

I CAME from a very small town in northern Wisconsin. It had been ravaged by the lumber barons. It was cut-over land, a term you hear very often up there. It was a one industry town: tourist business. During the winter, there was nothing.

A lot of people who suffered from the Depression—it was new to them. It wasn't new to me. I was number ten in a family of eleven. My father, who had one leg, worked in a lumber mill for a while. Lost it, held a political job for a while, Registrar of Deeds. Lost it. Ninety-two percent of the people in the country were on welfare in the early years of the Depression.

We could have gone on relief, but my father refused. Foolish pride. He would not accept medical care, even. I had, oh God, a beautiful set of teeth. To have one filled was $2 at the time, I think. Oh, my gosh, my teeth just went. Eventually, I got to work and saved most of them. But the fact that he wouldn't even accept medical relief—stubborn Dutchman!

He was a great admirer of Bob La Follette. He liked the idea of Bob's fighting the railroads and being against our entering the First World War. I came from German stock, that was a factor. People up here loved old Bob. They had been so downtrodden and knew they had been misused by the lumber companies. In 1924, my mother said to my father, "You know La Follette isn't going to win the Presidency. Why don't you vote for somebody who can win it?" He said, "I vote for what I believe in."

I remember seeing a hunger march to City Hall. It was a very cold, bitter day. My boss was looking out of the window with me. I didn't know what the hell it was. He says, "They ought to lock the bastards up." I thought to myself: Lock them up for what? All of a sudden, the printing business like everything else went kerplop. I was laid off in '31. I was out of work for over two years. I'd get up at six o'clock every morning and make the rounds. I'd go around looking for work until about eight thirty. The library would open at nine. I'd spend maybe five hours in the library.

The feeling among people was beautiful. Supposing some guy was a hunter. He'd go out and get a hold of some ducks or some game, they'd have their friends over and share it.

I can remember the first week of the CWA[3] checks. It was on a Friday. That night everybody had gotten his check. The first check a lot of them had in three years. Everybody was out celebrating. It was like a festival in some old European city. Prohibition had been repealed, of course. You'd walk from tavern to tavern and see people buying ponies of beer and sharing it. They had the whole family out. It was a warm night as I remember. Everybody was so happy, you'd think they got a big dividend from Xerox.

I never saw such a change of attitude. Instead of walking around feeling dreary and looking sorrowful, everybody was joyous. Like a feast day. They were toasting each other. They had money in their pockets for the first time. If Roosevelt had run for President the next day, he'd have gone in by a hundred percent.

I had it drilled in me: there are no such things as classes in America. I awoke one day. I was, by this time, working for a newspaper in Waukesha. They had a picture of this farm woman, standing in the window of her home and the dust had completely covered everything, and there was a dead cow. And here, at the bottom of the same page, they had a picture of Bernard Baruch. He had made some big deal in the stock market and was on somebody's yacht. I looked at one picture and then the other. No classes in America.

I was making sixty-seven cents an hour as a linotype operator. At about $27 a week, I was a big shot. I was rolling. And gradually got involved in the union movement. The printers played a big role in the early days of the CIO. This may seem unusual, a high class craft union went along with John L. Lewis against the old aristocracy of labor.

The union man today under forty knows absolutely nothing about the struggles. They don't want to upset the wonderful applecart they have. We used to sing, in the organizing days of the CIO, "Solidarity Forever." The Communists were active in it. Hell, we'd even sing "The Internationale" on occasion. Could I get a young printer today, who drives a big Buick, who has a home in the suburbs—could I get him to sing "Arise, ye prisoners of starvation . . ."? It's like when I was in the civil rights marches of 1965, they'd start chanting, "We want freedom." Here I am, a printer making $200 a week. It sounds silly as I chant, "I want freedom now." I know it's theirs I'm asking for, and, in a way it's mine. But it does sound silly, as *I* say it.

[3] Civil Works Administration. It presaged the WPA.

During the Depression, the La Follette movement grew, with Bob, Junior, and Phil. When the New Deal came in, they worked with Roosevelt. By this time, my father was getting pretty old and bitter. Being an extreme strict Catholic, he fell for Coughlinism.

It was quite a deal between him and his favorite son. He even wanted to sell *Social Justice*. I hated to do it, but I had to tell him: If *Social Justice* is quartered in this home, I'm not quartered in this home.

How do you explain the switch from Bob La Follette to Father Coughlin?

Even in the Depression, he wasn't able to accept the idea that there were different classes in America. The same as I couldn't when I was a child. And he was violently anti-Red. He objected to a lot that was going on: that's why he liked La Follette. But it was still the Great America. So there had to be some other reason for all the injustice.

He had great respect for the priestly collar, for one thing. While he was for Roosevelt in the beginning, he felt he was now in the hands of the Jews. The latent anti-Semitism had always been there.

Well, the rise of Hitler comes along the same time as the rise of Roosevelt. And after all, Hitler certainly took care of the Communists in Germany. I think it was his anti-Communism more than his rigid Catholicism that was the cause.

When Father Coughlin's silver market manipulations were uncovered, my father felt it was another plot. He just couldn't bring himself to believe that Coughlin was in it for anything except to help the poor people who were at the mercy of Roosevelt and the Jews. He was about eighty-two at the time and never gave up his belief. He followed Coughlin until the end.

When Coughlin was on, Sunday afternoons, everything in the house had to be absolutely quiet, not a whisper. You could walk down the street and every single Catholic house—it was Coughlin. To hell with the ball game or going out for a ride. . . .

Every time Coughlin would mention the name of a movie actor who was of Jewish extraction, and add his real name after his stage name, my father would gloat. And yet, my father was a good and kind man, and suffered along with his neighbors.

At the same time, he didn't see any benefits in social legislation: giving people something they didn't deserve, he felt. He liked Bob La Follette because he could see with his own eyes what Bob was fighting.

He was for Workmen's Compensation. Oh, my father was full of contradictions. . . .

In 1938, I threatened *The Freeman*—the Waukesha paper I was working on—to pull the boys out on strike, if they wouldn't raise our wages from ninety cents an hour to ninety-five. We finally got it up to $1 an hour. I was making forty bucks a week. I'm reading *Esquire,* seeing what kind of shoes I should buy, suits and stuff. I was really a big shot. I'd go out drinking on Saturday night, sometimes I'd spend as much as seven or eight dollars. Tavern keepers would welcome me with open arms. He's a big spender.

E. D. Nixon

For twenty-five years, he had been president of the Montgomery (Alabama) branch of the Brotherhood of Sleeping Car Porters.

"A Pullman porter can always get into a conversation anywhere. He walked into a barber shop, somebody'd say, 'I didn't see you around here,' or maybe they'd notice his pants with the stripe. Everybody listened because they knowd the porter been everywhere and they never been anywhere themselves.

"In cafes where they ate or hotels where they stayed, they'd bring in papers they picked up, white papers, Negro papers. He'd put 'em in his locker and distribute 'em to black communities all over the country. Along the road, where a whole lot of people couldn't get to town, we used to roll up the papers and tie a string around 'em. We'd throw these papers off to these people. We were able to let people know what was happening. He did know a whole lot of things."

I WORKED for the Pullman Company from 1928 to 1964. It was a hard job. We had a rest period: 10 P.M. to 2, for one porter, and 2 to 6, for the other. During that time, one man guarded two cars. From 6 in the morning to 10 at night, he was plenty busy with his one car: touch it up all the time, clean up, call a man at a certain time. You get that man off, you run back and tidy up the place, you run back and bring a new man in. By that time, they holler "All aboard!" you got to get that step up.

You have to touch up the men's room, the ladies' room, the vestibule. You carried a mop and a broom and the Company said: just bring me the handle back.

When I first went to work, they had a cuspidor set between every section. That means you had six on each side and three in the men's room and two in the ladies' room. Seventeen, they had to shine like gold. Twelve lowers and twelve uppers and three beds in the drawing rooms. Twenty-seven, they had to be made up all the time.

Maximum sleep was four hours a night. And some trips were Chicago to Los Angeles, Chicago to Miami. Before the Brotherhood, we had to cover 11,000 miles a month. No established time. Sometimes it took four-hundred hours to make it.

Passengers wrote up complaints. Sometimes conductors wrote up complaints. Newsboys could write up complaints, just so he's white. Here a man could leave his pocketbook at home. He'd swear he had it on the train: "That nigger porter took it." A whole lot of porters were searched and humiliated, and they found the man left it at home.

I was in New Orleans one day. The supervisor came in ahead of me. I had four bags, one in each arm and one in my hand. He opened the drawing room door. I said, "Thank you." He turned around and said in a rough manner, "I didn't open 'at door for you." I said, "Thank you again."

We got $62.50 a month. We had to depend a lot on tips. Some of the passengers would get hot about something. He wouldn't give you nothing and run down and tell the other passengers not to give you anything. "Didn't shine my shoes right. . . ." "Didn't get my pillow." They said it loud for other people to hear.

The porter instructor was a Negro man. The permanent inspector was a white man. They would have a mimeographed sheet. All he had to do was put a cross opposite any rule. The porter instructor would set there and watch you and write down when you turned your back. They turned in plenty on me because I was active in the Brotherhood. They were stool pigeons. They watched me my every move. They'd turn in what I said. A lot of men were scared off. But in spite of all that, we had a few here, there—kept the Brotherhood alive.

"The Brotherhood was born after several attempts by porters who were fired for it. The Company set up a Pullman Porter Benefit Association. Controlled by the Company. Three of the men were walkin' down the

133

street one day and heard Randolph speakin' on a soap box.[4] These three porters heard him and said, 'This is the man we need.'

"They didn't have any salary to offer him. Randolph took the chance. We had a women's auxiliary. They would have fish fries and raise some money. He stuck it out for twelve long years without a salary. Never knew when he'd come back to a place, because he didn't have the money to get there."

When Pullman fought the Brotherhood, almost all the Negro papers sold out to the Company. I think the Pittsburgh *Courier* was an exception. And *we* carried these papers. They'd have big red headlines lambasting Randolph. They'd point out that the Pullman Company been good to the Negro: decent jobs, opening schools for children, all that kind of stuff. Don't bite the hand that feeds you.

When I heard Randolph speak, it was like a light. Most eloquent man I ever heard. He done more to bring me in the fight for civil rights than anybody. Before that time, I figure that a Negro would be kicked around and accept whatever the white man did. I never knew the Negro had a right to enjoy freedom like everyone else. When Randolph stood there and talked that day, it made a different man out of me. From that day on, I was determined that I was gonna fight for freedom until I was able to get some of it myself. I was just stumblin' here and there. But I been very successful in stumblin' ever since that day. It was in 1928.

Shortly after, he became president of the Montgomery branch of the NAACP. His was the first private home that was bombed. In the late Thirties, "I got a call about a sheriff who beat a woman to death. I got a telephone call about two o'clock in the morning from a white man: 'I don't like what happened. I can't tell you on the phone. Come see me.'

"It was pouring rain. You might think I was crazy, but I drove forty miles out there. I walked on the front porch. Knocked on the door. Would I get a shotgun blast? I hear a man's voice, 'Is that you, Nixon?' He opened the door and told me what had happened. But he wouldn't sign anything. I don't blame him. If he did, they would've done something to him.

"The grand jury met. Same man called and said, 'You ought to have her sons there. They saw it.' I got ahold of the dean at Miles College:

[4] A. Philip Randolph, founding president of the Brotherhood of Sleeping Car Porters.

'Put them boys on the train. I'll get your money for you.' I met the train.
I said to the clerk, 'I want these boys to testify before the grand jury.'
She almost fell dead. 'The sheriff issues subpoenas,' she said. 'He's the
man who done the killin'.'

"I walked into his office. A short, fat fellow with hobnailed boots,
two pistols, handcuffs, bullets around his belt, blackjack in back pants
pocket, shirt all open. I said, 'You Sheriff White?' He said, 'I'm Sheriff
White.' I said, 'My name is E.D. Nixon. I represent the NAACP.' You
oughta seen him when I said that. 'I'm here to ask you to subpoena these
boys. They got a grand jury at three o'clock about the killin' of their
mother.' He looked at me. He didn't know what to say.

"He pulled out a pencil. He licked it. He took him so long to trace out
the boys' names. I said, 'You know the state pays eight cents a mile for
travel. Both these boys are entitled to transportation.' He said, 'It's a
hundred miles from here to Birmingham!' I said, 'That's correct. And
thirteen from Montgomery to where the case is, and three miles from
the college to the station. So you got 116 miles.' He said, 'Yeah, that's
right.'

"He started figurin' on a piece of paper. I could see he didn't know
what he was doin'. So I figured it out ahead of time. I wrote the figure
and I said, 'I believe when you get through figurin' yours up, this'll tally.'
He grabbed my sheet and said, 'Yeah, that's right, that's right.' He wrote
a voucher. I got the money.

"Of course, he was acquitted. The woman died 'from causes unknown.' But he couldn't believe his eyes. He just couldn't believe a
Negro had the courage to challenge him. I had nothing on me. If I had
a pocket knife and had been arrested, that's all they needed."

I was in St. Louis when Randolph spoke that Sunday in '28. He says,
"If you stick with me, the day will soon come when you'll be making
$150 a month." I couldn't see a man raising my salary from $62.50. But
I put a dollar in the collection anyway.

When I got home the next morning, the manager met me as I stepped
off the train. "I understand you attended a meeting of the Brotherhood
yesterday." A stool pigeon had told him. I said, "That's right." He said,
"If you continue to go, you won't have no job." Well, I won't let nobody push me around. I said, "I *joined* the Brotherhood yesterday. I
think I got enough money to carry any so-and-so to jail who messes with
my job." I never had any trouble after that.

In the course of my speaking, I got into hot water quite a bit. I took care of grievances. The southern white man couldn't see why he had to abide by a contract that was agreed upon by the Company. Despite the fact that Randolph started the Brotherhood in 1925, they were not recognized as a bonafide union until 1938. During that time, a whole lot of us were gettin' fired. Any time the Company felt you'd done *anything*— if you had anything to do with the Brotherhood, they got rid of you. Or punished you. . . .

I was once called in. The supervisor wrote me up, said I was talkin' to "some woman." The woman was my wife. I said, "Mr. Maloney, that woman is Mrs. Nixon. And I'm gonna demand you respect her as Mrs. Nixon, just as you would expect me to respect Mrs. Maloney as Mrs. Maloney. And I want my statement in the record." It knocked him for a deck of tombstones.

They found me guilty of dereliction of duty. They gave me eight days on the ground. You get no pay for that time. The Chicago office of the Company said eight days. The local man made it read: eighteen days. So I said to my wife, "They're askin' for a fight and they're gonna get it."

The Brotherhood appealed it to the Relations Board.[5] I was found not guilty, and the Pullman Company had to pay me for all the time lost. And that my record be clear of all charges.

We had a porter named Cooley. He was extremely large and weighed close to three hundred pounds. The Company wanted to get rid of him. The superintendent got on the train at Montgomery. He weighed three hundred and some odd pounds. Cooley gave him a pillow. He stretched out on the sofa and shut the door. When he got to Atlanta, he wrote a statement saying Porter Cooley failed to shut the toilets between Montgomery and Atlanta.

He told the conductor to write up Cooley as no good. The superintendent's letter was May 31st. The conductor dated his letter June 6th. And the superintendent quoted the conductor in his letter.

At the hearing, I said he must be a fortune teller. He could read what the conductor wrote seven days before he wrote it. I wonder if he would read my hand. I'd like to have him tell my fortune if he's that good.

[5] The National Labor Relations Board. An election was held in 1938, under the supervision of the Federal Government. "There were sealed ballots, and the Brotherhood won. We got a closed shop. Plenty folks didn't want to join the union, but they wanted the gains that the union got for them."

What won the case, though, was weight and width. The superintendent stated that Porter Cooley didn't lock the toilet doors from Montgomery to Atlanta. There were seventeen stops between. That means the superintendent would have to get out of that drawing room and walk to the other end of the car and back thirty-four times. He'd have to pass Cooley each time. If he weighed three hundred and some odd pounds and Cooley weighed close to three hundred, together they weighed close to six hundred pounds. You know the aisle of a Pullman car, it's about thirty inches. It just wasn't wide enough. He couldn't pass him once, let alone thirty-four times. I pointed this out. We won the case.

Sure, there are fewer Pullman porters today. That's because railroads are goin' downhill. The plight is much of its own fault. No regard for passengers. What a railroad sells is service. When a man bought a ticket, it was service he bought along with transportation: cordial treatment, sanitation, ticket claims all that. They ran away a whole lot of passengers. I wanted to go to New Orleans last week. There was only one train, leaving at 11:50 at night. My God, there used to be a train out of here every three hours. . . .

POSTSCRIPT: *He was a key figure in the Montgomery bus boycott. Mrs. Rosa Parks, the lady who was arrested for refusing to move to the back of the bus, was his secretary at the NAACP. It was he who issued the call to all the black preachers of the city. It was he who suggested the young pastor, Martin Luther King, Jr., as head of the Montgomery Improvement Association. The rest is history. . . .*

Joe Morrison

Half his working life was spent in the coal mines of southwestern Indiana—"as poor a part of the country as we could afford." He was born there. The remainder of his work days were in steel mills. He quit school at fourteen for his first job "in the fields."

"My father was a farmer and a coal miner, ten kids and I'm the oldest. He wanted me to do something else. Every parent worried about their kids gettin' killed in mine explosions. Just a few miles away, they had

gas, where mines exploded and we had one in 1927, killed thirty-seven men.

"The coal industry was hit in '26 and never did fully recover. Coal and lumber, they was the two things hit pretty hard. There was a dip in 1919, it picked up some. But in '26, there was another one. Coal and lumber never did recover.

"1929 is when it hit banking and big business. But we had suffering and starvation long before that. In the early Twenties, mines shut down, nothin' for people to live on. Children fainted in school from hunger. Long before the stock market crash."

ONCE I COUNTED the people that I give a lift to from Detroit to southern Indiana. It was fourteen people that I give a lift to that day. One was a woman with three children. Detroit was a one-industry town. When auto went down, everything went down. If there was a job in the auto plant, there'd be two hundred men for that job. (Laughs.)

In '30 and '31, you'd see freight trains, you'd see hundreds of kids, young kids, lots of 'em, just wandering all over the country. Looking for jobs, looking for excitement. . . . The one thing that was unique was to see women riding freight trains. That was unheard of, never had been thought of before. But it happened during the Depression. Women gettin' places by ridin' freight trains. Dressed in slacks or dressed like men, you could hardly tell 'em. Sometimes some man and his wife would get on, no money for fare.

You'd find political discussions going on in a boxcar. Ridin' a hundred miles or so, guys were all strangers, maybe two or three knew each other, pairs. There might be twenty men involved. They would discuss politics, what was happening. What should be done about this, that and so forth.

What was the spirit of the people . . . ?

Oh, they was ready for revolution. A lot of businessmen expected it. The Government sent out monitors. They had 'em in these Hoovervilles, outside the town, along the railroads, along the highways. In monitoring these places, they got a lot of information. The information was: revolution. People were talkin' revolution all over the place. You met guys ridin' the freight trains and so forth, talkin' about what they'd like to do with a machine gun. How they'd like to tear loose on the rich. . . .

You don't find much political talk any more among workingmen. You go to a tavern now, it's around ball games, something like that. Seldom ever politics or war. The old crackerbarrel discussions we had at home, always lively.

Up until since the end of World War II, you always found a bunch of young workers, up and coming, that read a lot. They liked to discuss history and things like that. They read Socialist and Communist publications. Of course, the Communists didn't come till a later period. The Socialist literature—I remember when I was seventeen down in the lead mines in Missouri—they'd get from them things, they could give a congressman a pretty good run for his money. Even in these small towns, they passed newspapers, magazines around. People that couldn't subscribe, they'd ask everybody to save their papers, and they'd pass 'em on and so forth. People read and talked more than they do now.

Maybe they're thinkin' today, but they don't talk. There's an apathy. They're so busy trying to keep their bills paid. And the unpopularity of their being interested in anything they're confronted with. People forget a lot. The younger generation has simply forgotten the history of these periods. It's being covered up.

The terror that's placed upon people—the McCarthy times. The guys begin to clam up and say nothin'. I was summoned before the House Un-American Activities Committee in the Fifties. When I went back to the mill, it was only a couple of guys that acted afraid, afraid to talk to me the first day. After the first day, it was O.K.; they got over it. All the men went out of their way to be friendly, to aid me in any way they could. But none of 'em didn't want to *talk* about it. We've reached a place where people just got over doing anything about things they didn't want to face. They're afraid of being branded, being called Red or something.

In '34 I got discharged over a hassle we had with the mine company. I was on the union's grievance committee. They had me blacklisted in the fields there. I never got a job until I went to work in the steel mills in '36. I bummed around a little in some temporary jobs, anything I could get. Had a big family, seven children, they were all small. So you just had to hustle for whatever you could get.

I went to work in a car shop. That's when the CIO started organizing steel. Half the organizers we had there came from coal. Among 'em were some good organizers. But among 'em was also pie cards,[6] they didn't do anything but make a lot of noise. You see it crop up today.

It was rough going. You'd get a little relief. There was some surplus commodities, flour and stuff like that. You'd get a day's work now and then on the farm. You might run into a week's work, a road job or something like that. That's the way people got along.

Mary, 22

MY FATHER lived on a farm. When the Depression came around, the first thing he did was go to New York City to look for a job. He took a job as a strikebreaker, because he really didn't know what it would mean. He didn't realize how bad this would be, or how dangerous. Or what striking people would think of this. He remembers being shadowed by people with guns and all sorts of things like that. He really got out of that job quickly. He didn't know what he was doing, he was that naive. . . .

Gordon Baxter

Attorney. An alumnus of Yale University and Harvard Law School, '32. "Children in eighth grade today have more knowledge of what's going on in the world than I had all during college. I was sitting there listening to William Lyon Phelps lecturing about Tennyson and Browning, the most terrible crap in the world, but I didn't have the judgment to know it was a lot of crap.

"Those times, people went through school insulated from everything except the immediate environment. Very few people doubted their ability to make a living. Success was measured by income: to get ahead fast

---

[6] An idiom for labor organizers who didn't give a damn.

*in the business world. If people thought of going into teaching, they
didn't say anything about it. They were regarded as kind of nuts.*

*"It was really in my last year at law school that I noticed something
was going on. At the New Haven football games, I met Yale graduates,
who a couple of years before were claiming it was easy on Wall Street.
Now the market crashed, and they were back at school, out of jobs.
The world rushed in on us suddenly. . . ."*

*In 1937, at the age of thirty-two, he became general counsel and vice
president of a large company, employing ten thousand. It was engaged
in the making of die castings, appliances and automotive parts.*

THERE WAS a wave of sit-down strikes. Newspapers and respectable
people said it was bad enough to have strikes, but it was clearly immoral
as well as unlawful to seize property. In those days, strikes were broken
by the importation of strikebreakers. Sitting down in a factory kept
strikebreakers from getting in. It was a new technique. When suddenly
the rules of the game, which the unions had always lost, were altered
by the sit-downs, there was an outcry.

You hear the same kind of talk about student demonstrators today.
It's all right for them to protest peacefully, but they must do it in accordance to the rules.

There was a sit-down strike at one of our plants. We had a plant
manager who dealt with these labor troubles. In his way, he was a nice
guy, but his appearance was that of a cartoon factory boss: cigar in the
corner of his mouth, a big square face and a big square frame. He had
ways of beating the strikers that were not generally published, but
known to manufacturers.

There was a police detail in Chicago known as the Industrial Squad,[7]
in charge of a lieutenant, Make Mills. When a strike occurred, Mills
would arrange to arrest the leaders. They'd beat them up, put them in
jail, make it pretty clear to them to get the hell out of town. Mills got
tips, $1,000, or if it was a serious thing, $5,000. He made a hell of a
lot of dough to get the agitators, as they were called.

These were organizers, some of whom didn't work in the factory.
With his plainclothesmen, Mills would get them in a saloon. They'd have
free drinks, then a fight would break out.

His uniformed men would come in and arrest the organizer, beat hell

[7] It was popularly known as "The Red Squad."

out of him, put him in jail. They got a lot of people out of town. There was an awful lot of rough stuff going on.

The factory was shut down. I was drawn into it. The union had filed a complaint with the National Labor Relations Board.[8] The issue was union recognition. The complaint: blacklisting.

The company sent letters out in very fancy language: we will pay the best wages, we will always discuss grievances with employees, but will allow no outside intervention. Newspaper editorials were urging employees to return to work. Each day of the strike was costing them money they'd never recover.

I was handed a stack of cards to take downtown to our attorneys. Some of those I examined had notations: "Union agitator, do not re-hire." Others were marked with little round dots. The employment manager told me they indicated a union sympathizer. Many of them had been or were to be fired. If any prospective employer were to ask about them, he'd be told: "Don't hire him—troublemaker, agitator." The word "Communist" wasn't used much at the time. "Red," though, was a common term.

I took the cards to Twynan, Hill and Blair. The operating head of the thing, Blair, came out of the Northwest as a successful railroad attorney. He represented many big companies and was a member of our board. A tremendous bore, a funny little guy, about five feet four, small mustache. All his clients were saints, under attack. He was about seventy at the time.

When he'd get agitated, it would upset his stomach, he'd bounce up and down in his leather chair and reach for mineral water. Then he'd run out in the hall, holler for his secretary and relieve himself by dictating letters.

He had a special phrase he liked: "This presents a situation pregnant with danger." Of course, it's a great sustenance for a lawyer. If a danger is pregnant, he's got to come to the rescue. The annual retainer doesn't quite cover this. He got a hell of a lot of fees out of this operation.

Blair told me the cards were harmless. It dawned on me that he didn't know of the existence of the Wagner Act. When I told him, he said, "There cannot be any such law. And if there were, I would not hesitate to advise you it would be unconstitutional because it would be an impinge-

---

[8] With the passage of the Wagner Act, the National Labor Relations Board came into being. It became illegal to fire or blacklist any employee on the grounds of union activities.

ment upon the freedom of contract." I said, "There is such a law. It's sometimes called the Wagner Act." He said, "I never heard of it." And I said, "It was adjudicated in the Supreme Court and its validity was upheld." He howled, "That is impossible!" He swiveled around and grabbed for his mineral water.

He called in an associate. "This young man tells me there is a law by the name of the Watson Act." "The Wagner Act." The other nodded. "There is? This young man goes further and claims the United States Supreme Court declared it constitutional." The other nodded. "That, sir, is impossible!" His associate said it was so. "It's a fine thing!" With that, Blair slapped the stack of cards on his desk, bang. "Well that's one more of these left-wing New Deal activities. Respectable citizens who built up this country can come in and testify, and their testimony won't be believed." The other said, "That's the way it would go." Blair said, "We sent the president of the company to deny these charges, and he wouldn't be believed?" I said, "Mr. Blair, one of the reasons he wouldn't be believed is because it would be a lie."

"What do you mean a lie?"

"Look at these cards. It identifies union men."

"Is something wrong with that?"

"Yes, it's prohibited."

"That has to be adjudicated."

"It was adjudicated. And all these people who were fired. It says on the face of it: Don't rehire."

"But they are *former* employees."

Well, this is the way it went. He called in a detective, who was on the company payroll and said, "Take these cards. I don't ever want to see them again. I don't want to know what happened to them, and I don't want you to ever know anything about them."

The National Labor Relations Board did find the company engaged in unfair labor practices. The union was recognized. A large sum of money was awarded in back wages to employees who were fired. There were tremendous legal fees, of course.

There was a curious aftermath. The people went back to work. But there persisted an attitude of bitterness and resentment. A continuing hostility. Each side wished the worst of the other.

During the ten years I stayed on, this feeling existed. Finally, the company sold its die-casting plant. They couldn't make any money out of it. It's a difficult business, but there are companies that do make it. I've often wondered whether the failure here wasn't due to this long, sustained bitterness. Every negotiation became a war, bitterness begetting bitterness, violence begetting violence.

Most people don't become vice presidents until their late fifties. I was one of the few college-educated men in the company. There was a lot of suspicion of me: I had to be watched. But a great many of the older men would take me out to lunch and ask me to tell them something.

This was at a time when people who went to Yale or Harvard went into brokerage, not into manufacturing. In contrast to now, the industrialists were basically men who came up from the bench. The hard way, they called it.

That had a lot to do with their tone and attitude. If anybody has the impression that a man who had come up the hard way had an easy way of looking at the working man, he's completely mistaken. His view was: I got ahead. Why can't you?

There's a parallel in this race business today. Look, my family came from the Old Country, and my grandfather sold pots and pans off his back, and I've moved out to the suburbs, and if my grandfather could do it, what the hell's the matter with these niggers?

The people who made it were very impatient with the agitators. Agitators were parasites, trying to tear down the structure. There was no law of agreed principles. It was nothing but a contest of staying power. It was a jungle.

People would regard a depression today as man-made. In the past, depressions fell in the same category as earthquakes and bad weather. An act of Providence or God. I don't think there'd be the acquiescence of the Thirties. I think there'd be a rebellion. I think even in these suburbs out here you'd get a rebellion. Exactly what they'd do about it, I don't know. I think there'd be a vigorous and, ultimately violent, insistence: if not my measure, then some other measure. Something and soon.

There was some of this in the Thirties, the left wing. Some were called Communists; some were Communists. They pointed up, as they called it, the contradictions: people starving, with farmers being told to kill off their pigs. There was anger and frustration with the inability to put the productive capacity to work to meet the needs of the people. There wasn't much of this talk in the Thirties—these were the nuts, the fringe. They wouldn't be the fringe today. . . .

Three Strikes

Bob Stinson

THE SIT-DOWN

"Everybody has to have something they're really sold on. Some people go to church. If I'd had anything I'm really sold on, it's the UAW."

Regularly, he visits the regional headquarters of the United Automobile Workers Union in Flint, Michigan. He's a small-boned man, in specs, sports shirt and a business suit.

"I started working at Fisher Body in 1917 and retired in '62, with 45 and 8/10 years service. Until 1933, no unions, no rules: you were at the mercy of your foreman. I could go to work at seven o'clock in the morning, and at seven fifteen the boss'd come around and say: you could come back at three o'clock. If he preferred somebody else over you, that person would be called back earlier, though you were there longer.

"I left the plant so many nights hostile. If I were a fella big and strong, I think I'd a picked a fight with the first fella I met on the corner. (Laughs.) It was lousy. Degraded. You might call yourself a man if you was on the street, but as soon as you went through the door and punched your card, you was nothing more or less than a robot. Do this, go there, do that. You'd do it.

"We got involved in a strike in Detroit, and we lost the strike. Went back on our knees. That's the way you learn things. I got laid off in the

fall of '31. I wasn't told I was blackballed, but I was told there was no more jobs at Fisher Body for me. So I came to Flint and was hired right off the bat. I'm positive my black marks in Detroit followed me later. (Laughs.)

"We had a Black Legion in this town made up of stool pigeons and little bigotty kind of people. They got themselves in good with the management by puttin' the finger on a union organizer. On the same order as the Klan, night riders. Once in a while, a guy'd come in with a black eye. You'd say, 'What happened?' He'd say, 'I was walking along the street and a guy come from behind and knocked me down.'

"The Black Legion later developed into the Flint Alliance. It was supposed to be made up of the good solid citizens, who were terrorized by these outside agitators, who had come in here to take over the plant. They would get schoolkids to sign these cards, housewives. Every shoe salesman downtown would sign these cards. Businessmen would have everyone in the family sign these cards. They contended they had the overwhelming majority of the people of Flint.

"Most people in town was hopin' to hell the thing'd get solved. They had relatives and friends that they knew working in the plant was no bed of roses. They did accept some of this outside agitator stuff that got in the paper. I think anybody who reads this stuff day after day accepts a little bit of it. The great majority of the people was neutral.

"There was fear. You kept your mouth shut when you was in strange company. Every time you put a union button on, you were told to leave the plant. You were fired so fast, it made your head spin.

"We'd meet in an old ramshackley building. No doubt, stool pigeons came. Frenchie was exposed. Somebody got up on the platform and said, 'I know this guy's a stool pigeon, 'cause I gave him information and it passed right from him to the foreman!' They trapped the guy. Nobody touched him. He just walked down the stairs."

He tells of constant betrayals by the AFL International to which they had belonged, and of the subsequent organization of the CIO, led by John L. Lewis.

THE FLINT SIT-DOWN happened Christmas Eve, 1936. I was in Detroit, playing Santa Claus to a couple of small nieces and nephews. When I came back, the second shift[1] had pulled the plant. It took about five

---

[1] The men who worked from 4:30 P.M. to 12:30 A.M.

minutes to shut the line down. The foreman was pretty well astonished. (Laughs.)

The boys pulled the switches and asked all the women who was in Cut-and-Sew to go home. They informed the supervisors they could stay, if they stayed in their office. They told the plant police they could do their job as long as they didn't interfere with the workers.

We had guys patrol the plant, see that nobody got involved in anything they shouldn't. If anybody got careless with company property—such as sitting on an automobile cushion without putting burlap over it—he was talked to. You couldn't paint a sign on the wall or anything like that. You used bare springs for a bed. 'Cause if you slept on a finished cushion, it was no longer a new cushion.

Governor Murphy[2] said he hoped to God he would never have to use National Guard against people. But if there was damage to property, he would do so. This was right down our alley, because we invited him to the plant and see how well we were taking care of the place.[3]

They'd assign roles to you. When some of the guys at headquarters wanted to tell some of the guys in the plant what was cookin', I carried the message. I was a scavenger, too.

The merchants cooperated. There'd be apples, bushels of potatoes, crates of oranges that was beginnin' to spoil. Some of our members were also little farmers, they come up with a couple of baskets of junk.

The soup kitchen was outside the plant. The women handled all the cooking, outside of one chef who came from New York. He had anywhere from ten to twenty women washing dishes and peeling potatoes in the strike kitchen. Mostly stews, pretty good meals. They were put in containers and hoisted up through the window. The boys in there had their own plates and cups and saucers.

Didn't the guys want a drink now and then . . . ?

That was one of the hard ones. Even though you had strict discipline in there, anybody wanted to climb through the window, you couldn't stop him. He could leave any time he wanted. There was always some of the boys who would take a day off, go out and see how the old woman was doing. When they'd come back in, if somebody didn't search 'em, why, there'd be a pint.

---

[2] Frank Murphy. He subsequently became a Supreme Court Justice.

[3] See Harry Norgard's interpretation in the sequence, "Strive and Succeed," p. 501.

The plant police would start bringin' in some women. That was damn quickly stopped.

We had 'em outnumbered. They may have been anti-union at the time, but it wasn't more than three or four years later before the plant guards' union was organized. I don't blame 'em. They were dependent on their supervisors for jobs just like we were.

Most of the men had their wives and friends come down, and they'd stand inside the window and they'd talk. Find out how the family was. If the union supplied them with enough coal. . . .

We had a ladies' auxiliary. They'd visit the homes of the guys that was in the plant. They would find out if there was any shortage of coal or food. Then they'd maneuver around amongst themselves until they found some place to get a ton of coal. Some of them even put the arm on Consumer Power if there was a possibility of having her power shut off.

Any of the wives try to talk the guys into coming out?

Some of 'em would have foremen come to their homes: "Sorry, your husband was a very good operator. But if he don't get out of the plant and away from the union, he'll never again have a job at General Motors." If this woman was the least bit scared, she'd come down and cry on her husband's shoulder. He'd more than likely get a little disturbed, get a hold of his strike captain. . . . Maybe we'd send a couple of women out there. Sometimes you just had to let 'em go. Because if you kept them in there, they'd worry so damn much over it, that'd start ruinin' the morale of the rest of the guys.

Morale was very high at the time. It started out kinda ugly because the guys were afraid they put their foot in it and all they was gonna do is lose their jobs. But as time went on, they begin to realize they could win this darn thing, 'cause we had a lot of outside people comin' in showin' their sympathy.

Time after time, people would come driving by the plant slowly. They might pull up at the curb and roll down the window and say, "How you guys doin'?" Our guys would be lookin' out the windows, they'd be singin' songs and hollerin'. Just generally keeping themselves alive.

Sometimes a guy'd come up to you on the street and say, "How the guys doin'?" You say, "They're doin' all right." Then he'd give ya a song and dance: "I hear the boys at Chevrolet are gonna get run out tonight."[4] I'd say, "Hogwash." He'd end with sayin': "Well, I wish you guys the best of luck because, God damn, when I worked there it was a mess." The guy'd turn around and walk away.

Nationally known people contributed to our strike fund. Mrs. Roosevelt for one. We even had a member of Parliament come from England and address us.

Lotta things worked for the union we hadn't even anticipated. Company tried to shut off the heat. It was a bluff. Nobody moved for half an hour, so they turned it back on again. They didn't want the pipes to get cold. (Laughs.) If the heat was allowed to drop, then the pipes will separate—they were all jointed together—and then you got a problem.

Some of the time you were scared, because there was all kinds of rumors going around. We had a sheriff—he came in one night at Fisher One and read the boys the riot act. He told 'em they had to leave. He stood there, looked at 'em a few minutes. A couple of guys began to curse 'im, and he turned around and left himself.

National Guard troops were there. Some from Pontiac, some from Detroit. I lived within a block where they camped. I would pass these young fellas every day. One boy, pretty young, he had a union button on. Was it his union button or was it his dad's? I walked up to him. "Your captain allow you to wear that button?" He says, "I don't know, but I'm gonna find out." (Laughs.) They were twenty-year-olds. Well-behaved boys. No rough stuff, nothing untoward happened.

The men sat in there for forty-four days. Governor Murphy—I get emotional over him (laughs)—was trying to get both sides to meet on some common ground. I think he lost many a good night's sleep. We wouldn't use force. Mr. Knudsen was head of General Motors and, of course, there was John L. Lewis. They'd reach a temporary agreement and invariably the Flint Alliance or GM headquarters in Detroit would throw a monkey wrench in it. So every morning, Murphy got up with an unsolved problem.

[4] Several other General Motors plants in Flint were the scenes of similar sit-downs. "At Chevrolet Four, there was a knock-down and drag-out fight. That's where the Battle of Bull Run happened. The boys took it over, and the city police and the sheriff's men decided they were gonna throw 'em out. Between the tear gas the police used and the nuts and bolts the strikers used, there was hell to pay. We run 'em off. When the tear gas got in the plant, the women's brigade smashed every damn window they could find to let the air in. It was vicious. (Laughs.) Hans Larson, he was shot in the Battle of Bull Run."

John L. was as close to a Shakespearean actor as any I've ever listened to. He could get up there and damn all the adversaries—he had more command of language. He made a speech that if they shoot the boys out at the plant, they'd have to shoot him first.[5]

There were a half a dozen false starts at settlement. Finally, we got the word: THE THING IS SETTLED. My God, you had to send about three people, one right after the other, down to some of those plants because the guys didn't believe it. Finally, when they did get it, they marched out of the plants with the flag flyin' and all that stuff.

You'd see some guys comin' out of there with whiskers as long as Santa Claus. They made a rule they wasn't gonna shave until the strike was over. Oh, it was just like—you've gone through the Armistice delirium, haven't you? Everybody was runnin' around shaking everybody by the hand, sayin', "Jesus, you look strange, you got a beard on you now." (Laughs.) Women kissin' their husbands. There was a lotta drunks on the streets that night.

When Mr. Knudsen put his name to a piece of paper and says that General Motors recognizes the UAW–CIO—until that moment, we were non-people, we didn't even exist. (Laughs.) That was the big one. (His eyes are moist.)

Gregory

He was born in Flint in 1946 and has lived in its environs most of his life.

THE SIT-IN strikes? No, it doesn't ring a bell with me. What were they? My grandfather worked for the GM plant in Flint. I had an uncle

---

[5] When Governor Murphy was being urged to use the National Guard to oust the sit-downers, Lewis orated: "I shall personally enter General Motors' Chevrolet Plant Number Four. I shall order the men to disregard your order, to stand fast. I shall then walk up to the largest window in the plant, open it, divest myself of my outer raiment, remove my shirt and bare my bosom. Then, when you order your troops to fire, mine will be the first breast that those bullets will strike. And, as my body falls from the window to the ground, you will listen to the voice of your grandfather as he whispers in your ear, 'Frank, are you sure you are doing the right thing?' "

working for Body by Fisher, another one for Buick. He used to talk about his work, my grandfather. About standing in line, waiting for a job. He did auto work for forty-five years. But he never mentioned the sit-in strikes.

Charles Stewart Mott

A vigorous ninety-four, he's the oldest member of the board of General Motors. In the early part of the century, he served as three-time mayor of Flint. As head of the Mott Foundation, he is responsible for many philanthropies. He says of himself: "Old man Mott is working days and nights, and Sundays, not knowing when to quit. I'd be busy if I were three people." He is weary of being reminded of his remarkable resemblance to the late British film actor, C. Aubrey Smith.

ALFRED P. SLOAN came to GM in 1932 and was made president. He was a master of corporate procedure. He brought order out of chaos. For every one share of stock in 1913, we had 562½ shares in 1935. We enlisted the help of the DuPont company. At one time, they held twenty-four percent of the stock. I don't know what we'd have done without them. Since that time, it's gone up and up and up.

I never became involved in the labor matters. Even in companies where I own all the stock, I leave those matters to those better able to handle it. I'm not the kind of person that worries, certainly not about something that's water over the dam. I get more pleasure out of the foundation business than anything I can think of.

At board meetings, labor matters were described but not discussed. We had a vice president in charge of labor relations, a very able chap. He was in close contact with the directors of GM to see that he didn't cross them up—that he does things the way they approve of. We meet the first Monday of every month. Sometimes, he'd appear to tell us what the situation was. We'd merely approve.

I knew Frank Murphy. (Laughs.) I don't like to speak ill of a dead man, but he certainly lacked an awful lot of things that might have been good. Frank was Mayor of Detroit in the early Thirties. I remember him saying: "The water department of Detroit is in terrible shape. We supply water to contiguous communities, and they can't pay. Water companies are tough things. . . ." Well, I own six or eight or ten, I guess, water companies. And they're the easiest things to run. I said to him, "If they take water and don't pay, all you have to do is apply to the courts and demand payment. You'd collect." He didn't understand. . . . He was Governor during the sit-down strikes, and he didn't do his job. He didn't enforce the law. He kept his hands off. He didn't protect our property.

You feel the National Guard should have evicted the sit-downers?

They had no right to sit-down there. They were illegally occupying it. The owners had the right to demand from the Governor to get those people out. It wasn't done. The same as today.

Communities allow all this hoodlum stuff. It's an outrage. When you have people breaking into stores, and you have police and the National Guard with things loaded, and they don't stop those people—it's terrible. They should have said, "Stop that thing. Move on, or we'll shoot." And if they didn't, they should have been shot. They'd have killed a certain number of people, but it would have been a lot less than would have been killed afterwards. It's an absolute duplicate of the Thirties, with the sit-down strikes.

What are your memories of Franklin D. Roosevelt?

Someone said to me: Did you see the picture on those new dimes? It's our new destroyer. It was a picture of Roosevelt. He was the great destroyer. He was the beginner of our downhill slide. Boy, what he did to this country. I don't think we'll ever get over it. Terrible.

Do you remember seeing lines of unemployed men . . . ?

I recollect there were such things.

POSTSCRIPT: *A Flint cab driver, on the way to the Mott Foundation Building observed, "He's a great man. If you live in Flint, that's one name you get used to. He's done great things for us. . . . Sure, I remember the sit-down strikes. Boy, did they wreck this town . . . the way they destroyed property. The papers here were full of it. I tell you. . . ."*

Scott Farwell

He is twenty-two. "My mother's family owned a large part of a large
city. We had a summer home of twenty bedrooms. It was somewhat
rough in the Thirties, but my sister went to a girls' school, where the
tuition today is $4,000 a year.

"I come from a WASP upper middle-class suburb and was raised on
the myth that everybody can make it. In reality, everybody can't make
it. If a guy makes a million dollars, he can do so only because another
thousand people are making $3,000 a year."

BOOKS TOLD US about guys jumping out of windows. But it didn't tell us
GM made fantastic profits all those years. Our textbooks tell us everybody got fucked. That isn't true. A lot of guys, Joe Kennedy, for instance, made tremendous profits during that period. The vast majority
got fucked up by the high guys. It's the textbooks that are fucked up.

My father talks a lot about his mistake in not going to college. If he
didn't fuck off those four years in the steel mills, he could've gotten
ahead and had more money than he has now. And he has plenty.

He's defensive about those four years as a worker. He sees it as a
youthful folly, as he sees what I'm going through. But now he sees it's
less and less of a youthful folly with me and that I'm totally ruined for
the rest of my life.

He blamed himself. Instead of saying society was fucked up, he's
really saying that he was fucked up. I don't think people were fucked up
during the Depression. I think if given half a chance, they'd have really
accomplished something. He never told me about the millions out of
work. He talked about how fucked up he was and didn't work hard
enough and he should have gone to school and got a doctorate.

When my father brings up these struggles, I manage to smash him
down. He doesn't give me that argument any more. They're slowly
ruining my sister, with clothes and all that shit. She's a groovy little girl.
My brother is a nice liberal guy. He will never consciously screw somebody else. But that doesn't mean he won't. When he gets that job, he'll
have to.

Mike Widman

THE BATTLE OF DETROIT

A Preface

Justin McCarthy quit college in 1933. He was working at a Ford assembly plant in an industrial suburb, near Chicago.

"*I sandpapered all the right-hand fenders. I was paid $5 a day. The parts were brought in from the River Rouge plant in Detroit. When I went to work in January, we were turning out 232 cars a day. When I was fired, four months later, we were turning out 535. Without any extra help and no increase in pay. It was the famous Ford Speed-up.*

"*The gates were locked when you came in at eight o'clock in the morning. They weren't opened again until five o'clock in the evening. People brought their own lunch. No commissary wagons were permitted on the grounds. Nobody bothered to tell me. So I didn't eat that first day. You were supposed to buy your own gloves. Nobody bothered to tell me that, either. Imagine my hands at five o'clock that first day.*

"*I was aware of men in plain clothes being around the plant, and the constant surveillance. I didn't learn till later these were the men of Ford's service department. Many of them, ex-cons.*

"*If you wanted to go to the toilet, you had to have permission of the foreman. He had to find a substitute for you on the assembly line, who could sandpaper those two right fenders as they went by. If he couldn't right away, you held it. (Laughs.)*

"*If you didn't punch that clock at 8:00, if you came in at 8:02, you were docked one hour's pay. There wasn't any excuse. If you did this two or three times, you got fired.*

"*I made the mistake of telling the foreman I had enrolled at Northwestern University night school. He said, 'Mr. Ford isn't paying people to go to college. You're through.'*"

A long-time associate of John L. Lewis, Mike Widman was appointed director of the campaign to organize the Ford Motor Company, the automobile industry's last holdout against the UAWU.

154

WE STARTED OUT on the sixteenth day of October, 1940. The three plants in Detroit, Hamtramck and Dearborn had about a hundred thousand men. We immediately zoned the town and located the Ford workers. The milkmen helped. There were about seven hundred of them, members of the CIO. They told us who their Ford worker customers were. But we had to shake the bushes to get them. There was great fear in the hearts of these men.

This was three years after Reuther and Frankensteen were beaten up by the service department.[6] This department was made up of men who served time in prison. They could be paroled to someone who insured them employment. Ford readily gave them jobs. It made him a fine espionage system. Bennett built it.[7]

As fast as the men signed application blanks, they were fired. We couldn't figure how the company found out so fast. So we tightened our security. I kept the cards in my safe until it got too small for all the cards coming in. There were hundreds of John Doe applications. They were just scared to death.

They'd come into our office when it first opened, they'd walk three, four times around the vestibule, look in all directions. Finally, they'd jump in the door and ask you to take them in the back room.

The life of a Ford worker was quite miserable. These service men were everywhere. The way they'd throw men out . . . today, anybody that wore a blue shirt got laid off. Tomorrow, if you had brown hair, black hair, anything. No recourse.

If they caught some of our people on the street, they slapped 'em around. When some of our boys first wore union buttons or UAW baseball caps, they were given the works. Some of our boys got fed up, and next thing a couple of service men were slightly hurt. That ended their parading in public. But this was later. . . .

Within sixty days after the campaign started, we challenged Ford, through Bennett, to have an election. Bennett refused to meet any "outsider," but he agreed to meet with employees on grievances. Bennett and I exchanged blasts through Jim Dewey, the federal conciliator, who acted as go-between. We blasted each other in newspapers. The more

---

[6] Shortly after GM had signed with the UAWU, Walter Reuther and Dick Frankensteen were assaulted at the overpass, near Detroit's River Rouge plant, while in the act of passing out union handbills. The La Follette Civil Liberties Committee confirmed the charge that the assailants were members of Ford's service department.

[7] Harry Bennett, chief of the service department.

stories got in, the more cards we signed. It was $1 initiation fee and $1 dues. In February, we took in $88,000 plus.

The first meeting I addressed, some thirty days after my arrival, had a grand total of twenty-three in the audience. Now we were having meetings of more than thirty thousand at the fairgrounds. We had broken down this fear.

We had forty organizers on the outside. Those were the men Ford had fired, so we put 'em on the staff. But the real secret of our success were the ones Ford paid for himself—the six thousand volunteers inside the plant.

We bought an old abandoned school building. This was lined up as our soup kitchen. We didn't want any strike, but we knew sooner or later, Ford would force us into one. We were prepared just in case. . . .

On April 1, it happened. The five men on our grievance committee had permission from the foreman to leave their job and see the division superintendent. He said, "Talk to the employment office." At the employment office, they were told, "You left your jobs. You're fired."

We asked the company, through the conciliator, to arbitrate this matter. The answer was: They're fired, and we don't care what you do. The word spread in the plant like wildfire. . . .

We called the strike for 12:15, just after midnight. The boys on the day shift stayed in the plant until four o'clock. Now both shifts were inside. We were still trying to get the five men reinstated. Again the company refused. So we let the midnight shift come in. Ford had about eighty-nine thousand workers in that plant all at the same time. What everybody said was impossible was about to happen.

We had organized a band.[8] The boys came marching out to the sound of music. We had surveyed the fourteen highways that led into the plant. It would take at least two thousand cars on each of 'em as a picket line to tie things up. One of the boys got the idea: We'll pull the trolley pole off the first streetcar coming in from Detroit. So we had the streetcars clear downtown for about six miles all stopped. The boys stacked up rubbish and cars and anything they could find. Everything was tied up.

Word came from the Governor. He wanted the highways opened up.

---

[8] Efforts were made from the beginning by the UAWU to interest the young workers. Bowling leagues, baseball teams and bands were organized. "We hoped for about eight teams, we ended up with ninety." There were five hundred applicants for the eighty-piece band. Uniforms, caps and shirts with UAWU insignia were issued.

We agreed, if Ford would keep the plant shut down while mediation was going on. At the insistence of the Governor, Ford agreed. We had fourteen picket lines, and I made fourteen speeches that morning. I explained what was happening. We opened up the highways and set up skeleton picket lines.

All the workers were out, except about five thousand Negroes. Ford was lenient in hiring Negroes at that time.[9] This was their first chance to work in the industry, and they were fearful of losing their jobs. They weren't really scabbing. It was just fear. They weren't doing any work. They were sitting there making all kinds of homemade weapons, short pieces of iron and rubber pipe. They were afraid somebody was gonna come in and get 'em. But we weren't trying to get them out. Ford was keeping them in there twenty-four hours a day. They never went home. Keeping them around the clock for five or six days was costing him a pretty penny.

Bennett went to the conciliator and said, "We want those fellows out of the plant." I called my pickets over to the east side. Dewey, the conciliator, had arranged with Bennett to get the Negroes on city buses, on the west side of the plant. So that's how it worked. There was no trouble.

Then comes the AF of L sticking their nose in, at Ford's insistence. I happened to meet their director, a teamster from Boston. I said, "Where the hell are you goin'?" He said, "I'm goin' to compete with you." I said, "You're too damn late. I've got the barn door locked." He said, "I've been ordered to do it."

Do you think Ford made a deal with the AF of L to keep the CIO out?

Exactly. They had never touched this place before. They weren't interested. They opened up six offices: One for white workers, who numbered more than seventy thousand; and five in Negro areas with less than ten thousand workers. With one purpose: If they couldn't win, they'd create a race riot or damage the CIO. Among our militants were many southern white workers, who were incensed. But they were disciplined.

The strike continued until the eleventh of April. It lasted about nine or ten days. When the company consented to the election, the boys all

[9] "I think he brought them in to show a philanthropic attitude. He also brought in a lot of deaf and dumb people and other handicapped. I signed up a good number of them. We had somebody who could talk on his fingers to them."

went back, without discrimination. But Ford wouldn't put those five men back. Rather than delay the return of the workers, I put 'em on my staff.

On May 21, 1941, we had the election. It took that long to get things straightened out. We carried seventy-two percent of the vote. We were certified. So negotiations started. They went on for about thirty days.

Ford, through Bennett and Capizzi, his lawyer, agreed to just about everything we asked for. He'd match what the rival companies were paying, and more. He was out to top them. He suspected—in his wild imagination—that they had put us up to this strike. (Laughs.)

I was dumbfounded when Capizzi said, "Mr. Ford doesn't want any dues collection in the plant. Would you accept the check-off?" We said, "That could be arranged." (Laughs.) He asked if we'd take in, without recrimination, the twenty percent who voted against us. We said, of course. They'll all be treated alike. He asked, "Do you have a union label you could put on the cars?" We offered to get one designed. For a while we put 'em on, but didn't keep it up.

Bennett surprised me by going completely overboard. He gave workers the right to vote on who they wanted as their foreman. (Laughs.) When I found this out, I hit the roof. "What the hell are you doing?" He said, "Your boys are gonna work for the foreman they like and won't work for the one they won't like." This was his reasoning. I said, "Do you think we'd let you appoint our committeemen? Appoint your own damn foremen." There'd be no stability. If the foreman says, "Hey, you're not performing your end of the work," the guy could say, "We'll vote you out at noon."

My union experience taught me that the direction of the working force is vested in management. The union shall not abridge the right, so long as there is no discrimination or unfairness. Ford was abridging his own right.

How do you explain this 180-degree turn in the attitude of Ford and Bennett?

I think Bennett was a realist. He saw he couldn't fight us any more. He told me: "I want to see this thing work out, and Mr. Ford wants me to make it work." I've a hunch Ford put him on trial: make this work or get out. And that was the end of the Ford service department.

It was a little tough for some of the fellows to accept at first. They were suspicious. There was a rash of wildcat strikes. I think it came out of this newborn freedom. Each little thing, they'd pull the pin in that department until the grievance was settled. I got a call. Bennett offered to send over a chauffeured car for me. That's all I needed was a car with a chauffeur, provided by the Ford Motor Company. (Laughs.) For a while, I handled each of the grievances.

From a very tough anti-union position, the company now tries to get along. In the old days, every time we saw a Ford go by, we'd say, "There's another tin lizzie." After the strike, we said, "Doggone, isn't that a nice little buggie?"

Howard

He was born in Detroit in 1947.

MY GRANDFATHER never mentioned strikes to me.

The Ford strike?

No.

John L. Lewis?

No. You see, he was really anti-union. He didn't want Negroes to come into the plant. That's why he wanted it unionized, to keep his job and keep them out. On the other hand, he was against unions.

Dr. Lewis Andreas

MEMORIAL DAY, 1937

In 1932, he was a founding member of Chicago's first medical center: group practice and low fees. Sympathetic to labor, he found himself involved. . . .

THE WAGNER ACT had become the law—the right of labor to picket, to organize. Professionals, social workers, theological students—all kinds of people got into the thing. Some of the workers didn't like this. They must have wondered what we were doing there. But they didn't mind me, because I was a doctor and trouble was brewing.

A few days before Memorial Day, 1937, some steel workers picketed Republic Steel on the Far South Side. I received a call: "We've got a very nasty situation here. There're probably going to be some injuries. There's not a hospital for miles around, not even a drugstore. Would you come and get a few first aid stations started?"

There was a tavern called Sam's Place. I took a few supplies and got a first aid station started. The men who picketed that day got clobbered. There were a few split skulls and a few fractures. Everybody got mad and then decided to try it again on Memorial Day.[10]

It was a holiday, so we had them from Indian Harbor and Gary and all kinds of places. Some were looking for trouble, but for many it was simply a family picnic sort of thing: little kids, people dressed up in their Sunday shirts. Many came just for the fun of it; they weren't expecting anything.

The police were standing in line in front of Republic Steel, quite a distance from the others. It was a hell of a hot day, about ninety. They had their winter uniforms on. The sun was strong, and all I could see were their stars glittering.

The people began wandering out. A long line. This was a mixed bunch. Some of them may have been planning to use the sticks they were holding the signs on for other purposes, for clobbering somebody. Nobody was armed. But the police got the idea these people were armed. At least, they were told so by Captain Mooney and Lieutenant Kilroy, who were managing this thing. Mayor Kelly was out of town.

I stayed behind. All of a sudden, I heard some popping going on and a blue haze began rising. I said: My God, tear gas. What do you do for that? I couldn't remember what the medical books said. I ran back to Sam's Place. About three minutes later, they started bringing in the wounded, shot. There were about fifty shot. Ten of them died. One little boy was shot in the heel. I took care of him. One woman was shot in the arm. They were lying there, bleeding bullet wounds in the belly, in the leg and all over. All sorts of fractures, lacerations. . . . I had absolutely no preparation at all for this. I was there alone, except for one guy sent by the Party. He tried to take over.

---

[10] The circumstances of the Republic Steel Massacre were recreated by Meyer Levin in *Citizens*, a novel in which Dr. Andreas is the principal character.

The Communists didn't like the idea. I seemed to be doing what they wanted to be doing. I had no sympathy with them, I couldn't get along with them. I couldn't tolerate their dogmatism, their lack of tolerance and worst of all, their lack of humor. They were so grim. I couldn't understand this blind business of apologizing for everything—for all the Russian business. That I couldn't swallow.

We all wanted a better society, but I didn't want to deal with these boys, and they kind of resented my intrusion into their business. One of them helped me a little bit, but I was practically alone.

I jumped on a chair and said: Get all the gun shots out of here right away to the nearest hospital. I can't handle them. Some of them had been taken to Bridewell and to other hospitals by the police.

Were many shot in the back?

I made charts of these gun shots. A great majority of them were shot from behind. Mel Coughlin, the assistant state's attorney, asked me, "Can you define the back?" In the courtroom, I just got up and turned around and said, "What you're looking at now—that's the back."

What happened was this: There were a few rocks thrown at the police when the shooting started. Or even before. They all turned and ran. I said in my testimony before the La Follette Committee: like the shutters of a Venetian blind. As they were running, the police shot into them.

The police weren't all bad. Some of them quit the force because of the incident. They couldn't stand what happened. I know this as a fact because some of the guys came up here as patients and told me.

There was a break in the trial at the Criminal Court. I had been testifying. I went out for a smoke. There were about sixty cops in the corridor, and I was nervous. Some big guy comes up to me and I thought: Oh-oh, here it comes. I prepare myself for the blow. He came up very close and said, "Every day I get a pain up here in my stomach. What do you think it is, Doc?" (Laughs.) I wasn't hostile to all these guys. They committed a brutal act. They were told to do this thing. They were told these people were armed. They were scared, they were trembling and they were shooting, at whom they didn't know.

Mayor Kelly tried to get me, when he heard about this. I had an excited call from Wesley Hospital: There are people going all over your records. What's the matter? I said, "They're trying to find out how many abortions I did during the last few years." I wasn't scared. A friend of

Kelly's told him to lay off, he'd be disappointed. I had a pretty clean record. He quit.

The misrepresentation in the newspapers was so great. There was a picture in the back page of the *Tribune,* for instance: a little old guy lying on the prairie in his white shirt, blood streaming down his face and Lieutenant Kilroy beating the hell out of him with his club. The caption said: "Striker Beats Up Police At Republic Steel Riot." A few of us said this will be called a historical fact some day unless we do something about it. So we decided to have a mass meeting at the Civic Opera House.

Paul Douglas was the chairman. Robert Morss Lovett[11] and Carl Sandburg and A. Philip Randolph came. I described the wounds and an organ was playing and almost everyone in the place was crying. Lovett got up and said, "Captain Mooney is a killer." Carl Sandburg got mesmerized by A. Philip Randolph and started chanting the words: "The Brotherhood of Sleeping Car Porters." He didn't say a thing; he got caught up in the rhythm.[12]

It's the tableau I remember: people walking out on the prairie and the police shooting them down.

He recounts the struggles of his group; editorials in the AMA Journal labeling them subversive, un-American; the denial of hospital facilities. "All through the Thirties, it was difficult. We had no way of calling peoples' attention to our work, because we were opposed to advertising as much as the AMA."

In medicine, people were having a hell of a hard time. Doctors themselves were pressed, particularly the younger ones. Doctors coming out now are almost sure to find a place. The kids coming up in medicine now have absolutely no conception. You talk Depression to these boys, nonsense. They're met on all sides with delightful offers. Their biggest job is to find which piece of French pastry to choose.

[11] A professor at the University of Chicago. He was an outspoken dissenter on many issues of the day.

[12] "I sat in the gallery that evening. During Sandburg's incantation, in which he seemed to be improvising a poem, a few of my neighbors, among whom were steel workers, became impatient: 'Get goin', get goin', for Chrissake!' They were shushed by others, in shocked stage whispers: 'That's Carl Sandburg. Quiet, please!' Came the response, low and hurt: 'I don't give a fuck who it is, he's holdin' up the works.' "

In the bad days of the Depression, there was really almost nothing. Competition with the older generation was terrific. One found oneself with a lot of training, knowledge, skills, ready to spring forth on the world—no customers. They weren't going to doctors because they couldn't afford it.

The poor got some care, could go to free dispensaries. The rich got good care because they could afford it. There was this big middle class that was not getting any care. The middle class got very much in the position of the poor people. . . .

The poor people would not hesitate to go to free clinics, there was no loss of self-respect for them. They were used to this business. But the middle class couldn't drag itself to that point.

People fairly well-off suddenly found themselves without funds. Insull-destroyed teachers, they were in a heck of a fix. A lot of teachers had been actively assaulted by the Insull sales force and lost all their savings. Particularly older teachers who were soon to retire. We had many teachers among our patients.

They couldn't afford to get medical care, and they couldn't bring themselves to sitting in a dispensary. They put off care until things got real bad. They probably lost their lives.

The spirit of the free hospital and the spirit of the free clinic was the spirit of the alms house. I was working at the Northwestern dispensary in '30, '31. We noticed a lady coming to us rather frequently. She'd come in a Cadillac, park three blocks away and walk over. She belonged to a class I used to call the well-dressed destitute. She had the clothes, she had the Cadillac, but she didn't have any money. She'd come over and get her care for nothing. If she had come up in the Cadillac, and the social worker saw her, she would have been excluded. People of that status would find it very difficult to accept charity.

"These simple things we stood for—group medicine and prepayment— have been achieved. I read some of the arguments for Medicare. They were almost verbatim the arguments we used thirty years ago, the same damn thing. With an innocent air of discovery they're just finding out about this stuff. This has been the habit of the AMA. They sing the praises today of what they condemned yesterday."

All of a sudden, I find myself taking care of an ex-president of a university. And there was a widow of the curator of an art museum, well-dressed, white hair, genteel. We were surprised. The kind of people we expected to find were the dispensary-goers. . . . It was a mixture of people, with one common denominator: difficulty in paying their medical bills.

And people starved on the street and on streetcars. I knew a resident at People's Hospital. Every day, he told me, somebody would faint on a streetcar. They'd bring him in, and they wouldn't ask any questions. They'd look the patient over briefly. The picture was familiar, they knew what it was. Hunger. When he regained consciousness, they'd give him something to eat. People were flopping on the streets from hunger.

They would just sit there. This was a kind of incoherent, senseless structure we were facing. Some of us figured it was collapsing. We decided we were gonna reconstruct the thing. This was sort of unique medical care in the new society. We were kidding around, really. Chewing the rag.

But there *was* a feeling of creativeness. We belonged to a thing called New America. Our outlook was socialism. The leadership was mostly from the Union Theological Seminary. It was up to us to create a substitute for the society that was disappearing. (Laughs.) We were arrogant, perhaps, but this was the feeling. Splendid ideas about what we could accomplish.

There was a feeling of perplexity. Unless something like the New Deal happened, people might have become violent. I remember an ominous march down Michigan Avenue one day. It was about '34. A very silent, scraggly march of the unemployed. Nobody said anything. Just a mass of people flowing down that street. In their minds, I think a point was reached: We're not gonna take it any more. I remember it particularly because of the silence. No waving of banners, no enthusiasm. An undercurrent of desperation.

It was the hopeful voice of F.D.R. that got this thing out of the swamps. He didn't have much to offer, but it was enough. He was a guy flexible enough to understand the need for experiments, for not being rigid and for making people feel there was somebody who gave a damn about them.

In the late Thirties, I'd say our society was saved again. By Hitler. Because the stopgap wasn't working, and things were sliding back. The war, in a sense, ended the Depression. It's like an incurable disease in which there is a remission. Like Hodgkin's disease. Everybody is happy, the gland gets smaller. And then the guy dies. The war stopped the second slide, which might have gone as far as violent upheaval. You see, people now undergo improvement with leukemia. They feel good, but they all die.

But there is something important about this treatment, about stopgaps: the hope that if the patient keeps on living, somebody will come up with something new. We saw this with pernicious anemia. A doctor friend had it. We kept him going for months and months with transfusions. His daughter said: Why do you guys keep this poor man living and suffering? I said: Because there's always a chance somebody will come up with something. This man died. But three months later, Murphy and Minot came out with Vitamin B_{12}. If this fellow had been kept alive with transfusions, he would probably be alive today. I'm in favor of stopgaps for a man or for a society.

Those were terrible days, remarkable days. We had achieved goals. We wanted to promote the interests of labor. Outsiders like myself and Bob Lovett and the rest felt their interests were along with ours. The Social Security Laws, Unemployment Compensation, all that was connected with the labor movement. Some of these goals—largely achieved. Today, I think, it is much more terrible. This terrible sense of wondering how we're going to get out of things. Then, we got out. And we felt good.

My habit of life has been changed by the Depression. I'm sitting here in this office . . . these wounds are permanent. My father was a doctor, and his life's savings were in one piece of property. It was foreclosed on him by the University of Chicago, and he lost every cent he had. They simply took it away because they had the legal right to take it away. And he taught at Rush Medical College[13] for twelve years for nothing. (Laughs.) So there was no help from Papa any more. I had planned research work, but the Depression got me into this—I don't have too many regrets. I would have been a nice rich guy probably, with a practice . . . I would have been one of many other fellows. As it is, I'm myself, unique, as they say. (Smiles.) I have no regrets. . . .

[13] An adjunct of the University of Chicago at the time.

BOOK TWO

Old Families

Edward A. Ryerson

Retired chairman of the board, Inland Steel Company. On the eighteenth floor of a modern structure, the Inland Building, is his office. Facing us, on the far wall, are portraits of family members: his grandfather, his father, his brother, his son, himself.

The early Ryersons had established iron furnaces out East in the 1600s. They supplied bullets and cannon for the Revolutionary War. His grandfather had come to Chicago in 1842 to sell boilermaker supplies for the growing city.

UNTIL THE LATE 1920s, everything was going pretty well with us. The Depression hit us like everyone else. People weren't buying steel. Most of my friends, who represented wealth, were all in some way affected. There were some smart guys, so-called, who claimed they saw the handwriting on the wall and liquidated their securities in advance. Most I knew suffered setbacks.

We'd have to readjust our way of living. We all did. We did more for ourselves. I did away with my chauffeur and so forth. I drove my own car, my wife did and all that sort of thing.

We had to cut ourselves down so that it would not look too far out of line. After all, I was in the midst of a very close relationship with a lot of people who had nothing. I was running the welfare field.

*During the Depression, he was head of the Council of Social Agencies
—later to be known as the Welfare Council—and chief of the newly created Public Aid Commission. He was on the board of Chicago Com-
mons, a settlement house. . . . "Very early, I was aware of the problems
of the distressed."*

Before Hoover's term ended—I called on him personally—I got for
the State of Illinois, the first federal money for relief ever granted. It
was a curious thing for me to do. I was bitterly opposed to federal funds
at that time. But I realized the problem was beyond the scope of local
government.

I first went to Springfield to obtain funds. I got $12 million. You can
imagine how far that went in relief programs in 1932. It lasted only
three months.

The legislature couldn't understand it. They had no comprehension
of what was needed. We had to battle. They didn't believe any public
money should be used in this way. It should all be left to the private
welfare agencies.

I think the Old Deal, the Hoover Deal, would have accomplished
many of the reforms of the New Deal. I was very close to Hoover, a
great admirer of his. He had asked me to take some appointments in
Washington, but I declined because of my other responsibilities. If he
had been reelected . . . but the public wanted a change. Hoover was
a humanitarian, more than any President we've ever had. Certainly in
my lifetime.

*In 1935, the Ryerson Company, distributors, merged with Inland Steel,
manufacturers. Inland was part of a loose association of companies
known as Little Steel, among others being Jones & Laughlin and Republic. Tom Girdler, president of Republic Steel, was the most recalcitrant in dealing with the Steel Workers' Organizing Committee of the
newly emerging CIO.*

That strike of 1937 was a terrible one. Were seven people killed?

Ten.

Tom Girdler was quite a different kind of person than anyone at
Inland. I knew him very well. He had great ability, but he was a little
too hardboiled to deal with. He never quite grew up to accept the fact

that conditions were different in this country than they had been years before. You remember the statement he made: he would never sign up with the CIO, he would go down and sell apples, or something.

Our philosophy was different. We recognized the difficulties. We recognized the seriousness of some things in the demands of labor. We all realized we had to deal with it in a different way than we were used to in the old days, when the industry was being run by the so-called steel barons, Gary, Schwab and so forth. Tom Girdler and a few others were a carry-over from that philosophy. I think they saw the light before they were through.

Sewell Avery was another. He was a colorful, brilliant, able man, before he began to go to pieces. He was in full command of his capacities up to the time he was carried out by the army.[1] A change came upon him after that. He felt the country was going to pieces under the New Deal. Bitter. I was sympathetic to him. But I didn't agree that everything was going to the dogs. I felt we'd pull out of it.

Diana Morgan

She was a "southern belle" in a small North Carolina town. "I was taught that no prince of royal blood was too good for me." (Laughs.) Her father had been a prosperous cotton merchant and owner of a general store. "It's the kind of town you became familiar with in Thornton Wilder's Our Town. *You knew everybody. We were the only people in town who had a library."*

Her father's recurring illness, together with the oncoming of hard times—the farmers and the townspeople unable to pay their bills—caused the loss of the store. He went into bankruptcy.

THE BANKS FAILED about the time I was getting ready to go to college. My family thought of my going to Wellesley, Vassar, Smith—but we had

---

[1] Chairman of the board of the mail-order house Montgomery Ward in 1944. He became involved in a dispute with the Federal Government. He insisted his company was not involved in war work and thus ignored the rules of the War Labor Board. The plant was seized and Avery, refusing to leave, was carried out by two soldiers.

so little money, we thought of a school in North Carolina. It wasn't so expensive.

It was in my junior year, and I came home for Christmas. . . . I found the telephone disconnected. And this was when I realized that the world was falling apart. Imagine us without a telephone! When I finished school, I couldn't avoid facing the fact that we didn't have a cook any more, we didn't have a cleaning woman any more. I'd see dust under the beds, which is something I'd never seen before. I knew the curtains weren't as clean as they used to be. Things were beginning to look a little shabby. . . .

The first thing I noticed about the Depression was that my great-grandfather's house was lost, about to be sold for taxes. Our own house was sold. It was considered the most attractive house in town, about a hundred and fifty years old. We even had a music library. Imagine my shock when it was sold for $5,000 in back taxes. I was born in that house.

I never felt so old in my life as I felt the first two years out of college. 'Cause I hadn't found a new life for myself, and the other one was finished.

I remember how embarrassed I was when friends from out of town came to see me, because sometimes they'd say they want a drink of water, and we didn't have any ice. (Laughs.) We didn't have an electric refrigerator and couldn't afford to buy ice. There were those frantic arrangements of running out to the drugstore to get Coca-Cola with crushed ice, and there'd be this embarrassing delay, and I can remember how hot my face was.

All this time, I wasn't thinking much about what was going on in this country. . . . I was still leading some kind of social life. Though some of us had read books and discussed them, there wasn't much awareness. . . . Oh, we deplored the fact that so many of our young men friends couldn't find suitable things to do. . . .

One day a friend of my father stopped me on the street and said, "Would you like a job? A friend of mine is director of one of those New Deal programs. She'll tell you about it."

Oh, I was so excited, I didn't know what to do—the thought of having a job. I was very nervous, but very hopeful. Miss Ward came. She looked like a Helen Hokinson woman, very forbidding, formal. She must have been all of forty-five, but to me she looked like some ancient and very frightening person from another world.

She said to me, "It's not a job for a butterfly." She could just look at me and tell that I was just totally unsuitable. I said I was young and conscientious and if I were told what I was supposed to do, I would certainly try to the best of my ability. . . . She didn't give me any encouragement at all.

When she left, I cried for about an hour. I was really a wreck. I sobbed and sobbed and thought how unfair she was. So I was very much amazed to receive a telegram the next day summoning me to a meeting in Raleigh—for the directors of women's work.

There were dozens of women there, from all over the state, of all ages. It seemed to me very chaotic. Everyone was milling around, talking about weaving projects, canning, bookbinding. . . . Everyone there seemed very knowledgeable. I really didn't know what they were talking about. And nobody really told me what I was supposed to do. It just seemed that people were busy, and I somehow gathered that I was in.

So I went back home. I went to the county relief offices at the courthouse. There were people sitting on the floor of a long hallway, mostly black people, looking very depressed, sad. Some of them had children with them, some of them were very old. Just endless rows of them, sitting there, waiting. . . .

My first impression was: Oh, those poor devils, just sitting there, and nobody even saying, "We'll get to you as soon as we can." Though I didn't know a thing about social work, what was good and what wasn't good, my first impulse was that those people should be made to feel somebody was interested in them. Without asking anybody, I just went around and said, "Have you been waiting long? We'll get to you just as soon as we can."

I got the feeling the girls in the office looked very stern, and that they had a punitive attitude: that the women just had to wait, as long as they were there and that you had to find out and be sure they were entitled to it before they got anything.

I didn't know a thing about sewing, bookbinding, canning . . . the approved projects. I'd never boiled an egg or sewed a stitch. But I knew seamstresses, who used to make clothes for us when we were children. I went to see them and got them to help me. I sought help from everybody who knew how to do things.

In the meantime, I would work in the relief office and I began interviewing people . . . and found out how everybody, in order to be eligible for relief, had to have reached absolute bottom. You didn't have to have a lot of brains to realize that once they reached that stage and you put them on an allowance of a dollar a day for food—how could they ever pull out of it?

Caroline, who used to cook for us, came in. I was so shocked to see her in a position where she had to go to the agency and ask for food. I was embarrassed for her to see me when she was in that state. She was a wonderful woman, with a big heart. Here she was, elderly by now, and her health wasn't good at all. And she said, "Oh, the Lord's done sent you down from heaven to save me. I've fallen on hard times. How beautiful you are. You look like an angel to me." In the typical southern Negro way of surviving, she was flattering me. I was humiliated by her putting herself in that position, and by my having to see her go through this. (Weeps softly; continues with difficulty.)

For years, I never questioned the fact that Caroline's house was papered with newspapers. She was our laundress for a while, and I remember going to her house several times. Caroline was out in the yard, just a hard patch of dirt yard. With a big iron pot, with fire under it, stirring, boiling the white clothes. . . .

She was always gracious and would invite me in. She never apologized for the way anything looked. I thought to myself at the time: How odd that Caroline uses newspapers to paper walls. I didn't have any brains at eleven or twelve or whatever to think: what kind of country is this that lets people live in houses like this and necessitates their using the Sunday paper for wallpaper. I'm shocked that I can't say to you: "When I was twelve, I was horrified when I first went into this house." I was surprised, but I wasn't horrified.

The girls at the office—when the clients had all gone—it's funny you treat them this way, and you still call them clients—when they had all gone, the girls would be very friendly with me. They would ask what I wanted to know and would show me the files. I was quite impressed with their efficiency. But when they were dealing with clients, they were much more loose. I didn't see why they had to be this way. Perhaps they were afraid the people in town would think they were too easy with the welfare people.

Because even then, people were saying that these people are no good, they didn't really want to work. Oftentimes, there were telephone calls, saying so-and-so Joe Jones got a bag of food from Welfare, he got an automobile, or his wife's working or something like that. I spent my time away from the job talking to my old friends, defending the program, saying: You don't know about the situation. They would tell me I was terribly sentimental and that I had lost my perspective. That was when I first heard the old expression: If you give them coal, they'd put it in the bathtub. They didn't even have bathtubs to put coal in. So how did anybody know that's what they'd do with coal if they had it?

We were threatened the whole time, because funds were constantly being questioned by the legislators. After I'd been there three months, the program *was* discontinued. By this time, I was absolutely hooked. I could almost weep thinking about it. I told Miss Ward, who had by now become my staunch friend, that this is what I want to do with myself: I want to do something to change things.

By this time, the girls in the office—Ella Mae was the one I liked best —were perfectly willing to let me interview people, because they had more than they could do. Something like 150 cases each. In two months, I was employed as a case worker.

As I recall, when a person came into the office and applied for help, you filled out a form, asked all those humiliating questions: Does anybody work? Do you own your own house? Do you have a car? You just established the fact they had nothing. Nothing to eat, and children. So you give them one food order. You couldn't give them shoes, or money for medicine—without visiting and corroborating the fact that they were destitute.

So, of course, you get out as fast as possible to see those people before the $4 grocery order ran out. You know, the day after tomorrow, I used to drive out to make house calls. It was the first time I'd been off Main Street. I'd never been out in the rural area, and I was absolutely aghast at the conditions in the country.

I discovered, the first time in my life, in the county, there was a place called the Islands. The land was very low and if it rained, you practically had to take a boat to get over where Ezekiel Jones or whoever lived. I remember a time when I got stuck in this rented Ford, and broke down little trees, and lay them across the road to create traction, so you could get out. Now I regard that as one of my best experiences. If somebody said to you: What would you do, having been brought up the way you were, if you found yourself at seven o'clock at night, out in the wilderness, with your car stuck and the water up to your hubcaps or something like that? Wouldn't you worry? What would you do? I could get out of there: I could break down a tree or something. It helps make you free.

I would find maybe two rooms, a dilapidated wooden place, dirty, an almost paralyzed-looking mother, as if she didn't function at all. Father unshaven, drunk. Children of all ages around the house, and nothing to eat. You thought you could do just absolutely nothing. Maybe you'd write a food order. . . .

"The WPA came along shortly after this. Roosevelt recognized that people cannot stay on relief forever. It degrades them, it takes away their manhood. I'm sure he'd be appalled that people today, who are on relief in Chicago, are allocated twenty-seven cents a meal. That's just about what it was in 1930. And it was inadequate then. . . ."

This family . . . the Rural Rehabilitation program came along, the RRA. I had the joy of certifying certain families from the relief rolls to go to the land bought by the government. To have better houses, to have equipment. And I saw this family move to a different house. Saw that woman's face come alive—the one who'd been in that stupor—her children clean, her house scrubbed—I saw this family moved from a hopeless situation. . . . The man had been a sharecropper. Apparently, he had once been a very good worker. There he was with nothing, till . . . I could go on about that. . . .

I had twelve families in this program. And Ella Mae had twelve. It was a beautiful farm, maybe two, three hundred acres. With houses, not two-room shacks. Ella Mae and I were involved in the thrilling task of selecting the families. Ella Mae would say, "I think Jess Clark would be good." And Davis, the man in charge of the program, would say, "That old, lazy bum? He's not gonna be able to do nothin'. You're just romantic." So we became personally involved in seeing these people prove their own worth. . . .

Every month the program was threatened with lack of funds. We didn't know if Congress was gonna discontinue it. A lot of the public thought the money was being spent foolishly.

With the program in danger of being killed from month to month, the state administrator suggested she accept other job offers. She attended the New York School of Social Work, under federal auspices; she married; there was an absence of six months from the county.

The first thing I did when I got back, I got out of the car and rushed over to the courthouse—to know how did those people perform. Did they make it?

I talked about this one white family. There was a Negro family, nine of them living in one room. The man was not young; he was in his sixties. But he impressed me as being a strong person—who would really make it, if he had a chance. Every one of the people we had certified had done well and had begun to pay back the loans. Not one of them had been lazy and done a bad job. They were absolutely vindicated. The people were vindicated, not us.

In 1934, she and her husband moved to Washington, D.C. They were there eleven years. "I'd been invited to a First Families of Virginia Ball at the George Mason Hotel. I'd been picketing it the week before, because they paid their workers some ridiculous wage, oh like seventy-five cents an hour. When I answered the invitation, I didn't just say Mrs. So-and-So regrets she's unable to accept . . . ; I wrote a letter and said I couldn't possibly go to a hotel where the wages were so unfair. My husband was very much surprised. He said, 'I never dreamed you would take that kind of stand.' Well, I never dreamed I wouldn't."

I'd like to think that even if we hadn't lost our house, even if I hadn't the job with the Civil Works Administration, I might have waked up someday. But maybe I would just have worked on the Community Chest or the St. Luke's Fashion Show. I don't know. Maybe I'd never have understood how people feel if I weren't subjected to it.

Maybe you do have to experience things personally. . . . Do people in Lake Forest, or Grosse Point, or Scarsdale have to have their houses burned down and bombed before they recognize the state of the society? As long as it happens a few miles away—or in the city, if you live in the suburbs—you just read about it. . . .

POSTSCRIPT: *"I went to a women's board meeting of a great university. On the way, I had taken the wrong exit from the superhighway and had to go through an area, where I was appalled by the look of the people, living in absolute hopelessness.*

"At the meeting, there were black and white women, well-off, intelligent women. Middle, upper, privileged people, the top one percent. I thought maybe when they refurbished the studio of a great sculptor—

177

who used to be here and is now gone—they could somehow begin to think about three blocks away, what's going on here.

"I said to one of these women, 'Have you driven through this neighborhood recently?' She said, 'Diana, dear, with all the new housing projects and everything, it's much, much better.' I realized at once that nothing I could say would make them understand. . . ."

Mrs. Winston Roberts

She came to Chicago from the South in 1906 as the bride of a wealthy young industrialist. His family was included in the city's most select social circle.

"It was a great shock to my genteel, poverty-stricken southern family. My friends were not at all impressed. My brother commented: I would, of course, have a diet of ham and bacon every day."

She immediately became part of Chicago's "best people." "I loved it. I ate it with a spoon. I had one of the first electrics. When you drove to Marshall Field's, the man at the door took your car and parked it someplace. Oh, life was very simple in those days." She was invited to Mrs. Potter Palmer's most exclusive soirées. ("It didn't mean anything. I was always happy. I wasn't aware of any of this snobbishness.")

She was spoiled by her indulgent husband. She slept late; her days were spent driving her friends about in her electric. The English nurse who cared for their four children suggested she see each of them for twenty minutes, an hour or so before dinner. "I talked to the children. When Winston came home, I was all dressed and ready. Then we had dinner and went out."

She occasionally saw a young man who told her about Jane Addams and Hull House and the surrounding poverty. "I thought he was odd. I thought other people were the funny ones. I thought: he's an awfully nice young man, but I'm not gonna ask him to tea again. I didn't think we had much in common. (Laughs.) Everything was handed to me. I didn't realize a lot of people didn't have it."

With the death of her husband, things changed. Though he was hardworking, his investments were haphazard. "They told me solemnly there was very little left."

I HAD four half-grown children and not much to get along with. I was looking, one day, in the hope that Winston had left a safety deposit key or some receipts. 'Cause they were surprised he had left so little. I came and said, "Is this it?" I can see my brother-in-law's face: "That's a streetcar check." I'd never seen one. I had the electric.

The first thing he said, "How much can you get on with a month?" I said, "Whatever I have. All you have is what you've got. Then you get on with it." There are a lot of things you can do to save money. I used to say, "It's hard to start up high. It's easier to start out low." So I got along low.

About 1930 a friend suggested we go into the negligée business. For a year, she and I were together. We made them and sold them. I could make wonderful clothes. I didn't learn it, I did it. I was never helpless. When I was a girl, the only way I could have a dress was to sew it. In the South, if you were a lady, you sewed. You didn't cook. You might not have money for shoes, but you had someone to come in and cook. They didn't charge anything. They took home with them anything that was left over.

She sold the electric car, and, with her children, moved to smaller quarters. After her business associate quit, she continued her enterprise for ten years.

I had a lot of fun making the third floor into a business place, with a tea shoppe in the corner. The customers would come in to be fitted and so on. I got a good sewing woman and went into business in a big way. We cleaned up the market on that kind of garment.

I called it my little dressmaker's home. All my friends felt so badly. They felt I was really giving up the world. You don't know how snobbish people used to be. But they tried to help me. I didn't feel a bit of shame.

I had quite a lot of friends and they were all loyal in keeping up with me. I gave them their money's worth in every way—charm and interest and—oh, I made all kinds of things. I had one woman who had a slightly illicit affair with a doctor. (Laughs.) I designed a velvet gown which she could wear when he came to see her in the evening. All kinds of things. (Laughs.)

But I was always a bit of a rebel. All my friends sent their children to the Latin School. So I sent mine to Francis Parker.[2] I'm very happy I did because I learned a lot of things.

You didn't feel your friends were patronizing you?

No, they were pretty mean to me part of the time. Because they wouldn't see I was giving them their money's worth. Some were afraid they'd get stung.

When we really almost had no money, I sold a lot of silver. It was very high then. Also, I had a lot more than I needed. That made the railroad fare to go East and join the children. They were all at Eastern schools now. Their education was paid for in grandfather's will. If I'd had them come to Chicago, I'd a had to pay their fare. I decided it would be cheaper to go to Washington.

It was a great, handsome hotel there called the Admiral. It had a lot of suites used for retired admirals and their guests: that's why they named it that, maybe. We took one of the apartments. They were very inexpensive. $5 a day for two bedrooms, a sitting room and a bathroom. It was in the early Thirties.

We had bought a lot of big boxes of cereal and big bottles of milk from the grocery. We'd get a certain number of things from the hotel. The elegant waiter would come with this beautiful tray, and then we'd all sit down and divide it up, who gets the Corn Flakes, who gets this, who gets that. It all came out beautifully. We lived like queens for weeks there, at that place.

I was there when we came off the money business. When the moratorium happened, the Bank Holiday. I didn't have any money, but I didn't mind. I was just as well off as before. And had the thrill of hearing Roosevelt say those wonderful things: We have only to fear fear itself.

How did your friends feel about Roosevelt?

In those days we didn't talk about things like that. (Laughs.) That was not conversation. A lot of people objected to Mrs. Roosevelt. I think she was wonderful. All my fine ideas I get from my children.

I became more serious-minded. But I never did get interested in the sufferings of the world as a lot of people. Like my daughter. I'm not quite so much that way. But I became aware of it. . . .

2 At the time, a highly advanced progressive school, headed by Flora Cooke, a friend of Jane Addams.

Noni Saarinen, Mrs. Roberts' Maid

She has worked for Mrs. Roberts thirty-two years.

She came to the United States from Finland in 1921. Work as a domestic, with all variety of chores, in all manner of households, has been her American experience.

IN 1930, it was slack time. He didn't have a job, my husband. Even now, the painter's work is seasonal. So I went to work those times when he wasn't working, and he took care of the boy.

Yah. He said he's walking upside-down, if you know what that means. (Laughs.) You start walking on the floor, and then you put yourself upside-down, how you feel. Because he couldn't provide for his family. Because when we got married, he actually said: "You're not gonna work."

One thing we ever got from bad times is the shoes from the Democratic Party. During election, somebody had brought the basket with the chicken and shoes for my son. One friend of ours used to tease when the boy had those shoes on. He says they are Democratic Party shoes. That's the only thing we ever got.

When Depression came, I got me a job with a family, and they had a chauffeur, cook, chambermaid, general maid, laundress. I was kitchen helper. They were wealthy. The lady didn't even meet me till two weeks after I was hired.

I didn't work very long there. On account of the banks closed, they had to put out so many help. Him and her were in Florida when it happened. The daughter and son was on Astor Street. He wrote a letter, said: Put some of the help off, we can't afford it any more, and you don't deserve it either.

We had so little money in the bank that even if the bank was closed, it didn't matter much. I don't take it hard. (Laughs.) When Mrs. Roberts was younger, I would tell her: Work is not that kind of thing you *must* do. You just do it the way you like it, for enjoyment. It's not punishment. I enjoy work.

I always went to our club, working people. Gatherings. We heard a lotta good speakers, who would tell life isn't like it should be. But revolution wasn't near, no nearer than it's now. (Laughs.) Not anywhere nearer than it is now.

The trouble with my life is that I been confined to housework, and I haven't been able to observe the world. My world is been closed. So my observation—even if I was capable—there was a fence around.

Julia Walther

A wide range of interest is evident in the books that fill the shelves, and in the painting on the walls. There is a touch of old world ambience to the apartment. The appurtenances, though expensive, are unobtrusive.

Through the window, across Outer Drive, where cars are exceeding the speed limit, we see the Lake, serene on this spring afternoon. . . .

MY FIRST THOUGHT—when you say Depression—is Samuel Insull. He was sort of a symbol. Somebody who made a fetish of success. He represented all that was most unattractive about the period that preceded the Great Crash of '29. He used his power in unattractive ways: such as building the Opera House and forcing the abandonment of the Auditorium, which is so much superior. . . .

People were forced into subscribing to the Opera Building.[3] It was held over their heads like a club . . . businessmen in Chicago, who were in some manner obligated to the Insull interests. They had to put a certain amount of money into it, otherwise Samuel Insull would withdraw his support.

The Opera House was finished the year of the Depression. I remember having to go to the opening night performance of *Rigoletto*. Everyone was sitting around there with grim faces, because the Depression had hit. Everyone knew the market was sliding. There we sat in those pink velvet boxes, grimly looking at each other, while forked lightning

[3] Insull, in the Twenties, was the leading patron of Chicago's opera company. The Auditorium Theatre, built by Dankmar Adler and Louis Sullivan, considered one of the finest opera houses in the world, had been its home. It was restored and reopened in 1967.

took place on the stage. In the rain and storm scene of the last act, Insull could let himself go, being president of Commonwealth Edison. You've never seen such rain on the stage or such lightning or such thunder.

The poor Arnold Fletchers had just been inveigled by Insull to buy one of those expensive boxes. We sat with the Fletchers in their box. They couldn't be happy about what was happening on the stock market that day. They couldn't be happy about their lives. Moreover, they couldn't be happy about the music on the stage. It was so awful. The whole performance was so terrible. The staging was dreadful. The scenery was Insull taste from beginning to end. And that curtain! That over-designed, over-decorated gilt thing. I can only remember it as a sheer nightmare.[4]

They all just hated Insull, the people in the boxes. At that moment, they hated him more than ever. And then they found themselves slithering down the toboggan. With the Insull crash, when his empire folded.

My husband's losses were really quite shattering. We felt they were perilous days. By 1926, Fred had built up the Corporation.[5] It had begun with a lumber company which had belonged to his father. The men who had been presidents of the merged companies were older than he and had more experience. They could hardly wait to get rid of him as soon as the Corporation was formed. In fear of this happening, he borrowed money in order to gain the fifty-one percent control.

When the Crash came, the banks withdrew their support, stock held on margin was called in. Fred, unable to meet this in the falling market, lost everything he had. He was completely wiped out. Fred always laughingly said, "The only million dollars in my life I ever saw were those I lost."

I felt the fever period was unreal. And the Depression was *so* real that *it* became unreal. There was a horror about it, with people jumping out of windows.

[4] Win Stracke was a young member of the chorus of Max Reinhardt's *The Miracle*. It was performed in Chicago during the 1926–27 season at the Auditorium. During a rehearsal, "Morris Guest, the impresario, walks on the stage, arm in arm, with Samuel Insull. Guest pointed out these huge pillars, he'd say 'Now these are replicas of the huge columns in the Cathedral de Notre Dame, and that window is an exact copy of the rose window of the Köln Cathedral.' And Insull said, 'The originals?' I can remember thinking how culturally stupid were men of finance. It was reflected later on in the Opera House."

[5] A company known, aside from its industrial products, for the sponsorship of cultural enterprises.

I remember the first time motoring under the Michigan Avenue Bridge, under those streets, where the *Tribune* is, and seeing not hundreds, but thousands of men, rolled up in their overcoats, just on the pavement.

I remember being so horrified, so overwhelmed. The only other thing that had as great an impact on me happened at the beginning of the First World War. It was 1914, the day of the Battle of Metz. My brother and I sat as children in the coupé of the train, leaving Germany. We could hear the big guns and the cannons. They started to load the wounded onto our train. They pulled in a colonel. They went into war those days with bright suits. This one happened to have one of the most beautiful verdant green, with scarlet stripes going down his trousers. The man had a chest wound and the blood kept dripping, just slowly drip-drip-drip-drip on the floor.

The men, lying under the bridge, was the same kind of first experience of something, of realizing that life was not the way you had thought it. Until you actually see someone dying, you can't know what war is like. Now I have an inkling of what the Depression was for some people, although I never slept under the bridge.

Do you think a Depression will ever come to America again?

I don't know. I've been told it can never happen again. However, there is one thing that does trouble me. I went to Germany in '34 and '38. I saw what Nazism did. I was troubled by Americans saying: "But this could never happen with us. The Germans are a strange people with whom we have nothing in common—beasts." I knew this wasn't true. This kind of thing can happen any place, given certain circumstances. . . .

There was a terrible depression in Germany. Along comes a man who tells them they're a great nation, all they have to do is believe in themselves and follow him. He promised them the sun, the moon and the stars. The German intellectuals and comedians made fun of him and the Nazis in their night clubs. I heard one in the Platzl in Munich. The audience loved it, adored it. But it didn't stop Nazism. They won over the lower middle classes. . . .

The Depression overwhelmed us, yes. It was terrible. But we had hope: This is not going to kill us. I don't think people can say that nowadays. If a Depression came now, I'd be afraid, terribly afraid. . . .

Member of the Chorus

Win Stracke

A Chicago balladeer. Founder of the Old Town School of Folk Music.

I WAS A SOLOIST at the Fourth Presbyterian Church from '33 to '40. The parishioners were very well-to-do people, whose families had come from New England to Chicago many years ago. I was just beginning to wake up to the fact that there was such a thing as politics and influences in our society. I hadn't really been conscious of a sort of class distinction between the supporters of Alf Landon and the supporters of Roosevelt.

I remember very clearly the Sunday morning before the election of '36. When I got up to sing my solo part at the services, I looked out over the congregation, about nine hundred or a thousand, and it was one sea of yellow. Everybody was decorated with large yellow Landon sunflower buttons. Just the impact of the thing suddenly made me realize there is such a thing as class distinction in America.

The pillar of another church, where I had previously sung, was a very wealthy Chicago industrialist. Great deference was paid to him. At one evening service, he gave a sermon. This was about 1933, in the depths of the Depression, and there was a lot of political protest around. He got up and said that he had searched the Bible from cover to cover and he could not find a single word or sentence or phrase to indicate that Jesus was against capitalism. (Laughs.)

185

In 1937, '38, I was working with an octet at the Old Heidelberg.[1] We were infuriated because the waiters would stand around reading the *Völkischer Beobachter,* the official Nazi paper. It had been a traditional practice, when a customer had a birthday, they would send up a bottle of Rhine wine—the sommelier would bring up a tray and proceed to pour a glass for every member of the octet. I would say, "We're very happy to salute Mrs. So-and-So," or whoever it was. Then we'd hold up our glasses and sing *"Soll Er Lieber."*

A couple of us said: Ah, the hell with drinking this Rhine wine. So we announced to the headwaiter: no more Rhine wine. The management was furious. We said, "If you don't like it, we'll quit." So we finally settled on the idea that they'd serve us Cuba Libras. From then on, we saluted birthday guests with Cuba Libras. (Laughs.)

I still had my job at the church. So I'd do the first show in my costume: a red jacket, white pants and long Prussian boots. Of course, we had those little pepperbox hats. Heidelberg cadets. I'd sneak in the back way of the Fourth Presbyterian, put a robe over my Heidelberg outfit and sing sacred songs. (Laughs.)

In the Depression, the business of being a singer had lots of hardships. We were all hurting for dough. During one job, a once-a-week radio broadcast, our compensation was a room in the Allerton Hotel. The idea being: if we showed enough initiative, we'd rent the room and thus have compensation for our singing. I was never able to rent my room. The hotel was only about thirty percent occupied, so they weren't giving anything away.

We had one sponsor of a Sunday morning radio program, who owned cemetery lots. We sang old-fashioned hymns and talked about the memorial park. We were paid fifteen bucks apiece. He persuaded us to make recordings, so he could save money. Somehow the old codger talked us into taking, not money, but cemetery lots. I still have seven of them. (Laughs.)

In 1939 I was a chorus member of WGN's "Theater of the Air." I saw and heard Colonel McCormick every Saturday night. There was a ten-minute segment where he'd expound on the defense of Detroit against the Canadians or how he first observed artillery from a balloon at the Battle of Chantigny.

One time I remember he was sitting on the aisle. Next to him was his

[1] A no-longer-existent Loop restaurant featuring excellent German cuisine and wines.

wife, next to her was his Great Dane, and next to the Great Dane was (laughs) Governor Dwight Green. When the Colonel began his speech, the dog started to snuffle loudly. The Colonel's wife reached over into the Governor's breast pocket, took out his handkerchief and held it over the dog's muzzle. After the talk, she just reached over, put it back in the Governor's pocket. (Laughs.)

In 1940, I was fired by the Fourth Presbyterian Church. I had become active, singing for various causes. I hadn't gotten too much static from this because they were worlds apart. The farm equipment workers were on strike against the McCormick Works. First time since the Haymarket affair. I sang at the union hall. During the evening a film was shown by a local finance company: how strikers could borrow money, during the emergency, and repay it, with interest.

I had heard the minister of the church had been visited by a woman, complaining of my activity. I received a letter from the chairman of the music committee, a member of an old Chicago family, saying my services were no longer required.

The funny thing about it is this man was head of the finance company whose film was shown. So my conclusion was: It's all right to loan money to strikers at interest, but don't sing for 'em for nothing. (Laughs.)

Before my last service, the minister took me up to his study and prayed for me. He asked the Lord to give me guidance, to straighten me out. After the prayer, he strongly suggested I leave town and change my name.

High Life

Life is just a bowl of cherries,
Don't make it serious,
Life's too mysterious.
You work, you save, you worry so,
But you can't take your dough when you go–go–go,
So keep repeating it's the berries.
The strongest oak must fall.
The sweet things in life,
To you were just loaned,
So how can you lose what you've never owned.
Life is just a bowl of cherries,
    So live and laugh at it all.

—words by Lew Brown,
music by Ray Henderson[1]

[1] Copyright 1931 by De Sylva, Brown & Henderson, Inc. Copyright renewed, assigned to Chappell & Co., Inc.

Sally Rand

A dancer.

"*I was twenty-six in 1930. A good age to start savoring things. I was born in the last naïve moment America was ever to enjoy . . . between the Spanish-American War and the First World War. Things were S.S.&G.—Sweet, Simple and Girlish.*"

Hers was a rural Missouri childhood and a Kansas City adolescence. When she arrived at the age to be giggly, her father, a West Point graduate, said, "the giggly girl causes grief." She was raised according to the old homilies: Virtue triumphant, Honesty prevailing. . . . "It poorly prepared us, who grew up in this innocent way, for the Thirties.

"*Suddenly, all the copybook maxims were turned backwards. How could it be that a man who had been at his job thirty years couldn't have a job? How could it be that a business that had been in business for a lifetime suddenly isn't any more? Friends of mine who had been to Harvard, Yale and Princeton jumped out of windows. With accuracy. The idea of the stock market quittin' was unbelievable. Only naïveté permitted us to believe this could go on forever. . . .*"

"*For those who lived with little money, it didn't make much of a difference. I never saw money until I was nine or ten years old. On $100 a month, my father supported us. We were clothed, sheltered, well fed. There was always enough of everything—except love.*"

When she was six, she saw Pavlova dance. "I sat up and wept uncontrollably. At that moment, there was born this true knowledge: I was going to be a dancer, a ballerina." She traveled with Adolph Bolm's ballet company throughout the Midwest, "bringing culture to the masses." (Laughs.)

In Hollywood, she worked as a Mack Sennett girl and was under contract to Cecil B. De Mille. "I followed him every waking minute. I was at story conferences, I saw every rush, I was a little ghost. When he went to the men's room, I waited outside." Her stage name had been Billie Bett. "De Mille took Rand off of a Rand-McNally map."

A close friendship developed with Mary Pickford. "Later when Doug

Fairbanks achieved a more sophisticated marriage with Lady Ashley,
Mary turned to religious contemplation. She wrote a book, Why Not
Try God? *Subsequently, she married Buddy Rogers."*

Sally Rand *traveled the Orpheum circuit with her company, "Sally*
and Her Boys." The impact of the Depression caused canceled book-
ings. Her wealthy friends went broke.

THESE BEAUTIFUL YACHTS that cost a half million dollars were sitting
around with barnacles on them. These are the people who had jumped
out of windows. Who's gonna buy a yacht? A man came up to me and
said, "Hey, any of these yachts for sale?" I said, "Are you kiddin'?
They're all for sale." This guy was a bootlegger. So I sold half-million-
dollar yachts to bootleggers. For five or ten thousand dollars. And took
my six percent commission on them. Beautiful.

They used to have their own fast boats, to go beyond the three-mile
limit, or eight-mile limit or whatever it was, to pick up their booze. By
now, all the federal agents knew their boats. So they took these yachts
and decorated them with pretty girls in bathing suits, like going out for
a little sail. Load up and come back.

The interiors of those boats were done in rosewood, gold handles on
the toilets and all that jazz, great oil painting in the salons. They're now
jammed up with loads and loads of wet alcohol. The interiors of them
were gutted and ruined.

Every hotel in the Loop was in 77–B. This was being in bankruptcy
to Uncle Sam—legitimately. I couldn't pay my bill. I didn't have any
food or whiskey or anything. I went to the management and said, "I
never ran out on a hotel bill in my life. I don't have a job, but I'll get
one. Meanwhile, I can't pay what I owe you." They said, "Don't worry.
Nobody's in the hotel anyway."

One of the boys in the show, Tony, said, "Don't worry. All my uncles
are stagehands and the rest of 'em are bootleggers. Pick out a night
club you want to work, we'll work." I looked at these freaks, with these
little postage-stamp stages. . . .

Up to this time, the most sexy thing I'd ever done is Scheherazade
in the ballet. I thought a girl who went on the stage without stockings
was a hussy. (Laughs.) I got a job, $75 a week, only because Tony's
uncles were delivering alky to Frankie, the owner.

Now I've got to find a number to do. I can't do a toe dance there. I
went down to Maybelle Shearer's costume shop. She had a lot of old

fans laying on the counter. I'd been wanting to do "White Birds Fly in the Moonlight" for a long time. I used to see these white herons come down on my grandfather's farm. I'm harking back to Pavlova and her bird dance, "The Swan." As a youngster, I tied wings on my shoulders. I'm glad I had the good taste even then to know this wasn't it. Then I saw pictures of Isadora Duncan. I may have been a fine dancer, but I wasn't ready to create. So, necessity being the mother of invention. . . .

I picked up a pair of these feathered fans that prima donnas used to hit the high note with. Any time any female puts a fan in her hand, she instantly becomes a *femme fatale*. A coquette. I've seen this happen down in the Ozarks at Baptist revival meetings. The lady in a poke bonnet and calico picks up a palmy fan and instantly becomes the Queen of Sheba. So I picked up the fan and looked in the mirror. I immediately tried my inscrutable smile and the whole thing. Suddenly I saw the fans did exactly what I wanted.

I ordered a beautiful pair from New York. The fans came C.O.D. and I couldn't spring them, having no money whatsoever. Ollie, a girl I knew, who was running a floating crap game, said, "Don't worry about a thing. Petey's coming in from Canada with a load. He'll be loaded." When Petey came back, the rear end of his Buick looked like a sieve. He'd been hijacked and no money to spring the fans. But he hocked his rings, and they sprung the fans for me.

I went to the club for my opening, but Frankie didn't remember me: "Who the hell are you?" So I called Tony: "He won't let me open." So Tony, Petey and another boy came into Frankie: "It'd be a terrible thing if this place got a stink in it." Frankie was horrified: "Wha-wha-wha-what?" So I rehearsed the whorehouse piano player, and Tony went over and clouted two of the Chez Paree's[2] best blue spotlights. So there I stood. . . . I intended to take my chiffon nightgown and make a classic little Grecian tunic out of it *à la* Isadora Duncan. I was saving that nightgown for an occasion, but it hadn't come yet. I didn't have a chance to get back to the hotel. . . . I was announced!

So I stood on the threshold of decision, in a pair of slippers and a pair of fans, period. Either I went on or Frankie would have every excuse to fire me. So I rationalized, I said, "All righty, who's gonna know what's behind these fans anyway?" And they didn't. That night I proved the Rand is quicker than the eye.

[2] For many years one of Chicago's leading night clubs.

No one was vaguely interested. They were waiting for the table singers. These were the folk who went around with a little push-around piano and sang sad songs while customers cried in their beer. It was weeks before anybody discovered I wasn't wearing anything. It was economically sound, because I didn't have any money to buy anything.

It's now the spring of '33. I'd met Charlie Weber, who was County Commissioner for forty years. Charlie had the beer concession at The Streets of Paris.[3]

Meanwhile, they had the Beaux Arts Ball at the Congress Hotel. There were bread lines, and people were starving. Yet, women in Chicago had the bad taste to have themselves photographed in gowns they were going to wear at the Ball. One was made of thousand-dollar bills. People went to Paris to get these gowns that cost thousands of dollars, wearing jewels, while people are starving in the streets, and people are marching in Washington and being shot at. It was such bad taste.

A friend was doing press work for me. We were socially conscious. She said, "Why don't you have your picture taken in the costume *you're* going to wear at the Beaux Arts Ball?" I didn't have a costume. She said, "How about Lady Godiva?" She sent out a blurb to all the papers.

We had to hire a horse. So I had a picture taken as Lady Godiva. It was like saying: How dare you have a dress of thousand-dollar bills when people are hungry? The girl sponsoring the ball was a little upset because of all the publicity my pictures got. So I went to the Congress, and they wouldn't let the horse in because he didn't have rubbers on his shoes. They put me and the horse on a table, and all the guys carried us in: Lady Godiva's riding into the ballroom floor on a white table top. The Hearst papers came out the next day with the whole double column, front page. All righty.

Now I'm harassing Charlie Weber for that job at the World's Fair, and he's not coming up with it. Because The Streets of Paris was sponsored by the high and mighty of this town, the social set. It was all French entertainment. Mr. Weber just didn't swing it big enough to get a job for me there. He suggested I crash the preview, the night before it opens. Mrs. Hearst was giving one of her famous Milk Fund dinners: "You'll get your foot in the door. . . ."

I hired the horse again, but the gates of the Fair were closed. No wheeled vehicle could come in until the next day when Mrs. Roosevelt

[3] One of the features of A Century of Progress (Chicago's World's Fair), 1933 and 1934.

would be there and the ribbon, cut. I took the horse out of the truck: "O.K., no wheeled vehicle, it's a horse." But no animals were allowed. O.K. Back into the trailer, we go up to the Wrigley docks. The Streets of Paris had a yacht landing there. The clientele is so posh, huh.

So I paid $8 for the tickets to the boat. He said, "Who's going with you?" I said, "Just a friend." So I brought the horse on the boat, and the man demurred. I said, "What do you care if it's a horse or a human?" At the yacht landing of The Streets of Paris, there was a little Frenchman who spoke no English. He figured that a broad that arrives in a boat with a horse is *supposed* to be there. So he opened the gate. The master of ceremonies, poor soul, figured: God, here's a woman with a horse and nobody told me about it.

Up to this time, the party'd been pretty dull. They had two bands. It kind of takes people's appetite away at a hundred dollars a plate. The fanfare sounded and the MC announced: Now, Lady Godiva will take her famous ride. Music played. Every photographer in the business, especially the Hearst ones, were there. Flashlights went off and the music played, and everybody was happy. They said: do it again. So I did it again. I had to get back to the show at the club.[4]

The next day I went down to The Streets of Paris to importune somebody for a job. I couldn't get in. There was a riot. All the people were waiting to tell them when Sally Rand was going to appear. You see, the Fair had opened. To hell with the cutting of the ribbon. Every newspaper in America came up that morning with Lady Godiva opening the Fair. The place was jammed. When does she go on? Nobody knew. (Laughs.)

A poor soul was walking the floor: "Nobody's gonna come in unless Sally Rand's gonna be here." I said, "I'm Sally Rand." Whaaat? They hired me at $90 a week. I had to go home immediately and get the fans. They had no piano, just a xylophone. That's how we got started.

They planned this Fair to bring business to Chicago, into the Loop. But you could have fired a cannon down State Street and hit nobody, because everybody was out at the Fair sleeping in their Fords. No business in the Loop. They figured they'd better get a Fair attraction down

[4] The Paramount Club. "Mildred Harris Chaplin was playing there with me. She said one night, 'I want you to meet a sweet and lovely man.' In the ladies' room, a girl said, 'You're certainly in high society tonight. Machine Gun Jack McGurn.' I left my coat and ran back to the hotel and locked myself in. Wow!"

there. It wasn't easy to bring the Streets of Flags or the Hall of Science. I was the most mobile. So they hired me in the Chicago Theater.

There was a big scandal on in City Hall. A reporter got a hold of this tax business that Mayor Kelly was stealing. Taking property for taxes and hadn't even sent out tax notices. It hit the front pages. So City Hall had to do something to attract attention away from their own nefarious business. They got an old jim-dandy slogan: Clean Up The Loop for Fair Visitors.

Their first net brought in a little prostitute who wasn't paying the right madam. And a guy selling rubber goods in a back alley. Everybody else was protected. They paid. Well, you're not gonna get a headline that way. You gotta get a hold of somebody big.

So on my opening night, this enormous policewoman, a giantess, came crashing through the scrim curtain. I thought she was a sex maniac. She came screaming. . . . Here I am locked in my dressing room with a tiny little reporter trying to get a story. The police sirens are going, and the whole detective squad is out there. It's the biggest thing since sliced bread. Finally, John Balaban[5] had to get his firm of lawyers to get me to come out of my dressing room. Why . . . I'm arrested!

By this time, it's all on the radio, and the lines are beginning to queue up. I went down to the police station, signed the necessary papers, came back, did my show. I was arrested again. Four times that day. Finally, a little policewoman said, "Honey, don't worry about it. It wouldn't make any difference if you were wrapped up in the back drop. They'd still arrest you." I was trying to conform to whatever the hell they wanted, but nobody would say.

That was the point. They had to get headlines to distract away from the tax thing. That was the whole bag. The lines queued up for eleven solid weeks, four deep. I was doing seven shows a day at the Chicago Theater and seven shows a day at The Streets of Paris. I got my first $1,000 a week that week, and the first thing I bought with it was a tractor for my stepfather.

In June, '33, $1,000 a week was a lot of money. I did the Fair again in '34. On the eleventh of November, 1934, mass hysteria took over. They completely demolished the Century of Progress. They tore down flags, they tore down street lights, they tore down the walls. It started

[5] Of Balaban & Katz, owners of a chain of movie theaters.

out being souvenir hunters, but it became mass vandalism. Anybody who witnessed it had this terribly frightening feeling. . . .

When we say "our society," it has a smug kind of ring to it. We seem to be a people who can't get out of our childhood. We don't believe what we see, what we hear. . . .

The rich still eat rich and wear mink coats, while people in Chicago literally freeze to death in the streets.[6] When I first went to India and saw dead in the streets, I couldn't eat. When I think of the garbage that goes into our garbage can, and here are people dying in the streets. And it's happening in our country, too. And I'm wearing a mink coat. Yeah.

I truly believe we shall have another Depression. I think people will just go out and take what they need. I don't think there will be any more people queueing up on bread lines waiting to be fed by charity, God damn it. I'm not condoning this, but we've let it happen. Take the television. It isn't food they're hungry for now, it's a different kind of food. Not only the Negroes. All the poor.

The middle class look upon the deprived smugly: the poor we'll have with us always. Oh yeah?

Tony Soma

New York restaurateur. In his early days as a young immigrant from Italy, he suffered privation. As a waiter in a Cincinnati hotel, during the nomination of William Howard Taft, 1908, "I got a black eye from a tall red American. He said I had no business being in America because I was a wop." Later, in New York, he became Enrico Caruso's waiter . . . "he was a bad tipper."

In the late Twenties and early Thirties, he was known as "Broadway Tony." His speak-easy was a favorite watering place for members of literary and theater circles.

THE DEPRESSION meant the glorification of "Tony's." I had three leases, three blocks east of Sixth Avenue. I sold them for $104,000. In '29. So

---

[6] "I read of the Negro girl, found in the alley, frozen to death. They brought her back to life after her heart had stopped beating."

for me, '29 was the biggest year I had in my American life. Glorification, money-wise and in friends, too. I had the greatest friends and from both continents, Europe and Hollywood.

Didn't some of them go broke?

They didn't went broke—they went crazy. They were still rich. Americans never broke. It's a question of figures. Oh yes, I had stock. Paper went into paper. City Bank stock when I bought it, $518. Went down to $35. The same stock, the same people. It was the figures that changed. To me, money was paper. My ego is meant all the moneys in the world. I am an egotist.

I am a capitalist myself, but I think money rules too many human beings. No, I am not enlightened, I'm just a capitalist. After all, this is a capitalist country, and I am entitled to live like a capitalist. But I know the propertied classes, the conservative element kept the Depression going. Roosevelt changed the country back into the United States today. We are still adventurous today. I would give credit not to F.D.R., but to Mrs. Roosevelt. She was the genius of that family. He was a vain man.

I thought I was going to be well protected, but I had at that time a lawyer—he did not understand the procedures of business. It was on the night of Repeal, the vestibule of Seventy-Seven[7] was piled up with cases of liquor, which we were not supposed to have. The name Seventy-Seven brand. A retailer was not supposed to have a wholesaler's license. Only one license. So I had a retail license, that was enough. But the Seventy-Seven Corporation could be many things. I always thought what I did was responsible. I should have had for myself a corporation. Today that's why they are millionaires. Double standard of laws being made for the protection of money and not for the protection of human beings. Still today.

My business was better than ever in the Depression. Never changed my mode of life. I'm a very humble man. Many, many of my customers were in the paper. They were my friends: Wolfe, Fitzgerald, any of the big names. I never suffered economically because I never looked at economics. To have credit in an individual like Robert Benchley and to have credit in a bank—Benchley was better than a bank.

[7] A celebrated club, bearing another name.

I give you an instance. I met him at Seventy-Seven to settle certain matters. In those days, they were the place you had to meet certain people that was of value to my business. We had a little contract, it was in four figures. He gave to me, he says, "Tony, if I die today, you can collect." Just a piece of paper. That's the type of customer. It was a kind of mutual sympathy.

Were you ever raided?

Raided? No, never. A visitor was here. They wanted to know what business we had to be open with liquor. Well, I don't do anything here, I'm drinking here. It was not by the authorities considered bad, unless you had bad liquor, unless you had dope, unless you had prostitution. My place was a place where you could go and sit down and have liquor with a bottle on the table. I never measured it. They were my guests and they had their friends. Absolutely, there was no crime.

I never suffered. Life is not to suffer. The Depression is still here for some peoples. Depression is a disease, a mental disease. There's bread lines today, but they're getting money. Paid by people that works.

In the old days, the poor were more ignorant.They didn't have television. They had to work sixteen hours a day, and they didn't have time. The Plaza Hotel, where I used to work sixteen hours a day, my pay used to be a dollar a day. The Knickerbocker, I was frisked when I walked out, whether I had something in my pocket. They found out once I had a box of candy, so they fired me.

Today the poor are not guilty, just sick, mentally sick. Poverty is always a sign of laziness.

During those days, did you ever notice homeless men?

No. I always lived between Forty-third Street and Fifty-ninth Street. I never bumped into slums.

Ever see apple sellers?

I was busy. I worked.

POSTSCRIPT: *Immediately following the conversation, he, a devoted follower of the Yoga philosophy, stood on his head and sang "La donna è mobile."*

Alec Wilder

Composer. Among the more than five hundred songs he has written are, "It's So Peaceful in the Country," "While We're Young," "I'll Be Around," "Trouble Is a Man," "The Winter of My Discontent," "Good-bye, John." Among his instrumental compositions, woodwind octets, concerti, and concert band music. He has lived at the Algonquin Hotel, New York, off and on, since pre-Depression days.

I KNEW something was terribly wrong because I heard bellboys, everybody, talking about the stock market. At the Algonquin they were grabbing as much as they could—horse betting, anything—and running to put this money on margin. It sounded nutty to me. About six weeks before the Crash, I persuaded my mother in Rochester to let me talk to our family adviser. I wanted to sell stock which had been left to me by my father, who was president of a Rochester bank. Maybe that's why I became a musician. I certainly didn't want to be a banker. Anything but a banker.

I talked to this charming man and told him I wanted to unload this stock. Just because I had this feeling of disaster. He got very sentimental: "Oh, your father wouldn't have liked you to do that." He was so persuasive, I said O.K. I could have sold it for $160,000. Six weeks later, the Crash. Four years later, I sold it for $4,000. John Balcom was his name, I'd never seen a face as red as his. It turned out he'd been an alcoholic. So all this advice came to me through the fumes of gin. He'd finally killed himself. Oh, gentle John Balcom! Solid citizen and everything. He cost me about $155,000. I could have done nicely with that. The sage old gentleman. So I did know something was wrong.

I wasn't mad at him, strangely enough. But I wanted nothing to do with money. The blow had fallen, and it was over. I was very skeptical and never invested. I became tired of people telling me: "Oh, there's a marvelous thing happening—and if you should have any extra money . . ." I'd say, "Don't talk to me about the market." I would have nothing to do with it.

I didn't even take money to a bank. I kept it all in my pocket. I didn't have a bank account for years. The money was drifting in. Taxes weren't as bad in those days, so you didn't have to keep track of what you spent. So I just kept the money in my pockets. It was crazy. To walk around with three or four thousand dollars and not be able to pay any bills by check. Just crazy.

I carried thousand-dollar bonds around in my pocket, and whenever I would run out of money, I'd cash one. Again, I was reinforced by money. It was a counter-active against any feeling of Depression.

I met a very beautiful girl just outside a speak-easy, on the sidewalk. She was reading the funny paper about midnight. It was all very romantic. She wanted to appear in a play a friend of hers had written. So I sold my New York Central stock for $12,000. I don't think the play cost more than ten or twelve thousand dollars to produce. Had I waited five years, I could have gotten—oh, $100,000. Of course, the play was a perfect mess. That was about '30 or '31. So I did know a little bit about the Depression. (Laughs.)

I loved speak-easies. If you knew the right ones, you never worried about being poisoned by bad whiskey. I'd kept hearing about a friend of a friend who had been blinded by bad gin. I guess I was lucky. The speaks were so romantic. A pretty girl in a speak-easy was the most beautiful girl in the world. As soon as you walked in the door, you were a special person, you belonged to a special society. When I'd bring a person in, it was like dispensing largesse. I was a big man. You had to know somebody who knew somebody. It had that marvelous movie-like quality, unreality. And the food was great. Although some pretty dreadful things did occur in them. I saw a man at the door pay off a gentleman in thousand-dollar bills to keep from being raided.

I recall the exact day Prohibition ended. I went into a restaurant that started serving booze. It was such a strange feeling, 'cause I started drinking in speaks. I didn't know about open drinking, to go in off the street and order a drink without having an arm on your shoulder. I'd gotten used to the idea of being disreputable. A friend of mine took me to some dump up in Rochester and gave me my first glass of beer. I don't think I'd have drunk it if it had been legal.

A very rich family up in Connecticut, before taking off for Europe, said to their children: No liquor in this house. So, under the rhododendron bush, the gin; under the hawthorne bush, the bourbon. It was all scattered just outside the house. No liquor *in* the house. All the drinking had to be done on the porch.

Roosevelt came in, and that was a cheery moment. Everybody seemed to know it. Even politically uninformed kids. I'm so sick of hearing how devious he was politically. So was Abraham Lincoln, for heaven's sake. To be a politician in a country like this, you've got to be devious.

His miraculous quality seemed to hit everybody. His fireside chats. It was very odd to me. Although his wit and speeches were beautiful, I never could understand how the public could pick up on his voice. It wasn't the kind of voice you hear on the street. But it grabbed them. They all mocked him, and the comedians kept doing imitations of "My friends." Yet the moment he said it—bang!—you were home. It was really a very extraordinary experience.

My mind doesn't move in political ways, 'cause I'm fixed on music. Away from the seamy side. Maybe it's cowardice. That could have been part of it. I wouldn't go up to a Hooverville and look at those shacks. I didn't want to know too much about it, because it depressed me too much and I couldn't write any music. That's no excuse, but. . . .

Carl Stockholm

Today, he runs a successful chain of dry-cleaning stores in Chicago. In the Twenties and early Thirties, he was a six-day bicycle racer.

WE HAD SEVEN tracks running on the Eastern seaboard. One rider could work twenty weeks in the summertime. A minimum of five times a week. I started in 1922 as a pro bike racer and was paid $100 a day. Later, it was from $200 up. Any good bike rider was worth that. The two-man race was the most popular. We'd go 146 hours straight.

It was a great place for show people because we ran all night. We used to have a great many people come in with top hats—society people. Tex Rickard[8] had a group of six hundred millionaires. They came in dressed for an event. We had song pluggers. They'd have a piano on the track, in the middle of the infield. They'd sing day and night. You got so you peddled automatically to the tune that was going on. I remember "Back To the Carolinas You Love." My legs still move to it.

[8] The celebrated fight promoter who became head of the Madison Square Garden Corporation.

We never wore helmets. We never had anything to protect us. We worked in a silk shirt and tights. If you fell, you got ripped up a little bit. It was a very tough game.

I went out with a lot of newspaper men. You'd hit four or five speakeasies in a couple of hours. Everybody seemed to feel he had to be seen in certain places. It wasn't unusual for a big sport to put up $1,000 for a sprint. They were all kind to the athletes.

Dion O'Bannion[9] was a great customer of mine. The bootleggers were the real big spenders. They bought the best seats. Everybody accepted them. In New York, Rickard was the big spender. He'd always come around with his cigar. He'd give the six-day race tickets to Mike Jacobs[10] to scalp. If you wanted a good pair of tickets, you'd go to Mike Jacobs. All the best tickets were given to the scalpers. If you wanted a good pair, it was worth $25.

After the stock market crash, we felt the pinch. In the middle of the Depression, the bike game went out of business. The tracks deteriorated. It cost a tremendous amount of money to replace the boards, so they were never replaced.

I quit racing in 1932, when they couldn't meet my fee. Frankie Harmon[11] and I rented the Chicago Stadium in the winter of '34, '35. We ran two six-day races. They were still drawing pretty well, but it was dying. You could see it. We gave away tickets for the afternoon sessions to ladies. Only a ten-cent tax was required for each ticket. We had many well-dressed ladies, but they didn't have the price for the tax. That was it. We always hoped this sport would come back. It never did.

Doc Graham

A mutual acquaintance, Kid Pharaoh, insisted that we meet. Doc Graham had obviously seen better days.

"My introduction to Chicago was when a guy got his head blowed off right across from where I went to stay. In that neighborhood where I

---

[9] A Chicago gangster who was killed by the rival Capone-Torrio group in 1924. His funeral was attended by 40,000 "mourners."

[10] Tex Rickard's successor.

[11] A Chicago sports promoter of the time.

*gravitated, there was every kind of character that was ever invented.
Con men, heist men, burglars, peet men: you name it, they had it.*

*"These are highly sophisticated endeavors. To be proficient at it—
well, my God, you spent a lifetime. And then you might fall, through
not being sophisticated enough. You may have committed a common
error, leaving fingerprints. . . ."*

I WAS a caged panther. It was a jungle. Survival was the law of the land.
I watched so many of my partners fall along the way. I decided the
modus operandi was bad. Unavailing, non-productive. After spending
ten Saturdays in jail, one right after another. I changed my modus
operandi.

What were you in jail for?

Various allegations. All alleged. I been a con man, a heist man—you
name it.

How does a heist man differ from a con man?

One is by force and the other is by guile. Very few people have en-
compassed both. I was very daring. When I came to the city and seen
groceries on the sidewalk, I swore I'd never be hungry again. My family
was extremely poor. My father was an unsuccessful gambler, and my
mother was a missionary. Not much money was connected with either
profession.

A family conflict . . . ?

Yes, slightly. He threw the Bible in the fire. He was right, incidentally.
(Laughs.) My mother didn't see it that way.

I'm sixty-one, and I have never held a Social Security card. I'm not
knocking it. I have been what society generally refers to as a parasite.
But I don't think I'd be a nicer fellow if I held two jobs.

My teacher was Count Victor Lustig. He was perhaps the greatest
con man the United States has ever known. Lustig's outstanding achievement was getting put in jail and paying a Texas sheriff off with $30,000
counterfeit. And the sheriff made the penitentiary also. He got to be a
believer. And he went into the counterfeit profession.

Another teacher was Ace Campbell.[12] He was the greatest card me-

[12] A pseudonym for a celebrated gambler of the Twenties and early Thirties.
He is still alive.

chanic that ever arrived on the scene. Nick the Greek[13] wouldn't make
him a butler. A footman. He couldn't open the door for him. Ace played
the crimp. A crimp is putting a weave in a card that you'd need a micro-
scope to see it. I know the techniques, but having had my arm half
removed, I had to switch left-handed, deal left-handed. I'm ambi-
dextrous.

An accident . . . ?

With a colored North American. The Twenties and early Thirties
was a jungle, where only the strong survived and the weak fell by the
wayside. In Chicago, at the time, the unsophisticated either belonged to
the Bugs Moran mob or the Capone mob. The fellas with talent didn't
bother with either one. And went around and robbed both of 'em.

We were extremely independent. Since I'm Irish, I had a working
affiliate with Bugs Moran's outfit. In case muscle was needed beyond
what I had, I called on Moran for help. On the other hand, Moran
might use me to help him in one of his operations.

The nature of one operation was: if you had a load of whiskey hijacked, we went over and reloaded it on a truck, while several surrounded the place with machine guns, sawed-off shotguns, et cetera.

Did you find yourself in ticklish situations on occasion . . . ?

Many of them. You see this fellow liquidated, that fellow disposed
of. Red McLaughlin had the reputation of being the toughest guy in
Chicago. But when you seen Red run out of the drainage canal, you realized Red's modus operandi was unavailing. His associates was Clifford
and Adams. They were set in Al's doorway in his hotel in Cicero. That
was unavailing. Red and his partners once stole the Checker Cab Company. They took machine guns and went up and had an election, and
just went and took it over. I assisted in that operation.

What role did the forces of law and order play?

With a $10 bill, you wasn't bothered. If you had a speaking acquaint-
ance with Mayor Thompson,[14] you could do no wrong. (Laughs.) Al
spoke loud to him.

There was a long period during the Depression where the police were
taking scrip. Cash had a language all of its own. One night in particular,

13 Another renowned gambler of the time.
14 William Hale Thompson, three-term mayor of Chicago.

I didn't have my pistol with me, and the lady of the evening pointed out a large score to me. (Laughs.) A squad car came by, which I was familiar with. A Cadillac, with a bell on it. I knew all the officers. I borrowed one of their pistols and took the score. Then I had to strip and be searched by the policemen, keeping honest in the end, as we divided the score. They wanted the right count. They thought I might be holding out on 'em. They even went into my shoes, even.

Oh, many policemen in that era were thieves. Legal thieves. I accepted it as such and performed accordingly. We didn't have no problems. It was an era where there was no bread on the table. So what was the difference whether I put the bread on the table by my endeavor or they put the bread? I performed with a hundred policemen in my time. I can't say nothin' for 'em, nothin' against 'em. I would say they were opportunists. I would say that they were merely persons that didn't perhaps have the courage to go on and do what I did. Nevertheless, they were willing to be a part of it. A minor part, that is.

The era of the times led into criminality, because of the old precept and concepts were destroyed against everyday reality. So when a policeman or a fireman was not being paid, how in the name of God could you expect him to enforce what he knew as the concept of law and order, when you see the beer barons changing hundred-dollar bills, and the pimp and the whorehouse guy had hundred-dollar bills, and the guy digging the sewers couldn't pay his bills? So how could you equate these things?

A good example is Clyde Barrow and Bonnie Parker. They were a product of the era. Dillinger—it wasn't that he was really a tough. No, he was just a product of survival. Actually, Dillinger was a country bumpkin. He realized the odds were stacked against him and performed accordingly. I knew Dillinger. Yeah, I met him on the North Side. And Dillinger was nothing like people wrote about him. The times produced Dillinger. Pretty Boy Floyd. Baby Face Nelson.

They were dedicated heist men and in the end were killed, to achieve their purpose. By themselves, they didn't need an army.

Al Capone sublet the matter. Capone quickly removed himself from the danger zone, aside from murdering Anselmi and Scalisi with a baseball bat. Bugs Moran to the end—he died for a bank heist in Ohio. They were from two different bolts of cloth. One was a dedicated thief. And one was an intriguing Mediterranean product of guile, et cetera. So you'd have to say that Moran was dedicated while Capone was an opportunist.

How did you get along during those hard times?

By every way known to the human brain. All my brothers were in the penitentiary. I had one brother in Jefferson City, another one in San Quentin, another one in Leavenworth, another one in Louisiana. At that time, I am a fighter. I started boxing in 1925. Fourteen years till 1939. And it's a bloodthirsty thing.

How'd you become a boxer?

Gravitation. Being on the road simulated that fate, trying to grab a buck and so forth. Five different years, *Ring* Magazine rated me the most devastating puncher in the profession, pound for pound.

What was it like, being a boxer in those days . . . ?

Survival. If it worked out that you were on top, you made a living. And if you were three or four shades below the top, you scuffled for a buck. Fighters were very, very hungry.

I made some pretty big scores. But I spent it practically all on getting my brothers out of penitentiaries around the country. At that time, the one in San Quentin stood me thirty thousand, the one in Jefferson City stood me twenty-five thousand. Those were big give-ups in those days.

I lived from the bottom to the top. I lived as good as you could live. I run the gamut of having a butler and a chauffeur to a flopjoint, into an open car over night.

He describes the boxing "combination" of those days; the fix; the refusal of his manager and himself to "play ball"; the boxer as an investment, cut up "like a watermelon."

I had many injuries in between. My hands, you can see. (He holds out his gnarled, broken knuckles.) In the meantime, I had to step out and make a dollar otherwise. It was never within the law.

I've switched craps, I've run up the cards, I do the complete bit. Every way known to the human brain. I'm probably a rare species that's left.

Was muscle always involved?

Muscle if you hope to leave with the money. Muscle everywhere, yes.

Because for some unknown reason, muscle has been going on since the Roman Army conquered the field with a way of life.

When you enter an endeavor unsuccessfully, then the planning was incorrect. The risk was above the gains, and you stumble along the way. And the windup is a rude awakening with numbers strung out over your back. Unsuccessful in your modus operandi. Sagacity, ingenuity, planning . . . it involves much weighing, odds against failure, odds against gain—if you care to be in a free society.

I spent much time in jail. That's why I'm a student of the matter.

(*At this point, Kid Pharaoh and he conducted a vigorous and somewhat arcane debate concerning the relative dishonesty of Hoover and Roosevelt. The Kid insisted it was Hoover who, by clout, was saved from "the bucket." Doc was equally certain it was F.D.R. who should have had "numbers strung out over his shoulders."*)

Do you recall your biggest haul during the Thirties?

It was alleged—

Who alleged . . . ?

The newspaper report came out as $75,000. We took eight and were happy about the whole thing.

What was your role during Prohibition?

I was a cheater. After studying under Count Lustig and Ace Campbell, I considered it beneath my dignity delivering a barrel of beer. Although I drink beer. I hustled with crap mobs, on the crimp, the weave, the holdout—the reason I didn't do the rum running is you can hire a mooch with muscle. But can you hire brains? Big firms have not succeeded in doing this.

I have met only several proficient men in my time. One of them was Jack Freed. (Cups hand over mouth, whispers.) D—e—a—d. He worked right up to the edge of his demise. This is in the evening, when you are not at home. He was dedicated to his labor. He spent half his lifetime in the penitentiaries. One of my closest friends. I, of course, assisted him, from time to time. He accused me of rattling my coat one night, making entrance. I, who have endeavored in every participation known to the human brain, where art, subterfuge and guile is involved.

I take it you were caught a few times—

Incarcerated. Nothing proven substantially. I was a victim of circumstances. What they were, I didn't say. Yes, I spent a year in Salinas, California, amongst other places. The highlight was when I was nineteen. If I get convicted, I'm going out to join my brother in San Quentin. My brother was doing twenty years there. If I'm not convicted, I'm going up to visit him. I'm going to San Quentin, one way or the other.

And you did?

I did. As a free man. I was fortunate enough in having one of the greatest criminal lawyers of all time defending me.

For someone engaging in your varied skills, do you sense a difference between the Thirties and today?

It's so different today, it's unfathomable. You can't conjure what the difference is. Today everything is a robot. Today everything is mechanical. There is very little ingenuity. Everything today is no-personal, there is no personality whatsoever. Everything today is *ipso facto, fait accompli.* In my era they had to prove their point. Today, you don't have to prove your point.

Back then Ace Campbell steered Arnold Rothstein,[15] with Nigger Nate Raymond, into one of maybe the biggest card games was ever involved. I was a small feature of it in the Park Central Hotel in New York. Ace changed the weave (laughs), and when Rothstein wound up a half-a-million loser, he said he was cheated. Rothstein became jaded after he lost the half a million, no longer had any interest. No interest in life. After the card game broke up, he said he was no longer interested in this, that or the other. He refused to pay off. So Nigger Nate Raymond held court with him. And that was the end of that.

Held court . . . ?

The S & W people[16] had the implements that they held court with. That's all. Rothstein didn't have to pay off. You understand what I mean? I know, because I assisted in the operation with Ace. But let that be as it may. It was unfortunate, yes. But that was his demise.

[15] A gambler and fixer of renown. He was involved in the Black Sox scandal of 1919.
[16] Smith & Wesson, revolver manufacturers.

Were the S & W people popular those days?

Naturally, it was part of your wearing apparel.

Aren't some of the survivors in legitimate enterprises today?

One of the fellows who was a pimp in Chicago is the boss of one of the grandest hotels in Las Vegas. I assisted him in a few small matters. But true to all pimping, he forgot me entirely as he advanced into the autumn of life.

After Prohibition, what did the guys do?

The ones that were adroit enough branched into other fields. If they didn't have any knowledge, they fell by the wayside. I achieved some small success in race tracks. Machine Gun Jack McGurn[17] couldn't stand the traffic. He got his brains blowed out, branching into other fields.

The night Prohibition was repealed, everybody got drunk. It was the only decent thing Roosevelt ever did in his Administration. I was not one of his admirers. I tried to fire him on four different occasions. If I ever had a person work for me that displeased me, it was Roosevelt. I voted against him four times.

What was it about him you didn't like?

Him being a con man, taking advantage of poor, misguided, gibbering idiots who believed in his fairy tales. The New Deal, the various gimmicks, the NRA . . . the complete subterfuge, artifice and guile. . . .

Some say Roosevelt saved our society. . . .

I dare say it would have been saved if Roosevelt's mother and father had never met.

Many people were on relief . . . on WPA. . . .

I didn't have a thing to do with that, because I was above that. Nevertheless, the people that were involved in it did it merely to get some meat on the plates, some food in the kitchen. It was no more, no less.

[17] It was alleged that he was one of Capone's executioners in the St. Valentine's Day Massacre. He was killed in a bowling alley in 1936, on the eve of St. Valentine's Day.

Survival. None of the connotations of social dissent that has crept in since then. Merely an abstract way of eating. . . .

What do you think would happen if there were a big Depression today?

Very simple. They'd commit suicide today. I don't think they're conditioned to stand it. We were a hardier race then. We'd win wars. We didn't procrastinate. We'd win them or lose them. Today we're a new race of people. They'll quit on a draw—if they see any feasible way to see their way out to quit with any dignity, they'll quit. Back then, you had a different breed of people. You got $21 a month going into the army or the navy. So them guys, they went to win the war. There's been an emancipated woman since the beginning of the war, also.

KID PHARAOH *interjects: "The American woman during the Depression was domesticated. Today, as we move into the late Sixties, if you go into any high school, you don't see any classes of cooking any more. You don't see any classes at all in sewing. None of them can boil water. They're all today in business in competition to the male animal. Why should a Playboy bunny make $200 a week? If a veteran goes to war, puts his life up . . . can't raise a family."*

DOC: *". . . a lot of country bumpkins in the city wanting to look at poor, misguided, gibbering idiot waitresses. That they've stripped down like a prostitute, but hasn't sense enough to know that it's on her alleged sex allure that the poor misguided chump is in the place. In the end it amounts to absolutely nothing. A hypothesis of silly nothingness . . . undressed broads serving hootch, that cannot fulfill. . . ."*

KID PHARAOH: *". . . his dick directs him, like radar, to the Playboy Club. In a high moral society—in Russia—guys like Hugh Hefner would be working in the library."*

During the Depression . . . if a guy had a few drinks with a girl . . . ?

If she had two drinks with him, and she didn't lay her frame down, she was in a serious matter. She could have one, and explain she made a mistake by marrying some sucker that she was trying to fulfill her marriage commitment. But in the Thirties, if you had a second drink and she didn't make the commitment where she's going to lay her frame down for you, the entire matter was resolved quickly to the point and could end in mayhem. She was in a serious matter.

In the Thirties, then, the individual con man, the heist man, had an easier time with it—all around?

Oh yes, it was much easier then. The Federal Government now has you on practically anything you do. They make a conspiracy whether you accomplish the matter or not. Today, it's fraught with much peril, any type of endeavor you engage in. A nefarious matter. It constantly comes under the heading of a federal statute. The Federal Government then collected taxes, and just a few interstate things, as white slavery, and that was about it.

Today, the Federal Government has expanded into every field. If you use a telephone, as an example, and you put slugs in it, that's a penitentiary offense. Strange as that may seem. So that will give you an idea how far the Federal Government has encroached on a citizen's prerogative.

You think Roosevelt had a role to play in this?

Definitely. He was perhaps the lowest human being that ever held public office. He, unfortunately, was a despot. I mean, you get an old con man at a point in high office, he begins to believe the platitudes that are expounded by the stupid populace about him.

What about the young people, during the Depression . . . ?

The young people in the Depression respected what laws there were. If they'd steal, they tried to do it with dignity. And what not. They respected the policeman. They looked at him with forebearance, that he was a necessary part of society. But, nevertheless, he didn't impede the mere fact of gain.

No, he didn't stop 'em.

The young today are feminized, embryo homosexuals. Stool pigeons.

What about the young dissenters?

If you gave 'em a push, they'd turn into a homosexual. When the German hordes fifty years ago surrounded Paris, Marshal Pétain brought out the pimps, whores, thieves, underground operators, he says: Our playground is jeopardized by the German Hun. Well, all Paris, every thief, burglar, pimp, he come out and picked up a musket. Stopped the German hordes.

Today you don't see any kind of patriotism like that. They're trying to tear down the courthouse, they try to throw paint on Johnson's car. How can you compare that era, coming into this? Those were men, and today you've got to question whether they're homosexual or whether they're not.

Since the Depression, manhood has been lost—the manhood that I knew. Where four or five guys went on an endeavor, they died trying to take the endeavor off. It was no big deal if they did die. If it didn't come off right, there was no recrimination. Everybody put skin off what they set on.

Today, the foible of our civilization is to attack the policeman with a rotten egg, throwing it at him. Or walking around with a placard, that they're against whatever the present society advocates as civilized. Those people today—the Fall of Rome could be compared with it. Because they were the strongest nation on earth, and they disinterrogated into nothing. Through debauchery, through moral decay.

They need a narcotic to do anything, they can't do it on their own. They need a drug. Back in my era, we could cold-bloodedly do it.

Jerome Zerbe

"They're doing eight pages in color of this apartment in the fall issue of Architectural Digest. *So anybody who cares can see it."*

In the apartment on Sutton Place are all sorts of objets d'art: *jades, prints, photographs, original portraits of friends and acquaintances, statues . . . "two Venetian ones I admired in Venice. Hedda Hopper gave them to me. She was my long-time and greatest friend. Everything was given to me. You see, being a poor boy . . ." (Laughs.)*

THE THIRTIES? My own poverty. My father allowed me an allowance of $300 a month. On that I went to Paris and started painting. Suddenly he wrote and said: no more money. And what does a painter do in the Depression without money? I came back to America and was offered a job in Cleveland. Doing the menial task—but at the time I was grateful—of art-directing a magazine called *Parade*. $35 a week. It was 1931.

I thought, to goose up the magazine, I would take photographs of people at my own home. In those days, you didn't have strobe lights and all that sort of thing. We had our little Kodak cameras, and would hold up a flash and would open up the flash . . . but I got photographs of Leslie Howard, Ethel Barrymore, these people. Billy Haines was a great star in those days.

We published them in *Parade*. It was the first time that what we call candid social photography was founded. I had known I'd start something. *Town and Country* asked me to go over various estates and I went over and photographed people I knew. They were all horrified at the thought and couldn't wait for the pictures. (Laughs.)

After my father died, and no money, I sold my library books to the Cleveland Museum and the Cleveland Art Library. With that money, I came to New York and started out. *Town and Country* had guaranteed me $150, which seemed a lot. This is '33.

One day, a gal from Chicago called me up and asked if I would have lunch with John Roy and herself at the Rainbow Room. So we lunched, and he said: "Jerome, it's extraordinary how many people you know in New York. Would you like to come to the Rainbow Room? I'll pay you $75 a week, if you'll come, take photographs, and send them to the papers, and you will have no expenses." The Rainbow Room, here at the Rockefeller Center. This is 1935. The famous room at the top.

So twice a week, I would give a party and photograph my guests, all of whom were delighted to be photographed. The first night of this, I was so pleased, because I had been so poor. I still had my beautifully tailored clothes from London. I still had the accoutrements of money, but I had no money. You know? It was cardboard for my shirt and my shoes when they got old.

So I went to the El Morocco to celebrate this new job. John Perona said, "I'll take you on the other three nights." That made $150 a week. Then he said, "Jerry, cut out this Rainbow Room racket. They're getting more publicity than I am. I will pay the same amount, if you leave your camera here. You won't have taxi fares, you won't have problems."

So I went to work for John Perona. From 1935 to 1939, I worked at the El Morocco. He's a legend. He's dead now. He was a fabulous guy, just fabulous. He and I fought all the time. And I was always quitting. I adored him.

I invented this thing that became a pain in the neck to most people. I took photographs of the fashionable people, and sent them to the papers. Maury Paul of the *Journal-American,* at least four times a week, would use a large photograph on his society page of important people.

The social set did not go to the Rainbow Room or the El Morocco, until I invented this funny, silly thing: taking photographs of people. The minute the photographs appeared, they came.

They became celebrities at that moment . . . ?

That's right. I would send the photographs not only to New York papers. I sent them to the London *Bystander,* to an Australian paper, to one in Rio . . . I sent them all over the world. So people would come in to the El Morocco and I would get a note saying: "The Duchess of Sutherland has arrived and would love to have her photograph taken." (Laughs.) You know?

My two favorite people of all times were Mr. and Mrs. William K. Vanderbilt. Rose and Will, I knew very well as friends, as well as people in the night club. They would arrange once in the spring and once in the fall. . . . Rose would bring two hats and three coats, and I would photograph her for the next six months. And dole the photographs out every two or three months. But I'd do it all in one night. She was perfectly happy with that. It was a perfect arrangement. Extraordinary people came to the El Morocco all the time. You couldn't get in without a black tie. Not possibly. There would be lines waiting on the street—one whole block—to get in.

We're talking now about the Depression . . . ?

No, the Depression was over by '34. I think, pretty much. But because I invented this goddam thing (laughs), the Byron Foys, people like that, would call up, reserve a table. They'd hold it just so long: then, if they arrived, Carino, who was the greatest of headwaiters, knew— and, by the way, might I say, when he died, he left an estate of $450,000. Taxes in those days were not great. And people would often pay up to $200 to get a good seat in the El Morocco, in those days.

They were the top, top social. These were the people whose houses, one knew, were filled with treasures. These were the women who dressed the best. These were the women who had the most beautiful of all jewels. These were the dream people that we all looked up to, and hoped that we or our friends could sometimes know and be like.

Do you recall the Crash?

No, because it didn't hit the family. My father had coal mines, and it didn't hit the coal mines until '31. He still gave me $300 a month, and I went to Paris and lived it up.

My father was president of the Ohio and Pennsylvania Coal Company. It was on the West Virginia border—Cadiz, Ohio. Where Clark Gable was born. I went down there, because at the time he offered me the presidency at $12,000 a year. It was an incredibly large amount of money. I'm talking about 1932 or 1933. I went down there and spent two weeks in the town. The mine was 897 feet, the shaft, underground, and the working surface was three and a half miles. I spent two weeks down there and came back and said: "Mother, forgive me, to hell with it."

The men loathed their slovenly wives, and every night they go and play pool or whatever it was. The houses were drab beyond belief. You'd think a woman would at least put up a plant—a flower or something. And suddenly I flew into town with two or three friends for several weekends. We disrupted the place like nobody's business. (Laughs.) We'd go to the bars, and these guys would say: "Jesus, where did you get your shirts?" Where did you get this or that? and I'd say: "Why don't you go to your houses and make them more attractive?" And they said: "Our wives are so goddam slovenly. We don't even want to go to bed with them." I'm talking about the miners. They came out at five o'clock at night absolutely filthy. I've got a photograph of myself, I can show you, as a miner. I can show you how filthy I was.

And they all went through this common shower, got clean. Would they go home? Hah! For food, yes. And their squawling brats. And take right off to a bar. They loathed their life. The manager once said to me, "I never knew what it was to have fun with people until I heard your laughter. . . ."

We all had such fun, of course, and he joined in the fun. And this brings up another story. . . . At the time I photographed King Paul of Greece, he became a great friend. He said, "Mr. Zerbe, you and I have many friends in common. Do you realize in our position we are never allowed to laugh? Everybody treats us with such respect. And I hear you have outrageous stories."

When you went to this mining town—the year . . .

1933. Of course, to me it was a horror. That stinking little hotel. The lousy food and the worst service. And I was spoiled. When I was a kid, Mother always said to me: "Jerome, I think it's much easier for you to have your breakfast served in bed." So I always had my breakfast in bed. And I always had the fire lit in my fireplace. I was a very spoiled brat, and I loved that.

Did your friends ever talk much about Roosevelt?

Listen, dear boy, Franklin Roosevelt in those days we didn't even talk about. John Roosevelt and the young Franklin were great friends of mine. I photographed them in my apartment. We never did discuss the old man, ever. Well, I never liked politics. I think all politicians are shits. Franklin—I admired him very much. I thought the American public was so frightfully gullible to allow this man, he was a dying man, to be elected for that last term. Oh, that voice!

"My dear friends. . . ." You know, it became such an irritation. It was so patronizing. It was so the great man talking down to us common little herd.

Was his name ever discussed at El Morocco?

Well, no, actually. I have a great respect for the family. I'm sorry the boys haven't done better. And they haven't. What President's sons have? What happened to the Hoover boys?

Did his name ever come up with some of the people you photographed?

Yes, but always with a rather hatred. They didn't like him. Eleanor was a great woman, who was a real, real schlemiel. You know, making the most of everything she could out of a bad everything. But there was always admiration for her.

Did the people you knew in the Thirties ever talk about what happened outside? You know . . . those on relief . . . ?

I don't think we ever mentioned them. They did in private at the breakfast table or the tea table or at cocktail time. But never socially. Because I've always had a theory: when you're out with friends, out socially, everything must be charming, and you don't allow the ugly.

We don't even discuss the Negro question. Let's forget they're only one-tenth of this country, and what they're putting on, this act—someday they're going to be stepped on like vermin. There's too much. I'm starting a thing: equal rights for whites. I think they've allowed themselves, with their necklaces and their long hair and nonsense, to go too far.

Now I've had the same manservant, who's Negro, for thirty-three years, which is quite a record. I suppose he's my closest friend in the world. He's a great guy, Joseph.

But aren't beads and necklaces worn by some of the beautiful people today, too?

I was thinking tonight . . . I have to go out to dinner, but I don't have my Malta Cross, which had blue enamel and diamonds, which is really very good. Because I loaned it to somebody. I'll have to wear what I really love, which is my Zuñi Indian. This is authentic and good, and people all accept that.

Do you remember ever seeing apple sellers in the city?

No, there were none of those. Not in New York. Never, never. There were a few beggars. You came to recognize them because they'd be on one block one day and one block the next. And finally one day, I saw this pathetic beggar, whom I'd always felt sorry for. This Cadillac drove up. I'd just given him a quarter. And it picked him up. There was a woman driving it. And I thought: well, if they can drive a Cadillac, they don't need my quarter. His wife had a Cadillac.

You don't recall bread lines or stuff like that?

I never saw one. Never in New York. If they were, they were in Harlem or down in the Village. They were never in this section of town. There was never any sign of poverty.

What does the phrase "New Deal" mean to you?

It meant absolutely nothing except higher taxation. And that he did. He obviously didn't help the poverty situation in the country, although, I suppose . . . I don't know—New Deal! God! Look at the crap he brought into our country, Jesus!

Do you sense a different feeling toward people on welfare today than there was in the Thirties?

Oh listen, we had no little bastards dressed as they are today, putting on acts these days. The children were slapped down by their parents. I think they're encouraged by their parents today. I think our country is in a very dangerous and precarious position, and I would predict, if I dared, that within twenty or thirty years, we're gonna have a complete revolution here in America. Probably a dictatorship.

I feel the signs. The portents are going that way. Look what happened at Columbia. Why, they should have turned the fire hoses on those little bastards and get them out right away. Instead of tolerating them.

Any final thoughts . . . ?

The Thirties was a glamorous, glittering moment.

Judy

She is twenty-five years old and does public relations work.

YOU GET THE IMPRESSION there was this crash, this big explosion, and everything goes down. And all of a sudden one day, the sun comes up, and there's a war. There's all kinds of people making planes and napalm and this kind of thing. Affluence is equated with war. I hate it, I hate everything about it.

If another Depression came, the first ones out of work would be people like me. There's a whole sub-society of people like me. We're the ones who open doors and give a bit of polish to things. We're a luxury. We're not really functional. And there are many of us. Except for teachers and nurses, most female college graduates are in this dispensable category. There are lots of women doing this agency kind of thing—ad agencies, social agencies, being somebody's secretary and not working very hard. There certainly couldn't be anything like us if there weren't an affluent society.

At the Clinic

Dr. Nathan Ackerman

Psychiatrist. Director of the Family Institute for Living; Clinical Professor of Psychiatry at Columbia; visiting lecturer and consultant at Einstein and at Lennox Hospital.

"In 1937, psychoanalysis was coming into vogue. I started with a fee of $2.50 an hour. Ten bucks an hour was a fabulous fee. The very rich paid $25 an hour and that was considered a freak. Up to that time, psychiatric practice was tied mainly to mental hospitals. You worked your way up to a decent salary."

IN THOSE DAYS, psychiatry was quite removed from social problems. Almost ivory tower. For one thing, the really poor didn't go to psychiatrists. It was not in any way concerned with poverty and reform. There was no connection between social health and mental health. There was social service for the poor, but hardly psychiatric care. Very few good clinics.

People who came for treatment were preoccupied with internal suffering. They were unaware of the external living conditions, as causes. The issues were specific. For the poor and the jobless, relief. The anxieties we treated were seemingly of internal origin. The doctor's business was the patient's internal distress, not the living conditions. We were all in the same boat, so the emotional pinch was not that great. Nobody growled much about it. Although among young people, there was ferment, a dream of a better way of life. Social ideals.

The complaints were specific. Familiar symptoms. A young man can't drive to a hospital without going into a panic, or drive by a cemetery. A phobia, an obsession.

Did any of the symptoms have to do with status in society, say, losing a job and thus losing face . . . ?

No, it was internal distress. Remember the practice was entirely middle-class.

I did a little field work among the unemployed miners in Pennsylvania. Just observing. What the lack of a job two, three, four, five years did to their families and to them. They hung around street corners and in groups. They gave each other solace. They were loath to go home because they were indicted, as if it were their fault for being unemployed. A jobless man was a lazy good-for-nothing. The women punished the men for not bringing home the bacon, by withholding themselves sexually. By belittling and emasculating the men, undermining their paternal authority, turning to the eldest son. Making the eldest son the man of the family. These men suffered from depression. They felt despised, they were ashamed of themselves. They cringed, they comforted one another. They avoided home.

Many complaints today are pitched to the level of social actions. We have a great ideal of acting out. Instead of patients coming with a constrained neurosis, today they are less prone to choke up their distress. They live out their emotions in conflict. They get into difficulty with other people. They create social tensions. They act out: drinking, drug-taking, stealing, promiscuity . . . In place of complaining, they explode. They live out some of their urges. They don't contain the disturbance within their own skin.

Thirty, forty years ago, people felt burdened by an excess of conscience. An excess of guilt and wrongdoing. Today there's no such guilt. In those days, regardless of impoverishment, there was more constraint of behavior. I cannot imagine looting thirty-five years ago. Despite want, the patterns of authority prevailed. Today, those standards have exploded. Looting and rioting have become sanctioned behavior in many communities.

219

Society was unquestioned and the miner accepted his own guilt . . . ?

That's right. The way of life was an established one. It did not explode in a chaotic fashion. Despite deprivations, there was predictability. You could make long-term plans. If you were willing to work your ass off, you could look forward to reward ten years hence. Even during the Depression, there was more continuity in the way of life. Today there's no such conviction. People can't predict five years hence.

In the Depression, most people knew where they stood. Whether they were haves or have-nots. Despite the want, there was a greater degree of organization. The violence was more contained. Today it is anarchic.

The complaints then were more concrete. The poor wanted food, clothing, the sheer necessities of life. Today the demand is for egalitarian status.

During the Depression, I saw a young Negro lad, seventeen. He came to my office. He had been a leader of a very violent gang of kids in Harlem. He had shifted roles from being a gang leader to a community leader, making peace between black gangs and neighboring white gangs. He was going through an emotional crisis. I tried to treat him, but he bolted. It was the anxiety of being treated by a white doctor in an office near Madison Avenue. The surroundings were too comfortable; the office was too comfortable; the couch was too comfortable. He took flight. It was a silent color barrier. Today, it is no longer silent. It is open; it is vocal. Today, consideration from a doctor or a teacher is not viewed as privilege but as a right.

Thirty years ago, the patients' complaint was familiar. Today, the common complaint is much more vague: they're unhappy, anguish in their aloneness. They don't know where they belong. . . . Feeling lonely, unappreciated and alienated was no basis for going to a psychiatrist in those days.

Money is not a complaint . . . ?

Not at all. They complain of feelings of disorientation. They are afraid of close relationships. They are not happy with their wives. They fail utterly in controlling their children. They are bewildered, they are lost.

Like the unemployed miner in the Thirties . . . ?

Yeah. Rootlessness. The miners felt that, even if for a different reason. They felt they were outside society. There is something similar in the lostness of middle-class people today. But this has nothing to do with money. It has to do with the social community.

I think a depression today would have a paradoxical effect, at least temporarily. Political upheaval, on one hand—and bringing people closer together, on the other. Greater consideration for one another. Something like the quality of caring in London during the blitz. Everybody's suffering was everybody's concern. They drew together and gave each other solace.

Sixteen Ton

You load sixteen ton and what do you get?
Another day older, and deeper in debt.
St. Peter, don't you call me, because I can't go.
I owe my soul to the company store.

—Merle Travis

Buddy Blankenship

A West Virginian émigré, living in Chicago. Illness has kept him jobless. Children, ranging wide in age from late adolescence to babyhood, step-children, son-in-law, grandchild and a weary wife are seated or wandering about the apartment: trying to keep cool on this hot, muggy summer afternoon. Hand-me-down furniture is in evidence in all the rooms.

I'VE BEEN in a depression ever since I've been in the world. Still, it's better and worse. '31, '32, that's about the worst we ever been through.

I told my dad I wasn't going to school any more. He said: Why, you just come on and go work with me. I went in the mines, and I went to work. From '31 to about the last of '32. The Depression got so bad, we

222

went to farming, raising our own stuff. He worked in the mines fifty-one years. He was sixty-three when he got killed. A boy shot him.

We lived eight miles from the mine, and we had to ride it horseback. I was riding behind my dad. Many times I'd have to git off and hammer his feet out of the stirrups. They'd be froze in the stirrups. It was cold, you know. When you come out of the mines, your feet would be wet of sweat and wet where you're walking on the bottom. And get up on those steel stirrups, while you're riding by eight miles, your feet'd be frozen and you couldn't git 'em out of the stirrups. I'd have to hammer 'em out. His feet were numb, and they wouldn't hurt till they started to get warm, and then they would get to hurtin'.

We got up at five in the mornin', start at six. We got out at ten that night. We'd work about sixteen hours a day, seventeen hours. The boss said we had to clean up. We didn't clean it up, the next morning there'd be another man in the mine to clean it up. The motor man would say: How many cars you got? Five more. Well, hurry up, we want to get out of here.

They was gettin' a dollar seventy-five a day. We'd get sixty to sixty-five ton a day—that is, both us, me and Dad. Then they changed me off and let me get a dollar and a half a day. I was trappin'.

Trappin'? The trap door was shut so the air would circulate through the mine. Then the motor come along, I'd open it up. I had to stay there till everybody quit. Then we'd walk about two miles and a half till we got outside. We walked about a mile before we got to where we could get our horses. We got down to the horses, why we rode about eight miles before we got to home. Summertimes it wasn't too bad. But in wintertime, boy, it was rough. You'd get snowbound and it would get so you couldn't get in and out. Ice'd be so bad . . . an' dangerous. Of course, we had to go to work. We didn't eat if we didn't go.

They had what they called safety devices, but it wasn't real safety. They had an axe and a saw and you cut your own timbers. You brought 'em in, strapped on your back. You went out on the mountain with your one-man saw. You sawed down a bush or whatever size prop you wanted and you tuck 'em in on your back. On Sunday, I packed timbers on my back, about two miles to the place . . . to set 'em on Monday. Company furnished the timber but you had to cut 'em. You had to lay your own track. . . .

I've seen several accidents. I've had to take four out of the mines dead. I didn't think about nothin' like that, though. I packed one for seven miles, and he got up and walked better'n I could. I was gonna give out, and he wasn't hurtin' any bit. There was some rock on him, and I took a jack and lifted it up and pulled 'im out. Just his breath knocked out of 'im. . . .

About '32, it got so they wouldn't let us work but two days a week. We saved $20 in the office. They laid us off two weeks till we traded that $20 in the store. We had to trade it out in the store, or we didn't get to work no more. It was a company store. What we made, we had to go next evening and trade it off. If we didn't, they'd lay us off. They didn't let you draw no money at all. It was scrip. They had a man top of the hill who took your tonnage down, how many tons you loaded, and it was sent up to the scrip office. If you made $20 over your expenses—for house, rent, lights and all—why, then they laid you off till you spent that $20.

This town you lived in . . .

It was a cave, a coal cave. Thirty-two families lived in the caves. It was nice buildings, built up inside, but they was just rough lumber. The company was the landlord, too. They owned it all. They still got company houses yet.

I worked about two years on the mines, then we went back to the farm from '32 to '37. It seemed like you lived a lot better on the farm than today. The works was bad, but you didn't have to pay some big price for the stuff. You raised your own hogs, you could have your own cattle. And you had your own meat, your own bacon, lard. You didn't have to buy nothin' but flour and meal. You raised your own potatoes. You never had money because you didn't make it to have it. It was a pretty bad time. It seemed just like a dream to me, the Depression did. I was young and didn't pay no attention to it. I didn't get the clothes or the underwear or stuff like that, but the eatin' part was good. I'd rather be back on the farm than anything I ever done.

Then we went to camp—minin'—in '37. The same mines. Roosevelt brought the mines arolling again. Things got to moving, and money got to circulating through. I worked the mine from '37 up to '57. Then it was a lot different. They had the union there and we worked just seven hours and fifteen minutes. We didn't work as hard as when the Depression was on. And they wouldn't let us stay no overtime, 'cause they didn't want to pay the overtime. I guess. We made some good money, me and my dad, both. He worked up to '41 and they cut him out. Age. He never did get a pension. He never worked long enough in the union to get a pension.

I took part in four strikes. They fined us one time for takin' a strike. A wildcat, that's what they called it. I helped organize about six mines. Now the company didn't like this, and they was kickin' on us all at the same time. They'd do anything, they'd kill and everything else. One place in West Virginia, they was shootin' us all to pieces. They had guns of all kinds there.

They had three hundred state troopers there. They was on the labor's side, and they took a lot of smoke bombs out of the men's pockets, the scabs. They said: "If you fellows wants to sign up or not wants to sign up . . . but go to carryin' no guns. You fellas ain't paid to carry 'em and ain't paid to use 'em, we're paid to use 'em. If you want to sign 'em up, you go ahead and sign 'em up." And they signed up.

It surprised everyone that these three hundred state police come—on our side. The captain said: If they don't want to organize, shut 'em down. He walked into the bathhouse and, boy, they had guns hanging out all around, the scabs. See, the company furnished 'em guns. They had machine guns and everything. They took the state police in there to take all them guns out. I know the name of the Governor if I could think of it—he was on labor's side.[1] That was '42.

As he remembers, past and present fuse. . . . "The mines were runnin' out, except this little wagon of a mine, and it didn't have no tracks. You had to get on your knees, coal was so low. Coal was just twenty-eight inches. Panther Creek, West Virginia. We drove tunnels clear through the mountain to the other side. We'd drive up as far as we could go without air, and we'd come back and get a sniff and drive it up again as far as we could again without air. We could get breakthroughs to the other place and get air, you see.

"They cut one tunnel there was twelve miles long one way and twenty-eight miles long the other way, 'cause it was a ridge one way. They took twenty-eight inches of rock from the top, make it high enough for the men to work. I traveled about seven miles a day back and forth on my knees. They'd be knots on 'em big as your double fist. . . ."

I liked the mines till it got so I couldn't work no more. My wind was too short, and there was too much dead air and I just choked up and

[1] M. M. Neely, Governor of West Virginia, 1941–1945.

couldn't do no good. I went to work for a dollar an hour . . . on the roads. Till that run out. And I come to Chicago.

Mary Owsley

Before setting off with his family for Oklahoma in 1929, to follow the oil boom, her husband was a dynamite man in Kentucky mines.

ONE DAY HE NOTICED on the side of the boiler a place as big as a saucer. They call it a breather—it's a weak place on the boiler. He told the boss that had to be fixed, because he didn't want to get killed. Monday morning, I saw him comin' back home. They hadn't fixed it, hadn't done a thing about it. He told 'em in less than three weeks there'll be an explosion. Sure enough, there was. Killed three men and two mine mules from that very thing. He left.

We lived in a company house. We had to buy every bucket of water we used, 'cause the company undermined things so bad, they ruined all the water wells. I bought my food from the company store, and we bought our furniture from the company store, and we paid three prices on it. I've seen my husband have to borry from his next pay check—what they call scrip—to buy just medicine and things like that. And we didn't live extravagant either. We paid over 260 some odd dollars for furniture from the coal company. We paid it all back but $20. And when he went and got another job, he bought a truck down there for the furniture. And they took the whole thing away from us. They wouldn't let us pay the $20.

Because he was a troublemaker . . . ?

No, because he quit that job there where the breather was on that boiler. That's the kind of troublemaker he was, you're mighty right he was. He wanted to live.

We lived in this coal mine camp, this next one, and there was a pump out in the middle between four houses. The four families of us shared that one pump. In the wintertime, that thing would get covered up with ice a foot thick. Us women had to keep a tub of water on our coal stove hot. The men would have to get up at three in the morning to get out there and melt the ice off the pump before they went to work. Just for the simple want of a shed built over a water pump. It might deflate the company's bank account.

Aaron Barkham

"I'm too young to retire and too old to work in the coal mines. When a man gets to be up around thirty-five, forty years old, been in a mine ten or twelve years, they want somebody younger. When they get the chance, they'll replace him."

He is from West Virginia. His father, a miner all his life, died in a coal camp. "Silicosis wasn't even heard of. He died of hardened arteries.[2] Dad belonged to the Oddfellows, and they paid Mother about $11 a month. We had a cow and a hog. When things got tight, we let loose of that. We had a hardscrabble farm, worn-out ground, not worth much. From the time I was four years old, that's all I knowed, hard times."

PEOPLE WORKED fifteen hours a day, loaded a four-ton car, they got a dollar out of it. If the company could, it'd take that. (Laughs.) I think they made about $2 a day, most of 'em. We had boarders from the coal camp, others weren't that lucky. My oldest brother, he was fifteen, he went to work as a breaker boy at the tipple.

Years before, he and my other brother, who was twelve, got the idea of sellin' moonshine. We'd pay a dollar a gallon and sell it for twenty-five cents a pint. So that worked all right. We sold sometimes three gallons a day. During Prohibition, and after, people that got the relief checks was the ones that bought the whiskey. We'd get it in half-gallon jars and put it in pint bottles.

That's where a playful little boy comes in. A little boy—I was about six, seven—could get aholt of somethin' and carry it right along the road where a man could get arrested. 1931 was when that started and come to about 1936. That was 'bout the only family income. The only obstacle I

2 "Several hundred autopsies have confirmed that many miners die of heart failure when coal dust clamps the small arteries in their lungs in a stiff unyielding cast which eventually puts a critical load on their hearts." Robert G. Sherrill, *The Nation*, April 28, 1969, p. 533.

had, I had with my own second cousin. He was a deputy sheriff. He was big and fat, and I could get around him. He chased me miles through the thickets.

Nine revenuers were split up into three bunches. Work in the woods, lookin' for stills. They'd put down a marker. It was my job to switch the markers. And they'd get all confused. Everybody bootlegged. It kind of got to be a legitimate business. You had to be foxier than the foxes, that's all.

That second cousin, he was on the political side of the fence. So when WPA come in, we didn't get any relief from the local politicians. My mother was a Republican. I think it was her pride that wouldn't change our politics. Not much use complainin' about somethin' like that. We had enough to eat from the bootleg. About four out of five was unemployed in the county till 'bout 1938.

I never did get a whole year of school—maybe five or six months. I started workin' when I was thirteen. In a sawmill at ten cents an hour. I worked for the guy that had all the timber monopoly for the company. I worked for the bulldozers. I finally got twenty-five cents an hour, but he raised the board to seventy-five cents a day. Get up at four o'clock in the mornin', we clumb on a big truck and was hauled about fifteen miles. We started about a quarter to five and worked till we couldn't see. Then we'd quit. It was nearer sixteen hours than it was eight hours. I know we'd get into bed and turn over one time, and they'd be yellin' for breakfast.

It got bad in '29. The Crash caught us with one $20 gold piece. All mines shut down—stores, everything. One day they was workin', the next day the mines shut down. Three or four months later, they opened up. Run two, three days a week, mostly one. They didn't have the privilege of calling their souls their own. Most people by that time was in debt so far to the company itself, they couldn't live.

Some of them been in debt from '29 till today, and never got out. Some of them didn't even try. It seem like whenever they went back to work, they owed so much. The company got their foot on 'em even now.

When the Crash come, they got about ten cents an hour—that is, if they begged the supervisor for a job. They had to load a seven-ton car for fifty cents. If they found three pieces of slate as big as your hand, they took that car, and you didn't get paid. That's what they called the dock. A man couldn't predict what's gonna fall on that car, goin' through maybe a couple of miles of tunnel, and everything fallin' anyhow.

One time they hauled a mule out. They fired the guy that got that mule killed. They told him a mule's worth more'n a man. They had to pay $50 for a mule, but a man could be got for nothin'. He never had worked another day since. Blackballed for costin' 'em that money.

I remember one time, the Red Cross shipped in about four ton of flour in twenty-four pound bags. Unloaded it in the company warehouse. It was a Red Cross gift. But the company said they have to work a day to get a sack of flour. That started it. Pretty much like walkin' the inferno.

An old woman, about sixty years, she come down from Canyon Creek. One time she was makin' a speech near a railroad track. She was standin' on a box. The strikebreakers shot her off with a shotgun. So she come down to Logan County where we was and made speeches and helped get them organized. But they had a time.

The county sheriff had a hundred strikebreakers. They were called deputies. The company paid him ten cents a ton on all the coal carried down the river, to keep the union out. He was beaten in the election by T. Hatfield of the feudin' Hatfields. He was for the union. They had pretty much a full-scale war out there for about three years.

They brought the army in. The county was under martial law, stayed till about '31. What strikes me is the soldiers along the company road, dispersin' people. When people'd gather together, they couldn't talk. Two guys could, but three couldn't.

About that time, a bunch of strikebreakers come in with shotguns and axe handles. Tried to break up union meetings. The UMW deteriorated and went back to almost no existence. It didn't particularly get full strength till about 1949. And it don't much today in West Virginia. So most people ganged up and formed the Ku Kluck Klan.

The Ku Klux was the real controllin' factor in the community. They was the law. It was in power to about 1932. My dad and my older brother belonged to it. My dad was one of the leaders till he died. The company called in the army to get the Ku Klux out, but it didn't work. The union and the Ku Klux was about the same thing.

The superintendent of the mine got the big idea of makin' it rougher than it was. They hauled him off in a meat wagon, and about ten more of the company officials. Had the mine shut down. They didn't kill 'em, but they didn't come back. They whipped one of the foremen and got him out of the county. They gave him twelve hours to get out, get his family out.

The UMW had a field representative, he was a lawyer. They tarred and feathered 'im for tryin' to edge in with the company. He come around, got mad, tryin' to tell us we were wrong, when we called a wildcat. He was takin' the side of the company. I used the stick to help tar 'im. And it wasn't the first time.

The Ku Klux was formed on behalf of people that wanted a decent living, both black and white. Half the coal camp was colored. It wasn't anti-colored. The black people had the same responsibilities as the white. Their lawn was just as green as the white man's. They got the same rate of pay. There was two colored who belonged to it. I remember those two niggers comin' around my father and askin' questions about it. They joined. The pastor of our community church was a colored man. He was Ku Klux. It was the only protection the workin' man had.

Sure, the company tried to play the one agin' the other. But it didn't work. The colored and the whites lived side by side. It was somethin' like a checkerboard. There'd be a white family and a colored family. No sir, there was no racial problem. Yeah, they had a certain feelin' about the colored. They sure did. They had a certain feelin' about the white, too. Anyone come into the community had unsatisfactory dealin's, if it was colored or white, he didn't stay.

I remember one family moved in from acrost us. They had a bunch of women. I remember where I saw out the window, it didn't look right. The Ku Klux warned 'em once. Gave 'em twenty-four hours. They didn't take the warning. The next night they whipped Hughie (that was the man), his wife and his niece, his uncle and his aunt, and whipped six more that was acrowdin' around. They whipped 'em with switches and run 'em out, all of 'em. They was white; they wasn't niggers.

One time a Negro slapped a white boy. They didn't give him no warning. They whipped 'im and run 'im out of town. If a white man'd slapped a colored kid, they'd a done the same thing. They didn't go in for beatin' up niggers because they was niggers. What they done was kept the community decent to live in. What they did object to was obscenity and drinkin'.

What about bootlegging?

Oh, they objected to raisin' a fuss in town. What you do private, that's your business. You're talkin' about mountain people now. This ain't the Deep South.

People'd get their temper rubbed off quick. In organizin' the union, we didn't go through the Labor Relations Board. We went through what we called "mule train." We'd figure how many people were workin' at that certain mine, and we'd just tell 'em to organize it or we'd close 'em. We'd give 'em three days. Sometimes they'd stand at the mouth of the mine with a club. There was seventeen thousand in the whole district. I have knowd every one of them to come out on account of one man bein' called out. And join the UMW.

At a UMW meeting, they'd iron it out themselves. I had to pull out a .38 once to get out of a union meetin'. Our chairman of the local was thick with the superintendent of the mine, and I made mention of it in the meeting. Some guys didn't like it: they followed him close. We was in a school building. I was up next to the blackboard, and the door was on the other end of the room. So they blocked the door. My wife's half-brother was sittin' about half way back. So he pulled out his gun and throwd it to me. I told 'em I'm goin' out and anybody stops me, I'm gonna shoot. They followed me outside, there was about fifty. They blocked the gate. So I told 'em I'm gonna shoot the first six gets in my way.

The next day I went back to work. I took my gun with me. They cooled off. It took 'em a week, they cooled off.

In my life, I've found people won't take anything. If things get real bad again, I'm afraid there'd be some millionaires made paupers because they'd take their money. They'd take it the rough way. The people are gonna take care of their families, if they'd have to shoot somebody else. And you can't blame 'em for that. You think I wouldn't take what you got if you had a million dollars and I had to protect my family? I sure would. I'd take your money one way or the other. Some people don't have courage enough to fight for what they have comin'. Until 1934, more than half the people of Logan County were scabbin'. Gives you an idea how they don't know. . . .

Explosions? Had one back in '35, killed a few men. They had one in Bartley, killed 136 men. In Macbeth the same year—when was that?—a fire and explosion killed eighteen and twenty men. Then in 1947, they had an explosion that killed a couple of men.

They sent me for a job in Virginia. Shaft was fifteen hundred feet deep. I went down and looked it over and went up and didn't go. Gas and dust. That was 1965. Supposed to have been the most safest mine in the world. They had an explosion about four months after that. Killed two men, injured nine more. . . .

POSTSCRIPT: *Suddenly, a light laugh: "I remember the first radio come to Mingo County, next to Logan. Wayne Starbuck, a cousin to me, brought that in in 1934. That was a boon. It was a little job, got more squeals and squeaks than anything else. Everybody came from miles around to look at it. We didn't have any electricity. So he hooked up two car batteries. We got 'Grand Old Opry' on it."*

Edward Santander

A director of adult education at a small Midwestern college. "I never had the slightest intention of being anything other than a schoolteacher. My whole life is bound up in this. The Depression played a role: if I could just add my two cents worth to making life better. . . ."

MY FIRST REAL MEMORIES come about '31. It was simply a gut issue then: eating or not eating, living or not living. My father was a coal miner, outside a small town in Illinois. My dad, my grandfather and my uncle worked in this same mine. He had taken a cut in wages, but we were still doing pretty well. We were sitting in a '27 Hudson, when I saw a line of men waiting near the I.C. tracks. I asked him what was the trouble. They were waiting to get something to eat.

When the mine temporarily closed down in the early Thirties, my dad had to hunt work elsewhere. He went around the state, he'd paint barns, anything.

I went to an old, country-style schoolhouse, a red-stripe. One building that had eight rows in it, one for each grade. Seven rows were quiet, while the eighth row recited. The woman teacher got the munificent sum of $30 a month. She played the organ, an old pump organ with pedals, she taught every subject, and all eight grades. This was 1929, '30, '31. . . . At the back corner was a great pot-bellied stove that kept the place warm. It has about an acre of ground, a playground with no equipment.

Out there were the toilets, three-holers, and in the winter—You remember Chic Sale?[3] You had moons, crescents or stars on the doors. You'd be surprised at the number of people in rural areas that didn't have much in this way, as late as the Thirties.

One of the greatest contributions of the WPA was the standardized outdoor toilet, with modern plumbing. (Laughs.) They built thousands of them around here. You can still see some of 'em standing. PWA built new schools and the City Hall in this town. I remember NYA. I learned a good deal of carpentry in this.

Roosevelt was idolized in that area. The county had been solidly Republican from the Civil War on. And then was Democratic till the end of Truman's time. F.D.R. was held in awe by most people, but occasionally you'd run across someone who said: "Well, he has syphilis, and it's gone to his brain." The newspaper in the area hated Roosevelt, just hated him. (Laughs.)

Almost everybody was in the same boat, pretty poorly off. I remember kids who didn't have socks. We all wore long-handles—you could get 'em red, you could get 'em white. These boys would cut the bottoms off their long-handles and stuff 'em into the top of their shoes and make it look like they had socks.

We had epidemics of typhoid and diphtheria. Houses would be placarded with signs. This one girl who came to school had had typhoid and had lost all her hair. There was absolutely no way they could purchase a wig for her. This was the shame of it. The girl had to go around baldheaded for as long as I knew her. It wasn't the physical thing because we all got used to that. But what did it do to her inside? Along about '34 and '35, the state began giving diphtheria and typhoid shots and all this sort of thing.

His grandfather was the patriarch of the family; a huge man, born in a log cabin; took home correspondence courses and became a hoisting engineer in the mines. He was a Socialist, a strong supporter of Debs and was elected a three-term mayor of Central City, near Centralia. "In those days, women had just received the right to vote. Many of them were hesitant. He urged them to vote, no matter what ticket, as long as they went to the polls."

[3] A "rube" vaudevillian, best known for "The Specialist," a routine based on outhouse humor.

There were any number of Socialists in this area. Today people don't think and discuss as much as they did in those days. I remember men with thick calluses on their hands from handling shovels. They would be discussing Daniel De Leon and Debs and Christian Socialism and Syndicalism and Anarchism. A lot of them came out of the IWW into the miners' movement. Many were first generation, Polish, Italian, Croatian. . . . They changed the spelling of their names as they've gone along. The ones who couldn't read, someone would read it to them. There were thousands of presses that would run off little booklets, like the group in Girard, Kansas.[4] My grandfather, father and uncle were self-educated men. There were less distractions then.

Was drinking a problem when the Depression hit?

I remember driving through one town that had less than a thousand people in it. There were ten taverns. But they always did put it away rather heavily. They were a hard-drinking society under any standards. Many of them made their home brew. One old fellow I remember would drink his own during the week. On Saturday, he would become royalty and go to town and drink what they called factory-made. (Laughs.)

My grandmother was a very saving woman. The women in our family took care of the money. When the Depression really hit us in 1936, when the mine closed down completely, there was no income. We tried opening a filling station and went absolutely broke on that. The only livelihood these men had was mining coal. Where would you go? Down in Harlan County, Kentucky? They were out of work, too. West Frankfort? Carterville? They had the same problems.

Natural gas was being used, and cities began having ordinances against dirty coal in those days. This mine was simply not making a profit. The family that owned it, pretty decent people, decided to sell. The miners, bullheadedly—who could read the handwriting on the wall, anyway?—decided they would buy the mine themselves. This was '36, '37. So they sold shares of stock. They collected $33,000. The owner's widow accepted it rather than a $38,000 bid from a St. Louis scrap dealer, who was going to close it up.

For eighteen months, these men worked for nothing to get the mine back in shape to show a profit. It started with four hundred men. The

---

[4] E. Haldemann-Julius blue books. They were sold for a nickel or a dime: philosophical, political, scientific and literary classics.

mine operated until the Fifties. By that time, only eighteen men were left. . . .

Some people go into strip mining. Fifteen or twenty of them get together and get the mining rights from someone. Then they put a ladder and a shaft in and strip down the area. There are very few pit mines left in this state.

This area was not ready to convert to any other type of work. The people who had the money were absentee owners. There was plenty going out but nothing coming in. When the mines decided it wasn't profitable to operate, they closed down. That took away whatever income this area had.

In the Thirties, UMW came along. The union was the only salvation the people had. It grew violent at times, quite violent. If mines did open with scabs, it wasn't long before someone was done away with.

Do you recall any mine disasters?

I can take you to a cemetery where there is only one mausoleum. Everybody else is buried underground. In this mausoleum is a miner who died in an accident at Junction City. He oft expressed himself that he had spent so many years below ground that when he died, he wanted to spend the rest of it above. This was always on their minds: an accident.

He remembers the Centralia disaster of '47. "When number Five blew up." 111 men were killed. He remembers '51, West Frankfort: 119 were killed. "Illinois had always been notoriously lax in its rules regarding the safety of the mines. Even the old-fashioned method of using birds to check the gas—not too many of them did this."

His uncle was killed in the Centralia disaster. He recalls: "All the mines had wash houses. After a miner got done washing up, he'd go home and sit in a galvanized tub and just soak. Because he'd have this coal dust under his fingernails and ground into his skin. In the morning, they hang their clothes up on a hook in the wash house. They'd pull a chain and the clothes would go up to the ceiling. . . .

"In this '47 thing, we'd all be sitting in the wash house. It was damp and cold. Someone would unwind the chain, and he'd let these clothes down. And the most profound silence. No weeping or anything like that. You've seen these pictures of women in their babushkas, waiting

patiently, hoping. . . . In this '47 thing, all were killed. When the rescue team got to one group, they were still warm.

"In Centralia, they turned about everything into a mortuary. In the funeral home where my uncle was . . . my cousin said, 'I've got to see him.' The man lifted up the sheet. It wasn't even human. 'Is this your father?' He said, 'No.' He lifted up another one—and my cousin said to me, 'I've had enough.' My father went and identified him by his wedding ring. There was only one open coffin in the whole place: the mailman, who had died a natural death."

People in the Thirties did feel a bit different. When the pig-killing was going on, the farmers would kill the pigs well enough, but they'd tell the people where they buried them, and they'd go dig 'em up and take 'em home. The farmers couldn't sell the pigs anyway, so they weren't out anything.

It isn't true that people who have very little won't share. When everybody is in the same position, they haven't anything to hide from one another. So they share. But when prosperity comes around, you hear: Look at that son of a bitch. When he didn't have anything, he was all right. Look at him now.

The Depression was such a shock to some people that when World War II was over—you'd hear men in the army say it: "When I get back, I'm going to get a good job, a house and a car, some money in the bank, and I'm never going to worry again. These people have passed this on to their kids." In many cases, youngsters rebel against this.

I never heard anyone who expressed feeling that the United States Government, as it existed, was done for. It was quite the opposite. The desire to restore the country to the affluence it had. This was uppermost in people's minds. Even the Socialists who talked about taking the corporate system out were just talking, that's all.

If we had a severe depression today—I'm basically an optimist—I don't think this country would survive. Many people today are rootless. When you have this rootlessness, we're talking about the Germany of the Twenties. You'd see overt dictatorship take over. You would see your camps. . . .

POSTSCRIPT: *"We used to talk a great deal about keeping solvent and the morality of not going into debt. I was almost thirty years old before I went into debt."*

Roger

He is fourteen. He was brought to Chicago from West Virginia eight years ago. His mother is dead. His father, whom he sees once in a while, is somewhere in the Appalachian community. Though he stays with his sister-in-law, his life is on the streets of the city. He's pretty much on his own.

If I say the word—"Depression"—what does that mean?

I WOULDN'T KNOW, 'cause I never heard the word before.

What do you think it means?

I figure maybe you're all tensed up or somethin'. That's the only thing I could think of "depression" meanin'.

Ever hear of the time when millions of people weren't working, in the 1930s—long before you were born . . .?

I heard about it. They didn't have no food and money. Couldn't keep their children fed and in clothes. People say, like a long time ago it was, coal miners worked real hard for a couple of dollars, and you couldn't hardly get a job. Especially in my home town and places like that.

Well, we still had it hard when we come up here. I was six. My father and my mother, they told me about how hard it was to get a job up here. That's why I tried to get him to go back to West Virginia, after I was up here a while. See, I never knowd hard times when we was down there. So I said to Dad, "Let's go back to West Virginia." He says, "There's no jobs for us down there, we can't make a living. We have to stay here." He said: "Some days, sometimes maybe if it get easy to get jobs down there, maybe we go down there."

It's so damn hard. Seems like everybody's takin' advantage of you. See, I never heard that word "depression" before. They would all just say "hard times" to me. It is still. People around this neighborhood still has hard times. Like you see, the buildins are all tore up and not a decent place to live. My house isn't fit to live in. These buildins ain't no good. If we tear 'em down, they ain't gonna build new ones for us. So we have to live in 'em.

We could move out in the suburbs for a hundred, maybe fifty, dollars a week, if we could pay that much rent. They should have just as clean buildins for $25 a week. For what we're payin' now, we should have clean homes and such. Not this. It's hard livin'. Hard times.

The Farmer Is the Man

Oh, the farmer is the man, the farmer is the man
Lives on credit till the fall.
With the interest rate so high
It's a wonder he don't die
For the mortgage man's the one
That gets it all.

—Populist song, 1896

Harry Terrell

His Quaker forebears moved westward early in the Nineteenth Century. A South Carolina ancestor was hanged by the British, following the Battle of Cowpens; he would not betray the guerrillas. . . . "But he wasn't quite dead. His wife revived him, and he lived to a ripe old age to tell the tale."

It is a rainy Saturday in Des Moines. As he recalls the late Twenties and early Thirties—in this plastic-oriented room of a large motel chain—he feels alien, though he has lived in this region all his life, seventy-seven years.

239

He had worked as a YMCA Secretary, but "I had naturally been a farmer, 'cause I never went off the farm until I went to college when I was twenty-two years old."

320 ACRES of farm land, fine land, that my uncle owned and cleared, he lost it. 'Cause they foreclosed the mortgage. Some of the best in the state, and he couldn't borrow a dime.

The farmers didn't have anything they could borrow on. He came down here to see me, because he knew that a fellow that had a job could get credit. He wanted to borrow $850. I knew my banker would give it to me. So I told him I'd get it.

He said, "Harry, I want to give you a mortgage to support this loan." I said I'd never take a mortgage from my mother's brother. But here's what he put up: a John Deere combine and tractor, about sixteen head of cattle, a team of mules and wagons and farm implements. For $850. So you can see how far this had gone. He couldn't get a loan, a man who lived in this state from the time he was two years old.

I was born across the road from the farm of Herbert Hoover's uncle. I knew the Hoover family, distant cousins of the President. My folks sold hogs for 'em, thoroughbred, pure Chester White hogs at two cents a pound. Even people like them, they had times just like the rest of us. That's the way it was going. Corn was going for eight cents a bushel. One county insisted on burning corn to heat the courthouse, 'cause it was cheaper than coal.

This was at the time that mortgaging of farms was getting home to us. So they was having ten cent sales. They'd put up a farmer's property and have a sale and all the neighbors'd come in, and they got the idea of spending twenty-five cents for a horse. They was paying ten cents for a plow. And when it was all over, they'd all give it back to him. It was legal and anybody that bid against that thing, that was trying to get that man's land, they would be dealt with seriously, as it were.

That infuriated all the people that wanted to carry on business as usual. It might be a bank or an implement dealer or a private elevator or something like that. They had their investments in this. The implement dealer, he was on the line, too. The only place he had of getting it was from the fellow who owed him. And they'd have a sheriff's sale.

The people were desperate. They came very near hanging that judge. Because they caught this judge foreclosing farm mortgages, and they

had no other way of stopping it. He had issued the whole bunch of foreclosures on his docket.

It all happened in Le Mars. They took the judge out of his court and
took him to the fairgrounds and they had a rope around his neck, and
they had the rope over the limb of a tree. They were gonna string him
up in the old horse thief fashion. But somebody had sense enough to
stop the thing before it got too far.

They had marches, just like we have the marches nowadays. They
came from all over the state. That was the time of the Farm Holiday.
There was a picket line. The Farm Holiday movement was to hold the
stuff off the market, to increase the price. It saw its violence, too.

They stopped milk wagons, dumped milk. They stopped farmers haul-
ing their hay to market. They undertook to stop the whole agriculture
process. They thought if they could block the highways and access to the
packing plants, they couldn't buy these hogs at two cents a pound.

They'd say: we're gonna meet, just east of Cherokee, at the fork of
the road, and so on. Now they spread it around the country that they
were gonna stop everything from going through. And believe me, they
stopped it. They had whatever was necessary to stop them with. Some
of 'em had pitchforks. (Laughs.) You can fix the auto tire good with a
pitchfork. There were blockades.

The country was getting up in arms about taking a man's property
away from him. It was his livelihood. When you took a man's horses
and his plow away, you denied him food, you just convicted his family
to starvation. It was just that real.

I remember one man, as devout a man as I ever met, a Catholic. He
was mixed up in it, too—the violence. His priest tried to cool him down.
He says, "My God, Father, we're desperate. We don't know what to do."
He was the most old, established man you could find. He was in the
state legislature.

I remember in court when they were going to indict a Norwegian
Quaker, when they were offering them lighter sentences if they'd plead
guilty, his wife said, "Simon, thee must go to jail."

Did they ever talk about changing the society . . . ?

No, the nearer to the ground you get, the nearer you are to conservative. His land is his life. And he's not for anything that might alter the
situation. I never found anything in the Iowa farmer to indicate he would
accept any form of government but his own. If my family, grandfather,

great-grandfather, ever heard my political beliefs, why, they'd turn over in their graves. I don't think that without the Depression this farm country would be anything but McKinley Republican.

You know, Hitler's men were awfully interested that I'd been through a farm strike in northern Iowa. I was in Germany, with my wife, as a tourist in 1937. I had been to Geneva for a disarmament conference. I met Hitler's agricultural attaché in Berlin. They were just putting controls on their farmers. He wanted to know how this violence was handled. He kept getting madder and madder. I said: "What do you do with these people?" He said: "They've got to come to terms with the government or we'll just wipe them out."

The New Deal came along . . .

The progress was very slow, though. Of course, Henry Wallace and his ever-normal granary was the man who saved the farmer. The farmer would have passed clear out of the picture. They took this corn and paid for it and stored it. They put a price on it that was above the miserable going price. It wasn't allowed for no eight cents a bushel.

The farmers broke the laws, as a last resort. There was nothing else for them to do. To see these neighbors wiped out completely, and they would just drift into towns and they would have to be fed.

Oh, these towns are pathetic. Today, I mean. You'll pass through towns and if you get off the highway a little ways, and went down the main street, it's one vacant building after another. Little ghost towns with an elevator and a service station.

It's an abject depression now for the small farmer. My brother-in-law still has the farm that his father took when he came out here as a young man. The reason he can stay in business is that he turns everything he got on that farm into cattle feed and turns it into beef. Beef prices are decent because beef is used by factory workers. But the grain farmer, the farmer who gets cash out of his crop, he's feelin' the pinch of poverty.

Many of the farm families can't get any of their family to farm it. The children are goin' to the cities. The farm is just going on the block and is added to some other big land holding in the community. The individual farmer is becoming a thing of the past. Larger and larger holdings, fewer and fewer people. Even a fellow farming eight hundred acres now, which he doesn't own, is right up against the buzz saw.

The war economy is not helping the farmer . . . ?

No, it isn't. Not the small farmer. He's getting the worst of it all the time. You never see a war help the farmer, except temporarily. Much as I hate to say it, the Second World War *did* end the Great Depression. I think we solve our problems by killing our boys and others.

But I can see a Depression ahead right now. If we go to pot, it would make that one look like a Sunday school picnic. A Depression today would cut deep, quick. Today, in the machine age, like everything—it would be sudden.

In the Thirties, my sister's family lived on their own production. They had gardens, they had eggs, they had flocks of chickens. Now the eggs are all produced in these large establishments. Machines turn out thousands of dozens. Then, they had their own and were more self-sufficient. Today, the milk is supplied by the same company that supplies this dining room here. They didn't have money to buy new clothes or cars or machinery. But they had enough to keep body and soul together. Today, the money would be gone. They wouldn't have the food. . . .

People today have been taught violence, the denial of humanity under money pressure. People are going in that direction. I don't think they'd tolerate those conditions that we came through. The younger people wouldn't take it, because they know it isn't necessary. But you can't have a lot of people in Congress that you got today.

Oscar Heline

For all his seventy-eight years, he has lived on this Iowa farm, which his father had cultivated almost a century ago. It is in the northwestern part of the state, near the South Dakota border. Marcus has a population of 1,263.

On this drizzly October Sunday afternoon, the main street is deserted. Not a window is open, nor a sound heard. Suddenly, rock music shatters the silence. From what appeared to be a years-long vacant store, two girls and a boy emerge. They are about thirteen, fourteen.

I ask directions. They are friendly, though somewhat bewildered. "An old man?" They are eager to help. One points north; another, south; the third, west. Each is certain "an old man" lives somewhere in the vicinity.

Along the gravel road, with a stop at each of three farmhouses; no sign, no knowledge of "an old man," nor awareness of his name. At each is a tree bearing the identical sticker: "Beware The Dog." One trots forth, pauses warily and eyes the stranger in the manner of Bull Connor and a black militant. The young farmers are friendly enough, but innocent of Oscar Heline's existence.

At the fourth farm, an elderly woman, taken away from the telecast of the Tigers–Cardinals World Series game, knows. . . . Several gravel roads back I find him.

THE STRUGGLES people had to go through are almost unbelievable. A man lived all his life on a given farm, it was taken away from him. One after the other. After the foreclosure, they got a deficiency judgment. Not only did he lose the farm, but it was impossible for him to get out of debt.

He recounts the first farm depression of the Twenties: "We give the land back to the mortgage holder and then we're sued for the remainder —the deficiency judgment—which we have to pay." After the land boom of the early Twenties, the values declined constantly, until the last years of the decade. "In '28, '29, when it looked like we could see a little blue sky again, we're just getting caught up with the back interest, the Thirties Depression hit. . . ."

The farmers became desperate. It got so a neighbor wouldn't buy from a neighbor, because the farmer didn't get any of it. It went to the creditors. And it wasn't enough to satisfy them. What's the use of having a farm sale? Why do we permit them to go on? It doesn't cover the debts, it doesn't liquidate the obligation. He's out of business, and it's still hung over him. First, they'd take your farm, then they took your livestock, then your farm machinery. Even your household goods. And they'd move you off. The farmers were almost united. We had penny auction sales. Some neighbor would bid a penny and give it back to the owner.

Grain was being burned. It was cheaper than coal. Corn was being burned. A county just east of here, they burned corn in their courthouse all winter. '32, '33. You couldn't hardly buy groceries for corn. It couldn't pay the transportation. In South Dakota, the county elevator listed corn as minus three cents. *Minus* three cents a bushel. If you wanted to sell 'em a bushel of corn, you had to bring in three cents. They couldn't afford to handle it. Just think what happens when you can't get out from under. . . .

We had lots of trouble on the highway. People were determined to withhold produce from the market—livestock, cream, butter, eggs, what not. If they would dump the produce, they would force the market to a higher level. The farmers would man the highways, and cream cans were emptied in ditches and eggs dumped out. They burned the trestle bridge, so the trains wouldn't be able to haul grain. Conservatives don't like this kind of rebel attitude and aren't very sympathetic. But something had to be done.

I spent most of my time in Des Moines as a lobbyist for the state cooperatives. Trying to get some legislation. I wasn't out on the highway fighting this battle. Some of the farmers probably didn't think I was friendly to their cause. They were so desperate. If you weren't out there with them, you weren't a friend, you must be a foe. I didn't know from day to day whether somebody might come along and cause harm to my family. When you have bridges burned, accidents, violence, there may have been killings, I don't know.

There were some pretty conservative ones, wouldn't join this group. I didn't want to particularly, because it wasn't the answer. It took that kind of action, but what I mean is it took more than that to solve it. You had to do constructive things at the same time. But I never spoke harshly about those who were on the highway.

Some of the farmers with teams of horses, sometimes in trucks, tried to get through. He was trying to feed his family, trying to trade a few dozen eggs and a few pounds of cream for some groceries to feed his babies. He was desperate, too. One group tried to sell so they could live and the other group tried to keep you from selling so they could live.

The farmer is a pretty independent individual. He wants to be a conservative individual. He wants to be an honorable individual. He wants to pay his debts. But it was hard. The rank-and-file people of this state—who were brought up as conservatives, which most of us were—would never act like this. Except in desperation.

There were a few who had a little more credit than the others. They were willing to go on as usual. They were mostly the ones who tried to break the picket lines. They were the ones who gained at the expense of the poor. They had the money to buy when things were cheap. There are always a few who make money out of other people's poverty. This was a struggle between the haves and the have-nots.

The original bankers who came to this state, for instance. When my father would borrow $100, he'd get $80. And when it was due, he'd pay back the $100 and a premium besides that. Most of his early borrowings were on this basis. That's where we made some wealthy families in this country.

We did pass some legislation. The first thing we did was stop the power of the judges to issue deficiency judgments. The theory was: the property would come back to you someday.

The next law we passed provided for committees in every county: adjudication committees. They'd get the person's debts all together and sit down with his creditors. They gave people a chance. People got time. The land banks and insurance companies started out hard-boiled. They got the farm, they got the judgment and then found out it didn't do them any good. They had to have somebody to run it. So they'd turn around and rent it to the fella who lost it. He wasn't a good renter. The poor fella lost all his capacity for fairness, because he couldn't be fair. He had to live. All the renters would go in cahoots. So the banks and companies got smart and stopped foreclosing.

Through a federal program we got a farm loan. A committee of twenty-five of us drafted the first farm legislation of this kind thirty-five years ago. We drew it up with Henry Wallace. New money was put in the farmers' hands. The Federal Government changed the whole marketing program from burning 10-cent corn to 45-cent corn. People could now see daylight and hope. It was a whole transformation of attitude. You can just imagine . . . (He weeps.)

It was Wallace who saved us, put us back on our feet. He understood our problems. When we went to visit him, after he was appointed Secretary, he made it clear to us he didn't want to write the law. He wanted the farmers themselves to write it. "I will work with you," he said, "but you're the people who are suffering. It must be your program." He would always give his counsel, but he never directed us. The program came from the farmers themselves, you betcha.

Another thing happened: we had twice too many hogs because corn'd been so cheap. And we set up what people called Wallace's Folly: killing the little pigs. Another farmer and I helped develop this. We couldn't afford to feed 45-cents corn to a $3 hog. So we had to figure a way of getting rid of the surplus pigs. We went out and bought 'em and killed 'em. This is how desperate it was. It was the only way to raise the price of pigs. Most of 'em were dumped down the river.

The hard times put farmers' families closer together. My wife was working for the county Farm Bureau. We had lessons in home economics, how to make underwear out of gunny sacks, out of flour sacks. It was cooperative labor. So some good things came out of this. Sympathy toward one another was manifest. There were personal values as well as terrible hardships.

Mrs. Heline interjects: "They even took seat covers out of automobiles and re-used them for clothing or old chairs. We taught them how to make mattresses from surplus cotton. We had our freedom gardens and did much canning. We canned our own meat or cured it in some way. There was work to do and busy people are happy people."

The real boost came when we got into the Second World War. Everybody was paying on old debts and mortgages, but the land values were going down. In the fall of '38, we bought a half section at $125 an acre. In '39 it was down to $65. It's gone up now more than ever in the history of the country. The war. . . . (A long pause.)

It does something to your country. It's what's making employment. It does something to the individual. I had a neighbor just as the war was beginning. We had a boy ready to go to service. This neighbor one day told me what we needed was a damn good war, and we'd solve our agricultural problems. And I said, "Yes, but I'd hate to pay with the price of my son." Which we did. (He weeps.) It's too much of a price to pay. . . .

In '28 I was chairman of the farm delegation which met with Hoover. My family had always been Republican, and I supported him. To my disappointment. I don't think the Depression was all his fault. He tried. But all his plans failed, because he didn't have the Government involved. He depended on individual organizations.

247

It's a strange thing. This is only thirty-five years ago—Roosevelt, Wallace. We have a new generation in business today. Successful. It's surprising how quickly they forget the assistance their fathers got from the Government. The Farm Bureau, which I helped organize in this state, didn't help us in '35. They take the same position today: we don't need the Government. I'm just as sure as I'm sitting here, we can't do it ourselves. Individuals have too many different interests. Who baled out the land banks when they were busted in the Thirties? It was the Federal Government.

What I remember most of those times is that poverty creates desperation, and desperation creates violence. In Plymouth County—Le Mars—just west of us, a group met one morning and decided they were going to stop the judge from issuing any more deficiency judgments. This judge had a habit of very quickly O.K.'ing foreclosure sales. These farmers couldn't stand it any more. They'd see their neighbors sold out.

There were a few judges who would refuse to take the cases. They'd postpone it or turn it over to somebody else. But this one was pretty gruff and arrogant: "You do this, you do that, it's my court." When a bunch of farmers are going broke every day and the judge sits there very proudly and says: "This is my court . . ."; they say: "Who the hell are you?" He was just a fellow human being, same as they were.

These farmers gathered this one particular day. I suppose some of 'em decided to have a little drink, and so they developed a little courage. They decided: we'll go down and teach that judge a lesson. They marched into the courtroom, hats on, demanded to visit with him. *He* decided he would teach *them* a lesson. So he says: "Gentlemen, this is my court. Remove your hats and address the court properly."

They just laughed at him. They said, "We're not concerned whose court this is. We came here to get redress from your actions. The things you're doing, we can't stand to have done to us any more." The argument kept on, and got rougher. He wouldn't listen. He threatened them. So they drug him from his chair, pulled him down the steps of the courthouse, and shook a rope in front of his face. Then, tarred and feathered him.

The Governor called out the National Guard. And put these farmers behind barbed wire. Just imagine . . . (he weeps) . . . in this state. You don't forget these things.

Frank and Rome Hentges

It is on the corner, the oldest house in Le Mars, Iowa. The decor is of another era. Frank is in the middle eighties; Rome is in the middle seventies. They had been clothing merchants before the Depression.

FRANK: (Laughs.) Oh, gee whiz. The Great American Depression.

ROME: The Holidays here.

FRANK: Farmer's Holidays, yeah. They marched up to the courthouse, where Judge Bradley was sitting on the bench. The farmers objected to, oh, let's say, the losing of the farm. I think they were right. They had a just cause.

ROME: That farm was probably worth seventy or eighty thousand dollars, and they'd foreclose on a $15,000 mortgage. That wasn't fair.

FRANK: That certainly wasn't.

ROME: I don't blame 'em for taking the stand they did.

FRANK: They took the judge off his seat and put a rope around his neck.

ROME: They were gonna hang him.

FRANK: Yeah, they took him out.

ROME: He was frightened.

FRANK: He was scared to death. Bradley was a very good friend of ours. We knew him very well. He later went to Des Moines.

Did they tar and feather him?

FRANK: No, not here.

ROME: There was some of that, but not around here. But they had the rope around his neck, and he was pretty well frightened.

FRANK: He was scared to death, because he couldn't do anything. All he could do was carry out the law. Whatever the law was. And I don't know. . . .

They put the rope around his neck . . . ?

FRANK: I wasn't there. I didn't see it.

ROME: They didn't hang him. But it really ruined his life. He was never

249

all right after that. I think he retired. He was not well at all. That's quite a shock for an older man.

FRANK: Oh yeah, when you're within an inch of having your life took by the mob.

ROME: This group of farmers—there were hundreds of them, I guess. And he was at their mercy. I don't know how they finally decided not to do it. Just after this judge deal, they were all arrested, and the country club was on the south edge of town. That's where they kept them, fenced in, in an enclosure there. There were hundreds of 'em.

How did the Depression affect you?

ROME: It was rough on us.

FRANK: Those that had the money lost the money.

ROME: Yeah, all those banks closed, you know.

FRANK: I guess we're about the only family left that lived here, aren't we?

ROME: We had several stores around in different towns. In Yankton and Watertown, South Dakota. And Mason City, Iowa. Carroll, Iowa. We just closed up the stores. About '33.

FRANK: We had about the best trade in the city.

You reopened after . . . ?

ROME: We never did reopen any of 'em.

What have you done since then?

ROME: Sit around. (Laughs.)

Orrin Kelly

He's been a salesman at the Plymouth Co-op in Le Mars since 1940. For the last eight years, he's been doing odd jobs at the place. He now works two hours a day.

IF THEY WAS GONNA CALL a farm sale, we would send a group there to stop the sale. There wasn't any rioting like there is now. We would just go there, and they would see maybe several hundred of us. And they would just call the sale off. There wouldn't be no demonstration. We'd just go there.

The Judge Bradley deal came on quite unexpectedly. I wasn't here at the time. I was in Des Moines the day it happened. They went up in Sioux City and stopped a farm sale up there. And the group came down to Le Mars, maybe a hundred or more farmers. They heard about this sale here. So they went up to the courthouse and tried to interview Judge Bradley. He was belligerent and defiant. And they took him out, not intending any more than just talk to him. But as things went on, they took him out in the country and threatened to lynch him, which they wouldn't have done, of course.

Of course, that brought in the militia. That was on a Thursday. Saturday morning, the militia came to Le Mars. I came home Saturday midnight. Sunday morning, the militia picked me up because I was chairman of the Council for Defense. I was in jail for lacking-two-days-of-being two weeks.

I had been to church and walked downtown. The editor of the *Globe-Post,* he came running out and said: "You'd better get out of town, Orrin. The militia's looking for you, in connection with the Judge Bradley deal." I said, "I have nothing to run for. I'm not going." He said, "I'll call a lawyer and have him defend you." So I walked up the street where the lawyer's office was. As I went up the stairs, the National Guard followed me. They said, "We're taking Kelly out of here." He tried to defend me: "You have to have a warrant. You can't pick Mr. Kelly up just like that." But they said, "We're taking him with us." So they took me down and put me in a patrol wagon and took me to a camp, the south part of town. And kept me there that afternoon.

I asked them if I could call my wife. They said, "You can't call your wife." Someone did call her. They allowed her to come in. Searched her.

That night, about six o'clock, a patrol wagon came around and took me to Sioux City. I was in the police station there till Wednesday evening. There weren't any seats in the wagon, and I had to kind of stoop down all the way to Sioux City. This was the thing that brought on this back ailment. A colored boy came into the cell. He looked at me and said, "What's the matter, boy? You're in pain. We better get you out of here." So he went out and started hollering at the top of his voice: "There's a man here dying."

251

So they put me in an ambulance and took me up to St. Vincent's Hospital. I had three men guarding me all the time. Two policemen from ten at night until seven the next morning. Then the National Guard came in. There was one man there all the time.

A funny incident took place, one of the first days I was there. There were two beds in the room. Two guards slept and one was awake all the time. This nurse said, "I want to take care of Mr. Kelly. Will you leave the room?" They said, "We can't leave the room." She said, "I don't want you here." So they had a little conference and finally went out.

The next day, my wife came down. We were expecting a baby at that time. That was 1932. When she got ready to go, she put her arms around me and cried a little bit. She had a package which was a prayer book and a rosary. As she stepped over to the door, she kind of tossed it over on the bed. I just kind of shoved it under the pillow. The three guards were talking outside.

The nurse came in and she slammed the door. Kind of pushed me all over, took the pillows out, and straightened the bed and went all over it. And went out.

One of these Guardsmen was an ex-army man. He was the only fella that talked to me. The next day he said, "Something funny happened here last night. One of the guys thought your wife had passed you a gun. The man who was supposed to come in here was afraid to. He wanted the nurse to go in. She said, 'I'll go in and find the gun.' That's why she came in."

The next afternoon, she said, "Those damn cowards out there were afraid to come in. I told 'em I'd come in. But I shut the door. If you would have had a gun on you, they would never a' found it."

On Sunday, when they first arrested you, where were you taken?

It was about a ten-acre plot. They put picket fences around there and some barbed wire on top. They set up camps and army cots. I was there before they set it up, on Sunday evening. They set it up on Monday. They interviewed the men there. It was a country club, that's been sold and it's all built up with modern homes now.

Who were the people arrested?

Any farmer that had any connection with the Farm Holiday. Just farmers. On the Sunday they picked me, two trucks came out to our farm, looked all over in the hay mound for me. They didn't know that I had been picked up downtown. One truck came out with three men and left. A couple of hours later, another one came out, went into the basement of my house. My father told them I hadn't been home since Wednesday. See, they had the names of all the members of the Association. This was all the result of the Bradley incident. I was the only one taken to Sioux City. I don't know why.

Were any of you brought to trial?

Just a hearing before this judge and a county attorney. They tried to pin it on me, said that I had written a letter about stringing somebody up. They said a friend of mine told them this. Afterwards, he told me he never said that at all.

Who do you think was behind this?

The Governor. He called out the militia. The insurance companies and the big farmers, they were behind it. And he was with them.

We had sixteen hundred members: picketing, stopping trucks, letting the livestock out. There was two Communists trying to get in with us. One of these was Mother Bloor. A very fine looking young man with her, always well-dressed. She was dressed in rags. She said this was her son-in-law. But whenever Mother Bloor would get any chance, she'd get up on some kind of box or something and try to talk to the farmers, and they would just boo her down. There was some rough stuff, sure. No injuries. No attempt at injury, like throwing things or hitting people on the head or anything like that. It's strange: we had a lot of businessmen in with us, on the picket lines. We even had a couple of produce men. We had a doctor here in Le Mars out on the picket line all the time. This doctor, one night we stopped a truck, and he just went out behind the truck, opened it up and started kicking the cattle out. It's so strange, because he was a very good doctor in town. But he was sympathetic to the farmers.

The majority were with us, but there were those farmers who were well fixed and making money off the conditions—buying up these farms and increasing their holdings.

I was at a couple of the auctions. Usually the auctioneer was sympathetic to the farmer. Only friends would bid. Somebody would bid five cents, ten cents, fifteen cents. And the auctioneer would say: Sold to so-and-so over there, ten cents an acre or something like that. And of course, that would be the end of it.

But many farmers did lose their farms. I had an uncle that owned three farms. When the Depression come along, he couldn't make it. Many would rent farms . . . the farm he once owned himself. Just one of those things. . . .

Do people living in Le Mars today know of this period . . . of the Judge Bradley incident . . . ?

Only the older people do.

Emil Loriks

On a farm in Arlington, South Dakota. He had served in the state senate from 1927 through 1934.

"In 1924, our grain elevator went broke. Farm prices collapsed. I remember signing a personal note, guaranteeing the commission company against loss. I didn't sleep very good those nights. The banks were failing all over the state. The squeeze was beginning to be felt. The stock market panic didn't come as any surprise to us. Our government had systematically done everything wrong. . . . We were going to take the profits out of war. The only thing we did was put a ceiling on wheat. We passed high protective tariffs, other countries retaliated. . . ."

THERE'S A SAYING: "Depressions are farm led and farm fed." That was true in the Thirties. As farmers lost their purchasing power, the big tractors piled up at the Minneapolis-Moline plant in the Twin Cities. One day they closed their doors and turned their employees out to beg or starve. My cousin was one of them. I took my truck to Minneapolis and brought him and his family out to my farm for the duration. They stayed with us until the company opened up again, two or three years later.

During my first session in the state senate, in 1927, five hundred farmers came marching up Capitol Hill. It thrilled me. I didn't know farmers were intelligent enough to organize. (Laughs.) They stayed there for two days. It was a strength I didn't realize we had.

The day after they left, a Senator got up and attacked them as anarchists and bolsheviks. (Laughs.) They had a banner, he said, redder than anything in Moscow, Russia. What was this banner? It was a piece of muslin, hung up in the auditorium. It said: "We Buy Together, We Sell Together, We Vote Together." This was the radical danger. (Laughs.) They'd been building cooperatives, which the farmers badly needed.

I was the first man to answer him from the senate floor. Eleven others took turns. He never got re-elected. In the lower house, we had about thirty or forty members of the Farmer's Union. It was quite an education for me.

Among the members of our Holiday Association were bankers, businessmen, the president of the Farm Bureau, of the Chamber of Commerce. (Laughs.) They didn't stick their necks out very far, but the meetings were always jammed. People were hanging out of windows. Our slogan was: "Neither buy nor sell and let the taxes go to hell." (Laughs.)

Oh, the militancy then! At Milbank, during a farm sale, they had a sheriff and sixteen deputies. One of them got a little trigger-happy. It was a mistake. The boys disarmed him so fast, he didn't know what happened. They just yanked the belts off 'em, didn't even unbuckle 'em. They took their guns away from 'em. After that, we didn't have much trouble stopping sales.

Thirteen highways to Sioux Falls were blocked. They emptied the stockyards there in a day or two. There was some violence, most of it accidental.

I'll never forget a speech by a Catholic priest at a Salem meeting, straight south of here about forty miles. It was the most fiery I ever heard. He said, "If you men haven't got the guts to picket the roads and stop this stuff from going to market, put on skirts and get in the kitchen and let your wives go out and do the job." (Laughs.) The boys used the police stations as their headquarters. (Laughs.) The police couldn't do much. The sheriffs and deputies just had to go along.

That judge situation in Iowa was a warning. In Brown County, farmers would crowd into the courtroom, five or six hundred, and make it impossible for the officers to carry out the sales. (Laughs.)

Deputies would come along with whole fleets of trucks and guns. One lone farmer had planks across the road. They ordered him to remove them. They came out with guns. He said, "Go ahead and shoot, but there isn't one of you S.O.B.'s getting out of here alive." There were about fifteen hundred farmers there in the woods. The trucks didn't get through. It was close in spirit to the American Revolution.

One incident stands out in my memory. It was a mass meeting in the city park at Huron. Ten thousand farm folks were in attendance. I had invited Governor Warren Green to appear. He stressed law and order. He seemed frightened. Then came the surprise of the evening: John A. Simpson, president of the National Farmers Union. He electrified the crowd with his opening remarks, which I remember verbatim: "When constitutions, laws and court decisions stand in the way of human progress, it is time they be scrapped." When the meeting was adjourned, the crowd did not move. In unison came a mighty roar: "We want Simpson! WE WANT SIMPSON!" They didn't budge until he was called back to the platform.

The Holiday Association was fairly conservative. There was a United Farmers League that was leftist. In the northern part of the state. The business community welcomed us to head off the extreme leftists, the Commies. We didn't have anything to do with 'em.

The situation was tense in ten or eleven states. You could almost smell the powder. When Governor Herring of Iowa called out the militia, Milo Reno said, "Hold off. I'll not have the blood of innocent people on my hands." He suggested they picket the farmyards instead of highways. We had a heck of a time getting the farmers off Highway 75. There were probably a thousand of them out there. Reno called a meeting at Sioux City. About thirty thousand farmers showed up. We decided to go to Washington and settle for a farm program.

If Roosevelt hadn't come in in '32, we'd a' been in real trouble. I'll never forget our meeting with him. He came to Pierre on a special train. He appeared on the rear platform. Next thing I know, we were ushered into a private room, some of us leaders of farm and labor. We had about an hour with the President.

He pointed to the Missouri River and said, "This is the greatest resource of your state. It's got to be developed." He told us how Sweden had developed their power resources for the benefit of the people—the low rates of electricity and so forth. He was extremely well informed.

I resigned from the state senate in 1934 to become president of the South Dakota Farmers Union. We had many battles. Before that, I'd introduced a bill to cut penalty interest in delinquency payments from twelve percent to six. So I was attacked. The local editor said my radical legislation would destroy the state. (Laughs.)

Reactionary forces have controlled South Dakota since statehood. Corporation interests like the gold mine out here. That's the first time I heard the word "communist." I stayed at the Waverly Hotel, so they called that a Communist headquarters. They started to use that word about everything they didn't like. I had to look it up in the dictionary. (Laughs.)

We have the world's richest gold mine out here, in the Black Hills. While in the legislature, I was one of the promoters of a tax on ore. The mine was owned by the Hearst interests. It was very difficult. We took the matter to the people by the route of a referendum. We won. We passed the tax. Our slogan was: "Tax gold, not Russian thistles." These thistles, thorny, hateful things, were stacked, during the drought of '33, and fed to our livestock. They have lots of proteins.

It was in '35—we had this campaign to raise a million tax dollars. In the town of Phillips, one evening, during a blizzard, I was met by a crowd of miners. They were given the day off and a stake to attend this meeting. They surrounded me and said this tax would cost six hundred of them their jobs. They were busted farmers and fortunately found a job in these Home Stake mines. I went back home feeling worried. But the tax was passed, and not a single miner lost his job.

They had been stirred up by the mining interests. They made grants to colleges all over the state. When the tax was on the verge of passing, they'd write the alumni, send along a check and a message: Wire your Senator to oppose this vicious, discriminatory tax. (Laughs.) Today, they're in a squeeze like us farmers, because the price of gold is fixed and the cost is going up. But they get a moratorium on taxes. We don't.

In 1938, I ran for Congress. I carried the votes in the cities and lost the straggling farm precincts. A week before election, Senator Case, Governor Bushfield and my opponent asked the Dies Committee to investigate me. A night or two before election, they put out a picture of me and the Farmers Union Board meeting with CIO people. Here was proof that I was a Communist.

After I lost the election, Senator Case apologized to me. He said his name was used without his consent. The papers also broke their neck apologizing—after the election. I had served papers on some of them. One said I had marched in a Communist parade. I've never seen a Communist parade.

Whimsically, he recalls the names of prominent and wealthy Dakotans, big grain men, who were members of the Holiday Association in the Thirties. "They're millionaires today and a lot of these have gone reactionary."

Once in a while I'll meet a farmer who'll thank me. He'll say: "You sure helped me out. I was busted, and I got that loan." But it doesn't happen too often. A lot of fellows that were rescued became Roosevelt-haters and extremely conservative.

Today, corporations are moving in. Agribusiness. Among their clients are movie stars and doctors. Good investments.

This cattle operation is like a crap game. They can write off their losses, charge depreciation. . . . The small farmer doesn't stand a chance.

Ruth Loriks, His Wife

ONE TIME we were driving up to Aberdeen. It was during the grass-hopper days in 1933. The sun was shining brightly when we left home. When we were about half way, it just turned dark. It was the grasshoppers that covered the sun.

We had a large garden. The chickens would go in there and pick what little grass which they'd find. Our neighbors said: "The grasshoppers have come in, they'd taken every leaf off our trees, they're even starting to eat the fence posts." I thought that was a joke. Well, the next day they moved on here, and they did line up the fence posts. My faithful hen sort of kept them off the tomatoes (laughs), but they were moving in.

One day at noon, we had one of our worst dust storms. I never want to see one again! The air was so filled. We could just see it float in, and we had good, heavy storm windows. A year before, we heard of the dust storms to the south. They were collecting wheat to send down there by the carloads. Some of the good folks said, "Better share, because we never know when we may have a drought." The next year, we finally did. I'm surprised to think we lived through it.

This neighbor woman lost her husband, and, of course, he was owing in the bank. So the auctioneers come out there, and she served lunch, and she stood weeping in the windows. "There goes our last cow. . . ." And the horses. She called 'em by names. It just pretty near broke our hearts. They didn't give her a chance to take care of her bills. They never gave her an offer. They just came and cleared it out. She just stood there crying. . . .

Clyde T. Ellis

Former Congressman from Arkansas. For twenty-five years, he was general manager of the National Rural Electric Cooperative Association.

THE DIRTY THIRTIES—the phrase was coined where we had the dust storms. My people came from Arkansas, where the years of drought coincided with the hard years of the Depression. Even the one good year was no good. Everything dried up . . . the springs, the wells, the ponds, the creeks, the rivers.

We saw bank failures everywhere. In my county, all but three of perhaps a dozen failed. The most valuable thing we lost was hope. A man can endure a lot if he still has hope.

Mountain people are more rigorous than others. We lived a harder life. We had to grow or make most of the things we needed. The country never did lend itself to mechanization . . . still doesn't. Rock. We had relatives who just gave up. Broke up homes, scattered to different states. From down in my county, many would go to what we called *De*-troit. Then they started to go to California, any way they could. Thumbing rides . . . I thumbed rides when I was peddling Bibles. It was during a summer, while still in high school.

I became a schoolteacher. It didn't pay much, but it was decent work. I taught in a one-room country school. By the time Roosevelt was elected, I'd been to law school. A group of us there decided if we were going to hell, we might just as well get active in it. We ran for office ourselves.

I ran for the state legislature. I didn't ask the machine. So I was viciously attacked at county meetings. The political and economic establishment were one. But I was elected. The majority in the House were new fellows who had beaten the sitting candidates. We called it the Revolution of 1932, and organized ourselves as Young Turks.

I'd been talking about electricity for the people. The little towns hardly had any—just a putt-putt plant that wasn't reliable. The rural people had nothing. We could see the fogs rise over the White River, and when the river was up big, we heard the roar. We knew there was tremendous power going to waste. We had read about hydroelectric plants elsewhere in the world. We talked about it, but there wasn't much we could do. The power companies were against it. Arkansas is probably the state most completely dominated by a power company.

We tried to do something about flood control—and in the process do something about electrification—because the TVA had come to be and it was multi-purpose: flood control and power.

We set to form electric co-ops, hoping to buy power from the companies. It would be too long to wait on the dams. They demanded an outrageous price. They were determined to fight the cooperatives all the way.

In 1934, I was elected to the state senate, and introduced another rural electrification bill. It was passed in '35, but it was still a struggle. It became a model for the REA[1] and other states used it around the country. In 1936, we got some electric co-ops organized.

Today, there are dams up and down the White River, and others along the Arkansas. Industry has come into the state and development is encouraged. And yet, there are some areas that have never recovered from the Depression.

"What I'm about to tell you is related to poverty. In 1942, I ran for the U.S. Senate on the issue of rural electrification—but just at that time, Bataan fell. There was only one thing our people were interested in— the lives of our boys. Almost all the boys were in National Guard units. These were the children of the poor, who joined immediately because it gave them a few dollars. My baby brother, Harold, had no work. He quit school, volunteered. He was killed. . . .

"They were the first to go. Our whole county was cleaned out of young boys in Corregidor. . . ."

[1] Rural Electrification Administration.

I wanted to be at my parents' house when electricity came. It was in 1940. We'd all go around flipping the switch, to make sure it hadn't come on yet. We didn't want to miss it. When they finally came on, the lights just barely glowed. I remember my mother smiling. When they came on full, tears started to run down her cheeks. After a while, she said: "Oh, if we only had it when you children were growing up." We had lots of illness. Anyone who's never been in a family without electricity—with illness—can't imagine the difference.

From there, I went to my grandmother's house. It was a day of celebration. They had all kinds of parties—mountain people getting light for the first time.

There are still areas without electricity. Coal oil lamps are used, with the always dirty chimneys. But there are more and more electric co-ops, which first sprang out of the New Deal. And the power companies are still fighting us. . . .

Emma Tiller

Her father had a small farm in western Texas. The first depression she recalls began in 1914. "We were almost starvin' to death. Papa had some very rich land, but those worms came like showers. The cotton was huge, you never seen nothin' like it. You could just sit in the house and hear the worms eatin' that cotton. You had to check all the cracks in the doors because the kids were scared and the worms would get in the house. . . ."

IN 1929, me and my husband were sharecroppers. We made a crop that year, the owner takin' all of the crop.

This horrible way of livin' with almost nothin' lasted up until Roosevelt. There was another strangest thing, I didn't suffer for food through the Thirties, because there was plenty of people that really suffered much worse. When you go through a lot, you in better condition to survive through all these kinds of things.

I picked cotton. We weren't getting but thirty-five cents a hundred, but

I was able to make it. 'Cause I also worked people's homes, where they give you old clothes and shoes.

At this time, I worked in private homes a lot and when the white people kill hogs, they always get the Negroes to help. The cleanin' of the insides and clean up the mess afterwards. And then they would give you a lot of scraps. A pretty adequate amount of meat for the whole family. The majority of the Negroes on the farm were in the same shape we were in. The crops were eaten by these worms. And they had no other jobs except farming.

In 1934, in this Texas town, the farmers was all out of food. The government gave us a slip, where you could pick up food. For a week, they had people who would come and stand in line, and they couldn't get waited on. This was a small town, mostly white. Only five of us in that line were Negroes, the rest was white. We would stand all day and wait and wait and wait. And get nothin' or if you did, it was spoiled meat.

We'd been standin' there two days, when these three men walked in. They had three shotguns and a belt of shells. They said, lookin' up and down that line, "You all just take it easy. Today we'll see that everybody goes home, they have food." Three white men.

One of 'em goes to the counter, lays his slip down and says he wants meat. He had brought some back that was spoiled. He said to the boss, "Would you give this meat for your dog?" So he got good meat. He just stood there. So the next person gets waited on. It was a Negro man. He picked up the meat the white man brought back. So the white guy said, "Don't take that. I'm gonna take it for my dog." So the boss said, "I'm gonna call the police."

So the other reaches across the counter and catches this guy by the tie and chokes him. The Negro man had to cut the tie so the man wouldn't choke to death. When he got up his eyes was leakin' water. The other two with guns was standin' there quietly. So he said, "Can I wait on you gentlemen?" And they said, "We've been here for three days. And we've watched these people fall like flies in the hot sun, and they go home and come back the next day and no food. Today we purpose to see that everybody in line gets their food and then we gonna get out." They didn't point the guns directly at him. They just pointed 'em at the ceiling. They said, "No foolin' around, no reachin' for the telephone. Wait on the people. We're gonna stand here until every person out there is waited on. When you gets them all served, serve us."

The man tried to get the phone off the counter. One of the guys said, "I hope you don't force me to use the gun, because we have no intentions of getting nobody but you. And I wouldn't miss you. It wouldn't do you any good to call the police, because we stop 'em at the door. Everybody's gonna get food today." And everybody did.

The Government sent two men out there to find out why the trouble. They found out this man and a couple others had rented a huge warehouse and was stackin' that food and sellin' it. The food that was supposed to be issued to these people. These three men was sent to the pen.

When the WPA came in, we soon got to work. The people, their own selves, as they would get jobs on WPA, they quit goin' to the relief station. They just didn't want the food. They'd go in and say, "You know, this is my last week, 'cause I go to work next week." The Negro and white would do this, and it sort of simmered down until the only people who were on relief were people who were disabled. Or families where there weren't no man or no one to go out and work on the WPA.

I remember in this Texas place, they had twenty-five people came in that day saying they wouldn't be back any more 'cause they signed up and they was gonna work on the WPA the next week. Some of 'em had to sort of stretch things to make pay day 'cause it really didn't come to what they thought it would. But they didn't go back after any more help.

You sort of like to know to feel independent the way you earn your own living. And when you hear people criticize people of things like this today it gets under your skin.

What bothered me about the Roosevelt time was when they come out with this business that you had to plow up a certain amount of your crop, especially cotton. I didn't understand, 'cause it was good cotton.

And seein' all this cattle killed. Bein' raised with stock, to me it was kind of a human feelin' we had toward them. We had this cow and calf raised with us. I'd see these farmers, terrible big cattle raisers and they didn't have the food to feed these cattle, and there was drought, so they had these cattle drove up and killed by the hundreds of head.

I would go down and look at those cows—to me it was sorta like human beings, because they would just groan and go on—when they was killin' 'em and they wasn't dead. I remember one day I went down there, and all of a sudden it hit me. I seen the war.

When I listened to those cows and looked at how they were carryin' on, then I seen how horrible wars were. I thought then: Why do they have wars? To me, those cows were like women, moanin' over their husbands, their children and the starvation and the places where they were, everything was wiped out. I ran up to the house and I sit up there a long time and then I went to cryin' because they was doin' these cows this way.

Sumio Nichi

A second-generation Japanese-American.

WE HAD A BIG FARM near Salinas, California. Lettuce, celery, cauliflower, broccoli. . . . In 1934, I bought a truck for $1600. Paid everything back within a year. I bought another. In 1936, I bought four trucks and trailers for $24,000. We had our own packinghouse. It got rough in '37 and '38. There were too many crops, over-production. In those two years, we lost almost everything. We wound up owing the bank $78,000. In '39, '40, '41, we covered up our losses. The day I was to report to the assembly center, in 1941, we brought that mortgage down to $9,875. The day I left for the internment camp, I walked into the bank, paid them $9,875.

We had an inventory of $80,000 worth of equipment. The people around, the whites, knew we had to leave. They were just standing around, waiting. I was thinking of storing it, but they told us we couldn't do it. It would be hampering the war effort. So they set up appraisers. I got $6,000 for it.

After the war—I wound up in the army, counter-intelligence, would you believe it? (Laughs.) I took a trip back to Salinas. I couldn't lease one acre of land. Nothing available. The people who took over our place, they're doing quite well. (Laughs.) So I came to Chicago, and here I am. (Laughs.)

Editor and Publisher

Fred Sweet

During the last years of the Depression, he was editor and publisher of the Mount Gilead Union-Register. *The town in central Ohio had a population of 2,500.*

OH, GOD, one of the reasons I went broke is that a farmer would say: "I want to put an ad in the paper. I had to sell the place off." He had so many head of Jersey cattle and a baler and a tractor and wagon and this and that. At the bottom of the ad, there was always the line: "And other articles too numerous to mention."

You'd go to the auction and what would you see among the "articles too numerous to mention"? A doll, a couple of books, a basket with the Bible in it, the kids' wagon. . . . Here you had the whole history of the family in all this junk. People pawing over it and buying it for a penny on the dollar.

I never had the heart—the guy wanted a forty-inch ad. Twenty-five cents an inch. That's ten bucks, isn't it? And he always wanted about fifty or a hundred handbills to put on telephone posts and fences. How could you charge a guy who's dead broke for those extra handbills? You'd feel funny about charging for the ad in the first place.

The paper had 843 subscribers when I took over. When I left, it had about 2,780. It was a great success editorially. But I was running a New

Deal paper in a Republican town. The two other papers got the legal advertising. I didn't have a share of that stuff.

You see, the judge of the Probate Court is a Republican. The law says he's got to publish certain kinds of ads in two newspapers of general circulation. If he'd been a Democrat, I would've gotten a piece of the business, see? But that was only one of the reasons I went broke.

There's one factory in Mount Gilead at the time. It's making hydraulic presses for airplane fuselages. 1940—the war's coming, but it's still Depression down here. Highly skilled mechanics are working for sixty, seventy cents an hour. In Cincinnati, Cleveland and Toledo, they're making $2.50.

Into town one day, comes a walking delegate from the union. He says, "I find there's nobody around here wants to be seen even talking to me. Everybody's scared." I said, "The back end of the shop is yours any time you want a bunch of guys to come down here. We'll pull the shades down and you can sit behind the press down there and nobody will see you." So our little newspaper office became the center where the plot was laid to organize the company.

The president of the company was the superintendent of the Presbyterian Sunday School. He dominated the whole town. But the men in the plant responded. Pretty soon, the paper was covering the organizing drive. I'm trying to play it right down the middle in the news columns. Every time the union's got something to say, I'd call up this guy: "Have you got anything to say?" I'd print 'em side by side. But in my own column, I'd express my personal thoughts.

Pretty soon, the head of the town's biggest department store comes over. "Fred, you gotta get off this union kick." I said, "It would be a good thing for this town to have a union." A couple of weeks later, he jerks his ad. Biggest advertiser. (Laughs.)

Pretty soon we've got the Legion with ax handles and all the rest of it. The county sheriff lets the highway repair trucks haul the Legionnaires with their Legion caps. The highway department supplies the ax handles, and they beat up the pickets.

Eventually, the place gets organized. On a Saturday night, this department store man comes in, takes me to his place, and puts me near the cash register. He says, "I want you to stand here and watch for a while." Here are these machinists coming in with their paychecks bigger than they ever had in their lives. They're payin' bills they've been runnin' for six months or a year, two years.

The guy's amazed. He says, "I shouldn't have taken the ad out. You were right. I was wrong." But it was too late. I haven't got any money. I'm consistently overdrawn at the bank. One day it's gotten to the point where the kid linotype operator is sitting on the front porch with a knife about this long in his lap. He's also got the paycheck he tried to cash at the bank. "I want my $15." Well, I simply failed in the country newspaper business. . . .

W. D. (Don) Maxwell

He recently retired as editor of the Chicago Tribune. *As much as any living journalist, he reflects the thoughts and spirit of the paper's singular publisher, Colonel Robert R. McCormick.*

"The first interview I really had was on a Saturday. I got a call from the Colonel's office. His first question was: 'How far is it from Vladivostok to Shanghai?' I said, 'Colonel, that's one of the few things I don't know. But if you'll excuse me, I'll run downstairs and look it up.' I called him back in five minutes and told him how many miles it was. He was pleased that I didn't bluff it.

"He had a push button on his desk. Whenever he'd use it, his secretary knew he wanted to get rid of the visitor. On one occasion, the head of the UP had come up to tell of an interview he had with MacArthur. He had a cropped haircut, like the boys used to wear in college. He talked and he talked, and the Colonel was listening intently. I heard the button, so the man had to go. The Colonel said, 'Don, I want to talk with you.' I assumed it was something important concerning MacArthur. He looked at me and said, 'Why does he wear his hair like that?'

"The Colonel and MacArthur were very good friends. He admired military men very much. You know, he wrote the life of Grant and all kinds of treatises. When he visited Russia as a boy, he went around with the Grand Duke Nicholas. He wrote about the efficiency of the Russian Army. It didn't prove to be valid later on, but at that time. . . ."

What was the Colonel's reaction to the Crash of '29?

I KNOW HE BOUGHT a lot of cattle downstate, so he'd be sure to have steaks (laughs), if things went completely to pieces. He also had money in different lock boxes in New York, so he'd have plenty when he went there.

Did he ever say anything when Roosevelt's name was mentioned?

I don't think anybody would mention it. (Laughs.) The way to get along with the Colonel was very simple. When he proposed something, you'd say: "That's interesting. I'd like twenty-four hours to think it over." If you came back with more arguments against it than for it, he'd say, "I think you're right." He wasn't infallible.

Hardly anybody ever got fired. An exception was Bob Jones, who quit. It was silly. The Colonel asked him to put a map in the paper. He was great on maps. During the war, we were probably the best map-making paper in the United States on battles and so forth. Well, Jones told the Colonel, "We just had it three days ago." That was not the right thing to say. The Colonel hadn't seen it (laughs), and if he hadn't seen it, why . . .

. . . It wasn't there.

That's right. Anyway, I became the news editor. That's in '30. You see, he was a patrician. So was Roosevelt. They weren't going to push around, either by the other one. The Colonel had control of his paper, and no boss could tell him: I like Roosevelt, don't print that. He hated Roosevelt's hypocrisy.

He was friendly to Roosevelt at the start. So was Patterson.[1] But when F.D.R. tried to wreck the Supreme Court and shove through the NRA, the Colonel was against him. It was an attempt to impose upon people something you could get by with in Russia. When a delegation of merchants came over and demanded the *Tribune* quit attacking the NRA, the Colonel listened to them, ushered them out and ordered a front page cartoon. It had a great big barbed wire fence, with poor people trying to get through. The caption was: "No Relief Anywhere. NRA."

Did the Colonel think up the cartoons himself?

He had an editorial conference every day, which the cartoonists and writers attended. He did all the talking. There wasn't much discussion. He'd have something he wanted written about or cartooned. John Mc-

---

[1] Captain Joseph Patterson, the Colonel's cousin, publisher of the New York *Daily News*.

Cutcheon never paid much attention to that.[2] Orr was a kind of hatchet man that would be the political cartoonist.

He fought Roosevelt from that time on. Not very successfully. We had a candidate named Landon that got nowhere. We had Willkie, though the Colonel wasn't sold on him. He fought hard for Taft two times. The Illinois delegation stayed right in line. He liked to have a state delegation that went down the *Tribune* line all the way.

At one time, the Colonel was so irritated with the New Deal, he ordered a star taken out of our flag. It was on a standard in the lobby of the Tribune Tower. The Rhode Island Supreme Court had upheld some New Deal measure. He wanted the star representing that state removed from the flag.

I called up our law firm. They said: "You better put it right back or you'll all be in jail. You can't deface the American flag." Now they let 'em burn it on the streets, like Spock and those other fellows. The Colonel would have taken after those kids that burn and desecrate flags.

There were numerous anti-WPA cartoons, as I recall. . . .

He didn't believe in this WPA. He thought it was a waste of money. Guys that should be doing something useful were sweeping leaves. We never fought relief as relief. We fought this boondoggling.

And those cartoons portraying New Deal professors in mortarboard hats. . . .

There's nothing that proved him more right. A lot of people agree with him today. If he was against professors, it was the kind that today join these rebels in destroying these universities. It's about as silly as joining with the rebels in the Civil War when you wanted to protect the North.

I'm thinking about the Brain Trusters. . . .

He was against Tugwell. As it happened, everybody else turned on Tugwell, too. The Colonel was against Wallace. He was against Ickes. Ickes hated him, and he hated Ickes. When they showed their animus and tried to get the Colonel, he counter-attacked. The first thing you know, we're on the aggressive and they're on the defensive.

[2] His were primarily non-political cartoons. His most celebrated, "Injun Summer," has been reprinted every season for many years.

Did those protest marches in the Thirties bother him?

Not too much. He'd be against 'em, but there's nothing like this stuff today. When Episcopal ministers led a rabble from down here to Georgia or something like that.

All of the Colonel's behavior fits in with the pattern of the patrician. I gave him the title, "The Duke of Chicago." As a duke, he was kind to the peasants and fought for their rights. You might say he treated his subjects very well.

Carey McWilliams

Author; editor, The Nation.

"I had been conditioned for the 1929 Crash. My father was a prosperous cattleman in northwest Colorado. In 1919, in the wake of World War I, the cattle market fell apart. From 1914 to 1918, Western cattlemen had experienced a bonanza. They continued to expand. They thought it was going on forever. It didn't. They all went to the wall, including my father. It had a tremendous impact on my family.

"My mother took my brother and myself to live in California, which is where you go under these circumstances. . . ."

THE LATE TWENTIES and early Thirties was a time of innocence.

After the stock market crash, some New York editors suggested that hearings be held: what had really caused the Depression? They were held in Washington. In retrospect, they make the finest comic reading. The leading industrialists and bankers testified. They hadn't the foggiest notion what had gone bad. You read a transcript of that record today with amazement: that they could be so unaware. This was their business, yet they didn't understand the operation of the economy. The only good witnesses were the college professors, who enjoyed a bad reputation in those years. No professor was supposed to know anything practical about the economy.

It was a mood of great bewilderment. No one had anticipated it, despite the fact that we had many severe panics in the past. The inno-cence of the business leaders was astonishing. There were groups pictured at the time as being vicious, arch-reactionary and so forth . . . the Liberty League, for instance. There was a bit of truth in it, but by and large, they were babes in the wood or comedians.

There were obvious symptoms before the Crash . . . ?

Oh, yes. There was a runaway stock market. The value of stocks was all out of relation to earnings. There was indication of severe trouble in Europe. Reparations had gone from bad to worse in Ger-many. Hitler was beginning to make noises in the early Twenties. Mussolini in Italy . . .

Could the Depression have been avoided?

In '29 I'm sure it could. If you started back at some point well before 1929, with modern fiscal management, with an understanding of the business cycle.

As a result of my father's experience in Colorado in 1919, and my own during the Great Depression, my confidence was destroyed in the operation of this economy. I've tried—unsuccessfully—not to ac-quire any property. I didn't have confidence in stocks and bonds. The whole thing was put together in a way that didn't inspire my con-fidence. And it doesn't now. This may be an unreasonable attitude on my part, nonetheless. . . .

There was a delayed reaction to the events of October, 1929. I was practicing law in Los Angeles. In a year or two, I saw the impact on clients—the kind of widows who are legion in southern California. Who had brought money out from the Middle West and had invested it in fly-by-night real estate promotions. They began to lose their property. I was bugged when I saw what was happening. There was a feverish activity in foreclosures.

When I got out of law school in 1927, I was not a political person. I was an H. L. Menckenite character. My interests became increas-ingly social and political as the Thirties began to unfold.

My first reaction to Roosevelt was very adverse. I remember par-ticularly my great disappointment in a 1932 speech he made at the Hollywood Bowl. I thought it was fatuous. He didn't have a ghost of an idea, really, of what the Depression was all about. He was going to balance the budget, he was going to do all kinds of things, unrelated to the problems he had to face. He, too, was an innocent. He had no program. He was pressured into doing the fine things he did.

The labor movement, the sit-ins, were responsible for the labor legislation. The Farm Holiday movement was responsible for the farm program. Dr. Townsend, Coughlin, Huey Long and company were responsible for the pressures that brought about social security. Roosevelt was responsive, sympathetic. In later years, I became a great admirer.

There were many pension movements in California, aside from Doctor Townsend's. It was fascinating to attend these early meetings. At the same time, you had some apprehensions about their character. They had elements of the demagogic. The Allen Brothers and "Ham and Eggs." The Utopian Society . . .

The critical year, in my own personal experience, was 1934. First, you had the San Francisco General Strike. Then you had Upton Sinclair's campaign for Governor. I had known Sinclair. We were good friends. I covered the campaign for the Baltimore *Sun*. It was amazing. He ran as the Democratic nominee and almost won. This man started out a year before the elections with a pamphlet and no resources—and a reputation of being an atheist, a Socialist and a free love advocate. The motion picture industry brought obscene pressure to bear on their employees, threatening to close the studios if Sinclair was elected. He rolled up a vote of 800,000.

He had this passionate conviction that he could in fact end poverty in California.[3] I remember six or eight years after the '34 campaign, way in the wilds of northern California, written on rocks or on approaches to bridges, you could see this slogan in chalk: "End Poverty In California." It was an enormously educational campaign. I think it would have been a disaster if Sinclair had been elected. He wouldn't have known what to do. But he did have the conviction that poverty was manmade, that you didn't need it.

Going around the state in those years, you saw California as synonymous with abundance. It's so enormously rich, especially in agriculture. Yet you saw all kinds of crops being destroyed. There were dumps in southern California, where they would throw citrus fruits and spray them with tar and chemicals. At a time when thousands of people

[3] EPIC (End Poverty In California) was the symbol of Sinclair's candidacy.

were in real distress.[4] So my Menckenisms began to fade as the Thirties progressed.

You could easily romanticize the Thirties. The racial attitudes were not very good. I was intimately involved with these issues, and the attitudes were incredible. Though there was no categorization of the poor as there is today—the former doctor, the man who lost his law practice, the businessman, everybody was in on it—there was no feeling that there was a national race problem.

I was appointed by Governor Culbert Olson in 1938 as Chief of the Division of Immigration and Housing. It put me in touch with all the minority groups in the state: Mexican-Americans, Japanese-Americans, Chinese-Americans, Hindus, Filipinos. Negroes were not as significant as a group in California as they are today.

In the second half of the Thirties, about 350,000 Dust Bowl refugees flooded the state. They were promptly stereotyped, exactly like a racial minority. They were called Okies and Arkies: they were shiftless and lazy and irresponsible and had too many children, and if we improve the labor camps and put a table in, they would chop it up and use it for kindling. Once I went into the foyer of this third-rate motion picture house in Bakersfield and I saw a sign: Negroes and Okies upstairs.

When the war boom began in California around 1939, these Okies and Arkies were the salvation of the state. They promptly went into shipyards and defense plants. Within a couple of years, the stereotype began to fade. Now these people think of themselves as old Californians. Of course, they look down on the recent migrants from the South. The stereotype is the same.

When they first came in, they had no racist feelings. They were too preoccupied with their own distress. At the time of their migration, there were many Mexicans on public assistance, meager, inadequate. As the Okies came in, the authorities thought they could get rid of the Mexicans. I was eyewitness to many deportation trains that left the Southern Pacific station, taking thousands of Mexican-Americans back to Mexico, with their families and bundles of belongings. Of course, they'd turn right around and come back. And the process would be repeated.

[4] Dorothy Comingore, a former film actress (*Citizen Kane*), recalls, "I saw heaps of oranges covered with gasoline and set on fire and men who tried to take *one* orange shot to death."

I inspected labor camps. The conditions were not to be believed. There were no programs of aid for these people. The camps were filthy. We had a labor camp population of 175,000 in August and September, the harvest season. In the spring, they'd force people off relief rolls to take jobs at twenty cents an hour. I induced Governor Olson to let me hold some hearings. We recommended they not be cut off relief unless they were paid twenty-seven and a half cents an hour. The reaction could hardly have been more violent had we bombed San Joaquin Valley. Outrageous, that they should pay twenty-seven and a half cents an hour.

At his request, the La Follette Committee came to California in 1939 to investigate the denial of elementary liberties to farm workers and to probe the role of the Associated Farmers. Earl Warren, then Attorney General for the state, refused to cooperate, defending sheriffs in "every rural county of the state." The mass evacuation of Japanese-Americans is recounted. Again, he opposed Warren, who was in its favor. ". . . his education and growth as a civil libertarian were unquestionably acquired in California. I smile when I see these signs: Impeach Earl Warren."

The impulse of the New Deal was over by 1938. Its most creative years were 1934 to 1938. There were a lot of good times, too, because money was not so terribly important. A friend of mine and I had a protégé, a young writer. We rented him a room in Los Angeles and put up $5 a week to sustain him while he was doing a couple of books. He managed to live on $10 a week. On so meager an amount, we were philanthropists, you see. (Laughs.)

If such times were to come again, it would not be the same. Our discontents today are more vague and ill-defined. At the same time, we have an apparatus of police controls that could develop into a kind of American fascism. It would not be European style.

I think the New Deal saved American capitalism. It was a bridge. But it never really solved the problems.

BOOK THREE

Concerning the New Deal

Gardiner C. Means

Co-author (*with A. A. Berle*) *of* The Modern Corporation and Private Property.

"In the summer of '33, I got a call from Rex Tugwell:[1] would I consider coming down to Washington?"

He became Economic Adviser on Finance to Henry Wallace, Secretary of Agriculture. Among his other New Deal assignments were his work as a member of the Consumer Advisory Board of the NRA and as director of the Industrial Section of the National Resources Planning Board. During the war, he was chief fiscal analyst in the Budget Bureau.

AT THE BEGINNING of the New Deal, they called it a revolution. Then they began to say it wasn't a revolution. Our institutions were being shored up and maintained. What really happened was a revolution in point of view. We backed into the Twentieth Century describing our actual economy in terms of the small enterprises of the Nineteenth Century.

We were an economy of huge corporations, with a high degree of concentrated control. It was an economy that was in no sense de-

---

[1] Rexford G. Tugwell is one of the original members of Roosevelt's "Brain Trust" along with Dr. Means' colleague, Adolph A. Berle.

scribed by classical theory. What Roosevelt and the New Deal did was to turn about and face the realities.

It was this which produced the yeastiness of experimentation that made the New Deal what it was. A hundred years from now, when historians look back on it, they will say a big corner was turned. People agreed that old things didn't work. What ran through the whole New Deal was finding a way to make things work.

Before that, Hoover would loan money to farmers to keep their mules alive, but wouldn't loan money to keep their children alive. This was perfectly right within the framework of classical thinking. If an individual couldn't get enough to eat, it was because he wasn't on the ball. It was his responsibility. The New Deal said: Anybody who is unemployed isn't necessarily unemployed because he's shiftless.

Roosevelt was building up new ideas in a milieu of old ideas. His early campaign speeches were pure Old Deal. He called for a balanced budget. When he got into office, the whole banking system collapsed. It called for a New Deal.

I was never told what to do at any time, during those early days. I made my own way. We had meetings that would run into the early morning. A dozen of us sitting around the table, thrashing out problems. They were more than bull sessions, because we were making decisions.

I answered some of the mail for Wallace. Great quantities came pouring in, letters from everywhere. I must have handled some two, three hundred. They were proposals from people, solutions to all sorts of problems. Some of them crackpot, some of them quite good. Everybody had a suggestion. The country was aware, as it never was before, that it was on the edge of something.

Talking a couple of days ago with a couple of old New Dealers, we agreed it was a very exhilarating period. There was no question in our minds we were saving the country. A student of mine remembered how exciting it was to him. He worked in the Department of Labor. He said, "Any idea I had, I put down on paper. I'd send it up and somebody would pay attention to it—whoever it was, Madame Perkins, Ickes or Wallace." This is how it was all the way through.

I remember a request from Mrs. Roosevelt. One of the big corporations had thumbed its nose at a stockholder. The woman had written to Mrs. Roosevelt: Have they a right to do this? She sent the letter to

Tugwell, who sent it to me. I wrote an answer for Mrs. Roosevelt to send to her. I remember I did have a suggestion for her.

One of the first things I did was get in touch with Mary Rumsey. She was head of the Consumer Advisory Board of the NRA. It was she who sold Roosevelt on the idea of having the consumer represented. The first thing she did when we met was take me down to her limousine —she was Averill Harriman's sister—and had her chauffeur drive us up and down the countryside as we talked. We spent all morning talking about the needs of the consumer, his protection. She was very perceptive.

Another thing I remember. I brought Leon Henderson into the NRA. We sent him up to discuss some problems with General Hugh Johnson, the chief. He was a blustery, flamboyant person. As Henderson started to talk, Johnson began to ride all over him. Leon swore back at him and pounded the table. Johnson loved it and made him his assistant. (Laughs.) This was the kind of climate in Washington at the time— highly personal and highly charged.

The NRA was one of the most successful things the New Deal did. It was killed when it should have been killed. But when it was created, American business was completely demoralized. Violent price cutting and wage cutting . . . nobody could make any plans for tomorrow. Everybody was going around in circles. The NRA changed the attitudes of business and the public. It revived belief that something could be done. It set a floor on prices and on wages.

Pressures had been coming from business to get free of the anti-trust acts and have business run business. Pressure was coming from labor for a shorter work week to spread jobs. It was a whole institutional matter. Roosevelt put the two together. Mary Rumsey brought in consumers' rights. So there were three advisory boards: Business, Labor and Consumer. Codes of behavior were set up. You couldn't sell below cost. . . . Labor got collective bargaining rights. It was, in a sense, a prelude to the Wagner Act. The wage increases were worked out between business and labor.

Most important, laissez faire in the Nineteenth Century manner was ended. The Government had a role to play in industrial activity. We didn't move into a fascist kind of governmental control, because we continued to use the market mechanism. In the two years of the NRA, the index of industrial production went up remarkably.

Things had been going downgrade—worse, worse, worse. More than anything else, the NRA changed the climate. It served its purpose. Had it lasted longer, it would not have worked in the public interest. Although toward the end, the consumer group was making progress.

Had the NRA continued, it would have meant dangerously diminishing the role of the market in limiting prices. You see, there was little Governmental regulation of the NRA. The Government handed industry over to industry to run, and offered some minor protection to others in the form of Labor and Consumer Advisory Boards. Industry became scared of its own people. Too much power was being delegated to the code authorities. It was business' fear of business rather than business' fear of Government, though they wouldn't quite put it that way. You might say, NRA's greatest contribution to our society is that it proved that self-regulation by industry doesn't work.

Laissez faire as such certainly did not come to an end with the New Deal. We still have a tremendous amount of freedom of decision-making in the individual corporate enterprise. The new element is the government's positive responsibility for making our economy run.

As for those first New Deal days, much of the excitement came from improvisation. Nothing was fully set in the minds of the people there. They were open to fresh ideas. Always. We wouldn't have been where we are now, were it not for Washington improvisations. . . .

This outflowing of people felt they were somehow on the way—though they were not sure how. A surprising number, we discovered, were sons of ministers, rabbis, missionaries. Yes, there was an evangelical quality, though it was non-religious. People who were personally concerned about a better world, came to Washington, were drawn to it. Even though where we were going was still to be worked out. There was an élan, an optimism . . . an evangelism . . . it was an adventure.

Raymond Moley

He is seated, on this Indian summer day, at his desk: one of Roosevelt's original Brain Trust. "I had served him in various ways, from the time he ran for Governor. I wrote my first speech for him in '28.

"My interest, as was his, was restoring confidence in the American

people, confidence in their banks, in their industrial system and in their Government. Confidence was the buoyant spirit that brought back prosperity. This has been, always, my contention."

DURING THE WHOLE '33 one-hundred days' Congress, people didn't know what was going on, the public. Couldn't understand these things that were being passed so fast. They knew something was happening, something good for them. They began investing and working and hoping again.

People don't realize that Roosevelt chose a conservative banker as Secretary of Treasury[2] and a conservative from Tennessee as Secretary of State.[3] Most of the reforms that were put through might have been agreeable to Hoover, if he had the political power to put them over. They were all latent in Hoover's thinking, especially the bank rescue. The rescue was done not by Roosevelt—he signed the papers—but by Hoover leftovers in the Administration. They knew what to do.

The bank rescue of 1933 was probably the turning point of the Depression. When people were able to survive the shock of having all the banks closed, and then see the banks open up, with their money protected, there began to be confidence. Good times were coming. Most of the legislation that came after didn't really help the public. The public helped itself, after it got confidence.

It marked the revival of hope. The people were scared for a little while—a week. Then, Congress passed the bill, and the banks were opened. Roosevelt appealed to them on Sunday night, after the week of the closing. It was his very first fireside chat. They put their money back in the banks, the people were so relieved.

A Depression is much like a run on a bank. It's a crisis of confidence. People panic and grab their money. There's a story I like to tell: In my home town, when I was a little boy, an Irishman came up from the quarry where he was working, went into the bank and said, "If my money's here, I don't want it. If it's not here, I want it."

The guarantee of bank deposits was put through by Vice President Garner, Jesse Jones (a Texas banker), and Senator Vandenburg—three conservatives. They rammed it down Roosevelt's throat, and he took credit for it ever after. If you can quiet the little fellows, the big fellows pretty much take care of themselves. If you can cover it up to $10,000,

[2] William H. Woodin.
[3] Cordell Hull.

all the little fellows are guaranteed. So it's O.K. You didn't have any bank trouble after that.

Now that wouldn't be agreed to by some liberals. But, after all, I was never a real liberal. I was an old-fashioned Democrat. I was a believer in our industrial system. It didn't need a complete rehauling. I thought if we could get it back into operation and normal conditions return, we'd be all right. This happened.

Tugwell thinks we should have gone much further in shaping the economy, but I don't. What we did accomplished its purpose. We don't know what would have happened if something else had been done.

The first New Deal was a radical departure from American life. It put more power in the central Government. At the time, it was necessary, especially in the farm area of our economy. Left to itself, farming was in a state of anarchy. Beyond that, there was no need to reorganize in industry. We merely needed to get the farms prospering again and create a market for the industrial products in the cities.

The second New Deal was an entirely different thing. My disenchantment began then. Roosevelt didn't follow any particular policy after 1936. Our economy began to slide downhill—our unemployment increased—after that, until 1940. This is something liberals are not willing to recognize. It was the war that saved the economy and saved Roosevelt.

We had a slight recession in 1937, which was occasioned by his attack on copper prices, specifically, and on business, generally. Of course, his Supreme Court packing plan shocked the people. They resented it. It was his first great defeat. Then he tried to purge Congress in '38. Everyone he tried to purge was re-elected, except one Congressman in New York.

I think if it weren't for the war, Roosevelt probably would have been defeated in 1940. You would probably have had a more business-minded Administration: less centralizing on the part of Washington. More normal conditions would have prevailed.

During those first hundred days, wasn't there a slight fear in some quarters that our society . . . ?

I never had any doubt that our society would survive—and survive in much the way that it had existed before. As Dirksen recently said: our society was not sick, it was mismanaged.

Remember, Roosevelt at the start was a very conservative President.

People didn't realize that. In the first place, he was a very prudent Governor of New York. He balanced his budget. He was not a spender. We resisted all the efforts of radicals, like La Follette and Tugwell, to spend a lot of money in public works. Roosevelt said: there aren't more than a billion dollars of public works that are worth doing. They wanted five billion dollars. So he compromised on three billion . . . a split between what he said and what they wanted.

What led to Roosevelt's shift from prudence to . . . ?

I think he was tired of reform. He began to bring in the radical elements, who up to that time had not been in support of him. Business went along with him in his early reforms, but after 1937, it began to be nervous about where he was going. He was improvising all the time. Hit or miss.

Unemployment insurance was unsound the way it was financed. When I wrote the original message in '34, the idea was to invest the receipts from the tax in municipal and state bonds and high grade industrials. Congress created a phony trust fund, which was composed of IOU's of the Government. It's unsound. You collect money from the taxes, then you spend it and you put your IOU's in the trust fund. If you did this in private industry, you'd be put in jail.

Unemployment insurance is a welfare measure. It isn't insurance in any sense of the word. More and more people were living off fewer and fewer people. That's when the unsound practices began. Until now, we've got it in a big way . . . even in a period of prosperity.

In 1935, I took a firm stand. I said welfare is a narcotic, because it will never end. We'll have to stop this business and put people to work. The best way to put people to work is to encourage the development of industrial science. The Government can't put people to work.

I began to have my doubts in 1935. I had many arguments with him. There were a lot of radicals. I had them in my group. Tugwell, for instance. He expressed sorrow that Roosevelt didn't turn more radical in 1932. As a matter of fact, he doubted very much whether he'd vote for Roosevelt.

The whole city, Washington, began to fill up with these young radicals. They stayed down, many of them there, with Frankfurter. They were scattered all over the lot. Still, it was conservative until '35.

Finally, in '36, in the middle of the year, I quit. I never went back to him again.

Was he trying to persuade you to stick with him?

Yes. He was a proud man, and it was very difficult for him to make the request, yet I couldn't do it. I didn't like the direction in which he was going. He was turning into a demagogue. He was out-Huey Long-ing Huey Long. He was afraid of Huey.

Huey was a good friend of mine. He was threatening to run for President in 1936. The poll showed that Huey would take ten percent of the vote. I'm sure Farley could confirm this. He would have cut into the Democratic vote all over the country. Roosevelt, in order to counteract that, moved toward the Long program. His tax program in '36 was pure Huey: soak the rich. Roosevelt was using the same demagogic tactics. It's possible Huey Long—if he weren't killed—would have busted open the Democratic Party even then. As George Wallace is doing now.

Of course, Huey had a much finer brain than Wallace. Only he abused his power. He was arrogant and he drank too much. You'd go to see Huey after three o'clock in the afternoon, and he didn't make much sense. He made sense in the morning. He had a rather contemptuous attitude toward Roosevelt. He didn't think Roosevelt was very smart.

I used to go up and see Huey in his apartment at the Mayflower. I said, "Huey, you have a great capacity. Watch out for the people around you." He said, "I haven't got any money. This is the way I live. I live simple." I don't think he enriched himself. But he did have a lot of thieves around him.

He spent himself. He tore his passion to tatters, as Shakespeare would put it. He didn't need to do that. He had too much brains to get violent. But that was his way of dealing with the people down South. One of the things he destroyed was himself. He didn't need to go swaggering around. He was much too good for that. It was one of the great tragedies.

I think Roosevelt was a product of his time, his environment, that sort of thing. He had all that with him. Huey didn't. He came from a poor family, sought power and got it. Roosevelt hated him because he was so different. It was the aristocrat distrusting this farm boy.

POSTSCRIPT: *"Huey Long came up to my office, one hot day in August, '33. He said: 'I want you to get a dean for my law school.' I had been teaching Public Law at Columbia. He said: 'I'll pay anything you say. I got a damn good medical school. I want a good law school.' I said:*

'I suppose the dean at Harvard gets $15,000.' 'Well, that's nothing.' I thought for a while. I had a student two years before at Columbia. His name was Wayne Morse. He was Dean of the Law School at the University of Oregon. 'Call him up,' says Huey. Huey talked to him and said, 'How much you getting? I'll double your salary.'

"Wayne sent me a telegram: 'What is this all about? Is the Senator able to appoint a law school dean?' I sent back a telegram: 'If he offered you the job, you can have it.' So he went to the President of the University of Oregon, who doubled his salary. Now what would have happened had Wayne Morse gone to Louisiana?"

C. B. (Beanie) Baldwin

He came to Washington from Virginia in 1933, as an assistant to the Secretary of Agriculture, Henry Wallace. He served in the Administration until the death of Roosevelt in 1945.

"When he first met me, Wallace said, 'We've been lookin' for someone with a southern accent in this office.'" (*Laughs.*)

THE NEW DEAL was an uneasy coalition. Fights developed very early between the two factions: one, representing the big farmers, and the other, the little farmers. The Agricultural Adjustment Administration came into being shortly after I got to Washington. Its purpose was to increase farm prices, which were pitifully low. All the farmers were in trouble, even the big ones. There was a proposal that it be set up independent of the Department. Wallace and Tugwell[4] were able to thwart that.

You might say there were three interests involved. There was the consumer thing, too. Rex brought Jerome Frank in as General Counsel for the Triple-A. To protect them. George Peek, the head of the agency —he resented bein' under Wallace—was only interested in high farm prices. They would never admit it, but George represented the big

[4] Rexford G. Tugwell, Under Secretary of Agriculture. It was he who suggested Henry Wallace as Secretary of Agriculture. A political scientist: "Rex was my intellectual mentor."

farmers. And there was the need to protect the sharecroppers and tenant farmers in the South.

Tobacco got down to four cents a pound. Nobody could produce it for that. The Triple-A people reached an agreement with the industry: to more than double the price of tobacco overnight. They wanted no restrictions on the price of cigarettes and smoking tobacco. The net profits would have been greater than the total price paid the small farmers and the labor cost in the manufacture of cigarettes and smoking tobacco, all put together. Naturally, our consumers' group and Jerome Frank raised hell. Wallace decided to turn it down.

Peek, who wanted to see the agreement ratified, went to Roosevelt, undercutting Wallace. The President called the Secretary, I happened to be on the phone: "Henry, I'm sorry we've got to make some compromises. I want you to approve this." They argued a little. Finally, Wallace said, "Mr. President, this is your decision." I brought the papers for Wallace to sign. We met in the lobby of the Mayflower. He said, "Beanie, this is the most appropriate place in the country to sign this damned agreement."[5] (Laughs.)

Wallace was actually opposed to crop restriction. Very few people know this. But we had a problem. Hog prices had just gone to hell. What were they—four, five cents a pound? The farmers were starving to death. They were at the mercy of the packers. We tried to reach an agreement, similar to the tobacco deal—which, despite everything, had worked out fairly well.

They decided to slaughter piggy sows. You know what a piggy sow is? A pregnant pig. They decided to pay the farmers to kill them and the little pigs. Lot of 'em went into fertilizer. This is one of the horrible contradictions we're still seeing.

They lowered the supply goin' to market and the prices immediately went up. Then a great cry went up from the press, particularly the Chicago *Tribune,* about Henry Wallace slaughtering these little pigs. You'd think they were precious babies. The situation was such, you had to take emergency measures. Wallace never liked it.

You had a similar situation on cotton. Prices were down to four cents a pound and the cost of producing was probably ten. So a program was initiated to plow up cotton. A third of the crop, if I remember. Cotton prices went up to ten cents, maybe eleven.

[5] The Mayflower Hotel was a favorite gathering place for the lobbyists of various interests.

This brought on other complications. The Farm Bureau was pressing for these benefit payments to be made to the land owners. We were fighting for these payments to be made directly to the sharecroppers and the tenant farmers, rather than flowing down through the land owners. In most cases, they'd get very little money.

People like Norman Thomas moved in, highly critical of the Department, and properly, I think. Paul Appleby[6] and I had meetings with him, told him what we were trying to do. He didn't spare us, either, and I don't blame him. The Southern Tenant Farmers Union picketed the Department of Agriculture. As I look back on it, a very poor job was done in protecting the sharecroppers and the tenant farmers. The bureaucratic process, even in a decent administration, defeats you. And where there's an uneasy coalition of opposing forces. . . .

"Roosevelt committed himself in the campaign of '32 to cutting government expenditures. It was the most conservative speech he ever made. So we got started with our hands tied behind our back. A lot of things New Dealers wanted couldn't be done without increasing expenditures.

"He had to shift his position. So he brought Harry Hopkins in. Unemployment had jumped to about sixteen million. Something had to be done. He got a substantial appropriation in '34 for relief and also for public works. The public works thing went to Ickes—the very careful, methodical guy who was gonna be sure that nobody took advantage of the building monies.

"Hopkins persuaded the President that the situation was so desperate that everybody in the country who wanted a job had to have a job. Even with very low pay. Almost overnight, he set up the Civil Works Administration.

"Harry was really a sloppy administrator. Ickes was a very careful guy. Hopkins was impatient and he knew you had to have something to eat on. He was the kind of guy that seldom wrote a letter. He'd just call and say, 'Send a million dollars to Arkansas and five million to New York. People are in need.'

"They set up this CWA very hurriedly. There was no means test. Any guy could just walk into the county office—they were set up all over the country—and get a job. Leaf raking, cleaning up libraries, painting the town hall . . . Within a period of sixty days, four million people were put to work.

[6] His associate, the other assistant to the Secretary of Agriculture.

"There was no real scandal in this thing, but it lent itself to all the reactionary criticisms that it couldn't be well-managed. With our mores, you just can't dump $20,000 into a county in the Ozarks and say: put people to work. That's contrary to everything our political establishment was brought up to believe.[7] This lasted only six months. Roosevelt and Hopkins had to end it. They weren't able to get Congressional support to continue.

"Roosevelt won another appropriation—three billion—through an omnibus bill. This brought on another ruckus. Ickes thought it should go for public works: Grand Coulee Dam, Bonneville, projects of this type. They're slow to get under way—wonderful, but they take time. Hopkins thought people should be put to work immediately, even though it might not be done very efficiently."

Among the agencies created was the Resettlement Administration. It was independent of the Department of Agriculture, with Rex Tugwell as head, reporting directly to the President. This was a unique agency and, for that time, fantastic. It was Rex who largely drafted the Executive Order. It had to do with the plight of the small farmer and the migrant worker.

"I was in it from the beginning. Rex brought me in to run the administrative end of it. When he'd delegate authority to someone he trusted, he'd back 'em to the hilt. There were all sorts of bureaucratic battles, but Rex would have nothing to do with 'em. He gave me just absolutely marvelous backing."

Harry Hopkins had established the Rural Rehabilitation Division. It had something to do with urban unemployment. One of the answers was sending people back to the farm, even though they had no farm experience. Tugwell objected and he was absolutely right. Farming requires a good deal of skill. These people just would have been lost.

Hopkins recognized it as a mistake fairly early—that this thing ought to be more closely tied to agriculture. So he agreed to transfer the operation to the Resettlement Administration.

[7] He had an occasion to visit "Cotton Ed" Smith, U.S. Senator from South Carolina, a vociferous opponent of many New Deal measures. Apropos of nothing, the Senator told him: "You seem like a nice, intelligent young man. I don't know why you work for the Government. Get out where you can make an honest living."

"With a paltry $5 million appropriation, the Subsistence Homestead Division was established. A lot of Utopians dreamed of this for years: setting up rural industrial communities. This was given to Ickes originally, but he never had much empathy for Utopians. (Laughs.) All sorts of the craziest ideas came out on how to spend this money. Ickes was glad to get rid of this, so he transferred it to us. Generally, Ickes liked to handle everything, but this was one he wanted out of." (Laughs.)

He describes a project in Hightstown (now called Roosevelt), New Jersey. A group of Jewish ladies' garment workers moved from New York City to this rural community. "The enthusiasm was terrific." It was a cooperative, some working on the farm, others in the garment plant. "They had a hell of a good first year, but you take people out of a highly competitive situation and try to set up a Utopian society, you're gonna have some difficulty. (Laughs.)

"Mrs. Roosevelt tried to get Dubinsky interested,[8] but he didn't like this co-op nonsense. The garment industry was against it, too. They called it a Socialistic, Communist project. Anyway, it failed."

The Rural Rehabilitation had to do with buying sub-marginal land. To retire it from cultivation, reforest it and convert it into a state park. Much of the land we were authorized to buy was in the Great Plains area, damaged by dust storms. Tugwell's idea was: These people should be moved to better land, not just kicked off bad land.

This is what Rex and I were most interested in. There were about six million farmers in the country. I think we helped over a sixth of the farm families. A million farms. The most exciting part was the resettlement projects.

Tugwell had a passion for the adjustment of people to the land. But being a good economist, he foresaw what was gonna happen to small farmers, who just couldn't meet the competition. So we set up a certain number of co-op farms, about a hundred of 'em around the country. About twenty thousand families. Everett Dirksen later described it as Russian collectivism. (Laughs.) We were trying to work out cooperatives, where farmers would have their houses grouped, as a matter of convenience. We varied the pattern from place to place—nursery schools for their kids, central markets for their products. . . . Maybe it was Utopian, but I don't think so.

[8] President of the International Ladies Garment Workers Union (ILGWU).

I'll just tell you about one of 'em. We bought this beautiful delta land in Arkansas for about $100 an acre. It's worth about $700 now. We set up this little community of five or six thousand acres. We brought in about fifty young families.[9] A carefully selected group of young families. . . .

We built these houses, put in a school, nursery . . . they had individual garden plots. It was diversified land—livestock, cotton, fruits, vegetables. They were paid so much a month, and at the end of the year, when the crops were in, they'd divide the profits. It had been operating about two years. They were doin' pretty well. . . .

Will Alexander spent several days on the project visiting with these families. He'd talk to them in the evening, when they were relaxed. They'd say, "Dr. Alexander, this is wonderful. You know, if we're able to stay here four, five years, we'll be able to go out on our own farm."

It came to us as sort of a shock. See, this hunger for land ownership . . . Although they were happy and more secure than they'd ever been in their lives, they were lookin' forward to gettin' out and ownin' their own land. You have to reckon with this kind of thing.

These projects were all stopped cold, after the death of Roosevelt, all liquidated. Congress saw to it. It's one of the really sad things. They had all sorts of problems, sure—but this certainly would have been an important answer to poverty, as we see it now. Over half the farm families have disappeared. They are contributing to the ghetto problems of the city, black and white.

Almost everything we did became controversial. Hopkins had built a couple of migratory labor camps in California. They were also transferred to us. They were very simple camps—well, *Grapes of Wrath* tells you about them better than I could.

"I got a call from John Steinbeck. He wanted some help. He was planning to write this book on migrant workers. Will Alexander and I were delighted. He said, 'I'm writing about people and I have to live as they live.' He planned to go to work for seven, eight weeks as a pea picker or whatever. He asked us to assign someone to go along with

[9] It was now called the Farm Security Administration (FSA). "Rex left, I guess, in '37. He became the chief target of the anti-New Dealers. I think he felt his usefulness had been impaired. I'm also sure he was tired." Dr. Will Alexander succeeded Tugwell.

him, a migrant worker. We chose a little guy named Collins, out of Virginia.

"I paid Collins' salary, which was perhaps illegal. He and Steinbeck worked in the fields together for seven or eight weeks. Steinbeck did a very nice thing. He insisted Collins be technical director of the film, this little migrant worker. And he got screen credit. . . ."

At these camps, the people ran their own affairs. We had our project manager there to help them.[10] This became the most controversial thing we ever did. Before we'd build a camp, we'd hold a public hearing. There was a lot of opposition, particularly from groups like the Associated Farmers.

I was on the stand during one of these hearings. A Congressman, Al Elliott of California, was cross-questioning me. I had all the information, photographs—the plight of migrant workers. He argued against the camp. The real reason the big farmers didn't want them built is that they were places where the migrants might get together and organize. Think of this guy, Chavez, today—things have changed so little in thirty years, it makes you sick to think of it.

When Elliott finished his slambang cross-examination, I said, "You haven't convinced me not to build the camp. I'm issuing instructions for it to be started." He stormed across the room. He was a heavyweight boxer, about six-three, weighing about 210. I weighed in at 155. (Laughs.) He hollered, "You don't represent the people of my district! *I* represent them!" I said, "I have a national constituency. And a very important part of that are the migrant workers of this big country. I'm telling you again, Congressman Elliott, I'm gonna build this camp." We built it. (Laughs.)

Oh, the battles we had! There were any number of people in Congress who made a career out of it. Senator Byrd of Virginia—my own Senator—he was really out to destroy us.[11] He introduced legislation to abolish the agency.

The Farm Bureau, representing the big farmers, sent a very inexperienced kid into the South to investigate what we were doing. He came back with all sorts of fantastic charges. All of which had been published. I had to answer. I was called on the carpet by Byrd's committee.

There was one thing I had authorized that almost tripped me up. I

---

[10] See John Beecher, p. 311.

[11] "He sent me a letter of congratulations when I was appointed administrator of Farm Security."

advised our field workers and county supervisors to include in the rehabilitation loans enough to pay the poll taxes of individuals who
couldn't vote.[12] Byrd thought he had me on this one.

He said: "You are using federal money to pay the poll taxes of people
in the South, is that true?" I said, "No, it isn't true." He said, "What
do you mean?" I said, "We make *loans* to people. Small farmers who
can't get credit elsewhere. We make these loans for a variety of reasons.
Number one, to buy their seed. Number two, to assure them enough
to eat till their crop comes in. Number three, to buy the necessary equipment. Then we have to make sufficient allowance so the kids can at
least have decent clothes. And—I have told our supervisors—if these
people can register and vote, we should include in the loan enough to
pay their poll tax . . . so, Senator, they can become citizens of the
United States."

Carter Glass, the senior Senator from my state, said I was violating
the Virginia Constitution: nobody could pay anybody else's poll tax. I
said: "We're not paying them; we're just lending them money as part
of a complete operation."

I thought I came out fairly well on it. I was due to go back two days
later. The next morning I picked up the Washington *Post,* and here's a
front page story: "Baldwin Criticized by Roosevelt for Paying Poll
Taxes." Jesus. I knew something had gone wrong. Roosevelt was opposed to the poll tax.

But I knew a guy who was interested in the poll tax question and had
entrée to the White House. I said, "Go see Steve Early[13] and get this
message to the President. He's completely misunderstanding what we're
doing." He rushed down.

I was back on the stand. And, boy, Byrd was just beamin'! He had
me locked. He started out: "Mr. Baldwin, I have a story in the Washington *Post* of yesterday morning saying Roosevelt is opposed to the
things you are doing, paying poll taxes." In the meantime, I'm filibuster-
ing—took forty minutes with another statement—hoping that guy would
show up from the White House. I knew the President was calling a
press conference at ten-thirty. I heard a rustle in the back of the room—
the place was jammed. This was the hottest story in town. The guy
rushed up with a little sheet of paper and handed it to me.

[12] "In states like Alabama, the tax would amount to as much as $40. It was a
bar to poor people voting, particularly Negroes."
[13] Roosevelt's press secretary.

Byrd was really at it now—the President had criticized me and said that I must desist from this activity at once. So I cleared my throat (laughs), and I said: "Senator Byrd, I've just been advised that the President in his press conference, only thirty minutes ago, completely supported my position on poll taxes." Well, my Senator from Virginia was the most miserable looking character you've ever seen. (Laughs.)

Oh, the harassment was constant. It was a colossal job, reorganizing the Resettlement Administration, getting all the agencies to mesh and run smoothly. I had a good staff. But I also knew, in order to save it, we had to have a pretty good people's lobby.

We were under fire in Alabama. Senator Bankhead, Tallulah's uncle, was pretty conservative, but he liked the agency and was quite friendly. He said, "We're in real trouble in Alabama. I've got fifteen letters, all my supporters, sayin' the Farm Security Administration should be abolished. Important men." He looked at me and sort of smiled: "Beanie, what are you gonna do about it?" I said, "Give me two days."

I called our regional director in Alabama and asked him to get all the county supervisors to call all their political friends and get some letters to Senator Bankhead. And I said, "I think you ought to get in at least three thousand letters. Have most of 'em written in pencil. It don't matter what they say, just from the people that we're helpin' 'em."

About ten days went by and Senator Bankhead called me. (Laughs.) He had a little stack of letters, about so high, in opposition. And stacks of letters about *this* high. (Laughs.) He said, "For God's sake, stop these letters. We're safe." (Laughs.)

Under Baldwin's administration of the FSA, photographers were employed to take pictures, showing the plight of the rural poor. Among the people involved were Dorothea Lange, Walker Evans, Ben Shahn and Margaret Bourke-White. "I had to cover up a lot of this—even though we were payin' 'em peanuts—because you know what a reactionary Congressman would say: 'Here are these bastards wasting my money. Why are they sending people out to take photographs.'

"We ended up with over a hundred thousand of these photographs. Along about 1940, I had become the most controversial person in the Department of Agriculture. Congress was after me. Because of these projects and because I was a protégé of Tugwell. I knew we weren't going to get by much longer. The only thing we wanted to do was to save these negatives. . . .

"*Roy Stryker*[14] *got in touch with Archibald MacLeish, who under-stood the importance of this. He agreed. So we moved all the films quietly into a safe storage space. When MacLeish became Librarian of Congress, we were able to get them in there, where they will always be.*

"*I think our most lasting contribution was this collection of photo-graphs. I think it more effectively dramatized the plight of poor people than anything else done in thirty years. It was accidental. We just hap-pened to hit on the medium. . . ."*

Pare Lorentz's two documentary films, The Plow That Broke The Plains *and* The River, *were produced under the auspices of the Farm Security Administration. Again, controversy. "We couldn't get into many movie houses at first. Finally we got into a lot of 'em."*

The Depression lessened, but it never really ended until the war. The New Deal was never enough. Looking back, it was a pretty conservative effort. Rex Tugwell once said to me, "Beanie, we were pikers." I'd ask for $800 million, we'd get a couple of hundred million, and we thought we did pretty well. Today, with our war budget. . . .

When Roosevelt's death came, the New Deal was dead as far as I was concerned. I have nothing against Truman, but he simply wasn't up to it. Morgenthau was forced out.[15] Ickes was forced out. Wallace was fired. It was a whole new game of cards. At this point, my fascina-tion with Government was gone.

James A. Farley

Postmaster General during Roosevelt's first two Administrations. He had been F.D.R.'s campaign manager in the elections of 1932 and 1936.

In 1928, Roosevelt was elected Governor of New York by less than 30,000 votes.[16] *In 1930, "I was chairman of the Democratic State*

[14] Head of the Historical Division of the Resettlement Administration. "He's the guy responsible for these magnificent photographs."

[15] Henry Morgenthau, Roosevelt's Secretary of Treasury.

[16] Alfred E. Smith, in 1928, running for President against Herbert Hoover, failed to carry New York State.

Committee and conducted his campaign for re-election, and he carried the Governorship by 750,000 votes."

On the wall, facing his desk, is a large portrait of Franklin D. Roosevelt—youthful, vigorous.

He glances up at the photograph. . . .

IT BRINGS BACK the last discussion I had with him. I urged him not to run for the third term. I predicted he was in for rough going. The world was in a bad way. He'd break a tradition that shouldn't be broken—that had existed from Washington's time. And he wasn't getting any younger. I predicted that he'd run for a fourth time. I just told him I thought that, if he won, he'd even run for a fifth time. I broke with him on the issue, of course.

I felt very keenly about it. He just didn't think anybody else was big enough to be President. And that's not said unkindly. He did not like to give up power, let's put it that way.

In 1936, I was more optimistic than he was. I predicted he'd carry every state but two: Maine and Vermont. I coined a slogan then: There used to be a phrase: "As Maine goes, so goes the nation." The day after election, at a press conference, I said, "As Maine goes, so goes Vermont."

I went across the country for him in 1931, starting about June 18, if my memory serves me correctly. All by train. I was gone about twenty-odd nights, and I was on the train eighteen nights. When you'd get up in the morning, the sheets were covered with coal dust. It was hot, no air-conditioning. Pretty tough going.

As the train stopped for refueling, say, at Grand Island, Nebraska, or Pocatello, Idaho, I'd get off and walk around the station platform. I'd talk with the railroad men and the others. They didn't know who I was. I'd ask them who they thought was the best man for the Democrats to nominate, and could he win, and so on.

I wrote Mr. Roosevelt a letter—I don't know if it was from Portland or Seattle—in which I said that nearly every Governor I met was a candidate for Vice-President because they were sure he could win.

It's one of those things. You go riding around town and talk to taxi drivers and other people, you can go into lunchrooms. The information is not always accurate, but the sentiment is obvious.

People wanted a change. Unemployment. And then, Prohibition. Arthur Brisbane, who was a great reporter for Hearst, supposedly a very astute newspaperman—and I'm sure he was—made this statement in the lobby of the Congress Hotel in Chicago: What difference does it make what plank the Democrats put in their platform? The Eighteenth Amendment won't be repealed during the lifetime of any person attending this convention. This was in July of '32. It was repealed early in December of '33. Goes to show you how fast public opinion moves.

Mr. Roosevelt showed great leadership. He surrounded himself—one of the best men he had around him in those days was Ray Moley. I was sorry that relationship was broken. And it wasn't Moley's fault, see.

I felt those fellas around Roosevelt—he told me in 1940 that the people around the White House thought he was the only one who could win. I looked at him and said, "Mr. President, you know damn well that they want their jobs, and if you don't run again, they won't be around here the day after the inauguration." I said: "Hull[17] can make a better race than you can, because the third term won't enter into it." Hull was strong, according to the polls.

Very few Presidents have people around them who talk up to them. If they do, they're not around very long. Moley talked up to him, and so did I, at cabinet meetings and otherwise.

I never knew about the court packing, until I read it in the paper. The *Evening Telegram,* that afternoon, the early edition. I wasn't in Washington when he called the cabinet together. I didn't happen to get down to the meeting. So I saw him a few days later. I said, "Why the hell'd you call that meeting without letting me know?" He said, "Well, I tried to get word to you, but it was understood you were in New York and I couldn't reach you." I said, "You probably figured I'd be against it." And he said, "Not necessarily." (Laughs.) It was a mistake. But I did make speeches in favor of the court bill, because I was a member of the Administration.

They say that Roosevelt in '32 saved our society. . . .

He saved our free enterprise system, he saved the banks, he saved the insurance companies. There ain't any doubt but what Roosevelt in those first hundred days . . . this was a tremendous job.

[17] Cordell Hull, Secretary of State during Roosevelt's first three terms.

*What do you think would have happened if he hadn't been elected
. . . if his New Deal legislation had not been enacted?*

God only knows. I remember, during the inauguration period, you couldn't get a check cashed in Washington. The hotels were afraid to cash a check, so many banks were failing. During the week of inauguration, Roosevelt closed all the banks and then gave orders to move as quickly as they could to open what were known to be definitely solvent banks. A quick survey. They didn't lose any time.

If a Depression came on us today, would the attitude of people be different?

The attitude of people today is bad enough even though they're gainfully employed. It's difficult for me to understand the attitude of youth. I never went to college, but I'd proceed on the theory that if you're not satisfied, resign and go to some other college. If I was a student at Columbia now, I wouldn't be dissenting out around and causing a lot of trouble. I'd go to a college where I thought the conditions were ones under which I could labor and graduate and get the education I sought. That's an old-fashioned idea, but that's the way I feel.

What are your memories concerning Mrs. Roosevelt?

I had a very fine relationship with her. She sought my help on many occasions and I tried to help her. She was well-intentioned. Despite what may have been said to the contrary, she never interfered with my political activities at all. She'd ask me for my advice and pass on some suggestions, and I'd accept them or reject them. We never had any difficulties.

She really was very kindly disposed toward me. After I left the Government, friends of mine would see her, and she'd always say that Franklin—referring to him the way she did—didn't handle my situation properly.

The only thing that annoyed her is what I had in my book.[18] I quoted her as saying that President Roosevelt was ill at ease with a person who was not his social equal. Well, he *was* a snob. We're all snobs. We're all kinds of snobs, see. Unknowingly, he talked down to others. A lot of them resented it.

[18] *The Jim Farley Story,* by James A. Farley (New York, McGraw Hill, 1948).

You see, he was raised in that kind of patrician society where they looked over their noses. He didn't realize it. He never thanked me for anything I ever did for him. When he was elected Governor, he wrote me. But after that, he never wrote me or thanked me for anything. And I did a lot of things. It never affected my relationship with him. I wouldn't let it. Up to the third term, it was as fine a relationship as ever existed between two men. I was sorry it broke up that way.

Joe Marcus

An economist, he had worked in the New Deal days on a Harry Hopkins project: a study of the effect of technology on re-employment opportunities . . . "in other words, why the stickiness of unemployment.

"In '39, you still had over ten million unemployed, out of a labor supply of forty million. You're talking about twenty-five percent of the population. In '36, there were fifteen million unemployed, if not more. Industrial production came back to the '29 level around '37, just for a few months. Then it slid off into the Depression again.

"The New Deal starts wondering about problems. Maybe it's monopoly, maybe it's technology. That's the work I got involved in."

I THINK it was '31 or '32. I was attending the City College of New York. Most were students whose parents were workers or small businessmen hit by the Depression. In the public speaking class, I was called upon to talk about unemployment insurance. I was attacked by most of the students . . . this was Socialism. I was shocked by their vehemence. If I remember, the American Federation of Labor at its national convention voted it down. The idea of social security was very advanced. Those who were really hungry wanted something. But the intellectuals, the students, the bureaucratic elements—to them it was a horrible thought. It was something subversive. At first.

But they learned quickly. It was a shock to them. When Roosevelt came out with the ideas, it was not a clearly thought-out program. There was much improvisation. What you had was a deep-seated emotional feeling as far as the people were concerned. A willingness to change society, just out of outrage, out of need. I think they would have accepted even more radical ideas.

Roosevelt was reflecting the temper of the time—the emotional more than the intellectual. It wasn't merely a question of the king bestowing favors. The pressure from below was a reality. It was not a concentrated campaign effort. There was no organization with a program that commanded the majority of the people. This was part of the political strangeness of our society. The actions below were very revolutionary. Yet some of the ideas of the people, generally, were very backward.

I graduated college in '35. I went down to Washington and started to work in the spring of '36. The New Deal was a young man's world. Young people, if they showed any ability, got an opportunity. I was a kid, twenty-two or twenty-three. In a few months I was made head of the department. We had a meeting with hot shots: What's to be done? I pointed out some problems: let's define what we're looking for. They immediately had me take over. I had to set up the organization and hire seventy-five people. Given a chance as a youngster to try out ideas, I learned a fantastic amount. The challenge itself was great.

It was the idea of being asked big questions. The technical problems were small. These you had to solve by yourself. But the context was broad: Where was society going? Your statistical questions became questions of full employment. You were not prepared for it in school. If you wanted new answers, you needed a new kind of people. This is what was exciting.

Ordinarily, I might have had a job at the university, marking papers or helping a professor. All of a sudden, I'm doing original research and asking basic questions about how our society works. What makes a Depression? What makes for pulling out of it? Once you start thinking in these terms, you're in a different ball game.

The climate was exciting. You were part of a society that was on the move. You were involved in something that could make a difference. Laws could be changed. So could the conditions of people.

The idea of being involved close to the center of political life was unthinkable, just two or three years before all this happened. Unthinkable for someone like me, of lower middle-class, close to ghetto, Jewish life. Suddenly you were a significant member of society. It was not the kind of closed society you had lived in before.

You weren't in the situation kids are in today, where you're confronted with a consensus of hopelessness . . . unless you just break things up. You were really part of something, changes could be made. Bringing *immediate* results to people who were starving. You could do something about it: that was the most important thing. This you felt.

A feeling that if you had something to say, it would get to the top. As I look back now, memoranda I had written reached the White House, one way or another. The biggest thrill of my life was hearing a speech of Roosevelt's, using a selection from a memorandum I had written.

Everybody was searching for ideas. A lot of guys were opportunists, some were crackpots. But there was a search, a sense of values . . . that would make a difference in the lives of people.

We weren't thinking of remaking society. That wasn't it. I didn't buy this dream stuff. What was happening was a complete change in social attitudes at the central government level. The question was: How can you do it within this system? People working in all the New Deal agencies were dominated by this spirit.

There was the old government bureaucracy that could not administer the new programs. Roosevelt, who was criticized for being a bad administrator, made a great deal of sense out of this. There were weaknesses, but the point is if you wanted to get jobs for people in a hurry, as in WPA, you had to find new people with the spirit, with the drive.

At one stage, Harry Hopkins met with his staff, a lot of people, in a huge auditorium. He explained they'd have to work day and night to get this particular job done. He asked for volunteers, who would start off tonight and work straight through. Practically everybody in the auditorium raised their hands. Youth and fervor.

Normally, administrative people were much older. But even the young of the old bureaucracy were stodgy. They came to work, left their jobs when the day was over, went out for their lunches. . . . Frankly, they didn't work very hard and knocked off whenever they could. What rightwingers say about Government employees was very true in many cases.

The New Dealers were different. I'm not only talking about policy people. I'm talking about the clerks, who felt what they were doing was important. You didn't take time out for lunch because of a job that had to be done. You had a sandwich on the desk. Their job made sense. . . . Of course, I'm romanticizing somewhat, but there was still this difference.

The civil servants were competent people, but they worked within rigid formulas. They worked their hours and when they were through, that was it. The idea of sitting up all night. . . .

The evenings were exciting. Social evenings were spent in discussing policy, in what you were doing. It wasn't bridge playing. It wasn't just idle drinking or gossip. . . .

His wife, Sue, interjects: "The wives took a very dim view of men getting off in a corner talking about the levels of unemployment. The women were clustered together on the other side, but the husbands were so busy, so involved. . . . We took a dim view, I must say. (Laughs.)

"Every once in a while, we'd say, 'What is it?' We'd be interested. But it was very hard, because they were so terribly involved."

(He laughs, then adds,) "It would get very technical, I must admit —shop talk."

SUE: *"We were interested in what our husbands were doing. We felt as they did, that it was terribly important. Although I remember once, when Joe's boss called about something. They wanted me to look for a piece of paper on the desk. He said, 'I hope you don't mind my taking your husband weekends like that.' I said, 'I certainly do.' (Laughs.) When Joe came home, he said, 'Oh, that was a terrible thing you said. After all, it's for the war effort.' This was in the late Thirties. (Laughs.) We understood the philosophical things—that was taken for granted. It's the technical discussions that were so annoying. Other wives, too, felt part of this effort. But on a social level, it sometimes got difficult. They got so immersed in technical questions, the ceiling could have fallen in and they wouldn't have noticed." (Laughs.)*

The ambitious young man today takes his work home, too. But it's a question of himself, personal ambition. Not concern with society. Of course, some of our best operators were personally ambitious, but the climate was something else.

There was no difference between leisure time and work time. This doesn't mean we didn't go for a movie or go for a walk in the park. But the people I knew did not build a meaningful life outside of work. And action related to it, in some way.

SUE: *"One of the nicest things in Washington, with all the other New Deal people, was that everybody lived on the same level. The notion*

301

of keeping up with the Joneses didn't exist. Nobody was pushing for anything, because everybody was involved. . . ."

It was an exciting community, where we lived in Washington. The basic feeling—and I don't think this is just nostalgia—was one of excitement, of achievement, of happiness. Life was important, life was significant.

Were there questions in Washington about the nature of our society?

I don't think revolution as a topic of the day existed. The fact that people acted as they did, in violation of law and order, was itself a revolutionary act. People suddenly heard there was a Communist Party. It was insignificant before then. Suddenly, the more active people, the more concerned people, were in one way or another exposed to it. It never did command any real popular support, though it had influence in key places. This was a new set of ideas, but revolution was never really on the agenda.

F.D.R. was very significant in understanding how best to lead this sort of situation. Not by himself, but he mobilized those elements ready to develop these programs.

There are some who say F.D.R. saved this society. . . .

There's no question about it. The industrialists who had some understanding recognized this right away. He could not have done what he did without the support of important elements of the wealthy class. They did not sabotage the programs. Just the opposite.

One of the first things the annual report of Morgan & Company dealt with, right after the war, was the question of full employment. This had been considered a Bolshevik idea five years earlier. Business leaders, in the early days of the war, saw the importance of developing more progressive programs. It was a way of rationalizing a corporate society. The New Deal did the same thing.

It was a very unusual Depression in the history of societies. It lasted so long and went so deep. Usually, when you get a depression—even a severe one—you get two, three years of decline and in another two, three years, you're back where you were. But *ten* years . . . Just think, in 1939, we were back to the industrial production of '29. And you had a ten-year increase in population. If it weren't for the war orders from France and England, there's a question if we would ever have hit that point. The war did end the Depression. That doesn't mean that something else might not have ended it.

Burton K. Wheeler

Former Senator from Montana. In 1924, he was Senator Robert La Follette's running mate on the Progressive Party ticket. They polled nearly five million votes.

I SAW the Depression coming. Joe Kennedy came to see me. He said, "I'm afraid I'm gonna wake up with nine kids and three homes and no dough." I said, "Do you want to be safe? Buy gold." He came to me again. "They've taken my gold." I said, "Buy silver bullion." He came down once more. "They're taking my silver bullion." I said, "Do you want to be perfectly safe? Go get a farm, where you can raise a cow and a pig and some chickens, and put some of those kids of yours to work. But don't get too big, because we might take it away from you." He said, "Is it as bad as that?" I said, "No, but it might get that bad."

He recounted his experiences as a visitor in Vienna in 1923, as the Depression there affected all classes. "I didn't think it would start as quickly as it did here in the United States."

Hoover was President when they passed the Reconstruction Finance bill. I opposed it. Its purpose was to bail out the bankers, the insurance companies and the railroads. I said, "The pressure's gonna be so great that anybody who's got a sick cow is gonna come to Washington to borrow money." Bob La Follette, Junior, said he's voting for it, because he's afraid there would be a crash. I said, "There would be, but the sooner it comes off, the better." This RFC would only prolong it. The greater our indebtedness, the greater the crash.

Old J. Ham Lewis came up to me.[19] He used to call me "boy." That made me mad. "Boy, give 'em the devil." I said, "Won't you make a

[19] J. Hamilton Lewis, pink-whiskered, pearl-gray-spatted fashion plate, was a Democratic Senator from Illinois.

speech on it?" He said, "No, I can't. I represent a damn bunch of thieves. Thieves, I tell you, who want to reach their hand in the public coffers and pull all the money out. My God, if I were a free man, I'd tear this thing limb from limb."

I'd get pretty discouraged when the men in the cloak rooms would come up to me and say, "I agree with you." Then go out and vote the other way. I remember one piece of legislation I was interested in. It involved a challenge to the big money powers. A Senator said to me, "I think you're right. I'm gonna vote with you." In the afternoon he said, "I can't." "Why not?" "My bosses called me up." "You have a boss that tells you how you've got to vote?" "Who's your boss? You've got one." I said, "The only boss I've got is the people." He said, "Don't give me that stuff. You've got a boss somewhere."

When Tom Pendergast[20] was indicted, Harry Truman came up to me. "Should I resign?" I said, "Why should you resign?" He said, "They've indicted the old man. He made me everything I am, and I've got to stand by him."

After Roosevelt's election, I introduced a bill to remonitize silver. All the bankers of the country were against it. They were able to control the money much better with the gold standard. Some of the big mining companies out West were interested in my bill. For the wrong reasons. They were interested in raising the price of silver, but not in its use in money. The president of Anaconda Copper thought I was right—better silver than paper. There wasn't enough gold to go around. I said, "Why don't you say so publicly?" He shrugged his shoulders. I said, "You don't dare say so, because you owe the National City Bank so much money."

He recounts his disagreement with Roosevelt in the matter of court packing. During "the hysteria of the First World War, I saw men strung up. Only the federal courts stood up at all, and the Supreme Court better than any of them. Not as well as they should have, but better than the others." The aid of Associate Justice Brandeis and a letter from Chief Justice Hughes helped him in defeating Roosevelt's effort. He nonetheless led the fight for some of F.D.R.'s social legislation.

I handled the Utility Holding Company bill. It was a hard-fought one. I was approached by a fishing companion: "These utility people are

[20] Political boss of Kansas City for many years.

gonna destroy anyone who gets in their way." A few days later, two of their chief lobbyists visited me. I said, "Have you got any guns?" They said, "No, your boy frisked us." I said, "I told him to." They said, "How much time you gonna give us?" "One week." "We've got to have a month." "I'll give you a week, and the Government a week. If you can't tell what's wrong with the bill in a week's time, that's too bad." They said, "You're pretty cocky." "No," I said, "I'm just tired of crooked lobbyists and crooked lawyers."

He was pressured by colleagues of Roosevelt to accept the candidacy as Vice President for the 1940 campaign. "Justice Murphy came from the White House. 'The President will call you up.' 'I won't take it.' 'You're the biggest damn fool I ever met. You'll be President of the United States.' 'I can't take it.'" He was opposed to what he felt were Roosevelt's "war policies."

I had seen Roosevelt in '39. I told him it would be a mistake if he ran for a third term. He agreed. He said to me, "Burt, along about January or February of next year, we'll pick out somebody who can win. I'm tired of supporting some of these old reactionaries." And then he said, "Farley would like to see Hull run, and he'd like to run as Vice President. He doesn't think Hull would live through it. That'd make him President. Cardinal Mundelein told me that even though he'd like to see a Catholic President some day, he didn't want to see him come in the back door." That Roosevelt was really a master.

David Kennedy

Secretary of the Treasury.[21]
"I came to Washington in September of '29 to attend law school. I joined the Federal Reserve Board in April of 1930. Marriner Eccles came in '33 as Governor of the Board.

[21] The conversation took place before his appointment by President Nixon. He was at the time Chairman of the Board of the Continental Illinois National Bank and Trust Company.

"He laughs about that. He said, 'I'm from Utah, too. Did you know me?' I said, 'Yes, I knew you, but you didn't know me. I was a boy, and you were a man in a dark office.' He said, 'Well, I can't be blamed for bringing you.' I said, 'No, but I can be blamed for bringing you.'"

MY FIRST WORK was with the story of bank failures. In 1933, when President Roosevelt came in and declared a Bank Holiday, we worked day and night. We had three days in which to license the banks which were solvent. We had to get reports from the various states, Federal Reserve banks, the Comptroller of Currency and individual banks. From all over the country. I never left the office those three days. I slept on the couch and had sandwiches brought in.

We had a number of very famous cases, considered on a twenty-four-hour basis, as to whether they should open or not open. It was a matter of judgment. Two major banks in Detroit remained closed, because it was determined they were not solvent. Borderline cases were permitted to open.

There were three days of openings. Major banks in large cities were opened one day. The next day, the Reserve cities—the rest of the banks on the third day. In those three days, the field examiners knew the banks and knew their stories. It was not just starting from scratch. They'd been studying them day by day as these problems were developing.

The Bank Holiday was probably the most dramatic happening in the history of the financial world. It shocked many people. What was going to happen? Was this it? But once it was considered in realistic terms, it was accepted by the people on Wall Street and around the country, as a period in which to get your house in order. It gave the bankers themselves a chance to consolidate their resources.

All through the Twenties, they were having about six hundred banks a year close. Before the Crash, when conditions were booming. People don't realize that. In '29 and '30, they got into the thousands. Closings every day. There was one bank in New York, the Bank of the United States—in the wake of that closing, two hundred smaller banks closed. Because of the deposits in that bank from the others.

We had the problem of reconstructing the banking laws. In a serious Depression or a forced sale in bankruptcy, what is anything worth? It's worth only what somebody will pay you for it. Values just tumble away down. So Marriner Eccles conceived the theory of intrinsic values, whatever that means. There must be some basis, other than paper, on which an examiner can determine whether a bank should stay open.

This was difficult to sell the accountants and the bankers. But the Banking Act of '33 was passed, and they started to follow that theory. It permitted the Federal Reserve to lend on any sound asset. Before, they had the commercial paper theory—you could lend on certain things. And banks ran out of collateral for borrowing purposes.

Then the FDIC[22] was established. It gave confidence to the man on the street that his bank would not fail, and if it did, he was insured up to $10,000. That was part of the Banking Act of '33.

The Banking Act of '34 was much more fundamental. It gave our whole Federal Reserve System a better basis. This caused a fight between Marriner Eccles and Carter Glass.[23] They had different philosophies. Marriner was one of the original advocates of pump-priming. Glass was of the older school. Marriner loves an argument, and he was able to get most of his recommendations approved. It was a great victory for him.

He recounts the defeatist attitude, as he saw it, of the early Thirties. "Every one that we talked to, in the schools, in the universities, would have very little vision of what this great country and its resources could do. We had studies going on, in housing, in education, in various public works, in order to stimulate the economy.

"We were all affected by the Crash. My salary was cut fifteen percent. I was supposed to get a raise. There were thirty-five applicants for the job when I was hired. I was promised a substantial increase at the end of my six months' trial period. The man in charge of my division came to me and said: There's a freeze on all salaries in the Federal Reserve. The Government had done it, and even though the Board was independent,[24] it'd go along. He said he'd make it up when the crisis was over.

"Finally, when the Banking Act of '33 was passed, he made two

[22] The Federal Deposit Insurance Corporation.

[23] Senator from Virginia; Chairman of the Senate Finance Committee.

[24] "It's completely autonomous. Of course, it's a creation of Congress and its members are appointed by the President, but it has an air of independence few other agencies have, because we're not under the General Accounting Office. There has been a continuous battle. Congressman Wright Patman believes the board should be under Governmental control."

exceptions. I was one of 'em. After three years, I got a $600 increase. I learned what the word 'substantial' means." (Laughs.)

1937 and 1939 were interesting periods. We hadn't come out of the Depression. It was deep-set. The Board increased reserve requirements of member banks because they had large excess reserves. We made studies showing that only a very few banks would be affected by this increase in requirements. Then we got a real turn-down.

There was a very, very serious recession in '37. Marriner spent a good share of his time trying to prove to the public that it was not caused by the Federal Reserve action. Critics said it was.

We had a serious break in the market, when war broke out in Europe in 1939. A problem in securities. The Federal Reserve Board said it would buy all the securities that were offered, no matter what the volume, at the market price. That stopped the avalanche of sales. The market settled down, and we got through that.

We really had not made a substantial recovery from the deep Depression of the early Thirties. Unemployment was still very high. The New Deal programs were not stimulating the way people thought. There was sort of a defeatist attitude—that the Government just had to do all this for the people. It was not until the war, with its economic thrust, that we pulled out of it. The war got us out of it, not the New Deal policies.

As a matter of fact, the policies pursued could have thrown us into real trouble. It was changing our way of life. You're spending money and going into debt, but you're not really finding ways and means to explore new projects. Like today, we're in an explosion of ideas.

Despite all the programs—PWA, WPA, FSA . . . ?

It took care of immediate suffering in part of the areas. I'm not criticizing it in that sense. But it didn't pull the thing up so that private enterprise could take its place and replace it.

You applied the word "defeatist" to Roosevelt's as well as Hoover's time. . . .

Roosevelt gave us quite a bit of hope, early. He probably saved us from complete collapse, in that sense. But he did not answer the things. Many of his programs were turned on and off, started and stopped . . . shifting gears. Because we had never been in anything like this.

Planning had not been done. So they'd go out and sweep the mountains and clean up the debris, and then the wind comes along and blows it back again. It gave some work. But the people that got the money, in some ways were benefited and in other ways were hurt. They didn't like to see the waste. . . . They had mixed reactions.

We have a ranch in Utah. In 1933, we had a serious drought. Anyone that lived out there can tell you it nearly broke all the ranches in the area. I was on the ranch this day with my father. We had cattle coming in from the range land, thirsty, without food, getting down to the water. We'd gather these up and sell them to the Government. They'd pay from $4 to $20 a head. If the animal was alive, you'd get $4. If it was a good animal, you'd get up to $20.

They drove up, the buyers from the agricultural department. There were seven of them in this one car, on Government pay. There was an argument over the value of one steer, which was as perfect an animal as any I'd ever seen. They didn't want to give but $16. My father said it was $20 or nothing. After some argument with the seven men, they gave it. Before the Government was in on this, we'd sell all our cattle to a buyer, one man. Here were seven. The people out there got the feeling this was just Big Government, a make-work thing. These things tended to create a defeated attitude.

Do you recall any change in the Washington atmosphere, during the time you were there, between the last days of Hoover and the early days of Roosevelt . . . ?

In the last days of Hoover, it was very gloomy. The financial collapse had just dampened everything. They didn't know which way to turn. Mr. Hoover, as a man, took a good deal of this blame personally upon himself. It was unjustifiable. Roosevelt, with his silver tongue, brought words of hope. He started many things going, but they were turned on and off. We had the NRA, the WPA and these things—they'd come and go. You never could get clear-cut decisions. One day, one thing; the next day, another. It was bedlam and confusion in Washington.

Ickes and those fellows not knowing which way to go. One day, he was in good grace; the next day, it was Morgenthau. And the next day, everybody was questioning Harry Hopkins and those fellows, because they had the ear of the President, and they were getting in there on the side. We'd get stories about tossing a coin in the air to decide the price of gold. . . . Whether it's true or not, I don't know. But we'd get these stories.

I was enthusiastic when Roosevelt came in. I thought: We're in serious trouble. Something has to be done, and here's a man that's going to do it. I voted for him his first term and his second. After that, I voted against him. It wasn't just on the two-term basis, although that was important. The packing of the Supreme Court and the fact that we were not making the progress I thought our country was capable of making. . . . I became terribly disenchanted.

He was a dramatic leader. He had charm, personality, poise and so on. He could inspire people. But to me, he lacked the stick-to-it-iveness to carry a program through.

The private sector was not called upon enough . . . ?

I felt we were relying too much on the Government to save us. There was not enough involvement in the private area to carry its share of the burden. I felt people were losing their initiative to get out on their own instead of: Please hand it to me. Of course, we hadn't seen anything then compared to what we have now in this respect. But today, we have all this private involvement that is so interesting and expansive. It offsets the other. I don't want to be too critical of Mr. Roosevelt, because he did, in our period of history, do something.

This is—to use a Rooseveltian phrase—an "iffy" question: suppose he didn't step in with these programs, what do you think would have happened?

We had to have some of them. If he hadn't done it, someone else could have. In one way, you could say he saved it because he was our leader and he surely had the support.

At the time of the collapse that stunned so many, was there some doubt about our society?

Not as it is today. It is a different sort of thing. It was bewilderment. Of course, we hadn't been used to the affluence we have today. I didn't think our people were poor, many of them. They ate well, and so on. But the unemployment continued on and on and on.

Today, attitudes have changed. There'd be some rebellion that you didn't have then. It was peaceful then. It was law-abiding. You could walk down the street and have money in your pocket, and no one would take it from you. You might have a beggar ask you for something. But there wouldn't be the kind of feeling that you'd have it taken away from you. There was more respect for law. Now there is this demanding thing. It's general, it's in all the world now.

POSTSCRIPT: *"When I first came to Washington, Doc Townsend visited me. He was a nice looking gentleman, gray-headed, thin. A good country doctor, I felt. Well, he had a crazy idea which you couldn't talk him out of: a tax on all the deposits that went through the banks. I said, 'Somebody would have to pay for it.' He said, 'Look at all those billions of dollars. We don't have to take but a small amount of it.' He didn't realize, however, you raise it, it's going to be a burden on somebody. But he was a spokesman for a great lot of older people, and he gave them hope. I thought he was a little daft on this concept. On the other hand, he served a purpose at the time. He gave old people the idea of a pension. And now they're organized."* (*Laughs.*) *"I respected the old man."*

John Beecher

Poet. Two of his anthologies, To Live And Die in Dixie *and* Hear The Wind Blow, *concern the Depression in the South.*

He is of Abolitionist ancestry, a great-grandnephew of Henry Ward Beecher and Harriet Beecher Stowe. His maternal grandfather, an Irish-American coal miner, was a member of the Molly Maguires, terrorist mine organizers in the 1870s. . . . "He was the principal subversive influence in my life. . . .

"My father was a top executive of a southern subsidiary of the United States Steel Corporation. Fortunately for me and possibly fortunately for him, he lost most of his money in the stock market crash of '29. He had a hard time recovering from it, psychologically.

"I remember how, after dinner, he'd just lie on the couch in utter despair, night after night, for hours. A man who was interested in music,

*read all kinds of literature, novels, plays, history, economics and so on
—there was this man so knocked out. We were afraid he was going to
commit suicide. His close personal friend did take a header out of the
fourteenth-story window. He was still getting an excellent salary, but
he felt—up to that time—the measure of a man's success was the amount
of money he accumulated.*

*"But he did recover. He became a kind of coolly critical intelligence.
He was ready for any kind of change in the system—perhaps this system
was not eternal, perhaps there should be a more cooperative society."*

I HAD my first job in the steel mills, back in the Twenties. You could say
the Depression commenced in this town, Ainsley, Alabama, a steel
mill suburb of Birmingham. We had the first bank to go bust in the early
days of the Depression. All the workingmen trusted the banker.

In the fall of 1929, I left my job as metallurgist on the open hearth
to teach at the University of Wisconsin. For Alexander Meiklejohn's
Experimental College. Of course, the students became turned on very
rapidly during the Depression. At commencement, you'd see fellows in
caps and gowns selling apples at the doors of the stadiums, where they
were handing out the programs. This was kind of a demonstration, just
to show . . . highly gifted chaps, you know, going to work in dime
stores, after they got their degrees. And lucky to get the work. So they
were radicalized by the Depression the way kids are radicalized today
by the Vietnam war and the whole drift of our society. . . .

In the summer of '32, I played hookey from the academic rat race. I
was doing a doctoral dissertation on the novels of Dickens and hard
times back in 1832. I decided to find out what was happening in my
own time. In my home town. I found out with a vengeance. This led,
actually, to my going out into the Depression. First, as a volunteer
social worker and then as a New Deal administrator.

For eight years, starting in '34, I worked as field administrator all
over the South . . . with white and black, rural people, coal miners,
steel workers, textile workers, a fertilizer plant people, turpentine camp
workers and sharecroppers.

Was theirs an attitude of resignation?

No, indeed. The ferment I discovered in Birmingham was just
tremendous. The people were ready, really, to take action. They, of

course, didn't know which way to turn. Few people believed, in '32, that Roosevelt was going to be the answer.

I remember passing through Chicago on my way to the South. I stopped off at Hull House to see my literary idol, John Dos Passos.[25] He thought we were on the road to revolution . . . that Roosevelt would, of course, be re-elected, but that he wouldn't rise to the occasion. He seemed to believe some kind of anarcho-syndicalist solution would be found. The American labor unions would lead the way. Of course, they were not leading the way. And Roosevelt surprised everyone by coming up with emergency programs which did take most of the bite out of popular discontent.

I remember in Ainsley that year, in the relief headquarters, a woman had been arguing and arguing to get some milk for her baby. You should have seen the things they were giving babies instead of milk. I remember seeing them put salt-pork gravy in milk bottles and putting a nipple on, and the baby sucking this salt-pork gravy. A real blue baby, dying of starvation. In house after house, I saw that sort of thing.

Well, this woman was determined to get real milk for her baby. She raised all the cain she could, until the top supervisor agreed to let her have a quart. When they handed it to her, she got back as far as she could and threw it up against the wall—Pow!—and smashed it. This was the kind of spirit, you see. Not unlike the kind of thing you see today amongst the black people. But it was white people then, principally. They seemed to be the most militant ones—at least down South.

As an administrator, I worked with Rex Tugwell's rural resettlement programs. Rex had written, when he was an undergraduate in Columbia, a poem in praise of socialism. They kept dragging up this undergraduate poem on Poor Rex. You recall how viciously he was attacked? Actually this program, of which I was a charter employee, wasn't as radical as I would have liked it to be.

It was a stop-gap, dealing with rural problems. Grants-in-aid, to small farmers, so they could hold on and continue to produce crops. I managed a group of five of these communities.

I switched to the migratory labor program. I set one up in Florida for migratory farm workers, who at the time were poor blacks, displaced sharecroppers from Georgia and Alabama. Also displaced whites who had been, largely, packinghouse workers.

[25] Dos Passos was covering the Republican and Democratic conventions for *The New Republic*.

We built a hospital, clinics, community centers, schools and a number of temporary camps. They were at least better than the grass huts, tree houses and all those terrible barracks in which they were living.

I was down in the same area last winter, almost thirty years later. I found those "temporary" camps still standing there, deteriorated and disintegrated. In one place the ground had dropped ten feet. These places were way up in the air, on piles, because the land had subsided. In 1968, they were still living in these camps we had built in the Thirties.

The migratory workers, then, were not really affected by the New Deal?[26]

No. When the war came along, all the domestic programs were swept under the rug. They turned our migratory camp over to the local communities. The kind of thing we hear so much about today: local control. So the local people got hold of it. . . .

We had built a big hospital in the Everglades for the black people. There wasn't a hospital bed for fifty thousand people, not one. They had all kinds of things wrong with them, and there was nowhere they could go, so we built a hospital. It was the first thing of its kind the Administration had ever done. It was designed primarily for the black people.

The minute it was turned over to the locals, in the days of the war, they evicted all the black people. They repainted the hospital inside and out and made it a white hospital. I was talking recently to one family in the black camp—in those days they kept everything separate. The black camp is still a black camp, and the white camp is still the white camp—still segregated.

They told me down there, this last winter, they're not allowed to have community meetings any more—or any kind of self-government that they had. They didn't even have dances any more in the community centers we had built for them. They were run by white managers and white deputies and all this sort of thing. The very thing we had been trying to get away from, a generation later had been reinstated.

The migratory labor program was the most advanced thing I encountered in the whole Administration. The resettlement communities were more paternalistic. They carefully selected families, according to

[26] See Cesar Chavez, p. 58.

criteria handed down from Washington. In the camps, we had to rely on the people to do it. So they made all the ordinances, and they ran all the camps and did a much better job than the bunch of bureaucrats.

(*Half-tells, half-muses a poetic remembrance.*) They were living on the canal banks in stinking quarters and barracks, sometimes thirteen people in a room. Or in tarpaper huts, in shelters in the weeds. Every morning before dawn, they climbed onto trucks, bound for the bean fields. Where all day, everybody that could pick, down to five or six years old, picked. Kneeling in the black Everglades mud. It would be dark night again when they got back to quarters. And all night long the gyp joints stayed open, where whiskey, dice and women ate up the earnings of the day.

That was the white growers' idea of how to hold labor: Keep the Negroes broke, they said. Instead of a church or a school, the grower would build a gyp joint at the center of his quarters. To get back at night what he paid out in the day.

When the Government came in and started to build a model camp for the Negroes, with screened shelters and shower baths and flush toilets, and an infirmary, a community center, a school and playgrounds, laundry tubs and electric irons—the growers raised hell. What was the Government's idea anyway, ruining the rental value of their canal bank quarters? And fixing to ruin their labor with a lot of useless luxury? Besides, the Negroes wouldn't use the camp. They liked to be dirty; they liked to be diseased; they liked to be vicious.

When the growers saw the Government was going ahead anyway, they said: You'll have to hire a bunch of camp guards, white guards, and have them control the camp with clubs and pistols or the Negroes won't pay the rent. Or they'll stop working entirely and they'll take the camp to pieces.

I was there. I was in charge of the camp. When the day came to open, we just opened the gate and let anybody in that wanted to come in. No hand-picking, no references or anything like that. It was enough for us that a family wanted to live there. We didn't hire white guards, either, and nobody carried a club or a pistol in all that camp that held a thousand people.

We just got them all together in the community center and told them it was their camp. They could make it a bad camp or they could make it a good camp. It was up to them. And there wouldn't be any laws or ordinances, except the ones they made for themselves through their elected Council. For a week, they had a campaign in camp with people running for office for the first time in their lives. After it was over, they celebrated with a big dance in the community center. Nobody got drunk or disorderly and nobody cut anybody with a knife. They had themselves a Council.

The Council made the laws and ordinances. The Council said nobody's dog could run around loose, it had to be tied up. The Council said a man couldn't beat his wife up in camp. And when a man came in drunk one night, he was out by morning. The Council said people had to pay their rent and out of that rent, came money for baseball equipment, and it kept up the nursery school.

Finally, the Council said: It's a long way to any store. And that's how the Co-op started, without a dollar in it that the people didn't put up.

Some of the men and women on that Council couldn't so much as write their names. Remember, these were just country Negroes off sharecrop farms in Georgia and Alabama. Just common ordinary cotton pickers, the kind Lowndes County planters say would ruin the country if they had the vote. (*He opens wide his half-shut eyes.*) All I know is: My eyes have seen democracy work.

An Unreconstructed Populist

Congressman C. Wright Patman

*The gentleman from Texas is serving his twenty-first term in Congress.
He is Chairman of the House Banking and Currency Committee. His
appearance is that of an ingenuous "country boy." Physically, he bears
a remarkable resemblance to actor Victor Moore as Throttlebottom in*
Of Thee I Sing. *Journalist Robert Sherrill has pointed out that appearance, at least in this instance, is quite deceiving.*

IN THE LATE TWENTIES, the farmers were in distress because all the
money went to Wall Street. They were using it up there, manipulating.
They were not using money out in the country. The same thing's happening right now—a repeat performance of the '29 deal. Less than two
hundred men are controlling everything—the fixing of interest, bonds,
everything. Members of Congress just don't step on the toes of these
bankers.

That's why in May, 1929, I introduced the first bill to pay three and a
half million World War I veterans cash money, direct from the United
States Treasury. It took from then till 1936 for these veterans to be
paid—$1,015 each, on the average. They were in such distress, we had to
agree on bond payments. They wanted to rob 'em on interest rates. The
way they treated those men. . . . They didn't want to pay 'em their

317

money. It was adjusted pay, really. Remember, the army only paid $21 a month. In June, 1932, the House passed the bonus, but the Senators resented the pressure and voted against it. Those poor fellas, instead of doing something rash, why, they'd sing "America." They took it.

You were a hero to the bonus marchers. . . .

Why, certainly. They brought a donkey on top of a freight train from Texas up here to my office. They educated him, they taught him tricks and things. They wanted me to run for President. I said, "No, let's just get this thing paid."

There was twenty thousand here at one time. I addressed them out there on the Capitol steps.

Who were the so-called bonus marchers? They were lobbyists for a cause. Just like the ones in the Mayflower Hotel. They didn't try to evict *them*. When the poor come to town, they're trouble makers. Why, certainly. They step on the grass and they're put in jail for stepping on the grass. The Mayflower crowd, they don't have any problem at all. They're on every floor of every building of Capitol Hill all the time.

The marchers were good, law-abiding citizens. They built these lodgings down here from waste paper and boxes and things. They had lots of streets and everything. Like Resurrection City. Those buildings were burned down by the army, the military, under the direction of Mr. MacArthur and Mr. Eisenhower. Mr. MacArthur was strutting down the street just like it was a big parade.

The next morning, after driving them out, using tear gas, you'd see little babies and mothers on the side of the road. . . . There was never such a horrible thing happen on earth as that. They killed some of the veterans. They all ought to have been charged with murder. These people had as much right to be lobbying here for their cause as the Mayflower crowd.

Andrew Mellon[1] was opposed to any payment. He said it would unbalance the budget. They always talked that way. Some of them called it the 'boodget' (laughs)—unbalance the boodget. That's what led me to go after him. I'm against a few people taking advantage of privilege, using it for their own selfishness and punishing other folks.

As soon as I returned to Congress, on January 6, 1932, I rose to impeach Andrew W. Mellon for high crimes and misdemeanors. The

---

[1] Secretary of Treasury from 1921 to 1932.

Republicans were so shocked and confused, they didn't stop me. I got an hour's time on the floor. I spoke of the conflict of interests. He owned banks, stocks and everything else, and here he was heading the Treasury. It was made a violation a hundred years ago for a Secretary of Treasury to even own a Government bond.

They voted to refer the proposition to the Judiciary Committee. I sat on one side of the long table by myself and Mr. Mellon and his twelve lawyers sat on the opposite side. The most high-priced lawyers in the United States, the best money could buy. I had a rough time for a couple of weeks. But I was always able to fall on my feet like a cat, because I had the information. I had it documented. I knew what it was. They didn't. See, these high-priced lawyers, the higher they're priced, the less they study. (Laughs.)

At the end of two weeks, it was Mr. Mellon's turn to be on the witness stand. The committee recessed until one thirty that afternoon. Well, about twelve thirty, the papers came out with huge headlines: "Mellon Resigns, Appointed To The Court of St. James." Some members of the committee wanted to impeach him anyway. LaGuardia was one. But the argument was made: Why take up time? He's not only out of office, he's out of the country. So they just let it go. They destroyed all the papers.

What papers? Your documents . . . ?

Why, certainly. Stolen from my office. They robbed my office time and time again. They had people up there in corners, where they could see anybody that went in and out of my office. They'd even go in at night. In the morning, I'd find papers piled in the middle of the floor. I'd try to get the officers around here to do something about it, couldn't get them to do it.

Which officers?

The security officers around Washington. The Treasury has some. Also the White House and the FBI type people. . . .

And it's all gone?

Listen, there's none in the Treasury. There's none anywhere. The truth is Mellon didn't resign. He didn't want to leave that office. He was willing to buck it. He thought he had enough money to win. But this was the beginning of the campaign where Hoover was gonna face Franklin D. Roosevelt. He knew he had to get Mellon out of office. He accepted a resignation that had not been tendered. It was the most courageous thing Hoover ever did.

While he was taking the oath as Ambassador, Mellon told a newspaper friend of mine, "This is not a marriage ceremony; it's a divorce." They put him out. For all effective purposes, he was impeached. Hoover gave him a pardon in the middle of the trial.

Weren't there pressures to defeat you during the Thirties?

Why, certainly. About every three or four elections, they'd lower the boom on me. They could see I was givin' 'em trouble on their city-slicking deals. I pictured them as money changers and was after them with sharp sticks. (Laughs.) They come in, spittin' me back. I had a lot of hard races. The big business fellas didn't need me. They got their own paid people around here. They threw plenty of money around and begin to get very popular.

We have two Governments in Washington: one run by the elected people—which is a minor part—and one run by the moneyed interests, which control everything.

Like the farmer down in Texas. He had a few oil wells. He began buying up all the land around the rivers. Folks got terribly wrought up about it. Him buying up all the land in the country. He let 'em know he wasn't buying up all the land. He just wanted to buy that land that adjoined his'n. (Laughs.) That's what we had. A few fellas that was buying up all the property that adjoined theirs.

It was the big ones closing in on the little ones for the kill. At one time, they thought they'd get a dictatorship here. General Smedley Butler was picked out to be the leader. He was gonna be their man on the white horse. They were gonna close in and take this country over. And they come darn near doing it. They just picked the wrong man.[2] They'll get this country in that position again if they can.

[2] In his autobiography, John L. Spivak, a journalist, recounts his investigation of the matter. During his visit to Butler's home, the General . . . "an extraordinary man, described 'what was tantamount to a plot to seize the Government, by force, if necessary.'" In 1935, "Butler, on a national radio hookup, denounced the Congressional Committee for suppressing parts of his testimony, involving the names of important men.

"Roger Baldwin, who did not look with friendly eyes on communists because they denied free speech and free press, issued a statement as director of the Amer-

You worried about it?

Yeah, I'm worried about that. A dictatorship could spring up here over night, if this country got so bad. If another Depression came, we'd have a revolution. People wouldn't take it any more. They have more knowledge. The big ones, they'd be looking for somebody that'd have the power to just kill people, if they didn't agree. When John Doe begins to get up, they'd just go down and shoot him. . . .

What were your relations with Roosevelt during the Depression?

I liked him very much. There was an air of optimism. When he got in—getting the fat cats out, getting the money changers out. But he was wrong on the veteran's pay. He was against it, too, Roosevelt. I didn't bother him because I knew Congress was gonna have to pass it.

They had a leadership conference at the White House. *The New York Times* had a headline: "Patman At White House On Program." They had a "must" list on the agenda. Defeating the so-called bonus bill was on the "must" list. I think Roosevelt honestly felt it would cause inflation. He was budget-conscious, too. But he had to change. He realized the facts of life.

Do you have the feeling that you've been pretty well kept out of the news these past thirty years or so . . . ?

Why, certainly. I should have been chairman of this committee twenty-five years ago. But they kept me off on account of that fight for the veterans. They knew I knew too much about the money business. They didn't want a man like that.

Oh, I made news when I authored the Full Employment Bill. They called me a Communist, a Socialist and everything else. But we got the bill through. They all now recognize it as a good bill.

---

ican Civil Liberties Union: 'The Congressional Committee investigating un-American activities has just reported that the fascist plot to seize the government . . . was proved; yet not a single participant will be prosecuted under the perfectly plain language of the federal conspiracy act making this a high crime. Imagine the action if such a plot were discovered among Communists!'

"Which is, of course, only to emphasize the nature of our government as representative of the interests of the controllers of property. Violence, even to the seizure of government, is excusable on the part of those whose lofty motive is to preserve the profit system. . . ." From *A Man In His Time*, by John L. Spivak (New York, Horizon Press, 1967), pp. 329–30.

When I get kind of low, I'd think about a verse I learned at one time, when everybody was fighting me. It went something like this:

> He has no enemies, you say,
> My friend, the boast is poor.
> He who hath mingled in the fray
> Of duty that the brave endure
> Must have foes.
>
> If he has none,
> Small is the work he has done.
> He has hit no traitor on the hip,
> Has cast no cup from perjured lip,
> Has never turned the wrong to right,
> He's been a coward in the fight.

I'd often repeat that, you know. (Laughs.)

POSTSCRIPT: *"I live near the Water Gate Inn, but I'm not in that fat cat area. (Laughs.) They pay a half million dollars for condominiums down there. Of course, they have to pay ten or fifteen thousand dollars a year just to keep the corridors clean. From my apartment, I can see where the Cabinet lives." (Laughs.)*

Peroration

Colonel Hamilton Fish

His office is on the far side of the lobby: a downtown Manhattan hotel.
Once upon a time, it may have been deluxe, many, many years ago. Eld-
erly people, a few, are seated in this bleak anteroom.

Inside the office, it is cramped with mementoes of better days: a bust
of Alexander Hamilton; the face of Lincoln; autographed photographs of
Warren Gamaliel Harding, Calvin Coolidge, General Douglas Mac-
Arthur and Senator Everett McKinley Dirksen; and the adjacent
bookshelf on which are sprawled numerous works dealing with military
matters, a photograph of himself: a bareheaded young football player,
Harvard, '08, Walter Camp's choice as All-Time, All-American tackle.

The Colonel, tall, lean, remarkably vigorous for his years, crosses his
legs. His eyes half-closed, he appears to be addressing multitudes.

THE FIRST BILL I introduced in Congress was in December, 1920. It was
a bill to bring back the body of the Unknown Soldier. It was signed by
Woodrow Wilson, the last piece of legislation he signed. That's almost
fifty years ago. There were at least fifty thousand people there. . . .

As a World War I vet, did you have any thoughts concerning the Bonus
March of '32?

I was always for the veteran. Veterans elected me. Those young fel-

323

lows in those days knew how to fight—I wasn't connected at all with the Bonus March. It was ill-advised and caused a political issue, which it never should have. I was for a bonus certificate. I wasn't for these handouts. There were extremists on this Bonus March. They love to be in a march. They got a whole lot of extremists down there and they caused trouble. I kept away from it.

I was chairman of the first committee to investigate Communist activity in the United States. It was known as the Fish Committee. It only lasted one year, from '30 to '31. We didn't go after personalities. We didn't send people to jail or anything like that. Congress can't send people to jail, anyhow. We did go after their organizations, to warn the American people. It was educational.

We had only $25,000 to make the investigation. Now they give 'em three or four hundred thousand. We didn't even need the twenty-five thousand, because the four other members were also lawyers. Our $25,000 included traveling expenses and so on. I think I'm the first member of Congress, and perhaps the only member of Congress, that ever returned any fund allotted to committees. I returned $5,000.

I'm sorry I did it now. Because I would have liked to use the whole amount to have our report printed by the hundreds of thousands. HR 2290 is still the best report—it's only about sixty pages—is still the best report on Communism in America.

I wrote and got through a bill creating the Un-American Activities Committee, which came a few years later, chairmaned by Mr. Dies of Texas. I have a letter from him. It's interesting, because Congressmen are prima donnas. They like to claim credit for everything for themselves: that he was responsible for the investigation of Communists, and so on and so on. But in fairness to Dies, he was certainly not, in this case, a prima donna. Because he sent me this letter, unsolicited, in 1962, from Texas.

In a ringing voice, he reads the letter. Tribute is paid him for his pioneering efforts and the information he provided Dies ". . . all records which our government had seized had mysteriously disappeared. I was able to get invaluable help from the work you did. . . ."

What did Congressman Dies mean . . . about the files disappearing?

What he said was the files were destroyed under orders from Roosevelt. I don't claim Roosevelt was a Communist. I don't even say he was pro-Communist. He was a Socialist. He said: Some of my best friends are Communists. Imagine the President of the United States saying that! And then going over and selling out to Stalin. What I wanted to do was to encourage Hitler to fight Stalin. Let them fight it out. And let the free nations sit down on the sidelines, just egging them on and saying: A plague on both your houses.

Dies did a very good job. Why do you think we have so little Communism in America today? Actually it's less than one percent, Communism in America. With fellow travelers, it's a little more, with extremists and others. Now why is this a fact? Because the Un-American Activities Committee—American labor took it up, the American Legion took it up—all the patriotic groups. If it hadn't been for that, you'd have had ten percent Communists. We'd all have hell to pay in this country here today. We've got enough troubles already.

After Dies, came McCarthy, maligned, practically crucified and almost killed. He was hated because he was so fearless. He's still hated because they tortured the truth about him. Whether he'll ever get credit, I don't know. Although McCarthy is probably our most hated man in recent history, he always had the majority of the people with him—from Cardinal Spellman down. They spent millions to destroy this man. They destroyed him by putting through that censure resolution in the Senate. I'd like to have been at the Senate at that time, because I've always been able to talk, I'd a' given them hell. They killed him, you know, they killed him. They began to gang up on me first. Then they ganged up on Dies. And they ganged up on McCarthy a hundredfold. What they didn't do to him was a shame.

Franklin Delano Roosevelt . . . I represented, of course, the district which he came from, Hyde Park, Dutchess County. I represented it in Congress for twenty-five years, ten years before he was elected President, until the next fifteen years, until he practically died. I was never beaten in that district.

Roosevelt did his best every time to defeat me in Congress. He spent a great deal of money with the columnists and the radio commentators. He would rather defeat me, I think, almost than be elected himself.

It developed on his part, a good deal of bitterness. 'Cause I criticized him openly. Never personally himself. I always denied he was a Communist or a pro-Communist and so on. I'd say perhaps he was a Socialist, but if he wants to be one, he has a right to be one. He became bitterer and bitterer.

He really began to hate me. I had nothing against him. I don't belong to that school of Republicans that go around calling names, a lot of bad names. I fought him aboveboard, and I'm not sorry. I'm sorry I didn't fight him harder than I did, because he did a great deal of harm to this country. It will take us maybe a hundred years to live it down.

It was very amusing. He'd send in "must" legislation—some radical measure. I'd get up—I got along pretty well with the Democrats—I'd offer an amendment to the bill, which would really destroy it. And it carried. He'd have his leaders up there the next day: "What's the matter with you people here? What's the trouble?" And they'd say: "Mr. President, that's your own Congressman that offered that amendment." They say he almost had apoplexy, almost died. And they'd come back to me, all these Democratic leaders—I knew them well—and laughing, saying, "You almost killed the President. He was trying to put the blame on us, and we put it on you." They'd say, he nearly dropped on the spot. This happened a half a dozen times, not once.

I was on the radio at least ten or fifteen times a year, on the big radios. That's what hurt him, 'Cause I'd accuse him: I accuse the President of this, of that, down the line. It infuriated him.

Roosevelt never went out of his way to attack me personally. He did talk about "Martin, Barton & Fish"[1] and inferred we were reactionaries. That isn't correct. I had voted for Social Security and the most progressive legislation. I always had the support of the American Federation of Labor. On social justice, I was left of center. He hired a columnist to attack me. Some of them absolutely slammed me, maliciously lied about me. Members of his Cabinet, like Ickes,[2] were taking cracks at me. I naturally answered them. I spoke about Messrs. Jackson,[3] Ickes and Roosevelt. I called them Three Blind Leaders. (Reads.)

Three blind leaders, see how they run,
They ran into a Depression
Which they claim is a mere recession.
Did you ever hear such deception
By three blind leaders, see how they run,
See how they squirm, see how they alibi,
Those three blind leaders.

[1] Congressmen Joseph Martin and Bruce Barton, Republicans.
[2] Harold Ickes, Roosevelt's tart-tongued Secretary of Interior.
[3] Robert Jackson, Roosevelt's Attorney-General; later Chief Justice of the Supreme Court; eventually, the United States' judge at the Nuremberg Trials.

When he first ran for President, I was very friendly with him. He ran on a very fine, middle-of-the-road or rather conservative platform. Perhaps the most conservative platform in history. My wife voted for him.

I supported Hoover. They asked me if I would take my keynote speech down to Washington and show it to President Hoover. He read it and approved it, all except the provision about the liquor amendment. I had put in a paragraph in favor of light wine and beer. I'm afraid that his wife, who was a white-ribboner and a complete Prohibitionist, opposed that. He brought it back the next morning and he said, "You'll have to delete that light wine and beer suggestion because I can't approve it." That changed the whole election, just that one thing. And, of course, the Depression.

People were unemployed and they were blaming Hoover. But certainly it would have brought him millions of votes. He lost by probably ten million and he would have halfed it. That would have made a great deal of difference, but it would not have elected Hoover, because they absolutely sabotaged his constructive programs. It would have softened the Depression and would have solved the Depression. They sabotaged that deliberately, the Democrats in Congress. Roosevelt was in on it. He wouldn't even confer with Hoover at the time. They wanted to continue this Depression so they could sweep the country. They wanted people unemployed, so they could reap the whirlwind of votes. It was shameful.

As soon as Roosevelt got in, he changed. He trampled his platform, brought into Washington a whole lot of young, socialistic, radical brain trusters, who sought to change the whole ideology of the United States. He had become finally an extremist.

During the first hundred days, I voted for practically every recommendation made by Roosevelt. The real break between me and my constituent was on the recognition of Soviet Russia. He recognized Soviet Russia without any support whatsoever in Congress. All former Presidents, everybody was against recognizing Soviet Russia at that time. But he went ahead and did it by himself.

Up to then, we had been on very friendly relations. He okayed a stamp for me, and Jim Farley, who was a friend of mine and has been ever since, put the stamp through. I had letters from Roosevelt thanking me.

I broke with him, and began to be one of the leaders of opposition to the socialism of the New Deal and this big spending. There were ten million people unemployed all the time during the New Deal. That history has not been brought out clearly. Most of your historians of that period were New Dealers on the payroll. He had a hundred million dollars to spend without making an account. He gave large sums of money to his friends, who were authors and writers. Everything pro-New Deal was written and almost nothing against it. It's changed a little bit since then. . . .

Warming to his favorite subject, he speaks of "Roosevelt determined on a pro-war policy. In the 1940 campaign, he made a pledge to mothers and fathers that their sons would not be sent to fight in any foreign wars. It was absolutely a dishonest, dishonorable, contemptible statement, because he had been planning to get us in all the time. The Germans didn't want us fighting them, so they disregarded twenty or thirty attempts that we made to fight, attacking their submarines, bombing their submarines, giving away destroyers to England. . . . When he found he couldn't get Germany to fight us, he turned and tried to get Japan into the war."

There were three reasons Roosevelt wanted war. One: you had ten million Americans unemployed after six years of the New Deal. The other one: to be a war President, you became a great man overnight. And then, he hoped to put through a United Nations, of which he would be the author—and the uncrowned ruler of the world. With his dreams, I could speak at length. But that's another matter.

Roosevelt would have gone down in history as a great President after the first two terms. But he made a mistake, going for the third term. Jim Farley and all the rest fought it. His tragic mistake was when he was a sick and dying man, caved in, mentally and physically, and he insisted on a fourth term. "I'm the indispensable man." All that bunk.

He had all this fanatical, radical legislation introduced. They were not based on American customs. They were all Socialistic, and Socialism always fails. I know as much about this as anybody, 'cause I debated Norman Thomas, whom I have a very high idea of, at least ten different times.

Of course, Socialism has tremendous ideals. If everybody was an angel, Socialism would be wonderful. If everybody worked for everybody else and for themselves and for the country, it might work. But it's never worked in any big country. Maybe a small country of five million. . . .

I'm for the right of everybody to speak: Democrats, Republicans, left, right, freedom people, extremists, so on. The only thing Communism fears is the word "freedom," and they fear that like the devil is feared by Christians. HR 2290 was the best report ever written on Communism. I'm only sorry I didn't keep that $5,000 and spend it to print a million copies.

POSTSCRIPT: *"Al Smith was a very dear friend of mine. He loved this country, and he hated Communism. I was asked by Republican leaders if I would go down and see Al Smith at the Empire State Building . . . and ask if he would run on the Republican ticket for the United States Senator against his old friend, Robert Wagner. It was shortly before Al's death. Much to my surprise, he said, 'You know, Ham, I'd like to run and beat Wagner. I would like to go to Washington and as a Senator, get up and oppose all the New Deal Socialistic legislation. And ridicule it. And I can do it.' "* It was a matter of Smith's failing health, apparently, that kept him from making the race. *"And he said, 'My heart is not as strong as it should be. And I have a very good job here, $50,000.' 'Well,' I said, 'Al, as far as the job is concerned, we've been in touch with Mr. DuPont, who pays the salary, and he will continue the salary, regardless.' "* The Colonel withdrew the request: *"Because I, too, believed he could be elected. But not at the expense of his life."*

329

Scarlet Banners and
Novenas

William L. Patterson

He is seventy-seven.

"My mother was born a slave in 1850. As the War Between the States seemed inevitable, her grandfather sent his white family to Massachusetts and his black family to California. My father was a West Indian."

After graduating from law school in California, he signed up as a third cook on a steamship: ultimate destination—Liberia. While pausing in London, he met George Lansbury, the old Labour Party M.P., who urged him to return to America because "it was there the great struggle would develop."

In New York, he passed the bar, with an assist by Henry L. Stimson. Within a short time, his was the leading Negro law firm in the city. He became interested in the Sacco-Vanzetti case. "Most of the young Negro lawyers did not see any connection whatsoever . . . but I asked myself what was the purpose of practicing law when social issues arose and I played no part. . . ."

As a member of a delegation to Boston to protest the execution,[1] he met Ella (Mother) Bloor and other Communists. "They were very

[1] He was in a demonstration on Boston Common. Upton Sinclair, in *Boston*, describes "how the mounted police tried to ride me down and chased me on horseback."

330

solicitous of my welfare. It was for me an experience with a new type of white American. However, it was when Mother Bloor linked up the Sacco-Vanzetti case with the oppression of the Negroes, I was struck by the clarity of her cause. I gave up the practice of law and joined the Communist Party."

For three years, he studied in the Soviet Union at the University for Toiling People of the Far East. Most of the students were young Asians, though there were "one or two Africans." He returned to America in 1930.

FOR A SHORT TIME, I was an organizer in Harlem. It was an interesting period that gave rise to the Negro literati. James Weldon Johnson was around. And, of course, one of the great men of the century, Dr. W.E.B. DuBois. Professor Alain Locke of Howard . . . and young Negro writers following the path blazed by money-mad white writers. Two exceptions were the poets, Claude McKay and Langston Hughes.

I was asked by the Party to go to Pittsburgh to take charge of a new school there—of miners and metal workers. It was in the heart of the Depression. Unemployed Councils and hunger marches were organized.

I'd been arrested in a demonstration in which a thousand Negroes and whites had carried the furniture of an evicted white family back into their home. In the trial, I defended the other arrested men, as well as myself. The jury brought out a verdict of not guilty.

I was arrested while speaking to black and white miners in western Pennsylvania and eastern Ohio. On one occasion, there was talk of lynching me. White and Negro workers placed their picket line around the prison and marched all night.

On another occasion, I was thrown into jail without any charges being made. At twelve o'clock at night, gun thugs came to my cell, saying they were going to transfer me to another jail. I knew the town had only one jail. I thought this was it.

I was put into a Ford, and we started out of town. The three men began to talk among themselves in a language I did not understand, but which I recognized as Slavic. I asked them in Russian what they were going to do to me. They were very much surprised in hearing a black man talk Russian. We began to discuss my stay in Russia.

We soon came to a wooded section in the road. The car was stopped, and I was told to get out. I thought I'd be shot trying to escape, as the charge was usually made. But one of them kicked me, and they drove off.

The Unemployed Councils were a creation of the Communists, though in the main their composition was made up of non-Communists. I recall men and women being shot, engaging in these activities. There were hundreds charged with sedition, conspiracy, on one pretext or another. But it was a period of great schooling.

Many times, the Councils started at a meeting in which it was proposed that delegations be sent to City Hall or to the state assembly—demanding food and work. These committees would come back and report to their community. Out of these events, came the Unemployed Councils. There followed the idea of hunger marches. To city halls, to city councils. I led one of a few thousand into Uniontown. When we arrived, the cossacks were there in great number. I mounted the steps and began to speak. In a short time, the city council and the mayor came down and called a meeting. A delegation went into the City Council. I spoke for them. They immediately voted $6,000 for relief. It was a small amount, but it was a small town.

"Roosevelt emerged to talk about the necessity of giving people relief. One thing that many do not recall was his statement that he was out to save capitalism from itself. He did. With his WPA's and his PWA's, he brought back a measure of stability to American society.

"However, many illusions arose. Roosevelt carried out, in a very adroit manner, a program in which he doled out hundreds of dollars to workers, while millions were given to banks, the railroads and other industries. As contrasted to Hoover, he did, in fact, offer a New Deal to working people."

What do you feel was the Communists' role in the emergence of the CIO?

"John L. Lewis has stated it more clearly than anyone else. Without the organization ability of the Communist Party, the CIO might never have come to life. Youth today has no comprehension of the tremendous role played by the Communist Party in that period. It forced the Roosevelt Administration to carry through some of the Social Security measures."

Wasn't the idea of black nationhood suggested, for a time, by the Communist Party . . . ?

"During the late Twenties, the concept of self-determination arose, as a means of sharpening the struggle. The rights of Negroes to have a part of the United States in which they constituted a majority. There were separatist movements at the time. They were sharply challenged by DuBois. Black Americans are not Africans. To consider themselves so would be to surrender their heritage to the very forces which have been their greatest oppressors.

"Black power today is self-determination in a new form: autonomy of the black ghetto. It must be a positive force. Where it creates the idea of separatism, it must be combatted."

I had been in Pittsburgh only a short time when the Scottsboro Case broke. In April, 1931, nine Negro lads were arrested, and the trial took place in Scottsboro, Alabama. They were riding a freight, seeking work. Some were seeking hospital care, which they could not get in their home town. It was a freight train going from Tennessee to Alabama, in which a large number of white lads, who were also jobless and penniless, were moving restlessly from one place to another. When the lads were arrested, both white and black were charged with vagrancy. Until the sheriff found out there were two white girls, in overalls, on the same train.

Under pressure, the girls were forced by the police to say they had been raped by the nine Negro lads. Both these girls had been forced, by economic conditions, into prostitution at an early age.

He received a call from New York that the International Labor Defense (ILD) was undertaking the defense. The secretary of the organization was going to Europe with Mrs. Wright, the mother of one of the boys —to mobilize international sentiment in their behalf. He agreed to become acting secretary of the ILD.

I immediately sought the services of Samuel Liebovitz. He was one of New York's leading criminal lawyers and he had never lost a death case. He told me, "I'll bring these boys back and throw them in your lap." I told him, "No, you won't. These are political prisoners. They are arrested and being tried for a purpose . . . to terrorize the Negro people."

Liebovitz handled the case in a masterly fashion. The freight train on which these lads were riding had forty-nine cars. Liebovitz had a replica made of this train, every car placed in the position it originally occupied. In the trial, he forced the complainants, these two girls, to show what car the rape had taken place in. He showed the judge that this car had been full of gravel, that the gravel had come up to the level of the car's sides. Had these girls been raped, their backs would have been lacerated. . . .

Judge Horton reversed the conviction. He fairly analyzed the evidence and showed that much of it was inadmissible. And yet the case of the Scottsboro Boys lasted for seventeen years, from 1931 to 1947. That's when the last of them, Heywood Patterson, the most outstanding and courageous of these lads, was released.

It was a *cause célèbre,* which brought into action millions of people all over the world. And led me, inexorably, I think, to see the role of the American Government in the persecution of the Negro people. The case went twice to the United States Supreme Court. There was evidence, both in law and in fact, sufficient to enable the court to dismiss the case. Instead, on each occasion, these boys were sent back to go through the torture and agony of their prison life, and the racist persecution to which they had been subjected. I began to see clearly this conspiracy to perpetuate racism as an institution in our life.

Didn't one of the girls eventually become a witness for the defense?

One of the most interesting features of the case. It showed the tremendous power of struggle to awaken both the consciousness and understanding of people. Ruby Bates, one of the young white girls, was a remarkable person. She told me she had been driven into prostitution when she was thirteen. She had been working in a textile mill for a pittance. When she asked for a raise, the boss told her to make it up by going with the workers. She told me there was nothing else she could do.

After she had been going with the white workers, the police called her in. They didn't want to arrest her for prostitution, but she had to have what they called Nigger Day. On a certain day, she had to go with black workers, so if they wanted to charge a black man with rape, to organize a lynching bee, they would have a man who could not deny he had gone with her.

Ruby and I had an opportunity of speaking together. We brought her to New York, when she expressed a desire to tell her story, the true story. She met Reverend Harry Emerson Fosdick. And I took her to see Elmer Rice, the playwright. When Wexley's play[2] appeared, she made a speech, and so did I.

She told how she had been threatened with imprisonment unless she charged these boys with rape. She told how Victoria Price, the other girl, had been implicated in a murder charge, and how this threat of prosecution was held over her head. She told how the authorities promised to give Victoria a house in Scottsboro, if she testified as they wanted. Ruby found it impossible to be a party to a crime of this magnitude.

Ruby Bates was a remarkable woman. Underneath it all—the poverty, the degradation—she was decent, pure. Here was an illiterate white girl, all of whose training had been clouded by the myths of white supremacy, who, in the struggle for the lives of these nine innocent boys, had come to see the role she was being forced to play. As a murderer. She turned against her oppressors. . . . I shall never forget her.

Max Shachtman

Formerly a Trotskyite leader, now a leading theoretician of the American Socialist Party.

UNTIL THE CRASH OCCURRED, it was thought there was something unique about American capitalism. Even the radicals felt it. They were in bad shape. The Communists were wracked by internal strife. The Socialists were stagnating. Ford was paying his workers $5 a day—unprecedentedly high wages. It seemed the class struggle was coming to an end, and radicalism might disappear. But the 1929 crisis created a revolution in thought: it affected liberals and, in many cases, conservatives, as well as radicals.

[2] John Wexley's *They Shall Not Die,* a play based upon the case. Ruth Gordon enacted the role of Ruby Bates.

What was called the collapse of American capitalism had an enormously stimulating effect on the American Communist Party. It underwent two phases in the Thirties: the first five years of the decade; and the second. This phenomenon had something of a third phase, too.

At the beginning, it purged itself. It has nothing to do with events in the United States. As always, in the case of the Communists, it reflected happenings in Russia. On the eve of "the collapse of American capitalism," the CP expelled a group of us for espousing "the counter-revolutionary policies of Trotsky." Other expulsions followed. The conflict resulted in at least a dozen different factions. This bewilderment kept the Party in a state of paralysis.

However, the oncoming of mass unemployment, on a scale hitherto unknown in this country, enabled the Communists to organize the unemployed and stage vigorous protests. They were initially the leaders of this movement. In New York, at Union Square, they were able to gather as many as 100,000 people at a rally.

Hoover was still President. Since he didn't offer even the mildest form of amelioration for the unemployed, the Communist Party seemed to be riding high. But its success was illusory. At bottom, the unemployed worker was uninterested in communism. He was interested in one thing only: a job. The CP could involve him in demonstrations, but it couldn't get him a job. It was the New Deal that subsequently did this—at least, for a few million.

With the election of Roosevelt, the Party entered a new phase. It envisioned the complete decay of capitalism and the impending triumph of international proletarian revolution. It engaged in the most militant policies imaginable. Everybody to the right—and some to the left—of the Party was considered the enemy. Socialists became social fascists. They were more vigorously attacked than the real fascists. During the first New Deal period, Congress was referred to as the fascist Grand Council.

Although it was of transitory nature, Communists were making progress among the unemployed. Unfortunately, they deepened the gulf between themselves and every other radical group in the country. "Red trade unions" were created. Their programs were revolutionary as all get out; their leadership was hot as a pistol. They had only one defect —few members. Consequently, their reputation among trade unions became really bad. There are few crimes as great in labor circles as dual unionism: dividing the ranks of workers in their confrontations with employers.

Nevertheless, capitalism looked pretty sick. Wide segments of the population were radicalized. In liberal and academic communities, Marxism, which had been considered passé, became popular again. There was more writing about Marxism—favorable, though not very perceptive, in many cases—during these years than at any other time in American history.

In the late Twenties and early Thirties, thousands of young people had joined the Socialist Party. They kept pushing the Socialists further and further to the left, in many instances borrowing the jargon of the Communists. This led to a split. The right wing, many older Socialists, pulled out. Especially after the Detroit Convention of 1934, when a platform was adopted in favor of the dictatorship of the proletariat.

These parallel developments among the Communists and the Socialists were influenced, aside from our domestic crisis, by two events in Europe.

The first: the triumph of fascism in Germany. Hitler had overthrown the Weimar Republic, without any real resistance by the world's two largest radical parties, outside Russia: the German Communist Party and the Social Democrats. They capitulated without firing a shot. There was conjured up a return to barbarism, in modern form, and the danger of a second world war. This was about 1933.

The second event was the Russian Five Year Plan, inaugurated by Stalin. The world outside knew little of its details. Later, it learned of the horrors associated with it. But what stood out in the minds of ninety-nine out of every hundred of American radicals was this contrast: there was no smoke in American factory chimneys; there, production was going on like mad; everybody was working. And of all the great powers, it was Russia that was intransigently anti-fascist.

Yet in spite of all this, radicalism did not take deep root in the United States. The Communist Party had added a few thousand members, but it was still insignificant in the political life of this country. Especially, when contrasted to the American Socialist Party at its peak in 1918. It had over a hundred thousand members.

It was in the second half of the Thirties that a big change occurred in the American Left. There was the New Deal and especially the birth of the CIO. Labor entered politics, as the unorganized were organized.

Radicals of all persuasion were deeply affected. The Communists and the Socialists, because of their experience, were virtually sucked into the movement. In many cases, they were the moving forces.

With the rise of Hitler and the Spanish resistance to fascism in the Civil War, a most decisive event followed. A radical turnabout in Communist policy. The People's Front—the United Front—came into being. The Party abandoned the theory of "social fascism." The United Front welcomed all radicals, all liberals and, for that matter, all "right-thinking" capitalists. (Laughs.) Everybody. The New Deal and Roosevelt were embraced. Speeches called for understanding of the National Association of Manufacturers. Had any radical suggested these ideas in preceding decades, he'd have been politically lynched. There were only two prerequisites: friendliness to Russia and hostility to Hitler.

As far as the Communist Party was concerned, it was quite effective. Certainly, unity among radicals is better than internal strife. It was the party of friendliness. How could anybody oppose it? You'd have to be against motherhood. . . .

Soon, the policy of working in the Democratic Party became accepted. This was natural. The labor movement was overwhelmingly behind Roosevelt and the New Deal. It wasn't a matter of taking it over. I don't believe all this right-wing nonsense about their capturing the Democratic Party. It was merely a matter of influence. In comparison with its utter isolation in the first half of the Thirties, this was an enormous advance for the Communists. But it was all an illusion. Its Achilles' heel was its subordination to Moscow policy.

The Party had been doing fine. It was against fascism, for the Loyalist government in Spain, for the CIO, for all the nice things in the New Deal. What the hell more do you want from a radical party? There's never been anything as nice as this in American history. (Laughs.) Then, virtually overnight, it destroyed itself. It backed the Hitler-Stalin pact.

The shock was volcanic. The labor movement drove them out of its ranks. It lost liberal support. It was reduced to insignificance. At the end of the decade, the CP appeared far more discredited, far more isolated than at the beginning of the Thirties. And from that, it has never recovered.

There was a burst of respectability with the invasion of Russia by Hitler. Once again, radical and liberal intellectuals flocked to its banner.

But it was a brief moment. Then came the Cold War. . . . Today, even the New Left looks upon it as obsolete, puritanical, conservative, establishment. . . .

It's funny, if it weren't so tragic. It's sad because of its effect on a genuine American radical movement. It looked for a moment, at the beginning, that it might become that. It never did.

The decline of the Socialist Party is even more regrettable. Especially to me. For the past ten years, I've been a member. This party did not understand—and now is only beginning to understand—the profound political revolution wrought by Roosevelt and the New Deal.

A new political coalition was created: labor, with its many ethnic minorities and Negroes. At first it was sentiment on the part of the blacks; now it is organized. I'm convinced this coalition is going to remain a decisive element in American politics for a long time to come.

This coalition worked. It did not produce socialism, but then that wasn't Roosevelt's intention. (Laughs.) He saved our society in a new bourgeois reform way. I hate to use this jargon, but there you have it. Capitalism remains.

So the Socialist vote continues to decline. The enormous sympathies it once enjoyed in the labor movement has thinned down to nothing. The Communists, because of Moscow, are ruined. The American Left is nothing as compared to its role in European countries. Nothing breaks my heart more than to say this: our stupidity in not recognizing the significance of the coalition, our failure to identify with this group, our isolation from the mainstream of American political thought, our special language, which no one understands. It's a pity.

I don't expect our power structure to build a radical movement. I expect the radicals to do that. Up to now, they have failed. As I watch the New Left, I simply weep. If somebody set out to take the errors and stupidities of the Old Left and multiplied them to the nth degree, you would have the New Left of today. . . .

The radicals of the Thirties have gone their separate way. Only a handful retain their old commitments. I feel more strongly about the ideals of socialism than I ever did. Still, many thousands of old radicals, like myself, vote for the goddam Democrats. And yet, as I look back on that decade, the Thirties, it was for radicals the most exciting period in American history.

Dorothy Day

The headquarters of The Catholic Worker: *it is on the Lower East Side in New York. On a wall of the kitchen—an all-purpose room of "any peasant's lodging," as a young man says—is a framed quotation of Father Daniel Berrigan: "Men are called to declare peace as once they were called to declare war."*

Her room, two flights up, is bare of any luxury. A cot, a couple of chairs, a shelf of well-thumbed books, including a great many paperbacks. There are occasional interruptions by young associates—questions of the moment: the putting up of a stray couple; an unexpected visitor; will I share their meal? Nothing fancy, but filling. . . .

She is a large-boned, handsome woman. Though a white-haired grandmother, touching seventy, her demeanor is that of a young, exhilarated girl. An intimation of weariness is now and then reflected. It passes quickly.

"My approach even as a child was religious. Some of my old friends from the Communist Party felt I was too religious to be really a good revolutionist. Pacifism was very much my whole point of view. I never could see a set of people killing off another set of people to bring a better society. People had to work nonviolently. I don't think I was especially influenced by Gandhi. I think it's the whole Christian message.

"My whole background before, as a Socialist and a Communist, was that things should be changed. There's always going to be human suffering, plain human orneriness. But it seemed impossible to me that we should be living with these extremes of wealth and poverty, where people lived like dogs and got nowhere."

IN DECEMBER, 1932, I was covering the hunger march, down in Washington, of the Unemployed Councils. And a farmers' convention which was more or less Communist-inspired. I went down there to cover it for *Commonweal* and *America*.[3] I just sat in that shrine and prayed that a way would open up for me to work more directly with these is-

---

[3] Two Catholic journals: the first, a lay monthly; the other, a Jesuit weekly.

sues. My prayer was obviously a fervent one. That was the year I met Peter Maurin. That was the year *The Catholic Worker* started.

She tells of Peter Maurin, the French peasant, who chose poverty as a way of life; a former teacher, he came to Chicago's Skid Row; worked the railroads, the wheat fields, the steel mills; was a janitor; engaged in all sorts of manual labor: "the man who digs the ditches, the man who cleans the sewers deserves just as much pay as the man who sits behind the desk. . . ." All reform, he believed, must come from the bottom up, not from the top down. His belief was in a "personalist communitarian revolution." It begins with the individual and his personal response to poverty. . . .

Ours is more the anarchist's point of view: the State is a tremendous danger. We were the first ones in the Church to oppose Mussolini and Hitler. We picketed the *Bremen*,[4] I remember, down there on the waterfront. The Communists were picketing at the same time. The Communists and the Catholics. . . .

It must have been in 1935. A group of Communists boarded the ship and tore down the swastika. Some of them were arrested, and one was shot. We were, both sides, issuing leaflets. Although atheism is an integral part of Marxism, according to Lenin, we still had these concordances. . . .

We joined them in a protest in front of the police station. We were dispersed by the police. When the Communists who were arrested were brought to trial, they proclaimed themselves Catholic workers. Most of them were longshoremen and they were Catholics, by birth. Cradle Catholics. It was amazing to hear them all get up and say they were Catholic workers. (Laughs.) Right away, they were identified with us. I found it very amusing.

We participated in the strikes that were going on. I remember a brewery strike. Why we picketed a brewery I don't know. (Laughs.) I'm practically a Carrie Nation about liquor. You see so much misery on the Bowery, you just have to carry on. . . . There was a department store strike. I guess we were the first Catholics policemen had ever seen on a picket line. They thought we were all Communists boring from within.

---

[4] A German ocean liner, bearing the swastika.

There was the Chinese-Japanese War going on that we started in 1932 or 1933. Then there was the Ethiopian War and the Spanish Civil War. Nonviolence had to be the role of the Church. How else could any one speak of the teachings of Christ, the Sermon on the Mount, the whole question of the Beatitudes . . . ?

Plenty of students came down and joined us, 'cause there were no jobs to be gotten. They came directly from college, with no experience. Mostly young men. That's what really began building up the *Worker*. We had thirty-two hospitality houses in the country before we were many years old.

There's a wide difference in point of view of the students then and young people today. State universities were cheap in those days. You could go to a state university and get yourself a degree easily enough. But there were no jobs. Now there are plenty of jobs and most young people are wondering what's worth doing. They don't want to be part of the system. The war hangs over their heads, the Bomb. They have a sense of constant crisis.

In the Thirties, bread and butter issues . . .

Yes. They didn't consider the whole social order as students are doing today. Or the whole peace issue . . .

In 1933, 1934, there were so many evictions on the East Side, you couldn't walk down the streets without seeing furniture on the sidewalk. We used to go ahead and try to find other empty apartments and force the relief stations to pay those first months' rent. We used to help people move into the apartments and get settled. And give them a hand.

Did you, like the Unemployed Councils, try to put people back in the apartments from which they were evicted?

No. We felt we couldn't use people in this way, to make a point. We tried to forestall the marshal, and get them moved out, so they wouldn't be ashamed and humiliated and debased. They had enough suffering without having this suffering piled on them, being made part of a demonstration.

What was the attitude of the Communist Party toward The Catholic Worker?

There were a few articles in *The Daily Worker* trying to combat our ideas. They considered it false mysticism. There was no contact between us, except that some were friends of mine. . . . When it came to a certain kind of strike or to a demonstration, such as the one in front of the German Embassy, there was a common cause.

We were never militantly anti-Communist. But we saw so many liberals going over in the Thirties, we had to put out the very strong differences in point of view. In a way, they were not to be depended upon. They could change their party line, it was the style, sort of. At the same time I can see what Cuba's accomplishing. I think every single Latin-American country will have another brand of Communism. The Church could be a Communist organization.

The Communists contributed plenty in the Thirties. Absolutely. They were the ones that led the heroic struggles and risked beatings and imprisonment and death itself to organize in the South, for instance, in textiles. They tried to organize the unorganized, wherever they were.

That hunger march down in Washington emphasized the need for all the things we have now. They were marching on Washington, three thousand of them, for unemployment insurance, old age pensions, aid to dependent children. Every type of social security that we have now was on the Communist program at that time. But this was the philosophy of the State taking over.

Did you campaign for Social Security at the time?

No, we were on the other side. The whole program of unemployment insurance, Social Security, was a confession of the failure of our whole social order. And confession of failure of Christian principles: that man, in fact, did not look after his brother. That he had to go to the State . . .

There's a terrific conflict here. The Federal Government again and again has to protect people against injustices—in the South, for instance. And yet, ideally, it should not be the business of the State. Popes and anarchists have emphasized the principle: subsidiarity. The State should never take over the functions that could be performed by a smaller body. The State should only enter when there are grave abuses. The Tennessee Valley Authority is a good case in point. It concerns the welfare of a great many people in a great many states. And begins a new social order right there—a communal order, to a great extent, autonomous.

The relation of The Catholic Worker *to the New Deal . . . ?*

We were against it. On the one hand, we had to go ahead. It was a time of crisis, as a flood would be. So we did try to get the people on welfare. Did try to get their rent taken care of. But what you had to do first of all is to do everything *you* could.

You were not opposed to the reform measures of the New Deal, per se?

No. But if it could be done by a smaller group, it would be better. We see the evils of gigantic associations. Their abuse of power. There must be decentralization. It's a tremendous problem. Autonomy as against immediate need. We emphasize our anarchism.

What do *I* do? That's how our houses of hospitality started during the Depression. A girl came in. She had read a letter we sent to the bishops about the Church's tradition. She had been evicted from her furnished room. She had a couple of shopping bags and was sleeping in the subway. We didn't have any room, we were all filled up. We didn't know of any place that could take her. The girl looks at us and says: "Why do you write about things like that when you can't do anything about it?" It shamed us, you know? We went and rented another apartment. Then we got a whole house. We were pushed into it. Everything we've done, we've been pushed into.

We never started a bread line. We didn't intend to have a bread line or a soup line come to the door. During the Seamen's Strike of 1937, six of them showed up. They said: "We're on strike, we have no place to stay, we have no food. We're sleeping in a loft on the waterfront." We took in about ten seamen. We rented a storefront, while the strike lasted for three months. We had big tubs of cottage cheese and peanut butter, and bread by the ton brought in. They could make sandwiches all day and there was coffee on the stove.

While we were doing that for the seamen, one of the fellows on the Bowery said, "What the hell are you doing down there feeding the seamen? What about the men on the Bowery? Nobody's feeding them." So when the men would come in for clothes or a pair of shoes or socks or a coat and we didn't have any left, we'd say, "Sit down anyway and have a cup of coffee. And a sandwich." We kept making more and more coffee. We brought out everything we had in the house to eat. That's how the first bread line started. Pretty soon we had a thousand men coming in a day, during the Depression. It started simply because that Bowery guy got mad.

Our good Italian neighbors recognized poverty. They'd bring all their leftovers to add to the soup. Storekeepers and neighbors. They'd bring over pots of spaghetti and their leftover furniture and clothing and things like that. The very ones who were poor themselves. We lived in their neighborhood and they accepted us.

They were also the ones who had little statues of Mussolini in their windows and gave him their wedding rings.[5] So you can't go ahead and say these are the bad guys and these are the good guys. You can't ever say it. They talk about the Left and the Right, yet all men are brothers. The Communists have a better understanding of this, but they want to bring it about through the use of force. Isn't it a shame? They do have the vision. Would they wipe out these people with Mussolini in the window?

When we moved into a more respectable type neighborhood, they used to throw things at us when we passed by, saying we were degrading the neighborhood. As soon as people get a little more comfortable, this is what happens. . . .

The attitude is much worse today. In the Thirties, everybody was in the same boat. It was a general disaster. Ignazio Silone once said, "Everybody's disaster is nobody's disaster." The individual did not suffer as he does suffer now. Those on welfare today are despised as they were never despised before.

Another Depression might be a relief to many people. They know our prosperity is built on war. It might be so much better than war. People won't have to keep up a front any longer. They wouldn't have to keep up the payments any more. There would have to be a moratorium. The threat of Depression is nothing to worry about. I wish to goodness the stock market would collapse for good and for all. I'd like to see a nonviolent revolution take place and an end to this Holy War. . . .

Fred Thompson

"I'm just as old as the century." He is a member of the IWW (Industrial Workers of the World, popularly known as the Wobblies). He joined in 1922.

[5] In 1935, during the Ethiopian War, Fascist Italy was collecting gold, silver and copper. In exchange for their wedding rings, women received steel rings, inscribed: "Gold to the Fatherland."

In his younger days, he had been a construction worker: tunnels, irrigation ditches, dams, quarries, laying track. "We always boxcared from one job to another, never paid any fare. I had heard of the Wobblies . . . weird stories, that they were a bunch of nuts trying to change the world by burning haystacks and stuff like that.

"I found a tremendous difference between this myth and the reality. They were a very serious bunch of men with understanding: even if we do win our immediate demands, the boss and I will still have a fight. Let's run the works for our own good, so we won't have to fight any more. They had this notion: someday . . . But, right now, let's clean up these camps, let's raise the wages.

"There's a belief that the IWW was killed by the repression following World War I, when a lot of us, including myself, were arrested for criminal syndicalism. The facts don't correspond. Our membership was at its peak in the summer of 1923.

"In 1924, we had a catastrophe, when an internal factional fight split us in two. But we built up again, following the Colorado Coal Strike of '27."

IN THE THIRTIES, our biggest growth was in Cleveland. As soon as this Depression got going, we hammered away at one theme: people who didn't have a job would do far more for themselves by going to every worker who still had a job, and saying, "If you strike, we won't take your job away from you. We'll come there and beef up your picket line." We put out a leaflet, I remember writing it myself: Bread lines, Picket lines. The theme was that bread lines lead to despair and picket lines lead to hope.

I was on a soapbox circuit. I used to go from Duluth down to Minneapolis, over to Milwaukee, down to Chicago. We'd usually hit places like the iron country in Michigan and Minnesota. In Chicago, we'd hit Swedetown, around the North Side. They'd be mostly men. The home guard. The fellows who weren't migratory workers, who didn't ramble around, who had a stationary job.

Henry Ford changed things for the IWW. We used to be rather strong with people who worked the wheat harvest. They went there in boxcars. But the combines[6] shut out the demand for extra harvest labor. Plus the fact that people became "rubber tramps," in broken-down tin flivvers. This meant our organizing technique was no longer workable. We had to go to the flivver jungles.

[6] Machines for harvesting and threshing wheat.

In '22, at the construction camps, you didn't see any females around unless they were visiting with their business agent (laughs), for short durations. You didn't see men and wives.

In '27, I had a little holiday that the State of California gave me for criminal syndicalism. When I came back, two years later, I found the whole industry had changed. Every camp had provision for married couples, but their children had to be working.

Quite a few people were living in nearby towns, if there were decent roads between town and job. The automobile made it possible for a man to live a fairly settled life and fill these out-of-town jobs. The migratory worker had practically disappeared in '26. You didn't hear much about him again until the Dust Bowl days. And a new kind of mobility arose.

Did the Communists or Socialists try to win away your members to their causes during these years . . . ?

The radical movement waxes and wanes. They jostle each other. We like to grab each other's members and things like that, sure. But the overall anti-capitalist movement grows and declines together. They all get bigger at the same time, they all get smaller at the same time. (Laughs.)

In general, there was cooperation—not entirely so. The IWW has always tried to avoid being dogmatic, doctrinaire. We don't ask a guy: what are your political beliefs? We ask 'em: what kind of work do you do? What industry are you in? We have never prevented any person joining because of his beliefs.

The Communists wanted us to join them in 1920. They had a misapprehension over in Moscow, where they got their orders, that we were a secret underground. Heywood[7] went over and tried to explain to Lenin that we had a great big printing plant in Chicago, where we put out twelve different weeklies and a bunch of magazines and so forth. We had trouble with the Government, but we were certainly not hiding. They knew we were doing these things. (Laughs.)

The IWW did not engage in internecine warfare, say, the way the other groups did . . . ?

We were forced into a certain amount of it. By 1923, the Communist Party had decided that we should be allowed to exist in agriculture and

[7] Big Bill Heywood, a top leader of the IWW.

in the woods, but should not be allowed into any other industry. And if their members did join us, they should do what they could to disrupt us. Naturally, that gave us some concern. But even at that, we tried to get them to see the common sense, is all.

What did happen to the IWW membership in the Thirties?

We had lean years. But we did get to far more people. People had time, all kinds of time. In the early Thirties, up to '35, everybody might be flat broke, but they'd find a way of gettin' to a meeting.

In the depths of the Depression, did you hear much talk of revolution?

Oh, there was a lot of talk. But there was no anticipation that we were about to take over the works and run it. The IWW felt only an organized working class could do it. A working class that wasn't allowed to eat the food it produced . . . that had to go with patches on its ass after it had made too many clothes . . . was a working class that could be browbeat. A working class that had to beg for a soup bone wasn't a class that could take this world and run it. They had to organize first.

I ran into some ill-informed people who used the word revolution very carelessly—that things were so tough, we were going to have a revolution and so forth. I didn't run into any person who had given serious thought as to how you make one. I'd want a revolution. Sure, I'd like one now. But the circumstances are not propitious for havin' one, and they weren't in 1931, '32. It isn't just a bunch of starving people that are going to make a revolution. It's gonna be a people that have been asserting themselves. . . .

How did the IWW feel about F.D.R.?

When he died, I remember an obituary in our paper: "He was hated by those he had helped and loved by those he had harmed." A good many Wobblies felt that was hitting it right on the head. He made a big hullabaloo about what he was gonna do for labor. After he had labor by the tail, he seemed to figure he could disregard it and favor our enemy instead.

What were your feelings toward the New Deal?

Here was an economic system that had quit work. The logical remedy would have been for a working class to assert itself: we want at least enough of what we produce so we can keep on working. But you didn't have that kind of labor action. Consequently, the pigs who had been stopping the things from working by their own greed didn't disgorge anything. But certain adjustments were made that allowed people to eat. At the time of Hoover, you could use federal funds to feed animals, but not to feed people. It was up to your neighbors, he said.

You think, then, Roosevelt hurt the radical movement . . . ?

I don't know as he hurt it. He changed the situation. He did cause most people to feel if you could only find a good man and put him in office, he'll fix everything for you, and you can go back to sleep now. He certainly didn't help radicalism.

The kind of labor movement that grew up, that we have today, still has this birthmark. Unionism by permit—the NLRB, things of that sort.

In the early Thirties, there was a resurgence of an almost dead labor movement. There were various radical activities: the Trotskyites up in Minneapolis, the Communists over there in Toledo, the Socialists there, Wobblies in Cleveland, Detroit and so on. The union literature was like the labor literature of a century ago—looking toward a successor to capitalism. Industrial democracy. In which you have a cooperative commune, you have a brotherhood of man. Even though the issue of the moment was five cents more an hour or better files for metal finishers to work with. . . . The literature carried a vision.

But then you saw, in the coal towns of Pennsylvania—Lewis and the CIO—great big banners: "The President Wants You to Join the Union." It worked. So radicalism was replaced by something else. The Government had set up a way. Just sign your name, your authorization card. You can do it quite secretly, you don't have to be a hero any more. We can all vote in a union election, and nobody will know how you voted. Of course, the boss will have to recognize the union, and nobody will really have had to stick his neck out.

When I was a kid, if somebody asked me to define a grievance, I'd say it's something we don't like. Today, a grievance is something not in accordance with standards of arbitration. We're even *told what* the hell to be dissatisfied with these days. (Laughs.)

When I was a kid, the union was *us* guys, what *we* collectively did. Nowadays, people don't speak of the union as *us*. Almost everywhere, the union is *it* or *they*.

There is a growing perception that we should have something other than capitalism. But people aren't excited about it. It's a strange thing. I hardly find anybody today who doesn't agree that the ledger should not determine how we live. Most people think it's terrible that the pollution of Lake Michigan is being decided by how much it'll cost companies to cure it. People are realizing that an environment is being created that will be as dangerous for capitalists to live in as well as for working people . . . that it's insane to let major things be decided on the basis of black figures and red figures.

I find temperate people saying today that the business-motivated system isn't a safe thing to have around. (Laughs.) But I think there is less intensity of feeling.

I think a sense of powerlessness, of fatalism, has been growing from the Thirties. Then, we just felt we didn't have the power, the organization. We never felt we were *inherently* incapable of achieving it.

The thing that gives me the most cheer are the young people today. You find them all over the world, having a sense of common fate. They're the least bookish radicals I've ever known, but the most literate. In the Thirties, a guy read some kind of book and he wanted everything to go according to that text. Today, these college kids use books simply for insights. They don't have a dogma. They're far more flexible, far more open-minded, far more feeling. *They* have the feeling. . . .

Saul Alinsky

Director of the Industrial Areas Foundation.

His work involves the creation of power bases in the community, autonomy in the neighborhood. Although his efforts have been primarily with poor whites and poor blacks, it is now extending to middle-class areas.

"There was a radical continuum that went on in the Depression. Today, there's a chronological cut-off for the kids. They don't believe anything happened in the past. It's a wonder these kids don't re-invent the wheel. Don't they realize that John L. Lewis was fifty-seven when he started the CIO? I think the McCarthy period broke the continuity—the handing over of the torch. There is a radical gap.

"I don't believe anybody has all the answers, I didn't believe it in the

Thirties, and I don't believe it now. Whenever anyone comes up with a pat prescription for paradise, I worry. Paradise, nothing! I don't want to be in paradise. I can't imagine a world without problems. It'd be hell."

I HAD A FELLOWSHIP in criminology at the University of Chicago. My job was to get insight into crime. So I got in with the Capone mob and was with them for two years. I had enough of those classes in social pathology, social disorientation and all that crap.

How'd you get the boys to accept you?

I hung around the Lexington Hotel. It was their headquarters. I laughed at all the terrible jokes of Big Ed, one of the boys. He liked me and took me around. Different guys taught me the various operations. Jesus, did I learn! I learned what a fucked-up world this really is.

If you wanted to do something about crime, you had to start with the nice people, the respectable ones. I'd go around with a guy who headed the committee against vice. He owned a tenement, with call girls on every floor.

I found organized crime to be a huge, quasi-public utility. This was during the last years of Prohibition. People wanted beer, they wanted whiskey, they wanted broads, they wanted gambling and all the other stuff. It was a corporation. Everybody owned stock in it: City Hall, Democrats, Republicans, the world. . . .

Somewhere along the line, my interest in criminology waned. I remember my student days when I was starving and pulling funny rackets on restaurants, just to survive. Once, I came close to kicking in the goddam window of Henrici's.[8] People were in there eating steaks about this thick and my stomach was empty. As a kid was telling me of an A & P store he robbed and another of a gas station he heisted, Hitler and Mussolini were robbing whole countries and killing whole peoples. I found it difficult to listen to small-time confessions. Most of my time was spent in anti-fascist and CIO activities.

That's how I found myself Back of the Yards. It was the nadir of all the slums of America, worse than Harlem is today. You had this dingy, gray mile-by-two-miles of track, south of the big slaughterhouses. Clapboard frame houses, one behind the other. Many of them with outhouses. The neighborhood was practically all Catholic. You never saw

[8] It was, once upon a time, one of Chicago's finest restaurants.

so many churches. It made Rome look like a Protestant Gothic town.

At this point, I decided to get the hell out of academic work and go in for mass organization. I had certain concepts I couldn't follow through on as a professional. If you're an academic and you're controversial, you're in trouble. You had to organize around issues, and all issues were controversial.

I wanted to test out my ideas. Ideas on organization for change. If they would work in Back of the Yards, they would work anywhere. If you wanted to do something about crime and despair, you had to do something about its causes.

There were a lot of fascist groups in the area. It wasn't accidental. If you cut away a lot of your so-called political science analysis of why a totalitarian society develops, it comes down to this: If you're out of it, the demagogue comes along and says, "Follow me." If you haven't got a goddam thing to lose, you follow him. Isn't that what happened in Germany?

There was a Benedictine priest, who was leading the Coughlinite movement around there. He was making speeches denouncing international Jewry. He had psyched out, because nobody had paid him any attention. He had about fifty followers. This was his only place in the world. So I made him chairman of the neighborhood's anti-fascist committee. He now had a thousand followers instead of fifty. He became one of the best anti-fascist apostles of the democratic process. He was given a sense of personal identification.

I'm going around organizing, agitating, making trouble. At the end of three months, I had the Catholic Church, the CIO and the Communist Party working together. It involved the Packinghouse Workers Union. I even got the American Legion involved, because they didn't have a goddam thing to do. They all had one thing in common: misery. Powerlessness.

I'd go in to see this Catholic priest. I'd say, "I heard your sermon denouncing the union, calling it Communist. You know something, Father? Your people nodded and then walked out and joined the union. Know why? They're unemployed, their families are shot to hell and you're not doing a God damn thing about it. You sit on your ass in the sacristy, and you're no longer a shepherd of your flock. Everybody is disregarding you. You want to be a leader? Get back with your people, get out in the streets and fight for the union. The enemy is the meat packer; the enemy is low wages." So he'd do it. Purely on the basis of self-interest.

You don't talk Judaic-Christian moral principles to a priest, a rabbi or a minister. They wouldn't know what the hell you're talking about.

I had difficulty with only one priest. He was Irish. The Poles of the area had church wedding ceremonies involving bells. It broke down to a buck and a half a pull. The Irish priest passed the word around that he'd perform with bells at a buck a pull. The Polish shepherd went off his rocker. He said to me, "You're the guy who talks about people getting together, that we'll have power and so on. If you can get that Irishman to come back to the regular price, we'll join your organization. Otherwise, forget it."

So I went down to see the Irish priest. I made the mistake of posing the question on purely spiritual grounds. He told me to mind my own business. So I said, "O.K., I looked over the receipts of your last summer's carnival. Your big fund raising affair. You made $18,000. I'll see to it, when the time comes for your carnival, the CIO, the American Legion, the Chamber of Commerce and every other church in this community will have some kind of affair on the same date. We'll rip your carnival apart. The most you can make at a buck a pull, assume you get all the wedding business, is ten grand. You'll drop eighteen." He ordered me out.

About ten minutes later, the phone rings. He reconsidered. On moral principles, of course. He was up to a buck thirty-five a pull. So I got three Polish churches to join the Back-of-the-Yards Council. So it went: different tactics for different circumstances.

John L. Lewis heard of it. He wasn't happy. The CIO was merely one component, and he wanted it to be the dog with the community as its tail. But he was converted. He offered me a job at $25,000 a year. All I had to do was go around the country organizing CIO unions into industrial communities. I turned him down, though I admired him, and my heart was with the CIO.

Three weeks later, Roosevelt called me to the White House. What a personality! What presence! He offered me a job as assistant director of the NYA. My job was simply to organize young Democrats across the country. Again, though my heart was with the New Deal, I said no.

These were the two most remarkable men of the decade. Why did I reject these offers? Easy. The secret of the Back-of-the-Yards Council —and all the other organizations I worked at since—was: The people weren't fronting for anyone. It was *their own* program.

HARD TIMES

In the Thirties, I learned what is to me the big idea: providing people with a sense of power. Not just the poor. There is nothing especially noble about the poor. Everybody. That time may have been our most creative period. It was a decade of involvement. It's a cold world now. It was a hot world then.

The Doctor, Huey
and Mr. Smith

George Murray

A journalist, Chicago's American.

From 1938 to 1945, he had been associated with the Townsend Movement as editor of its newspaper and, subsequently, as its general manager.

AT THE TIME I came over, there were twelve thousand Townsend Clubs all over the country. The little old lady secretaries of these clubs would write up minutes of the meetings in pencil or pen: we heard such and such a speaker . . . a lady baked a cake and we raffled it off. Club notes. My chore was to take all this indecipherable handwritten material and make little stories out of them. One-paragraph stories to give recognition to each club. It kept me busy all week long. I became editor.

He recounts his experiences with Dr. Townsend, the country doctor out of Nebraska. "He was so slender, so thin, never weighed more than 120 pounds, had a good thatch of white hair.

"In 1933, at sixty-seven, he was Health Commissioner in Long Beach, California, and selling a little real estate on the side. He was dealing with old people. He was aware of their lack of money and of anybody's interest in them. He wrote a three hundred word letter to the

editor of the Long Beach Telegram. *His idea: a gross income tax of two percent on everybody in the country, no exceptions. Proceeds to be divided among all people over sixty, the blind and disabled, and mothers of dependent children. They had to spend it within thirty days. He wasn't a great economist, but he had something figured out in his mind.*

"It caught on so quickly, he didn't know what to do. It wasn't a movement at first. But then ten thousand letters came in a month. People from Long Beach sent this clipping all over the country. Other papers picked it up. He turned his real estate office into headquarters. From then on, it was part of the American scene."

I remember the national convention in Indianapolis. 1939. H. L. Mencken was covering it for the Baltimore *Sun*. He liked Doc. At the press conference, Mencken was cheering Dr. Townsend on. A reporter turned to Mencken and said that all the established newspapers were against this crackpot plan, and "The way you talk, Mr. Mencken, it sounds as though you're for it." I remember Mencken saying, rolling his big cigar in his mouth, "I'd love to see the Townsend Plan enacted tomorrow morning. I'd also like to see New York City bombed from the air. I love a spectacle."

My work was unlike ordinary newspaper reportage. You also had to be a promoter. The plan was carried on by contributions. We would set up a Doctor's Birthday Party on January thirteenth every year. Then we'd have a Founder's Day on September thirtieth. Then we'd have a Homecoming Day. On these three occasions, the ladies would bake cakes and all. There'd be cake sales. We had organizers in each of the forty-eight states. Yet it wasn't organized as it might be by a computer. This was something that had grown unexpectedly, and nobody thought it would last. It was just thrown together. . . .

It was strictly a grass roots movement, nothing else. But it served its purpose. It brought the Social Security plan into being. When he signed the bill, late in 1935, Franklin D. Roosevelt was apologetic. He said: the Social Security plan has not been fully worked out yet by the actuaries. But he had to enact it to forestall the Townsend Plan. People were just screaming. They wanted pensions.

Dr. Townsend was called everything. He was called a charlatan, a man draining money from people, the hard-won pennies of the old. He never took a nickel out of it. He founded the newspaper and took a salary, $90 a week. Many years later, it was $150 a week.

He wasn't an economic genius but his common sense and instinct caused him to hit upon this plan. He was never strong in the cities. His strength was always in the rural areas and small towns. That's where the twelve thousand clubs were. Men like Father Coughlin and Gerald L. K. Smith sensed if they could get these people, they could put over any program they wanted. Dr. Townsend was a genius in politics, if nothing else. When these men came around him—and I'm sure they wanted to use him for their own purposes—he never said no. He never said yes, either. He always said, "That's very interesting." He would try to use *them*. He had a lot of native shrewdness. Nobody was going to take his clubs away from him.

The movement was at its height just before the war and went downhill after that. It lost its momentum. The Townsend Plan was a Depression movement. Now it became a piebaking movement, just old people. But in the Thirties, it had direction: it was going to influence the Government, and it did.

Senator Russell Long

United States Senator from Louisiana.

It was my good fortune to be the son of a man like Huey Long. He always provided wealth for his family, even in the Depression. I was born and raised in a laboring man's neighborhood, and I knew what wretchedness was. Even though our people were poor, you might say we did pretty well for the kind of folk we came from.

Huey Long had a great sympathy for the Negro, even though, unfortunately, very few were permitted to vote in Louisiana. He did not carry the racial fight for the black man in Louisiana. He thought he was carrying as many crosses as he could, the way it was. He didn't want to be crucified on that one.

I was about seventeen when he died.[1] I heard some of his speeches and I could see its effect on his audience. He'd go to places where he'd

[1] In 1935, he was assassinated by Carl Austin Weiss in the capitol building at Baton Rouge.

never been before, where they had never heard him. When he finished, he had 'em.

He had been a traveling salesman when he was a youngster and his approach as a political speaker was pretty much the same. Selling. He'd warm the crowd up with some jokes. After a while, he'd start explaining one point, then another, carrying his audience with him—to where he'd really score. He'd return to humor, an anecdote, and then bear down again. He had the audience so tense, you'd think something was gonna snap. Suddenly, he'd relieve the tension by reaching the climax, followed by quick jokes . . . and everybody just relaxed. He'd make them laugh and cheer, from the serious to the ridiculous. He wouldn't move the crowd to tears. That wasn't his approach. But he certainly sold them points they'd never been sold before.

I enjoyed being in the crowd and hearing those speeches. One time, he was due to make a speech in the large football stadium in New Orleans. He was listening over the radio to the other speeches. Then he fell asleep and snored. He was tired. I could hear the crowd three blocks away. When he showed up, you might as well quit talking. The crowd shouted, "Let's hear Huey!" And that was it.

He never worried about how long he talked. He'd tell everybody to call their friends and neighbors and turn on the radio. He'd say, "I'm not gonna say anything important for the next few minutes, so make those calls." Because he wanted them to hear about all the stealing and corruption he'd found in Washington . . . that somebody else was engaged in.

You'd walk down the street, you couldn't escape the sound of his voice. Every home in New Orleans would have him turned on. His voice could be heard all over town till maybe one o'clock in the morning. New Orleans stayed open all night. It was that kind of town.

He was really catching on around the country. His plan was pretty well patterned after the old Populist philosophy. Money had gotten down to where a few people had practically all of it. He thought it was time you spread it among everybody. His share-the-wealth program was for one-third of the nation's money to be divided among all the people, even though you did permit the other two-thirds to be captured by the upper one percent. It had a lot of popular appeal.

His critics would say: In three or four years, the wealthy would have the money back in their coffers anyway. The Long people would answer: Maybe so. But think what a good time we'd have in the meanwhile. (Laughs.)

Huey Long had great impact on the Roosevelt Administration. Dr. Altmeyer told me about it.[2] He was one of the people who put together the Social Security program. He said, when they'd meet at the White House to discuss the program, Roosevelt was talking more about Huey Long than he was about Social Security. It was designed in a large measure as a backfire against Huey Long.

It was to cut the progress Huey Long was making that Roosevelt moved to the left with liberal New Deal measures. He began as a reactionary. When Roosevelt sent down the economy bill, cutting government salaries and veteran's benefits, Huey made a speech, "The Victory over the Helpless." In one talk, he read from a veteran's letter: ". . . with the new Roosevelt program, I won't be needing these. So you can wear 'em." The fella enclosed his false teeth. (Laughs.) The crowd just roared.

Roosevelt didn't buy all of Huey Long's program, but he certainly moved in that direction. His welfare programs paralleled in many respects what Huey Long was advocating. When the NYA was put into effect, Roosevelt gave my father credit as being a forerunner. We had a program very similar to it in Louisiana.

Westbrook Pegler wrote in his column that Huey Long had the support of the LSU student body because he had one-third of 'em on the payroll. About a third of the students did have scholarships to help work their way through college. He wanted to go far beyond that. He wanted to provide *every* young man and young lady who could make passin' grades, the chance to work their way through college.

This was in the early Thirties. A lot of people who today are bank presidents came to LSU with nothing more than a shirt on their back, and not so much as a change of underwear. Today they are prominent people.

Huey Long started out in favor of Roosevelt, and then they went their separate ways. Roosevelt, I think, made a mistake in underrating Huey. My guess is if my father had lived, he'd have run for President on the third party ticket in 1936. He might have kept Roosevelt from winning. I guess he was thinking in those terms. He probably would have caused Landon to win. If that had been the case, he'd have been a real prospect to win four years later.

Some people have suggested that this was a selfish approach, putting his own ambition above the good of the nation. His reply would be: If

[2] Dr. Arthur J. Altmeyer. He was Commissioner of Social Security for a number of years.

the public would suffer with Roosevelt or Landon, the sooner both are out, the better. Certainly, if Roosevelt hadn't moved left, Huey Long would have captured the public's imagination. He wasn't doing so bad as it was.

He knew Doctor Townsend and he knew Father Coughlin. I'm not sure they spent much time together, but they were all aware of what the others were doing. They were speaking from the same point of view. While each had a different approach, there was no fundamental difference.

I imagine he had many more good innings left, if the Good Lord had let him live. He was thirty years ahead of his time.

Evelyn Finn

I LIVED IN BATON ROUGE when Huey Long was shot. I coulda been up there at the capitol when it happened. My brother and I used to go there a lot. They had night sessions, because it was cooler at night. This time I said, "Oh, I'm tired of seein' 'im." So he went by himself. We was home listening to the radio and we heard the news. My brother came home. He'd been up in the spectators' gallery. He said, "There was a terrible commotion. They wouldn't let us out for a long time. I wonder what happened." I thought, "Well, no wonder. Huey Long was shot." He came home and didn't know it.

In 1933, she left St. Louis for a few years. Temporarily, she abandoned her work as a seamstress to run the family grocery store in her home town, Baton Rouge.

The grafters, Huey's boys, till they got caught up with, they went to town. There was a fella came into the store. He was foreman of a WPA gang—it was called somethin' else before that.[3] Anyway, they was buildin' these beautiful homes on WPA money. The servants that worked in these homes, I'd cash their checks. They'd say: "We're So-

---

[3] CWA (Civil Works Administration).

and-So's maid, we're So-and-So's yard man." All these politicians paid their servants with WPA money, get it?

Negroes'd go in town and get their rations. But they couldn't eat it. Full of worms and weevils. They would tell me when they come into the store. They couldn't use half of what they got. But they went and got it. Otherwise, they wouldn't get anything. Because who dished it out would say: "If you don't take it, there's no use to give it to you." That's what they'd give the Negro.

One day, a couple of fellas came around. They said they were Huey Long's boys. Election was comin' up. We had a lot of votes in the family. They explained all the wonderful things Huey Long was doing. Our road was mud. I said, "You only come around when you want votes."

The next morning, there was a big truck-load of gravel, comin', with five or six men on it. They had plenty of manpower, the WPA did. The foreman said, "We give everybody what they want." Oh, that Huey! He was somethin'.

Gerald L. K. Smith

"Rev. Gerald L. K. Smith, D.D. . . . the gustiest and goriest, the loudest and lustiest, the deadliest and damnedest orator ever heard on this or any other earth."

—H. L. Mencken, Baltimore *Sun*, 1936

A rugged, though slightly subdued, seventy-one, he and his wife, Elna (after whom the Foundation is named . . . "she came into a handsome inheritance") are impresarios of a religious enterprise in Eureka Springs, Arkansas. Once a celebrated spa, it had become ghostly until the energetic appearance of Mr. Smith. It is something of a shrine now, offering The Passion Play, *with the latest in stereophonic equipment (". . . if this noble spectacle is anti-Semitic, the New Testament is anti-Semitic." A General Motors executive pronounced it better than Oberammergau's.), a gallery of sacred art, and* The Christ of the Ozarks.

This last is a remarkable phenomenon: The Christ of the Ozarks, *a seventy-foot statue on the peak of Magnetic Mountain. The sculpture is astonishingly white, ". . . we ordered a special kind of mortar." It is visible from four states. The Saviour's outstretched arms appear to be blessing them with equally Wondrous Love: Arkansas, Oklahoma, Missouri and Kansas.*

At twilight, Mr. Smith is at the foot of the hill, his head bowed, his Stetson at heart, his Lincoln Continental nearby. From within the circle of The Christ, hymns pour forth. The voices of Kate Smith and Tennessee Ernie Ford are stereophonically loud and clear.

"Let it never be said that Gerald Smith is using the name of his Saviour to make a fast buck. But if I were a young man, I'd take options on land out here. . . ."

Mr. and Mrs. Smith ("We have been married forty-seven years, and I love her as much now as the day she became my bride.") are gracious hosts: a country dinner and effusive conversation. He is grievously wounded at having been "quarantined," these past years, by the mass media, though he is an admirer of Ronald Reagan. . . .

He still keeps a hand in secular as well as sacred affairs: "Three girls are busy every day, as I dictate articles for more than two hundred right-wing publications." His own journal, The Cross and the Flag, *founded in 1942, is going fairly strong . . . celebrated for its pungent philippics against the "Jewish Establishment" and recalcitrant blacks.*

We are in a stately Victorian house: stained-glass windows, profuse with religious artifacts, portraits, statuary, Tiffany lamps and chandeliers, Persian rugs. . . . "Every stone in this house has been personally cut by hand." What was once the prayer room of the original occupant, a Confederate officer, has been transformed into a bathroom: "I don't think God makes himself available only at certain hours like eleven o'clock Sunday morning." In addition to paintings of The Saviour, there is, facing the entrance, a portrait in oil of Henry Ford, the elder.

I WAS INTRODUCED to the Depression while I was in Shreveport, Louisiana. I was pastor of the most sophisticated church. The leadership included the top men in the community. Then the curtain fell. I had the experience of standing at the door of the church on Sunday mornings, meeting weeping men and women who had lost everything.

In the meantime, Huey Long had risen to power. He referred to Louisiana as the last stand of the feudal lords. Human slavery was still being practiced. When a Negro or a poor white was arrested, he would be assigned by the judge, district attorney or sheriff to the deputy, who happened to own a plantation or sawmill. It was a matter of common practice.

Then came the Depression, and sophisticated people became penniless. Fifteen thousand homes were coming up for mortgage foreclosures in the city. The building and loan company decided to foreclose, before the HOLC could advance loans.

I couldn't stand the tears of these people, and I offered aggressive resistance to this. I urged the company to postpone these foreclosures. They said it was none of my business. Lo and behold, I was waited on by the leaders in my church. They brought pressure on me to resign. They were silent partners in this thieving enterprise.

I called my friend, Huey Long: "The hypocrites in my church are planning to steal $50 million." In about thirty minutes, the phone rang. It was the head of the building and loan association. Weeping and wailing, he said, "Dr. Smith, what can I do?[4] You have no idea what Huey Long said to me. He's going to ruin me. He has told me to do anything you want me to do." I said, "All you need to do is cross the street to the courthouse and cancel the foreclosures." They were canceled. It confirmed my great affection for Huey Long, and it lost me my job as pastor of the King's Highway Christian Church.

"I've been asked, 'Why did you leave the formal ministry?' I said, 'Because I want to go to Heaven.' I insist on being called Mr. Smith. I don't like a man that hits me and says, 'Don't hit back, I'm a clergyman.' Take all these preachers causing all this trouble, stirring up the anarchists and all. They go out and tell these people what to do. Take off your collar and just be a private citizen in this controversy. So when someone hits back, they're not slapping a priest or beating a clergyman."

Huey Long and I developed a mutual respect for each other. When his power was at an apex, he said to me, "If God was Governor of Louisiana, he couldn't find enough honest men to make a chairman for each county. If anything happens to me, Gerald, you're the only one of this gang that shouldn't go to the federal penitentiary. These boys who were barefooted when I found them just can't keep their hands out of the public till."

Huey Long developed a philosophy in which I helped him along. He

---

[4] "Below the Mason-Dixon Line, all preachers are called 'Doctor,' whether they've been to school or not."

was the only man of this century who knew how to think like a statesman and campaign like a demagogue. His share-the-wealth program
sounded like demagoguery to reactionaries, but it was sound. The
barons of monopoly came into the state. They bought up all the natural
resources: the oil, gas and timber concessions—everything from oil to
trees, from sulfur to fish. Huey Long said the wealth on top of our
ground and underneath must be shared with the people. He said: No
man should be allowed to accumulate a fortune of more than $5 million
without a progressive levy against him. Imagine. We appealed to intelligent conservatives.

My strategy was to project Huey Long as candidate for President
in '36, as Wallace was in '68. It was the understanding we'd split the
Roosevelt vote. But we would have a say about who the Republican
candidate was. If Huey Long had lived, we would never have nominated this protoplasmic substance, Landon.

The conservatives lost because they didn't know how to support a
statesman. They only knew how to buy Senators and Congressmen.
When the real crisis came, we had no one to defend the cause, because
the man that can be bought isn't intelligent enough to think for himself.
His footwork is too slow.

I remember saying to the Republican leaders personally—in the days
of the Mellons—we're willing to split the Roosevelt vote, but we can't
promise to lose. Our man is becoming so popular so fast, he might win.
Jim Farley said if Huey hadn't been killed, he would have been President of the United States.

When Georgia was upstaging Louisiana and wouldn't let us into the
football conference, Huey threatened to impose an extra penny tax on
Coca-Cola. The Cannons, who own Coca-Cola, run Georgia. Naturally,
Louisiana was brought into the conference.

Everybody came to us. The most subtle, the most cunning Communist leaders on the face of the earth, from Moscow and New York,
visited us. They knew we were sincere friends of the people. They
wanted to sell us on the Marxist philosophy. The moment we repulsed
them, they called us Fascists. The moment we repulsed the reactionaries, we were called Communists. We were dealing with men who
felt other men should go to work for a dollar a day and go to church
in overalls.

We think our Congressmen pass laws and levy taxes. That is done
by the money changers. We raise interest from four percent to six, six

to eight, eight to ten. A conservative insurance company tried to persuade people out here to finance enterprises at twelve percent. When I was a boy, they'd shoot the three balls off a man's store and put him in jail for that. (Laughs.)

"You say money changer, and they think you mean Jew. The word anti-Semite is a dirty word given to people who take issue with aggressive Jews. My theory is the aggressive Jew is not an honest representative of his community. If I were to attack Rap Brown, would you accuse me of being anti-Negro?[5] I don't think the Jews should control Palestine any more than they should control New York. I don't mean they should be driven out. Not one ounce of their liberty should be affected. Their citizenship should not in any way be jeopardized, but they shouldn't control everything, either. . . ."

"Here we have these liberal regimes. Yet it's the greatest tyranny man has ever known. Cannibals are swallowing cannibals and dinosaurs are swallowing dinosaurs. The conglomerates. Under the leadership of the great impoverished statesmen like Harriman, the Kennedys, the Rockefellers, the Roosevelts (laughs),[6] we have developed the most super-monopolistic octopus of the human race today. . . ."

Huey Long died in my arms. We were walking through the hall, and this man shot Huey. The boys killed the killer, before he turned loose on the others. He missed me.

It was the largest public funeral in history. It took three acres of ground just to lay the bouquets. They came from everywhere on the face of the earth. There were people backed up eight miles on the other side of the Mississippi, couldn't get across the river.

[5] "Nigger, as used down South, wasn't a dirty word. Today we can't even say 'chiggers,' we say 'chigg-roes.' " (Laughs.) "Now we have to say 'black,' don't we?"

[6] "The only way they could fill the football stadium was for Huey to attend the game. In one case, he agreed on condition that the newspaper, begging him, cancel Westbrook Pegler's column. Pegler started out as a Gerald Smith hater and Huey Long hater. Later, he turned on the Roosevelts. A few years ago, in Tucson, he said, 'The greatest mistake in my life was not joining Gerald Smith 25 years ago.'

"I used to have a lot of fun with Eleanor myself. I said she was a very generous woman. She left her teeth at the Elks' Lodge. (Laughs.) I used to talk about the children. We were raised up to believe that if you married cousins, the children would be silly. It was never more graphically demonstrated than with the Roosevelt family. (Laughs.) When Eleanor came back from the South Seas and said the boys in the hospitals looked sad, I said, 'If I looked up into a puss like that, I'd have a relapse.' " (Laughs.)

I sat down beside the bed and wrote the eulogy by hand. Later on, I had it photostated.

It concludes: "His unlimited talents invariably aroused the jealousies of those inferiors who posed as his equals. More than once, yea, many times, he has been the wounded victim of the Green Goddess; to use the figure, he was the Stradivarius, whose notes rose in competition with jealous drums, envious tom-toms. His was the unfinished symphony."[7]

He recounts his one-man efforts, after Huey's death, in battling the Long machine—"the aggressive pigs in the trough." It was their compact with New Dealers that most incurred his wrath: the promise of several millions to be spent in the state, withheld during Huey's life—on the condition of their backing Roosevelt in the 1936 convention. . . . "Out of the nine men in the machine, I was the only one who refused. I arose in the meeting and said I had catapulted to prominence on the wet grave of Huey Long. There was nothing they had I wanted. So those others, who hadn't reported their income taxes, who had stolen money, were coerced by the Internal Revenue Department and lined up. I coined the term: The Second Louisiana Purchase.

"I went to the people. It was one of the most dramatic nights in Louisiana history. I took the last dollar I had and bought time on every radio station in the state. I announced I was going to speak in the plaza and seventy thousand people came out. I spoke past midnight. I talked about the blood of Huey Long sold on the auction block. It was months before the crooks dared leave their homes or drive through the country, because of what people heard me say that night."

Many believe that Huey Long was largely responsible for the quick passage of the Social Security Act. . . .

Modern politicians would like to romanticize things. Social Security is the substitute for the real thing. Henry Ford, for instance, never believed in charity. He believed in a job rather than a pension.

Yet . . . why was a man like Henry Ford so fond of you?

Henry Ford wasn't entrenched wealth. He turned a bolt into a nut, a nut into a fender, a fender into a car, and a car into a genius-like formula.

---

[7] "It was a political speech to himself," said Senator Russell Long. "He anointed himself as Huey Long's successor. He made a great impression."

That is American wealth. He wasn't part of a combine designed to destroy everyone else. He wasn't part of the money market.

I gravitated to Detroit and started the Christian Nationalist Crusade. Frank Murphy was coming up fast. He played possum while the CIO destroyed Mr. Ford's factory.

You came to Detroit just about the time the CIO was being organized . . . ?

Oh, I was for organized labor. For years, I was an honorary member of the American Federation of Labor. But I believed that labor was moving in the same direction as capital—toward giant monopoly.

"I came so completely into the confidence of Mr. Ford that he specified: Everyone who sold merchandise to the Ford Motor Company contribute to the Christian Nationalist Crusade. We were seeking to enlighten all schoolteachers, all clergymen, all public officials.

"Then one day I was waited on by Mr. Ford's personal secretary, my personal friend. He said he'd been waited on by a personal representative of the White House and that unless Mr. Ford withdrew his support of me, they'd seize the factory and operate it in the name of the wartime emergency. . . ."

In 1942, he ran for the United States Senate in Michigan. He came within twenty thousand votes of winning the Republican nomination. "Both parties united against me." But not Henry Ford.

The time came for a coalition of the people—1936. There were three big mass groups: Huey Long's following, Doctor Townsend's and Father Coughlin's. I was instrumental in effecting this coalition.

Townsend was a sincere, good, unselfish man. I was in Washington when they were crucifying Townsend—the wolf pack. They called in a bunch of neurotic women to testify against him. Hired perjurers, they tried to say it was a racket. They had a Roman holiday with the old man.

I said, "Doc, they're going to destroy you. You treat them with courtesy. You should hold them in contempt." He had two or three hangers-on, who were turning pale. They're the ones who watch over the dues. (Laughs.) I said, "I would stand up, pronounce my contempt, walk out and *defy* them to come and get me." He said, "If I had a young man like you beside me, I'd do it." I said, "You've got him."

So the stage was set. We didn't tell any of those shortstops there, it would scare 'em.

The old man stood up. He pronounced judgment and contempt on the whole Congressional committee. He defied the gavel. I just took him by the arm, and we ran out. In the meantime, I was in touch with Henry Mencken. I told him I'd kidnapped the old man and would bring him to Baltimore: "Find a place to hide him."

Mencken was delighted. We hid him for three days in defiance of the committee. The sympathy for old people was such that if any Congressman had offered a motion to cite him for contempt, he would have committed political suicide. If I may say so, that was the budge that made the Townsend movement a political factor.

He asked me to speak at his convention in Cleveland. You can hardly realize how the multitudes moved.[8] It was a Populist movement.

The little machine makers who organized the program said the meeting must be unbiased. We must have a Republican, a New Dealer and so forth. I was scheduled to speak at ten thirty. The Roosevelt friend was set for eleven thirty, and the Republican for twelve thirty. So I spoke for three hours. (Laughs.) Every time the chairman made a move toward me, the crowd wanted to lynch him.

Recalls Mencken: "Twice at Cleveland [author's note: the other event, the Coughlin convention], I saw the rev. gentleman torpedo even the press stand. In that stand were journalists who had not shown any human emotion above the level of cupidity and lubricity for twenty years, yet he had them all howling in ten minutes. . . ."

Everybody was hungry when I was through. The meeting was over before they got to anyone else. Of course, Dr. Townsend loved and revered me in those days. Later on, we had a little quarrel. I felt as he grew old and vegetated, he was exploited. But I respected him to the very hour of his death.

In the meantime, Father Coughlin had developed a great following. He asked if I would deliver the principal address at his convention, aside from his own. The gathering was as big as Townsend's. At the baseball stadium in Cleveland.

One day I was out at Royal Oak. We were discussing a tour. Out of

[8] "In those days, I spoke at the Rose Bowl to 110,000 people. Think of that."

the clear sky, Coughlin's door opened, without a knock. There stood Bishop Gallagher, his superior. Beside him stood the proverbial Prelate —tall, wide-brimmed black hat—serious, pallid, no color. As though he were about to announce the Governor had denied clemency.

Gallagher tapped Coughlin on the shoulder and said, "Come with me, Charlie." They were gone about twenty minutes. Coughlin came back as white as my shirt. He said, "The arm of Jim Farley is long. I'm finished. Our Church has always wanted an ambassador, but Protestant America won't give one to the Pope. The Vatican is willing to settle for a Fraternal Delegate. Mr. Roosevelt has served notice there will be none, unless I am silenced." He never spoke out again.

Imagine a man, who had been speaking to twenty million people every Sunday, imagine such a man being silenced. What frustration!

So I was left alone. Huey Long was dead. Doc Townsend was dead. Coughlin was silenced. General Wood lost himself in his business. Lindbergh told me, "I don't know how to fight Walter Winchell and those others. . . ." But that didn't stop *me*. My background wasn't that of a pantywaist. I've been mobbed and rotten-egged. Once in lower Louisiana, I grabbed a heckler by the collar, drew him up and held him through the entire speech. Everytime I'd make a point, I'd shake him. (Laughs.)

Did I ever tell you about that time in Georgia? A state with a lynching tradition. I was going to speak in a nearby town. We set up the sound equipment in front of the courthouse. Here came the mob. All the little farmers were there, all the little rich. The backbone of America are these little rich.

They grabbed the cable of our sound truck, threw it over the limb of a tree and screamed, "Hang the son of a bitch!" I stepped into the shadows of a store building. The sound men all ran and hid. The mob released the brake and the truck wound up somewhere in a ditch. They began to yell: "Where is he? Where is he?"

I jumped up on a big square of cement and I yelled at the top of my voice: "Here I am. The man that touches me touches a man of God. Who dares be the first?" (His voice breaks; with difficulty he stifles a deep sob. Across the room, his wife weeps softly. A long pause.) They went away.

A few nights later, I got a phone call about three o'clock in the morning. The voice said, "I am the man that led the mob. I'm a member of the state legislature. Mr. Smith, I am convinced you're a good man. If I

369

can't have your forgiveness, I won't sleep another night." Isn't that something?

POSTSCRIPT: *From the airport at Fayetteville to Arkansas Springs is a stretch of some fifty miles. On the car radio was a continuous flow of hymns—the singers all white—interspersed with commercials. At no time was a black face visible, during the drive. Of young people, there were remarkably few, aside from little children in the company of their pilgrim parents.*

The Circuit Rider

Claude Williams

His resemblance to the poet, Ezra Pound, is startling.

"I've been run out of the best communities, fired from the best churches and flogged by the best citizens of the South."

He was born and raised in the hills of western Tennessee, "so far back in the sticks they had to pump in daylight to make morning." He began as a fundamentalist, preaching "to save their never-dying, ever-precious souls from the devil's hell eternal." He drilled himself in chapter and verse.

After four years in the town of Lebanon, as an evangelist, he was invited to the Vanderbilt School of Religion. It was a seminar for rural preachers. The teacher who most influenced him referred to Jesus as Son of Man—"he cleared the debris of theological crap and let Him rise among us as a challenging human leader."

I ASSUMED the pastorate of a Presbyterian church in Rome, Tennessee. I took as my text: "Go ye into the world and preach the gospel to every nation." We must treat everybody as persons. An elder said to me that night at dinner: "Preacher, do you mean that damn burrhead is as good as I am?" I answered, "No, but I mean to tell you he's as good as I am." So I had to find another pulpit.

At Auburntown, I said, "Friends, I've enjoyed this pastorate and the people, but I must tell you I think of God as a social being. The Son of Man is worthy of discipleship and the Bible is a revealing book of right and wrong." After that revival meeting, I had to find somewhere else to go.

I come to grief because of a trip I made to Waveland, Mississippi. In 1928. An interracial meeting. I was together with black people for the first time in my life. At the table I was aware of food sticking in my throat before swallowing it. A friend taught me to emphasize the "e" in Negro—to avoid old terms like "nigra," "uncle" and "auntie." I went down to preach to a black church. There were some whites sitting to one side. As the people came out, an old black man was the first I shook hands with. This was in violation of all my upbringing.

I was recommended to a little church in Paris, Arkansas. It was a coal-mining town. They were trying to organize against all odds. We staged a strike and won. As soon's it happened, I began to get money from Moscow. (Laughs.) But I learned this "money from Moscow" spent quicker and bought less than scrip coupons at a plantation robbersary—that's the real name for commissary.

Miners began to come around, from as far as thirty miles. They built the thing with their own hands. We thought of building a proletarian church and a labor temple. I canceled my insurance policies to buy the cement for the foundation—they quit paying my salary. From fifteen active members, we now had over a hundred. One of the elders, a merchant, was furious. "You've got these cantankerous miners—these blatherskites." They accused me of Red-ism and corrupting the minds of the youth. I lost my church. The presbytery met and "dissolved the relationship of the Reverend Claude Williams and the church for the good of the Kingdom of Heaven."

We went down to the town theater for Sunday services. It was filled. Many young people, miners and unemployed. This was '32, '33. Black people were coming to my home for conferences. Someone said, "You ought to pull the shades down." I said, "No, I want to pull the shades up and let the hypocrites see brotherhood being practiced." I was pretty rash.

The church was $2200 behind in my salary. I refused to leave the manse. They evicted me and sued me for the interest on the money they owed me. One official was the editor of the local paper, the Paris *Express*. We called it the Paris *Excuse*. One was an insurance salesman and another was a retired colonel, who painted his house red, white and blue. So I was driven out and went to Fort Smith.

We staged a hunger march, a thousand or more. The Mayor sent word: The march won't be held. I sent word back: This is America. The march will be held. He said, "We'll turn the hose on you." I said, "You do your duty, and I'll do mine." While we were in the opening prayer, they swarmed down on us. A lot of us landed in jail. The vigilantes were on me pretty regularly. So in the spring of '35, I went to Little Rock.

I worked with black and white unemployed. And taught at the first school of the Southern Tenant Farmers Union. In June of '36, I went to Memphis to prepare a funeral for a black sharecropper who had been beaten to death. His body disappeared. I went to investigate.

Before we got to Earle, Arkansas, five deputies were waiting for us. They took me out of the car. They got me down, four men held me down. This man had a little four-inch leather strop. He was a master. He gave me about sixteen licks. The woman with me kept count. They made a jelly out of me. Then they said, "Let's get some of that fat woman's butt." They applied the lash to her—five or six licks. They were careful not to damage her hose, as they led her through the barbed wire. They didn't know whether to dump me in the river or let me loose. They made me sign a statement that I hadn't been hurt. When I refused, they said, "If you're not through, we're not." I signed. They couldn't use it because it was an admission that they'd had me. They took me to Highway 70 and headed me for Birmingham. A car followed me for miles. I got away from 'em at Brinkley.

That was my real induction. I learned it's one thing to preach radical from the pulpit—people will come to atone for their wrongs by enduring a radical sermon—but when you identify with the people in their battle that's when "you get your money from Moscow." I've been in this fight for forty years. I've spent many a night behind the barbed-wire fence.

"I was defrocked in 1934. But in '42, the Presbyterian people asked me to go to Detroit because of so many southerners there in the auto plants. The established church couldn't reach 'em. I was to be industrial chaplain. They wanted me to put my feet on the desk and get a $5,000 expense account. But I got there out among the people. That's when the presbytery people began to get complaints. G.L.K. Smith and Carl McIntyre and some of the others put so many pressures on, they fired me.

"I returned to the South and continued my work in Birmingham. They

preferred charges against me for heresy. It was confirmed by the Presby-
terian General Assembly. I returned to Detroit and was ordained in a
Negro church."

I've used the Bible as a workingman's book. You'll find the prophets—
Moses, Amos, Isaiah and the Son of Man, Old Testament and New—
you'll find they were fighting for justice and freedom. On the other side,
you find the Pharaohs, the Pilates, the Herods, and the people in the
summer houses and the winter houses. These people like John the
Baptist are our people and speak our word, but they've been kidnapped
by the others and alien words put in their mouth to make us find what
they want us to find. Our word is our sword.

I interpreted this for the sharecroppers. We had to meet in little
churches, white and black. It was in the tradition of the old underground
railway. I translated the Bible from the vertical to the horizontal. How
can I reach this man and not further confuse him? He had only one book,
the Bible. This had to be the book of rights and wrongs. True religion
put to work for the fraternity of all people. All passages in the Book that
could be used to further this day I underlined in red pencil. The Book
fell open to me.

The rabble-rousers hated me. I had the longest horns in the country
because I was using the very book they were using. I turned the guns the
other way, as it were. I interpreted as I thought the prophets would inter-
pret it, given the situation.

"We have a religious phenomenon in America that has its origin in the
South. Established churches followed urban trends. People out here
were isolated and delivered religion on the basis of what they saw. Store-
bought clothes—which they could not buy out of poverty—became
worldly and sinful: 'We had rather be beggars in the House of the Lord
than dwell in king's palaces.' They were denied schooling. They were
called rednecks and crackers and damn niggers. But the Bible was God's
Book. Refused access to medical aid, faith healed the body as well as
the soul: 'We seek another world.' It was a protest against things
economically unavailable. I interpreted this protest and related it to the
Bible—instead of calling them hillbillies and rednecks.

"At one gathering five or six Klansmen were around. I said, 'I want to
speak about the Ku Klux Klan.' All the people who are in the Klan are
not vicious. My brother was a member. You try to reach people at the

*consciousness of their needs. I quoted Peter on the day of Pentecost:
'Save yourselves, don't wait for somebody else.' Peter made contact
with every person in the language in which he was born. I won over a
number of Klansmen.*

"*I translated the democratic impulse of mass religion rather than its
protofascist content into a language they understood. That's what got me
in trouble with the synod. I was on trial. They asked me how I felt about
the divinity of Jesus. I said, 'I believe in the divinity but not the deity of
Jesus.' They didn't know the difference. The divinity is God's likeness,
the deity is Godship. I had the Son of Man as a carpenter.*

"*The preachers tell a story from the Bible, entertain for an hour or so
and then come back to it. Young radicals try to clarify every issue in one
speech. People are confused, go out and scratch their heads. And the
kid says: What's the matter with those dumb people? The demagogues
are smarter—they entertain. I've tried to beat them at their own game.
But you've got to know where to check the emotion.*"

In Winston-Salem, when we went out to organize the tobacco workers,
the leader said: "If you crack this in two years, it'll be a miracle." We
went to the oldest church. It was a bitter night. The pastor was a white
woman, sitting there with an army blanket around her shoulders and a
little old hat. I knew she was the bellwether. Unless I got her, I got nobody.

I gave the gospel of the Kings: Good News is only good when it feeds
the poor. This woman pastor got up and drawled: "Well, this is the first
time I heard the gospel of three square meals a day, and I want in on it.
I love to shout and now I know every time I shout, I know I need
shoes." First thing I know, she was touching cadence and going way off.

I jumped up and said, "Wait." (He unwinds into a rapid-fire
sermon.) "I charge you before the Lord and Saviour, Jesus Christ, who
will judge the quick and the dead. Preach the Word. Thy word is truth,
truth is thy word. Being instant, inside season, out of season, reprove,
rebuke, for the time will come, Sister Price, the time will come for the
kings. When they heap to themselves teachers, and theologians en-
dowed by robber barons, to take people from the people, boys and
girls, and teach them to take orders, and not to discuss controversial
subjects as to offend—and to say: 'Don't believe there's such a thing as
poverty. Boss John has your best interests at heart. And if you die of
fatigue or malnutrition or pneumonia or lack of medical care, your

375

most precious soul will be borne on the wings of lily-white angels in a home 140 million light years away.' Turn away from truth and we'll be turned away. Sister Price, we can't turn away from truth. We'll sing a song." (He sings.) "Let the will of the Lord be done—in the home, in the school, in the church, in the union. . . ."

I had to translate this emotion into action. But if I'd let her go on shouting, we'd never have made it. In three months, they called a labor board election. We won. We called on the Bible and the Son of Man.

The Gentleman from Kansas

Alf M. Landon

Two-term Governor of Kansas; elected in 1932; re-elected in 1934. Republican candidate for President in 1936.

We are in Topeka. As we are approaching Landon's office, there's casual conversation with the cab driver. He is thirty years old. He was born and raised in this city.

"There's Alf Landon." (*He was sauntering up the pathway.*)

"Never heard of him."

"Don't you know who he was?"

"Can't recall the name."

"Folks never told you . . . ?"

"No."

"They ever tell you about Roosevelt?"

"Roosevelt was in service. He was Rough Riders."

"Teddy Roosevelt . . . ?"

"Right."

"Did they tell you about Franklin Roosevelt?"

"No. Not so much about that. Most people called him Teddy."

"Did your folks ever tell you about the Depression?"

"Things were hard to get, things were bad, fight for what you got."

Alf Landon is a sprightly and genial eighty-two. Booted, he appears as though he'd just come in from the wheat fields. The walls of his office are decorated with mementoes and photographs; friends and colleagues of another day: Colonel Frank Knox (his 1936 running mate), Congressman Joe Martin, H. L. Mencken, World War I buddies, college football team mates, his father and a young Alf. . . .

THOSE WERE hard times for Governors, especially in '33. For sixty days, there was not standing room in my reception hall. Men with tears in their eyes begged for an appointment that would help save their homes and farms. I couldn't see them all in my office. But I never let one of them leave without my coming out and shakin' hands with 'em. I listened to all their stories, each one of 'em. But it was obvious I couldn't take care of all their terrible needs. If I could make some suggestion, I did that. It was a harrowing experience. I've never forgotten it.

On top of the Depression was the drought. It set in around '30 and lasted till about '37, '38. Black blizzards. Even here in Topeka, visibility was three blocks at most. In the spring of '35, I saw President Roosevelt. He sent M. L. Wilson out here—Assistant Secretary of Agriculture. We spent two days driving across Kansas. At times, we couldn't see past the radiator. I told him all about our flood problems and drought. As a result, President Roosevelt established a farm pond program. Federal aid. Prior to that, farmers did the best they could. The state today is dotted with these farm ponds.

And the farm mortgages were coming due. That's why my reception room was so jammed. As part of Mr. Roosevelt's program, I appointed a conciliation committee of three men in each county. To extend time wherever possible. In many cases, I personally called the local bank or insurance company and succeeded in working out a moratorium. Since the bankers got their holiday, why shouldn't the farmers? We were among the first states to declare mortgage moratoriums. The courts declared it unconstitutional, so we worked out the committees. We practically stopped all the sales. And there were no riots in Kansas.

My relations with Mr. Roosevelt were always very pleasant. I never went to Washington that I never failed to call on him to pay my respects. But I always respected the pressure on his time. The President never failed to clear his appointment list for me. Once I kept Mrs. Roosevelt and General Marshall waiting. Some enthusiastic Republicans would criticize me. Didn't bother me.

The New Deal accomplished practices in land management that farm colleges had been teaching. These programs were necessary at the time.

In '36, I advocated a long range land-use study, which we'd never had. There were two uses that were hardly considered: reclamation and recreation.

How come the Republicans chose you as the 1936 candidate?

The campaign started in the grass roots. I didn't pay too much attention to it. Some friends of mine formed a committee. My campaign strategy was this: I would not fight against any favorite sons. But it was like a brush fire, I guess. The Ohio delegation wanted to name me. They said the campaign would be underwritten by the head of a big banking chain. I said, "That's the very reason I won't enter Ohio. I'm not gonna be under anyone's obligation." I've never been owned by anybody.

We put a $2500 limit on contributions to our campaign. Roy Roberts[1] said he never saw so much money being waved under the noses of candidates in his life. Hoover addressed the convention. It was in Cleveland. Frank Knox told me afterwards there was a plan to get together on Hoover. He was eager to run again. But he didn't have much delegate support.

Why would they seek you out—an old progressive Republican, an old Bull Moose man . . . ?

(He had started out as Bull Moose county chairman in 1914. In 1922, he bolted the Republican Party to support the Emporia editor, William Allen White, as independent candidate in a campaign against the Ku Klux Klan.)

I don't know.

Did you express much disagreement with the New Deal program?

Not too much. In my telegram to the convention, I wanted a declaration in favor of the gold standard. The platform committee—Eastern establishment, if you want to use a current phrase (laughs)—was all for a little snack of inflation. I challenged them. "The wild jackasses" of the prairie states were with me. I interpreted the plank on Social Security very liberally. This was before the roll call started. I made it known that the platform didn't suit me. But they nominated me unanimously.

[1] For fifty-six years, he served, in sequence, as reporter, editor and president of the Kansas City *Star*.

(Laughs.) I assume my feeling fitted the feeling of the delegates more than it did the platform committee.

I was accused of being too much of a me-too New Dealer by some of the staunch Republicans. They couldn't see the necessity of staying in tune with the times. They were out of touch.

This so-called welfare state is a unique combination of socialism and capitalism, and we'd better make it work. I've said this many times. I had not used the word "socialism" in any speech I made during the campaign. I was not afraid of "creeping socialism" as much as I was of creeping inflation.

I always felt if we kept our money sound and recognized the rights of labor to protect themselves as well as their women and children, and of farmers to organize, we'd work out of this. I've always been in favor of collective bargaining. And co-ops for farmers.

If you take Mr. Roosevelt's program today in light of what both Republicans and Democrats are standing for, he'd be pretty conservative. I've never condemned Roosevelt's objectives, just his Administration.

Do you feel the New Deal saved our society?

By and large? (Pause.) Yes.

In a nutshell, the basic problem of any government today is to keep alive circulation from the bottom to the top. Through collective bargaining and cooperatives.

You sound to me like a Populist nominated by the wrong party.

(He laughs. He discusses the early Populists and their contributions to many of the reforms, accepted today. He expresses particular admiration for Bob La Follette.)

Weren't the eastern bankers worried about you?

I don't know. A lot of 'em were for me. They knew how I felt. Maybe they were just desperate. (Laughs.)

If I'd been Mr. Hoover in '30, when Senator La Follette—Bob, Jr.— introduced a bill for a $10 billion appropriation in public works, I would have passed it. We needed those dams that were subsequently built for flood control and the pollution of rivers. Hoover vetoed it.

I didn't feel too bad when I lost in '36. I probably could have gone to the Senate, but I felt the Republican Party needed one leader, who was not a candidate for public office. Politics with me was an avocation, not a vocation.

Did you ever feel you were going to win?

Once. When I was in New York for the Madison Square Garden meeting, Henry Allen, the former Kansas Governor, received a call from the editor of the *Literary Digest:* Come over and see our polls. Landon's going to win. That night, I got as far as picking my Secretary of State—and then I woke up. (Laughs.)

Could you explain the Digest *poll?*

No. (Chuckles.) I think they deliberately weighted it.

On my way to New York for the big parade down Fifth Avenue, I stopped off at Newark. I asked Governor Edge what chance I had in New Jersey. He said, "No chance." He asked, "What's the chance in the country?" I said, "No chance." A young fellow was sitting in the corner. I thought he was in Edge's party. He was a reporter. Edge jumped up excitedly. "I'll call his publisher. I know him, he's a Republican. I'll stop it." I said, "Sit down. I'll handle this." The young fellow was scared. I called the editor and I said, "Your reporter is perfectly entitled to that story. And if you print it, I won't deny one word of it. But you might as well call off the election. I'm not going to call your publisher or anyone else. Your reporter is standing here, and it's up to you." They didn't print it.

The campaign did have its good moments. I was invited to speak at the Union League Club. Their annual Lincoln Day Dinner in 1936. I said, no, I'm not coming. I was told no one had ever been nominated at a Republican convention, who hadn't spoken to the Union League Club. I said, "So what?" (Chuckles.)

I did speak there the following year, after I'd lost. I met Ray Moley there. He said, "Do you know what Roosevelt was most afraid of in the campaign?" I said, "I didn't think he had anything to be afraid of." Moley said, "He was afraid his radio delivery had become so perfect that people would think it's artificial." I said, "Good. There might be some benefit in the antithesis of our radio deliveries." I was pretty rough. I guess I got too much antithesis. (Laughs.)

I was endorsed by every Democratic ex-Presidential nominee, except Cox. When I got to New York for the big meeting, my room was jammed. Al Smith was there. I'd never met him before. As he was about to leave, I said, "Governor, I just want you to know that I understand you walked the floor many hours before you decided to support me, a Republican—thinking of the men and women that have worked for your nomination for Governor, have driven through rain and snow to get out and vote for you, tacked up your cards on trees and fence poles all over the state. I realize only your belief that America is in great danger ever induced you to support me." Al's eyes filled with tears. He said, "I thought you'd understand." And he turned and walked out.

You felt he really felt that . . . our country was in great danger?

Yes.

Did you feel that?

No.

On the way back to the airport, a forty-eight-year-old cabbie responds. He's a World War II veteran.
"Does Alf Landon's name ring a bell?"
"Oh yeah. He ran for Governor. I was a kid. He even run for President."
"Who did he run against?"
"I don't remember that. I remember he ran just because he was a Kansas governor."
"Franklin D. Roosevelt."
"Oh yeah. That's right."
"What about Roosevelt?"
"He brought this country out of it. You bet. I remember it. I'm afraid we're gonna have another one. . . ."

A View of the Woods

Christopher Lasch

American historian; author of The New Radicalism in America *and* The Agony of the American Left.

THERE WAS SOME TALK about the possibility of revolution in the early Thirties, during the worst years of the Depression, especially in '34, when men like Huey Long and Coughlin and Townsend identified themselves with the groundswell of dissidence. There were various kinds of spontaneous action, by the farmers of Iowa, for instance. There was fear in some quarters that a kind of revolutionary crisis was developing. This fear—if not of revolution, of some kind of upheaval —created a sense of urgency in the White House and in Congress, too. It may have provided the impetus for the reforms that were pushed through in late '34 and '35.

In retrospect, I don't think there was a revolutionary situation in America in the early Thirties, certainly not the kind of situation that would have led to socialism if the New Deal reforms hadn't been carried out. There was a demand for vigorous, authoritative leadership. Industrialists clamored for central control, even nationalization of some industries. Harold Ickes, in his diary, talks of industrialists descending on Washington, demanding that the Government take over the oil industry. I think if a semblance of vigorous leadership hadn't been forthcoming on the part of Roosevelt, there might have built up the kind of pressure that swept Mussolini into power in Italy. It is conceivable, in other words, that the government might have been forced into extreme measures, but I doubt that these would have taken a left-wing direction.

The NRA was a clear example of how the New Deal worked. All points of view were entertained. All kinds of advisors were summoned up. People got together and at one point were simply put into a room. Roosevelt said: You have to come up with something, whatever it is. The result was a compromise between things labor wanted and things business wanted. It's a pretty fair indication of the one-sidedness of the kinds of compromises that were arranged in the early New Deal. Business got a suspension of anti-trust laws and labor got a kind of token recognition.

All during the Twenties, corporations and trade associations had campaigned for a new anti-trust law which would exempt price-fixing arrangements of this kind. They didn't manage to get it until '33, with a combination of the Depression and a new President who wasn't as dogmatically committed to laissez faire as Hoover had been.

If the Supreme Court hadn't declared the NRA unconstitutional, Congress would probably have voted down its renewal. Because there was too loud an outcry from small business and old-line progressives like Borah.[1]

The prime purpose of NRA was to raise prices and stimulate investments. This could not be done without cartel-like arrangements. Its other purpose was to keep industrial peace by throwing a bone to labor.

There's a whole school of historiography that talks of two New Deals. The first, represented by the NRA and the AAA, a kind of economy of scarcity, and the second, aimed at raising production and recognizing the rights of labor.

But there were no clear lines of policy followed. The whole New Deal, as far as I can see, was really chaotic. All kinds of experiments were being tried constantly. The immediate aim of all the reforms was

[1] Senator William E. Borah of Idaho.

simply to end the Depression by whatever means came to hand. It's a case study of what can happen if you don't have a clear policy.

Yet that's not quite the point I want to make about the New Deal. When people look back at the feverish activity of the Thirties, it resolves itself into a conflict between two different points of view within the business community, within a shared body of assumptions about American society.

That it would stay capitalist, there was no doubt. Other alternatives were excluded from the beginning, as a range of serious ideas that might be considered. But within these shared assumptions, two distinct points of view could be discerned. On the one hand were the so-called enlightened businessmen who reflected the view of large, progressively-minded corporations, who recognized the need for regulation, the need to admit labor as a partner in the industrial enterprise—as a junior, and distinctly inferior, partner.

They proposed to recognize labor's right to bargain and to enact welfare programs, if for no other reason than to head off more drastic proposals.

On the other hand, there were the people who clung to a laissez faire ideology, who resented all these measures, partly because—the NRA being a beautiful example—they were clearly detrimental to the interests of small, independent outfits. They were clearly in the interests of giant corporations, in spite of New Deal rhetoric.

What were the excluded alternatives . . . ?

I'm not sure they were real alternatives at the time. Socialism, for instance, was written off from the very beginning. This point of view was not offered by anyone in the New Deal as far as I know.

To talk in retrospect is to do so coldly and, in a sense, to falsify what people experienced in the Thirties. While one can say, in the relative comfort of the Sixties, that the New Deal measures were palliatives, they were more than that to the people living in the Thirties. They were, in many cases, matters of life and death.

Hardly any of the observers of the Thirties sensed a revolutionary mood among the people. Almost all describe the same sense of dismay and disorientation, futility and shame. Being unemployed seems to have been experienced more often as a humiliation than as evidence of class exploitation. A matter of personal fault. A crisis in capitalist society doesn't necessarily produce revolutionary changes or even a sense of alternatives, unless people have an awareness of some other kind of social order in which disasters of this kind wouldn't happen. Depressions have been regarded as natural disasters, much in the same way as earthquakes and floods, and not as social catastrophes, which they are.

People first have to think about alternatives in a very serious way. The fact that there was so little discussion of alternatives, prior to the Depression, partly explains why people reacted as they did.

It doesn't make any sense to criticize Roosevelt's Administration for not raising the question of Socialism. You couldn't very well expect him to. When you talk of alternatives like Socialism not being seriously raised in the Thirties, it's no criticism of Roosevelt, but of the American Left.

The difference between the pre-World War I Socialist Party in America and the Communists of the Thirties is instructive. Both regarded the union movement as their primary concern. But the Socialists organized workers in their capacity as Socialists. Through this activity they created an awareness of other kinds of social arrangements. The Communists went about organizing as though it was an end in itself.

The failure applies to the whole American Left. If the pre-World War I Socialist Party had been around in the Thirties, working the way it did in that earlier period, devoted to propagating Socialist consciousness—at the same time, being aware of the immediate interests of its constituency, the workingmen, mainly, and not taking the position that every reform was bad because it put off the day of reckoning—if such an organization had been around in the Thirties, things might have been very different.

What you had was a Left, very much like today's, vacillating between hopes of an immediate revolutionary crisis and a kind of reformism that made it impossible to discuss alternatives.

People who talk in terms of revolution today underestimate the capacity of American capitalism, its resiliency and inventiveness. Whatever else you may say about the New Deal, there was an inventiveness. Aside from its tremendous resources, American capitalism has the capacity to foreclose other alternatives.

Robert A. Baird

He is president of a large conglomerate in a city of the far Northwest. One of the most powerful men in the region. He engages in many charitable enterprises.

MY FATHER had been a salesman all his life, a very successful one. Even though he had only a fifth-grade education. In the great financial period of the middle Twenties, he sold bonds. The house he worked for went broke. The president of the company overextended himself and committed suicide.

My father went back to selling trucks, but there were no trucks to be sold. There were times when we didn't know whether we'd have anything to eat at night. I tell that to my children today, and they think the old man's flipped his lid.

My dad lost the house he was buying, and we rented for a while. He went through bankruptcy, which was a common thing at the time. He grubbed a great deal with all his remarkable energy, but he was plenty worried. Could he provide for his family? I have a great understanding of the Negro male today, because I saw it first-hand with my father.

But he had no doubts. He believed in the system he had grown up with. He was an inspirational man, like many good salesmen are. You have to believe in it. Because he had only a limited education, he believed all his sons and daughters should go to college. And we did.

When the Crash came, he talked about the fortunes that were lost that day. He felt there's nothing really wrong with our system. Just a few speculators. It was a popular theme in those days. He was wrong, of course. Radical changes were called for. And Roosevelt made them. But this was the kind of salesman's spirit in him.

Things kept going downhill in Detroit. The automobile plants laid off so many men. They began organizing the unions. They were organizing everything there for a while. I remember being in Stouffer's Restaurant and someone blowing a whistle and all the waitresses sitting down. People were reacting against the suffering. What could be a better way?

I can remember the trouble at Ford's, the clash at the Rouge plant.[2] A big demonstration. The chant of the crowd that was marching: We wanted bread, you gave us bullets. It's funny how a little thing like that sticks in your mind.

When I got out of college, I went to work at the Packard plant. I hoped eventually to get into the industrial relations end of the business. After working in the plant for six months, I could understand the men and their grievances. I was working on the assembly line. I can still remember my badge number. FSG348. This was '37.

I learned a great deal about employee relations. I learned how not to treat men. They did a lot of things at the Packard plant in those days that earned them the animosity of their workers.

They used to take a train into the plant. They'd often do it when the workers were coming to work. So you were held up fifteen or twenty minutes by the train. If you were a minute late, they docked you thirty minutes' pay. That was the way it was. There were no ifs, ands or buts about it. I can remember talking to my foreman about it. It made no difference.

We were making new models of the 1938 car for the New York Auto Show. On the assembly line, you work at a certain pace. If they change the speed, and don't tell you about it, pretty soon you're working in the next man's space trying to keep up. This chassis has gotten ahead of you. This goes all down the line. Finally, you have to shut it down. Nobody wanted to shut the line down, because you got hell if you did.

I can remember how they speeded up the line and we got in everybody's way, and finally they hollered: Shut the line down. Steve, the big foreman, weighed about three hundred pounds, came swearing all the way down the line: What was the trouble? The union was new then. The steward said: We're not working.

An hour later, out comes the plant manager with the foreman. The steward explained. The manager said he was sorry. He apologized to the men. He said, "We have a train waiting to take the cars to the New York Auto Show. Next year's business depends on us getting a good start in the show." The steward said, "Why didn't you tell us? We'll knock

2 In 1937, there had been clashes at the River Rouge plant between the service men at Ford, who had been holding out against the CIO, and UAW organizers. The La Follette Committee held hearings, subsequently, and confirmed the union's charges of company violence.

these cars out." They got those guys going at twice the speed. Nobody complained.

It illustrated to me something I never forgot. If you tell people what you want them to do and why you want them to do it, they're very co-operative. I've always said around here: We could sell any reasonable program to our union if we looked at it from their standpoint, and made a reasonable explanation. But if you try to push them around, they aren't going to stand for it.

I got laid off in December of 1937. It was the down draft of the Roosevelt recession. In Detroit, when the automobile industry goes down, everything goes down.

I wrote a series of letters to companies that had interviewed me when I was in college. A large mail-order house said if I wanted to come to their city, they had a job for me. So I came over on the bus. It cost $6 to ride from Detroit to this city. I got the job.

I had about an hour and a half to kill before going back to the bus station. So I stopped in to see a fellow at this company. He had also interviewed me while I was at school. I thought it would be nice to know him. He talked me into working here. So I called up the other company and said no.

Tom, His Younger Son

At twenty-one, he is now somewhere in Canada, in defiance of his 1-A draft status.

MY FATHER talks about the Depression didactically. He tries to draw little lessons from it. He has an anecdote every time the subject comes up. It's sort of a heroic past for him. It makes him an extremist: you have one analysis you can fit everything into. He has an extremist definition of what the goal of a nation should be . . . what a guy should be preparing for at school. Since most people feel this way, it's not called extreme. But it is.

All the clichés that you hear. Americans are always saying, "I'm not enjoying what I'm doing now, but I'm making money. I'm preparing to do a thing which will be more important in the future." In the meantime, make a buck. That's pretty extreme. They all agree and reinforce one another, the people who lived through the Depression.

They won't allow any argument about other ways, which *they* call extreme. In any major corporation, you can't depend on getting the same profit every year. You'll fold. The only way a corporation, which sells stock, can keep existing, is to increase profit. This seems to me unlikely as a policy that will last a hundred years. Yet, the welfare capitalism they built can't be denied. . . .

My father is slick. He tries to say something we will dig. The other night, we played Billie Holiday, and he started naming some of her other songs. You see, he's really saying, "I am one of you." He uses the same sort of mechanism at work.

He's become a king in welfare capitalism, because he knows how to work with labor. He's always said that unions are the greatest. I'm sure he was a real slick worker, when they were changing their roles from real unions to company-minded unions. Which they are today. He learned all this in the Depression. It was his war.

Peter, His Older Son

He is twenty-four. A college graduate, he works full time as an SDS (Students for a Democratic Society) organizer. He travels along the West Coast, recruiting members.

As a PERSON, my father is a good person. He means well. His motives are all of the highest. He feels sincerely that the way you do good for the people of the world is to expand welfare capitalism.[3] The important thing to understand about a man like my father is that in a society like this, whether a person is a nice guy or a bad guy, is irrelevant. People play certain roles. It's not so much their attitudes as the roles they play.

[3] "It's a funny country. If you call it by its right name, you're branded a radical. In most countries, people name their economic system. We should talk about our economic system as capitalism, as others call theirs socialism. Then you either defend it or attack it. We use the parliamentary name, democracy, rather than the economic name, capitalism. That's a product of our public relations drive. . . ."

Although he's the kind of guy you wouldn't mind having dinner with, he plays a bad role in this society.

I'm sure the Depression was important in molding my father's life. A lot of older people look at young people today and say, "Those punks, they never felt the Depression. Look at the things they're doing." I don't think this attitude makes any sense. My brother and I grew up with a certain kind of history, and he grew up with another. I don't condemn him for his experience. I condemn him for the role he plays today.

In the Depression, people were up against the wall. Fear. So when you're up against the wall like that, any kind of solution is grasped at. In the case of those people, it was military spending, war.[4]

We didn't see the Depression. We have grown up in a time when going to school is like going to a factory. It's not totally parallel: we are materially privileged. But the conditions students face are increasingly like Depression factory conditions. We're not treated as intellectually curious beings. We're being manufactured. We're being channeled for certain roles. We're lined up, sorted into jobs . . . as well as being kept off the job market as long as possible. So growing up becomes a later and later thing.

Because of their education and the nature of communications, many young people identify with the other people of the world. We had grown up in a post-Depression, affluent society feeling this is the way it is everywhere. Then came the rude awakening: two-thirds of the world is starving and exploited by the same corporations that run our universities. My father is a member of the board of a leading university out here. He's also a board member of a bank that does lots of business with South Africa.

He's a philanthropist in many ways. That, too, is part of the approach of the individual who has made it. This is part of the whole psyche of competition: I made it—now I can help others. What competition really

[4] "It may be that many contradictions in our society have been resolved by New Deal legislation and other stop-gap measures, as well as union bureaucracy. This may stop much militancy. But this country can no longer be defined by geographical borders as it was before the Depression and World War II. You've seen the Chase Manhattan ad: Our Man in Rio. Our man everywhere. It's a world-wide system, and it's breaking up. In places like Vietnam—and Guatamala and Mozambique. . . . Whether a revolution takes place here or not, it will affect us. Capitalism ain't what it used to be. . . ."

means is: there is a stacked deck. Some people will fight against others for a few crumbs, while the guy with the stacked deck makes most of it.

My father does want to understand us. He wants to think we're following the values he taught us. But when what we do becomes more than a childish pastime, he feels threatened. He can't really face it, because what we're saying is: We want to build a society in which roles like his are no longer possible.

(Softly.) He used to tell me that of all his kids—there are five of us—I could have been the one to make it. Perhaps even his successor as president of the conglomerate. He always felt I had the brains and drive to be a ruler. I think he's disappointed in me. I don't think he's quite given up hope that I'm going through a stage and will come out of it. . . .

Much of his ambition, drive and energy comes from the Depression, I'm sure. But I also have a lot of energy and I did not have that experience.

He always downgraded campus radicals in the Thirties. He called them a minority—psychologically disturbed young people. . . .

POSTSCRIPT: *Peter has since become one of the leading spokesmen of the Weatherman faction of SDS.*

Campus Life

Pauline Kael

WHEN I attended Berkeley in 1936, so many of the kids had actually lost their fathers. They had wandered off in disgrace because they couldn't support their families. Other fathers had killed themselves, so the family could have the insurance. Families had totally broken down. Each father took it as his personal failure. These middle-class men apparently had no social sense of what was going on, so they killed themselves.

It was still the Depression. There were kids who didn't have a place to sleep, huddling under bridges on the campus. I had a scholarship, but there were times when I didn't have food. The meals were often three candy bars. We lived communally and I remember feeding other kids by cooking up more spaghetti than I can ever consider again.

There was an embarrassment at college where a lot of the kids were well-heeled. I still have a resentment against the fraternity boys and the sorority girls with their cashmere sweaters and the pearls. Even now, when I lecture at colleges, I have this feeling about those terribly overdressed kids. It wasn't a hatred because I wanted these things, but because they didn't understand what was going on.

I was a reader for seven courses a semester, and I made $50 a month. I think I was the only girl on the labor board at Berkeley. We were trying to get the minimum wage on the campus raised to forty cents an hour.

These well-dressed kids couldn't understand our interest. There was a real division between the poor who were trying to improve things on the campus and the rich kids who didn't give a damn.

Berkeley was a cauldron in the late Thirties. You no sooner enrolled than you got an invitation from the Trotskyites and the Stalinists. Both were wooing you. I enrolled at sixteen, so it was a little overpowering at the time. I remember joining the Teachers Assistants Union. We had our own version of Mario Savio. He's now a lawyer specializing in bankruptcies. We did elect a liberal as president of the student body. It was a miracle in those days.

The fraternity boys often acted as strikebreakers in San Francisco—the athletes and the engineering students. And the poor boys were trying to get their forty cents an hour. The college administration could always count on the frat boys to put down any student movement.

It's different today, the fraternities and sororities having so much less power. . . .

Robert Gard

Professor of Drama, University of Wisconsin.

I SET OUT for the University of Kansas on a September morning with $30 that I'd borrowed from my local bank. I had one suit and one necktie and one pair of shoes. My mother had spent several days putting together a couple of wooden cases of canned fruits and vegetables. My father, a country lawyer, had taken as a legal fee a 1915 Buick touring car. It was not in particularly good condition, but it was good enough to get me there. It fell to pieces and it never got back home anymore.

I had no idea how long the $30 would last, but it sure would have to go a long way because I had nothing else. The semester fee was $22, so that left me $8 to go. Fortunately, I got a job driving a car for the dean of the law school. That's how I got through the first year.

What a pleasure it was to get a pound of hamburger, which you could buy for about five cents, take it up to the Union Pacific Railroad tracks and have a cookout. And some excellent conversation. And maybe swim in the Kaw River.

One friend of mine came to college equipped. He had an old Model T Ford Sedan, about a 1919 model. He had this thing fitted up as a house. He lived in it all year long. He cooked and slept and studied inside that Model T Ford Sedan. How he managed I will never know. I once went there for dinner. He cooked a pretty good one on a little stove he had in this thing. He was a brilliant student. I don't know where he is now, but I shouldn't be surprised if he's the head of some big corporation. (Laughs.) Survival. . . .

The weak ones, I don't suppose, really survived. There were many breakdowns. From malnutrition very likely. I know there were students actually starving.

Some of them engaged in strange occupations. There was a biological company that would pay a penny apiece for cockroaches. They needed these in research, I guess. Some students went cockroach hunting every night. They'd box 'em and sell them to this firm.

I remember the feverish intellectual discussion we had. There were many new movements. On the literary scene, there was something called the Proletarian Novel. There was the Federal Theater and the Living Newspaper. For the first time, we began to get socially conscious. We began to wonder about ourselves and our society.

We were mostly farm boys and, to some extent, these ideas were alien to us. We had never really thought about them before. But it was a period of necessity. It brought us face to face with these economic problems and the rest. . . . All in all, a painful time, but a glorious time.

Chance Stoner

A financial consultant on Wall Street.

"I actually in my own life did not see any difference between the Twenties and the Thirties. I was living in a small Virginia town, and it was poverty-stricken. You had five thousand rural bank failures in the Twenties. . . . My father was a typewriter salesman who did the best he could. . . ."

THEY GAVE me a $100 scholarship to the University of Virginia. That's in 1931, which was damn good. And my mother gave me $100. I had a pair of khaki pants, a pair of sneakers and a khaki shirt. That was it.

The first year on the campus, I organized a Marxist study class. The students fell into two groups. About nine hundred of them had automobiles. About nine hundred had jobs or scholarships. The other nine hundred fell in between. We had real class warfare. The automobile boys and the fraternities—we had thirty-three little Greek palaces on fraternity row—they had charge of the student government. So I organized the other nine hundred, and we took the student government away from them and rewrote the constitution.

I spent half my time on radical activities. I was trying to organize a union in Charlottesville—and bringing Negroes to speak on the campus. We had the first black man to speak there since Reconstruction. He was an old Socialist.

This threw the dean into a fit. He still believed in slavery. He forbade the use of any university building. I was then writing a weekly column for the campus paper. So I attacked the dean: "What manner of small-minded men have inherited Mr. Jefferson's university?" (Laughs.) It was reprinted all over the Eastern seaboard. On the front pages of newspapers, including *The New York Times*. (Laughs.)

The president sent for me. He had a stack five inches high of clippings. He said, "Now look what you've done." (Laughs.) I said, "It's not my fault. The man's been properly invited, he's qualified and he's going to speak at the Episcopal Church chapel." The dean was one of the deacons of the church. So we had quite a time of it.

There were writings on the sidewalk of the university: "Down With Imperialistic War. Scholarships Not Battleships." Again I was invited to the president's office. He asked me if I couldn't stop people from writing all over the sidewalk. I said to him: We're perfectly willing to abide by a general rule. If the secret societies and fraternities aren't permitted to write on the steps or sidewalks, we won't either. So he walked me to the window and outside in great purple letters was the slogan: "Down With Imperialist War." He said, "Couldn't you *please* at least get the spelling right?" (Laughs.)

In 1935, we had the first official shutdown of all university classes for a peace demonstration. Guess who the featured speaker was? J. B. Matthews. He later ran the Un-American Activities Committee, as staff director for Martin Dies. He was the man who invented the complete file and cross-reference system, and the theory of associations and fronts and all the rest of it. A very remarkable fella. He started out as a Protestant minister, came to socialism and wound up with Martin Dies. Joe McCarthy was impossible without J. B. Matthews. And we shut down the university for him. . . . Oh, well. . . .

I was a troublemaker then. (Laughs.) I wish I still were.

BOOK FOUR

Merely Passing Through

Edward Burgess

Like most guests in this once-elegant hotel, he's a pensioner. His room is overwhelmed by old-time appliances. There are light-housekeeping facilities. A table radio . . . "I used to build 'em, battery set. I still got things to do. I got a set of tools there that would knock your eyes out, worth about $200. All kinds of tools. . . ."

He is eighty-two. During the Thirties, he had a steady job as a printer at Donnelly's.

I SPOTTED this Studebaker in the window at Twenty-sixth and Michigan. So I says to May, let's buy that car. So we just stopped in, give 'em $600, all we had with us, and bought the car. The sales manager—his name was Compton—I told him that's the one we want. So we just had a couple of fellas push it out and put air in the tires and a couple of gallons of gas and away we went, down South Parkway. So we went all around, down Field Museum. . . . It was a six-wheel job.

The foreman down at Donnelly, he said, "You sure did your bit for the Depression." He bought one, he bought a new Ford. I said, "If everybody would spend ten cents more a day than they ordinarily spent, we'd sneak out of this in a hurry." (Laughs.) I said that. My theory,

I felt that way. Because we were makin' money. We never got laid off or nothin'. There was no cause to feel otherwise.

When did you become aware of the Depression?

I really didn't pay no attention to it. The way I looked at it, without advertising there'll be no business, of any kind. And you can't have no advertising without printing it. See what I mean?

Did your standard of living change during the Depression?

It didn't change mine. I never did spend money foolishly. Never drank very much, just a little bit here and there. But I was kind of liberal, too, in a way. Always tried to help the other fella. Never hurt me any.

I co-signed a couple of times for loan companies and things like that. Fact I did that for a fella in Fort Wayne, and he skipped out. And I had to pay it, $55. When my dad died in 1919, he was on a train going to Ohio. I wanted him buried with my mother. I always tried to help out the other guy.

You don't remember bread lines?

No, we didn't have that here in Chicago, that I know of.

Billy Green

Among his enterprises in the Thirties: bookmaker.

I DIDN'T get hurt too bad. I didn't own any stocks. I didn't believe in the market then, I'm not too crazy about it now, if you know what I mean. (Laughs.) The stock market is like shooting craps or playing horses. You hear about the ones that win, but you never hear about the ones that lose. There's more losers than winners, I promise you.

Any time you're guessing, you got to lose. The only way to win is to have the other fella guess. That's my theory: never be a guesser. Never take a position in life. You give the other guy the first guess, and you always come out best. You can't make a mistake that way. You always wind up the winner. I've proved that on many, many occasions. Many occasions.

All the people around me in them days—successful businessmen—the stock market just knocked 'em right out of the box. Oh, do I remember the panic. Bedlam.

I never worked, always went in business for myself. I was lucky. You got to have that Guy Upstairs with you. You got to have his arms around you. I made a buck.

From an orange juice stand to a hotel, I branched out into a bowling alley. Made some investment in real estate. And here I am, with nothing to do. Call it semi-retired. But I'm always interested in a new proposition. Action.

I got no reason to be discontented. It's just lookin' fer somethin' that I don't think I'm gonna find. You just can't call your shots any more. Everything is regimented today. Understand? Maybe it's from the Depression days, who knows? So what I'm lookin' fer don't exist, strange as it may seem. You follow me? But I have no complaints. I'd be the last guy in the world to complain. Because, like I say, life's been good to me. God has been good to me. You gotta have Him.

Scoop Lankford

He is seventy-five years old. He spent thirty-one years of a life term in a state penitentiary: 1919 to 1950.

THE DEPRESSION hit that prison pretty bad. We were practically not eating. We really scratched. One time they wanted us to eat some kind of fish. They called it halibut. This had black skin all around—didn't have that little white side, you know. This was baby shark they tried to feed us. It smelled so the entire building was stunk up. (Laughs.) So they all threw it on the floor and refused to eat it.

If you know what it was like for you, just multiply. The quality of food was low to begin with. We would get some kind of meat once a day. It was kind of scraps you wouldn't even keep in a butcher shop. Just tiny pieces all boiled up in a pot. It was rich enough so one man would get about a fourth of what his system needed. More people died during that Depression there than they ever did at any other time.

It wasn't starvation. They called it malnutrition. It woulda been starvation if they died quick from malnutrition. They just barely gave you enough to keep you alive. You lost weight. They made you lose weight until the doctor got after them and said they have to get at least one meal a day. A thousand men woulda died if it hadn't been for that doctor.

Did the guards ever talk to you about the Depression?

They were as bad for it as we were. A lot of them was eating in there on the sly. I've even actually given to them a piece of corn bread to take out. Nearly all of 'em were family men.

You wouldn't know there was a Depression as far as the talk was concerned. There was nothing to say. We at least had a place to eat and sleep. The prison itself was a protection from the outside. The people outside, they had to hustle. We were just down almost as low as we could get. We had to dig a hole in low to get any lower than we was. (Laughs.)

We fared lots better when the war was on. Food and more food, during the war. Yeah, the fellas talked about it. They said, "Long live the war!" That was our attitude: Long live the war. 'Cause we were eating pretty good.

Three o'Clock in the Morning

Wilbur Kane

He is a thirty-nine-year-old journalist. It is at his home, out East. The time: about three o'clock in the morning. We have been drinking rather heavily. . . .

I WAS seven, eight. My mother was holding up the New York *World Telegram*. It had to be like 1937. With this huge headline across the front: Shanghai Falls. I remember the bitterness of my mother. I remember her bitterness about Ethiopia, too. Bubble gum cards about the Ethiopian War, I remember them. You had Ethiopians in ghost suits, sheets. And the Italian soldiers, they were always stabbing these guys in their ghost sheets.

I stayed with my grandmother that summer. She lived in a small town in Pennsylvania. It was suburban Allentown, if you could believe it. She was one of the two people in town who subscribed to *The New York Times*. She was considered a Socialist—which she was.

We had relatives, Peter and Millie Gore. Millie was a wonderful fat lady, and she'd sit on the front porch and she gave everybody food and beer all summer long. Uncle Peter would talk about World War I. He told this story about the black guy in his company, and he ran away from the Germans. He said he shot the nigger, killed the nigger. I was just absolutely petrified. I mean, I was really smashed! It was the first time I had ever heard that word. But I knew what it meant. And I never liked Uncle Peter again.

And this family, the Stahls, they moved next door. And they were really Nazis. They had this little girl who I hated. Who was a little female Nazi. And the second Joe Louis fight. . . .

He beat Schmeling . . .

Yeah, but they didn't know that, see? They invited us over to listen to it, my grandmother and me. On the radio. And they had all this stuff, they'd gone over to Bethlehem to get it, the knackwurst and bratwurst and all the other kind of wursts you can get. And they had it on big plates. And we're all gonna sit around and we're gonna eat liverwurst and watch this kraut beat the shit out of this black man, see? And they were gonna rejoice. All I can remember was praying to God that *somehow* Joe Louis would win. *Somehow* he would win. (Laughs.)

I can remember the faces, how they looked when Joe Louis came out and just *creamed* him. I mean, like in forty-five seconds.[1] They couldn't get the knackwurst in their fat faces, that's how they looked. They couldn't even swallow beer. I was screaming and jumping up and down and my grandmother was whispering to me: "I know how you feel, but you shouldn't show it. You've got to be polite." (Laughs.)

She dragged me out that night, saying, "You're rude, you're rude." She pulled me out of that place, because I was jumping up and down screaming, "It serves you Nazis right, it serves you Nazis right." She said, "You're right, but you can't talk that way." And I said, "If I'm right, why can't I talk that way?"

Oh God, I remember a couple of other things. I remember Franklin Delano Roosevelt. I remember his voice. It was a great voice. And I loved it. But some of us have learned that he was full of shit, too. That he was a fucking liar, that he was no good.

Why do you say that . . . ?

Because he just didn't deliver. Let's face it, let's talk about Munich. Let's talk about all those things that were just words when I was a little kid. And he and Churchill and Daladier and Laval, they built up the Nazis so they could kill the Communists. And that's what they really

[1] Joe Louis regained the heavyweight championship of the world from Max Schmeling, by virtue of a first round knockout. Date: June 22, 1938. Previously, Schmeling had K.O.'d Louis in the twelfth round. Date: June 19, 1936.

did at Munich, that's what Munich really meant. And all this appeasement myth is just a myth.

It's just that they thought they could use the Nazis against the Communists, and that's what it really got down to. And they killed forty million people to find out how fucking wrong they were. And they have plunged us all, my *whole* life, my *whole* generation into an *endless, terrible* misery. And they were all stinking, fucking, no good shits.

They put us into that God damn war which they could have stopped in the 1930s. They could have walked in, they could have killed that Hitler. But they preferred that Hitler, they really did, they preferred him to the Communists. And no matter how rotten the Communists were, at least, in some vague, triply removed sense they represented the principle of life. No matter how distorted. As opposed to these other bastards, who represented nothing ever *but* death. And promised nothing but death. And my whole life has been cursed by these men.

I'm slightly drunk, but I don't retract anything I've said, because I would say it when I'm sober. . . . I can't make any distinction between the war and the Depression and the Thirties. It all kind of merged, and you were growing up and all that. . . .

A Cable

Myrna Loy

Film and stage actress.

MUNICH, that was '38, wasn't it? I was at Malibu, down at the beach. I heard Jan Masaryk on the radio, speaking from London. It was about four o'clock in the morning there. I was so moved by this man. I was upset by the sell-out of Czechoslovakia. On an impulse, I sent him a cable. It was the first one he had received from anyone in the world.

Later on, he came to this country and he looked me up. It had meant so much to him. He said it cheered him in the darkest hour of his life. That was Munich. He said one of the reasons he broadcast to his country was that if he could reach me out on the Malibu coast six thousand miles away. . . .

My wire was published in the London *Times*. Then it got to Prague. And then to Berlin. As a result, my pictures were banned in Germany. I didn't know that until 1939. In Amsterdam, I met a man who had fled Germany. He said I was on Mr. Hitler's blacklist. (Laughs.) "You're on the second page," he said. (Laughs.) I said, "My God, I didn't know that."

Some months later, one of the men at MGM[1] came to me very, very

---

[1] Metro-Goldwyn-Mayer.

upset. "I have something here that I am ashamed to give you." It was a call-down about having mixed my politics with my work: How about watching out for this? He said, "What do you want me to do with this?" I said, "Tear it up."

When the Depression came, I had a very good job in Hollywood. It was just at the beginning of my career. It was really distant to me. Everybody around me was working. You get up at five-thirty. You're in the studio at seven. You're made up and ready at nine and work until six. They now call those The Golden Years of the Movies. Perhaps they were. People needed films, needed some diversion. I wasn't deeply involved in politics myself. I kind of dialed out. I didn't come to life until Roosevelt. . . .

I was told I was F.D.R.'s favorite actress. I had never met him. Later on, when I was in Washington, at a cocktail party, Henry Morgenthau[2] said, "The old man thinks we're keeping you away from him. You've never come to see him. Tomorrow morning, put your hat on the dresser, and I'll call for you." The next morning he called to tell me the President had gone to Canada.

Later on, they sent for me to attend his birthday celebration. I bought myself a John Frederick hat. I came tootling into the White House with a big bunch of violets and this black hat. I looked down the hall and I saw Mrs. Roosevelt. I walked up to her. She said, "Oh, my dear, my husband is going to be so distressed." He had gone to Teheran. (Laughs.) Here was this glamor girl all done up. I fell in love with her then and there. I was very lucky to have spent quite a lot of time with her. I miss her very much. There aren't too many people you miss that way. . . .

[2] Secretary of Treasury.

BOOK FIVE

The Fine and Lively Arts

Hiram (Chub) Sherman

At sixty, he is an established Broadway actor. Much of his time, whether "at liberty" or while engaged in a play, has been spent on the Council of Actors Equity.

I LEARNED in the Twenties that you could exist on very little. To paraphrase Tennessee Williams, you can depend on the kindness of strangers. When the Depression actually began in '29, I was just on my way to New York. It wasn't any demarcation point in my life. There were no stocks to be lost, 'cause we didn't have them.

There were no jobs in New York. I worked in summer stock and touring companies. In 1931, I played a season in Newport, Rhode Island. It was as if the Depression had never existed at all. All the functions were duly reported as going on at the Viking Hotel and the Casino Theater. Sitting in the middle of the Casino, covered with flowers, were Mrs. Vanderbilt and Mrs. Moses Taylor, arriving in their limousines. I hadn't seen men in panama hats, blue blazers and white shoes since. There was discreet drinking in china cups during Prohibition in all the best hotels in Newport. One could sit there nursing a teacup filled with bootleg gin or whiskey. But it was all elegant. In teacups, china cups.

413

It was rock-bottom living in New York then, it really was. Cars were left on the streets. There were no signs about restricted parking. (Laughs.) If somebody had a jalopy—a few friends you know would have some old car—it would sit there for months on end neither molested nor disturbed. It would just fall apart from old age.[1]

You didn't count your possessions in terms of money in the bank. You counted on the fact that you had a row of empty milk bottles. Because those were cash, they could be turned in for a nickel deposit, and that would get you on the subway. If you took any stock in yourself, you looked to see how many milk bottles you had, because that counted. Two bottles: one could get you uptown; one could get you back.

I remember being employed once to stand in front of St. Patrick's Cathedral on Fifth Avenue, Easter morning. With a clicker in each hand. A fashion woman had engaged me to note the acceptance of patent leather purses and white hats. Each white hat I saw, I clicked my right hand. And each patent leather purse I saw, I clicked my left hand. Then I had to go home and tote up what the clickers said. White hats were in that spring, patent leather purses were out.

I remember also what you'd pick up odd dollars doing. There were sightseeing buses—see Chinatown, see the Bowery, see New York. They were lined up right on Times Square. If you've ever noted a sightseeing bus, there'll be a couple of people sitting on the bus. And they'd say: It's leaving right away, guided tour, just leaving for the Bowery and Chinatown. Well, the people inside were usually shills. They're engaged for a quarter or fifty cents to sit there and look eager. I shilled in Times Square sightseeing buses. (Laughs.) As people came on, you got off: "Excuse me for a moment." And then you got into another bus. It's a sitting job.

The summer always provided work for actors. I don't know why this happened, I can't explain it. But there was a great proliferation of turning barns into summer theaters. During the Depression, that's when it came.

In 1936, I joined the Federal Theater.[2] I was assigned to Project

---

[1] Ben, a nineteen-year-old college student: "My grandfather owned a car, but it never left the garage. He had it jacked up for two years. Gasoline was just too expensive. He told how he polished the car once a week. How he took good care of it, but he never drove it. Couldn't afford it."

[2] One of the Federal Arts Projects (WPA) under the auspices of the New Deal. "It was an idealistic concept to encompass the whole country—to make the unem-

891. The directors and producers were Orson Welles and John Houseman. The theater we had taken over was the Maxine Elliott. A lot of theaters went dark during the Depression, and the theater owners were happy to lease them to the Government.

One of the marvelous things about the Federal Theater, it wasn't bound by commercial standards. It could take on poetic drama and do it.[3] And experimental theater. The Living Newspaper made for terribly exciting productions.[4] Yet it was theater by bureaucracy. Everything had to go to a higher authority. There were endless chits to be approved. There were comic and wasteful moments all over the country. But it was forward-thinking in so many ways. It anticipated some of today's problems. The Unit I was in was integrated. We did Marlowe's *Doctor Faustus*. Mephistopheles was played by a Negro, Jack Carter. Orson Welles played Faustus.

Our next production was *Cradle Will Rock,* words and music by Marc Blitzstein. And we rehearsed those eight hours a day. We worked every moment, and sometimes we worked overtime because we loved it.

Cradle Will Rock was for its day a revolutionary piece. It was an attack on big business and the corruption involved. It was done à la Brecht. We had it fully rehearsed.

On opening night, when the audience was assembling in the street, we found the doors of the Maxine Elliott closed. They wouldn't admit the audience because of an edict from Washington that this was revolutionary fare. And we would have no performance. Somebody had sent down the word.

Well, when you have an alert company, who are all keyed up at this moment, and a master of publicity such as Orson Welles, this is just grist for their mills. (Laughs.)

It's a nice evening in May—late May or April. Balmy evening. An audience not able to get into a theater, but not leaving because the directors of 891, Orson Welles and John Houseman, were haranguing

---

ployed actor an entertainment worker. To do his share." It employed not only legitimate theater actors and dancers, but vaudeville and circus performers as well.

[3] T. S. Eliot's *Murder in the Cathedral* was the most celebrated case in point.

[4] Documentary theater, based upon circumstances and controversial issues of the time: *Triple-A Plowed Under* concerned the New Deal's farm program; *Power* dealt with rural electrification; *Third of a Nation* (a phrase taken from the F.D.R. Inaugural Address of 1937) commented on the housing crisis.

them in the street: "Don't leave!" They expected to get a reversal of the edict. We're told not to make up. We're told not to go home. We don't know what's going to happen.

No reversal came from Washington. So Orson and John Houseman got their friends on the phone: What theater could we do this in? Somebody suggested the Jolson Theater. An announcement was made to all these people, without benefit of microphone: if you go to the Jolson Theater you will see the show. And we marched. Walking with our audience around into Broadway and then up Seventh Avenue to Fifty-ninth Street, we acquired an even larger audience.

Walking down the middle of the street?

Oh yes. Walking with no police permit. (Laughs.) Just overflowing the sidewalks. Obviously something was afoot. The Jolson Theater hadn't had a booking for months and was very dusty. But it was open.

Word came from Actors Equity that proper bonding arrangements had not been made. The actors would not be allowed to appear on the stage. Because now you're not under the aegis of the Federal Theater. You're under some obscure private management. You don't know what, because you haven't found out yet.

This didn't daunt us. We had a colloquy right in the alley. We decided, well, if we can't go on the stage, we could wheel out the piano and Marc Blitzstein could do what he had done in so many auditions: describe the setting and such, and we'll all sit in the audience. Equity didn't say we couldn't sit in the audience. When our cues come, we will rise and give them. So, that we did.

The theater filled. I don't know how the extra people, who didn't hold tickets for the opening, how they got in. I've often wondered. Did the box office open or did they just say: come in for the laughs? But it was packed with people.[5] The stage was bare, the curtain was up, and you suddenly missed all your fellow actors. You couldn't find them. We were in different parts of the house.

Eventually the house lights lowered a little. Marc Blitzstein came out and laid the setting and played a few bars and then said: "Enter the whore." I didn't know where Olive Stanton, who played the whore, was. Suddenly you could hear Olive's very clear high voice, from over left. A spotlight suddenly found her and she stood up. She was in the lower lefthand box. One by one, as we were called up, we joined in. We

[5] The Jolson Theater was larger than the Maxine Elliott.

turned around if we were down front, and faced the audience. People were scattered all over. It was a most exciting evening. The audience reaction was tremendous.

One of those summers, '38, '39, I don't know which—Marc Blitzstein corraled most of us who'd been in the original company and asked us if we'd give up Sunday to go give a performance of *Cradle Will Rock* in Bethlehem, Pennsylvania. I thought this was marvelous. Because we're now going to take *Cradle Will Rock* to the workers, to the people for whom he wrote this piece. We were all corraled into a bus and off we went on a nice, hot summer's day. I thought, well, pretty soon the mills will close down and the steel workers will pour into this amusement park, as twilight comes, and they'll hear this marvelous saga. No one showed up.

A few men drifted in, and the first thing you find out is that many of them do not understand or speak English. And this was written in, supposedly, common American speech. Here we were preparing an opera for the proletariat, and the proletariat neither wants nor understands it. It's a rather shocking occurrence. But you don't give up.

You're in a hot, sort of open auditorium. And Will Geer,[6] never to be discouraged, scrounging around for an audience. He found a picnic of church ladies over an adjoining hill. They were spreading out their picnic baskets and he asked: "Would you like to be entertained with an opera?" They allowed as how they would, and they packed their gingham table cloths, all the sandwiches and brought them over to this little amusement place. And sat down.

Marc Blitzstein came out and announced the name of this piece was *Cradle Will Rock,* the setting was Steeltown, U.S.A., and it begins on a street corner at night, and enter the whore. When he said those words, our audience got up and packed up their picnic baskets and left us. We never did do *Cradle Will Rock* in Bethlehem, Pennsylvania.

We were to report back to the Federal Theater, to Project 891. We had no assignment at the moment. But all of us in the stock company had to spend eight hours a day in the Maxine Elliott Theater. We could bring no food in the theater. We had a lunch hour. We could read, but we could not write. We couldn't deface anything, we couldn't rehearse. We sat. Forced sitting, with nothing to keep you interested, is one of the most grueling punishments I've ever been through. I've never been in jail as yet, I expect to. But prisoners are paid for work.

[6] Veteran character actor.

417

I don't know if I'm partisan to the underdog or whether I'm the underdog. My political convictions were my own. But this is not the case in life. You're stigmatized, anything you do. I was active in my union, I was playing benefits—there was Spanish relief, you know, the Spanish Civil War. My life was very full. I didn't sleep very much. I got excited about everything. They were tearing down the Sixth Avenue Elevated and selling the scrap iron to Japan. I was going to protest. . . . (Laughs.) There was a cause every second.

I was horrified one morning to find that a Congressman from Kansas had stated in the Congressional Record that I was one of the seven Communists that dominated the Council of the Actors Equity Association. I thought that was unusual. So I sent the Congressman a wire and I said: I read this news story, and if you'll repeat your accusations outside the halls of Congress, I would sue you for loss of employment. I never heard from him again.

I found the Equity Council in an uproar and I was asked to resign. I said I have no intention of resigning because a man has made such a statement, and he's never answered my telegram. "If you don't like me, don't elect me next time to the Council. But I'm certainly not walking out." Several councillors walked out in protest to me being there. I was so politically naïve, I wouldn't know then how to go about joining the Communist Party. I wouldn't know just how to do it. (Laughs.)

There comes a time when you cannot think seriously about Left and Right. And people would come up to you, your dearest friends, and say: "Listen, tell me, really, are you?" I'd say: "Am I what?" They'd say: (whispering) "Are you a Communist?" Now if you say no, you're immediately accused of lying. I don't know why this is. But as soon as you say no, they look at you as if—oh boy! If you say yes, you're also lying, because no Communist says yes when asked. I found myself in this terrible bind, being assailed at every corner by people asking me.

One old Equity member—I was really at the breaking point—during a recess in the Equity Council meeting said: "Look, I really want to know." And I just couldn't care less at this time. He said: "I want to talk to you." And I said: "Yes?" And he said: "Tell me, are you a Communist?" I thought: I can't say yes and I can't say no. I said quickly, I said: "We're not allowed to tell." And there wasn't a laugh on his part at all. It was just as if I'd sealed my death warrant, being facetious. It haunted me for years, that remark. (Laughs.)

I remember going into a theatrical office looking for work. You'd go up and say: who's casting today? And the sign hanging over the railing: NO COMMUNIST NEED APPLY. It was hanging there. Indignantly, I ripped off the sign and went to the girl at the desk and said: "Why don't you reduce this to the basic fact that no actors need apply? You're not doing anything anyway." Making the little gesture. It probably got hung back on the door again.

So then the war broke out and the Depression, as we know it, ended. . . .

It didn't for me.

I enlisted in the navy—I was a bit too old for the immediate draft call. After being vilified in the halls of Equity I was told I was a marvelous human being and that my seat on the Council would always be waiting for me. Five years later, I got out and went back and said: "Where's my seat?" And they said: "You'll just have to run like everybody else."

I had incurred a few debts before the war with high Depression living, and they were still waiting for me after the war. Not the seat, the debts.

The average actor clings to whatever job's providing money, the longest time possible. I've now come to an age where I can't do that any more. I find I want very little in the way of possessions out of life. Here we are in a hotel room, and there're unanswered letters piled up on my desk. And that's my life. I don't care. I've got a suit on, and that's about all I want. I'd like to answer the letters before I die. (Laughs.) But I don't know that I will.

Neil Schaffner

It is a comfortable trailer home in Wapello, Iowa. He and his wife, Caroline, both retired, spend their winters in Florida.

Though both had "trouped" from childhood, the Schaffner Players were organized in 1925, and "we never missed a year—come war, catastrophe, the Depression—till a heart attack laid me low" in the late Forties. It was a tent dramatic company, touring the towns of Iowa. After its first ten years, other Midwestern states were "trouped."

419

The Schaffner Players were among the more celebrated of such companies that performed in the rural areas of the country, since before the turn of the century.

The fare was primarily comedy, though a serious theme was occasionally part of the "repertore." "All these plays always had a good moral, a thought to carry away." In most of them, he appeared as Toby. With red wig and freckles, he was the rural comic hero, who always outwitted the city slicker. Whether he appeared as a GI, an FBI man or a country editor, he always was Toby. His wife was, invariably, Susie, recognized by her pigtails, freckles and equally pungent wisecracks.

The company would usually work a week in one town, a different play each night. Their regular appearance was always a major event in the entertainment life of the community. "Crowds would line up sometimes two, three hours before the performance was scheduled to start." The box office was always busy. . . .

WHO TOLD EVERYBODY the Depression was on on the sixth day of July, Nineteen Hundred and Thirty? In the middle of May we opened our season in Wapello. We had heard talk of hard times being back East. We couldn't see it. We had normal crowds at the show. A normal amount of candy and popcorn was being sold. We ended up our usual big week on the Fourth of July at Ollie, Iowa. We moved down to Fairfield, where we had always had big crowds.

On the night of July sixth, we played to about $30 gross business. That week, we took in $200 with a show costing us $1500. We couldn't understand it. Somebody must have told everybody to quit going to shows. Well do I remember that day.

I jumped into a car and drove to Belle Plaine, where J. Doug Morgan had a show. He said, "I did the smallest business in the history of the Morgan Show." How everybody found out the Depression was on that day I'll never understand. All of a sudden, the plug was pulled out of the bathtub.

I have a wife, a baby and a mother-in-law. All I've got to sell is my ability as an entertainer. But it appeared nobody had any money to buy. The audience had become benumbed. They just accepted it as a horrible thing. You'd accept anything you couldn't do a thing about. The show was an escape from the trials and tribulations of everyday scratch for existence. The company had to survive. It was a ground hog case —root hog or die. We had to keep going, and that's all there was to it.

Mediapolis had always been one of our very good towns. We heard a rumble that people on relief were going to our show. They were threatened to be taken off the rolls. That night I made a little speech: "Many of our dear friends, who have always come to our shows, don't have the money. If anyone comes to me and tells me he can't afford it, I'll be happy to have him come as my guest." It took all the thunder away from these birds. I couldn't see whose business it is if people would sacrifice a hamburger to see a show.

We had to work all kinds of gimmicks to survive. At Burlington, I made a deal with the merchants. 110 paid me a dollar apiece. I gave them all the tickets they wanted to give away to their customers. That's how circle stock was born. Out of the Depression. A company would have a base and book six or seven towns nearby. A different town each night. They'd explain to the merchants, "We'll be in your town every Tuesday night." Another town, another night. We give them all the tickets they'd want for a dollar, which they'd give away. That plus ten cents would admit you.

Since time immemorial, "repertore" shows opened: ladies free. As a result, we'd have a big crowd on Monday and on Tuesday hardly anyone. We reversed the nights. So we had good Tuesdays and bad Mondays. I'd send postcards out to all the rural mailboxes: an absolutely free season ticket. But it had to be used every night. So the farmer would give it to someone, if he couldn't go. And we'd get a dime for the chair.

During the early Depression, Chatauqua was murder. They were our biggest competition. They started out as educational programs— lectures, Swiss bell ringers. They were subsidized by the local citizens. But then they changed to entertainment. They tried to tie up all the choice lots in town for their tents. Sometimes they'd get in with the mayors and try to raise our license fees. But we survived.

Talk about desperate ideas. We decided our titles weren't catching. So we changed *Rebecca of Sunnybrook Farm*—that is, my version of it —to *Her Unwelcome Relative*. A play I wrote called *Chain Stores,* we changed to *What Mothers Don't Know*. We sat up till broad daylight thinking up these titles. Business doubled.

In about '32, I paid $150 royalties for *The Family Upstairs*. The audience enjoyed it, all right. They'd say, "I tell you, Toby, it was the best show I ever saw. Enough to last me for a month." So they never came back.

I made a serial out of the whodunit, *Jittering Spooks*. After opening night, we'd invite the audience to remain and give them the opening act as a free gift. On the second night, the second act, and so on. Anything to get them back. . . .

Talk about bad luck. They had a terrible dry spell. On this hot night, I announced, "Toby predicts that tomorrow you'll have rain." They hooted and howled. It did rain. They marveled so at it, they never came back to see the show.

We worked all kinds of dodges. This guy comes up one day with the idea of a balloon ascension in front of our tent. For $10. So I made the deal. I advertised the free balloon ascension. He gets up there, and it floats five miles out into the country. The crowd follows him, and the sonuvaguns never came back.

Sure, I made gags about the Depression. The traveling salesman called on the farmer. He sees him out in the field with a fishing rod, casting. So he turns tail. He visits another farmer tying a rope around a pullet. The farmer says, "That other guy's gone daffy. It must be the Depression's done it." So the salesman asks, "Why are you wrappin' the rope around the pullet?" The farmer says, "When I get this outboard motor started, I'm gonna join 'im." (Laughs.)

The Depression ended for us in 1936. We did a Toby-Susie act on the radio, five times a week, fifteen minutes. Then, went on the "National Barn Dance for Alka-Seltzer over NBC. 550 stations. We got thousands of letters. Stores wouldn't wait on customers when the show was on. They had loudspeakers where the men were pitching horseshoes. Farmers would come in out of the fields to listen. . . .

POSTSCRIPT: *"The Federal Theater had no connection with us. It was an idea of Mrs. Roosevelt. She thought it would alleviate unemployment among actors. Instead of putting William A. Brady in charge or some other recognized theatrical man, they chose Hallie Flanagan, who had gone to Vassar. It became a haven for all the short-haired gals and long-haired boys and weirdies of all kinds. And legitimate actors were walking the streets.*

"A friend of mine ran the project in Peoria. He made a profit. This horrified Miss Flanagan. She said: 'This is art, not commercial theater. You're not supposed to show a profit.'

"They could have solved actors' unemployment at very little cost. All they had to do was make a survey. If they said to each manager of each show: Add one more actor to your company. Uncle Sam will pay his salary. That would have been the easiest way. But, no, they couldn't do that. That's the practical way. . . ."

Paul Draper

Solo dancer.

I HAD no money before the Depression. I had no money then. So I wasn't aware of anything affecting my life. I was a dancer. I worked up in the rehearsal hall every day, looked for jobs, and auditioned.

In '33, we were performing on what was known as half-salary—breaking in. Whenever we got through with the break-in period, this manager would replace somebody in the act—make up another name for the act, and it would become another break-in. So we always worked on half-salary. I wasn't aware of it for a long time. I worked on half-salary for years.

Vaudeville was still alive. We used to do five shows a day at movie houses. You did thirty-five shows a week. I was always being hired for 19/35 of one week's work. Some act would get sick, and they'd say: Who can come in without rehearsal? I was at the time a flash act soloist. I used to work on a marble table top and had one number, "Bye Bye Blues." I was not hard to place in a show.

A flash act goes on and off. It is without personality in any way. It is only the *act*. A juggler or acrobats. A dancer was, at that time, a flash act. It was only the exhibition of one's physical skills. You could always be fitted into a show without interfering with anything else.

In the late Thirties, he perfected the tap dance technique to the accompaniment of classical compositions. He became a night club headliner and, subsequently, a concert performer. "I was no longer on the marble pedestal. I had achieved a sort of status."

My political awareness had nothing to do with the Depression. It was the Spanish Civil War. It was around 1937, '38. I danced to raise money for the Spanish Loyalists. Of course, I had a little more stability as a performer and could afford the luxury of outside interests.

If I have any nostalgia of the Thirties, it does not concern the social-economic changes which took place. It's the memory of the Persian Room.[7] It was a very smart room. Everyone was in evening clothes. You weren't able to get in without a black tie. If the host didn't like the way someone looked, he would say there are no more tables.

I used to work there three months straight. You'd often get the same audiences, but it was all right. On last nights, every table had champagne. We all stood up, made a toast and sang "Auld Lang Syne." This was '37, '38, '39.

We thought of the poor, at that time, as quite divorced from us, who were not poor. By the exercise of one's charity, life could be made all right. You would always have the poor with you, they were the unfortunate, and you made donations. You could handle them. It was mildly unpleasant, but not fundamentally upsetting.

Now, for the first time, we face the dreadful reality that we are not separated. They are us. They are something we have made. There is no conceivable way today to say: Fish, and you'll be all right. In hurt, in anguish, in shock, we are becoming aware that it is ourselves, who have to be found wanting, not the poor.

Robert Gwathmey

A Virginia-born artist living in New York. He is Visiting Professor at Boston University.

"Our family had a polite name, poor but polite. We never went hungry. We had a little garden and everything. We had dogs, cats, pigeons, every damn thing. We had wealthy relatives, but I only saw them at weddings and funerals."

RICHMOND, Virginia, didn't feel the Depression to any great extent. It's

[7] An expensive dining room-club in the Plaza Hotel.

a tobacco town. A strange thing, I don't give a damn how deep a Depression might be, people seem to insist on smoking. That sort of sustained the city, I'm certain. Richmond had only one bank failure.

But there were many people committed suicide in Richmond, at the time. The most important citizens began to go to church. And they became rather superstitious about palmistry and the occult. The ouija board was a big deal then. They couldn't afford to go to a movie, perchance, so they'd say: We'll all play the ouija board tonight. The questions people would ask! They wouldn't ask: May I speak to my grandfather? or something like that. They would ask: Is So-and-So's bank going to fail tomorrow? Things were that current. Call it mystique if you will, but things came down to the rock-bottom.

I got out of art school in 1930. That was the proper time for any artist to get out of school. (Laughs.) Everybody was unemployed, and the artist didn't seem strange any more. I got a job teaching at a girls' school in Philadelphia, Beaver College. This was 1932. I taught two days a week and spent the rest of the time painting. The WPA was founded then, '33, '34.

The Artists' Union in Philadelphia came into being. Although I was not on the WPA, I was vice president of the union. We'd say: Tomorrow is a better day. It was an affirmative time. We did much political agitation. We made posters for the Roosevelt campaign, for Loyalist Spain, for May Day parades.

Many Congressmen called the WPA boondoggling, barrel rolling and what not. So many energies were spent going down to Washington, interviewing Congressmen, asking them to sustain the WPA. . . .

The total cost of the Federal Arts Project was only $23 million. Many of these paintings, sculptures and prints were given to museums, courthouses, public buildings. . . . I think that today those in museums alone are worth about $100 million.

Not only did this twenty-three million support young artists just out of school, but artists in transition. I'll wager if there were five hundred gallery artists who made it, who are represented by dealers, about four hundred were on WPA.

Nobody was buying art in those days. The Whitney Museum had $35,000 a year to buy contemporary art in the Thirties. We thought that was just the greatest thing ever. Now a man will pay $35,000 for a single painting.

Guys on the project made something in the neighborhood of $94 a month. Then a guy might have a sweetheart on the project, so that would be almost $200 a month. You could live very well.

But the most important thing was: the artist had a patron who made no aesthetic judgments. Occasionally, you'd find a director in a given neighborhood who played favorites. . . . So artists for the first time, I dare say, had a patron—the Government—who made no aesthetic judgments at all.

The director of the Federal Arts Project was Edward Bruce. He was a friend of the Roosevelts—from a polite family—who was a painter. He was a man of real broad vision. He insisted there be no restrictions. You were a painter: Do your work. You were a sculptor: Do your work. You were a printmaker: Do your work. An artist could do anything he damn pleased.

You did have supervisors. They were artists who had already made it. They would visit your studios maybe two days a week. When the work was done, it belonged to the Government, of course.

I painted this thing called "Tobacco." If I'm going to paint tobacco, let me do some work on tobacco. It was 1936. I spent a summer on this tobacco farm in North Carolina. They had three sharecroppers on this farm. I said I'd give each of the three guys a day a week. Harvesting tobacco is difficult. It's almost communal in a way. Here are six farmers. There are six days in a week, one day for rest, right? These six get together, and they would prime tobacco.[8] Mondays on this farm, Tuesdays the next farm, and so forth.

I picked tobacco because I wanted to know the whole story. An instant observer could do all this surface quality. To be involved, it has to have a deeper meaning, right? We're all total fellows, aren't we? Right. I insist on being a total fellow. I couldn't sit there and make a sort of representational and calling it priming tobacco, if I hadn't done it myself. I had to.

I lost my job at Beaver College. I used to discuss articles out of *The Nation* at lunch time, where the teachers gathered. They didn't say this was the reason. I'd done simply this. Four girls were graduating. They wanted to come to New York to do some grad work. I drove them up, and we went to see some of the schools. Also, we saw Marc Blitzstein's *Cradle Will Rock*. Then we went to an Italian restaurant, and we had a cocktail and ate and returned to Pennsylvania.

[8] "You prime tobacco when you pull the leaf off the stalk. It may have thirty-five or forty leaves. You take the leaves off the bottom, 'cause it matures there first. . . ."

The president wrote me a letter—we were with my wife's people in North Carolina at the time; she was pregnant: "It has come to my attention that you have been in a drinking establishment with your students. You have been unfaithful to your president and your institution. . . ."

The president of Beaver College was a Presbyterian minister, but he acted like a traveling salesman. He lost his job because he ordered furniture from the purchasing agent for his married daughter and didn't reimburse the college. The guy that fired me.

I don't mind losing jobs. Every time I lose one, I get a better one. I got one at Carnegie Tech. I taught for three years there. I came to New York in 1942 and have been here ever since.

I wouldn't expect a man in 1930 to think like a man in 1968, would you? Of course not. But there are many people who will take a point of view as artists: I'll be an idealist. I'll be a romanticist, I'll be this or that or the other. You've got to be what you are, churning up the day in which you live and pull out of that experience something that is representative in artistic terms.

Artists have to live, right? Eat, sleep, breathe, build. The great difference is when you have a government as a patron or anyone else as a patron, who made no demands on you at all, there were no enlarged notions of making that extra buck. That was a very free and happy period. Social comment was in the wind. Now the wind has changed. But despite the direction any artist follows, he is still pure politically.

Artists have a chance of being good people 'cause they work alone. I go to my studio. I don't work on a belt line. When your work is done, after dinner, you meet people and you become talkative. You've been alone all day. Now give me that first drink, will you? Right?

Some fear Government as an arts boss because of the dangers of political censorship. . . .

I think it's the craziest thing. We live in a democracy. We call it a democracy, right? I can vote. I can agitate for my franchise, right? Why should I be fearful of my Government. I am a part of it, am I not?

Perhaps, there could be a dictatorial Government—that's another story. Like Hitler, say: You can only paint blondes with strong breasts. . . .

It's fearful to think that today's times are so affluent for me. I live real, real well. I'm in the upper ten percent. But when I see poverty, it's still poverty. I hate it.

During the Depression, we were all more or less engulfed. Today when people say poverty, they turn their head. They don't want to admit poverty exists. They're living too high, so on-the-fat, right? If you're living on-the-fat and see poverty, you simply say: They're no good. In the Depression, there was a little more Godlike acceptance of the un-employed guy, because you could be he.

Knud Andersen

The studio of a portrait painter and sculptor. Piercing eyes are fixed upon us: a self-portrait of the artist as a young man. The eyes of others illuminate the twilight of the room. They are in oils: Senator Henrik Shipstead, among others. Of this portrait, Harold Laswell said, "The blue eyes of the subject do not stare vacantly into the future, but intently into reality. . . ."

He had come to Chicago from Norway forty-five years ago: "It was a grand adventure, the arts in the new land." Powerful men in the worlds of politics and finance had commissioned him to do their portraits, in times past.

His eyes wander from work to work, from face to face, as he remembers. . . .

YOU SEE, to me the Depression was a blessing. When the shock of los-ing what you had worked for comes, I found refuge in my art. To stew in a deplorable situation . . . where people were affected . . . some to suicide . . . I lost myself in my art. The pain that came with eco-nomic loss, I felt would pass. These things, like the eclipse of the sun . . . People first observed it and committed suicide . . . not realizing that this would pass.

I felt quite prayerful, and so I was at peace. Of course, the knock on the door of economics . . . disturbed. But you survived. I constantly counseled myself on the best way of survival.

Did you join the Federal Arts Project?

No, no, no. It was so disappointing, I couldn't participate. If it is done in the right way, the gifted artist benefits from the state and contributes: thus, body and soul are nourished. Then I would have participated. But the program went against my grain. I did not recognize true artistry in evidence.

Oh, the Depression years were hard. I managed with a commission now and then.

Days without food . . . ?

Those are days I don't recall. Self-respect never allowed anyone to know I was in that state. I had quite a duplex studio. I had Bach and Beethoven. Nothing else mattered. I worked in the cathedral of the spirit. My body may have needed food, but I was unaware.

Once in the studio, a rat ran across my arm and bit me. Luckily, a visitor had left a bottle of whiskey, without my knowing about it. The bottle came of good use, I told him afterwards. I poured the whiskey over the wound. These are accidents, like the Depression. I avoid bringing accidents to mind.

Little Brother Montgomery and Red Saunders

The first is a jazz pianist and the other a band leader, who devotes much of his time to finding jobs for black musicians.

MONTGOMERY: I was making a dollar a night on Sunday nights. And a spaghetti dinner. Playing house rent parties. On a Saturday night, I was playing for $3. No supper there. Weekends is when the stockyards workers would go. Tuesday night, I was playing for $2. My weeks were filled up with two, three dollars a night.

Monday night, that was the biggest night I had. $4. They had Blue Monday parties, the sporting people. Everybody who'd been out all Saturday and Sunday night, gamblers and hustlers. If they'd been hustlin' anything, they'd be poppin', buying moonshine, having fun, on Monday. From five o'clock in the morning until the wee, wee hours, way through the night.

SAUNDERS: Those Blue Monday parties had a meaning. The night life, the gambling, the prostitution and the pimps—they weren't just something that happened. They were a necessity. Survival. Women had to sell their bodies for twenty-five cents, fifteen cents. You find fewer black pimps today, because the black woman is more independent.

In a flat, everything would go. In one room, they were playing a piano and drinking whiskey. In another room, they would have Georgia skin, poker or whatever game. In another room, they'd have whores, hustlers. Everything went. A person had to have some kind of life.

MONTGOMERY: They were houses where people lived. With a piano in the front room, where people danced. And moonshine, twenty-five cents a half pint. Pulverized alcohol. No admission. The money came from the sale of moonshine and supper. Spaghetti and chili . . . The house'd be packed, all kinds a ways. Six, five, sometimes four rooms, a hundred, eighty people would be in it. They were givin' a party to get their rent together.

Lots of times we were raided by the police. Catch moonshine or catch 'em gamblin'. They had some bad policemen around at that time. They had Jesse James, Big Six, Callahan's Squad. . . .

We had a lot of house party piano players in them days—a guy called Forty-Five, Cripple Clarence Lofton, Pine Top Smith, 'Sippi Wallace, a guy called Toothpick. Piano'd be ringin' all night. Guys would come in, weren't workin', they'd play. You'd find all kinds of piano players, great ones. Boogiewoogie began in house parties. But we didn't call it that then. Doodley Joe, we called it . . . 1928, '29, '30. I paid $4 a week for a room. We made $15 a week. We got along pretty good.

SAUNDERS: There was a pickup in business when beer came in in '33. They could go out publicly and drink. And the price was right. Beer was fifteen cents and you could get entertainment. With Repeal, you began to see a new light. You had to have these rent parties during Prohibition because there were no night clubs, to speak of. They were black speakeasies.

MONTGOMERY: I left around the early Thirties and organized a band around Jackson, Mississippi. Sometimes we'd play at a dance and make fifteen cents apiece. (Laughs.) You'd travel maybe two, three hundred miles in a secondhand Cadillac, and a beat-up Lincoln. The whole band. We'd get to a place and couldn't make gas money. Places like Meridian, Hattiesburg, Vicksburg, all up in the Delta. 1935, '36 and up to around '38.

The main times is when they're pickin' cotton. They got a dollar a hundred for pickin'. (Laughs.) Some people could pick two, three hundred pounds a day. We played in tobacco barns down through the South. I remember one band was burned up in one of those warehouses. We played a white dance tonight and a colored dance tomorrow. But we didn't mix.

SAUNDERS: In those days, the black artist was at the mercy of the promoters. In later years, MCA[9] and others took them on, but at first they weren't booking black bands. The hotels and ballrooms were for white bands. This was a time when radio was great. White musicians were having a field day, making all kinds of money in studios, in concerts and legitimate theaters. Big money. The poor black musicians just had the beat-up Lincoln. They were what you called starvation bands. Did you know black musicians created the one-nighters?

They didn't have any homes. Out of five years, they'd maybe sit down ten weeks. They lived in the auto. The location jobs were for the Benny Goodmans and the Tommy Dorseys, hotels and ballrooms. The only time they would sit down would be like the Apollo in New York, the Regal in Chicago, the Howard in Washington. . . .[10]

MONTGOMERY: Even their music was taken from them. Clarence Williams wrote "Sugar Blues" and that was called Clyde McCoy's. "Dorsey Boogie" is Pine Top's, which he played at house rent parties. . . .

Jack Kirkland

Writer-producer. His play, Tobacco Road, *based upon Erskine Caldwell's novel, ran "almost eight years."*

IN THE SPRING of '32, I woke up with a violent hangover. An agent gave me this book to read for that afternoon: "You're a southerner, you'll dig this." I went home with my hangover and read it and said: this is a play. So I took the book under my arm and went to live in Majorca for three, four months. I was quite broke at the time.

[9] Music Corporation of America.
[10] Black Theaters, featuring live artists. The films were merely stage-waits.

He completed the play in Hollywood, where he wrote films at "very big salaries." One was a highly successful Shirley Temple movie. "Shirley Temple's responsible for Tobacco Road, *really." (Laughs.)*

It opened December 4, 1933. I couldn't get anyone else to produce it. They all were afraid of it. They thought it wouldn't run. So I put up all the money myself. No one else had a nickel in it. I gave away a great deal of it to associates. . . .

The whole thing cost about $9,000 to produce. The reviews in the dailies were not too good for the play, except the raves for Henry Hull's performance. I just had to get up another five or six hundred dollars a week to carry the play. Until the *Daily News*[11] had the editorial. Captain Patterson[12] fell for it and wrote an editorial. And the next day we were in. Later on, the monthlies came out—George Jean Nathan, Bob Benchley, Dorothy Parker, all came out for it.

Did you have any doubts during the five weeks before the editorial and the magazines appeared?

No. Or I wouldn't have spent that money. The play was dealing with poverty. The audience understood and they were concerned. Of course, it was based on a period preceding the Depression. It had existed for some time in the South. Cotton was five cents a pound, and all that sort of thing. There was shock value, sure. But I think its success was determined by its reality and honesty.

Mrs. Roosevelt helped. She loved the play, because it was about social conditions. When it opened in Atlanta, she went down there in case any trouble happened. But there was none whatsoever.

Did you encounter much censorship trouble?

No. Mayor LaGuardia threw out burlesque, but he wouldn't throw out good theater. Later, in Chicago, they called us intellectual New Yorkers.[13]

[11] New York *Daily News.*
[12] Publisher of the paper.
[13] A couple of years after its Broadway opening, the play came to Chicago. "We opened to rave notices. They carried me down the aisle on their backs, the audience did. Opening night in Chicago was just the greatest opening night I'd ever known. A couple of months afterwards, I was in California. I heard, over the air, we were closed by Mayor Kelly. He exercised his power capriciously in revoking the theater's license. As I understand it, Mrs. Kelly walked in with her priest, and she was offended by it." The case was in the federal courts; a District Court decision in favor of Kirkland; a reversal by the Circuit Court of Appeals . . . , "so

From then on, the Depression was a swinging time for me. Everything was so reasonable, and my income was so big. (Laughs.) I never had it so good. When you're involved in making a living, gambling all your money, it was just something that passed in front of you without any feeling about it. And I was getting married quite often in those days, too. (Laughs.) Besides my artistic occupations, I had some marital preoccupations. (Laughs.)

Heaven knows I saw Hoovervilles—out of train windows. It was appalling to look at, even through train windows. But it didn't touch me.

A great many people felt it, especially the young. That's why so many at that time joined the Party. It wasn't a lack of love for the United States so much as thinking some other system would correct this blasting horror of hunger. They were soon disillusioned. . . .

But it was a more generous time then. There wasn't this miasmic fear of unnamed things out there. Then it was specific: hunger. We had a more specific enemy to overcome. We were all in such a mess. When you're in trouble, you never go to rich friends to help you, you go to poor friends. I was more fortunate, so I was able to help out friends.

Don't forget, we were all younger. There was a spirit of adventure then, too. When you're thirty years old, you don't have much fear. You don't have the same kind of fear I would have now after thirty, forty years. As I'm talking to you now, I'm seeing it with the eyes of a young man. Oh, it was a magnificent time for me. There was certainly no lack of girls. (Laughs.) I'm awful glad I was young at that time.

Herman Shumlin

Theater producer-director. Among his works: Grand Hotel, The Little Foxes, Male Animal, Watch on the Rhine, The Children's Hour, Inherit the Wind, The Deputy.

Two or three blocks along Times Square, you'd see these men, silent, shuffling along in line. Getting this handout of coffee and doughnuts,

we moved down to St. Louis. We kept our full company on full salary in Chicago for five or six weeks, waiting for a decision. . . ."

dealt out from great trucks, Hearst's New York *Evening Journal,* in large letters, painted on the sides. Shabby clothes, but you could see they had been pretty good clothes.

Their faces, I'd stand and watch their faces, and I'd see that flat, opaque, expressionless look which spelled, for me, human disaster. On every corner, there'd be a man selling apples. Men in the theater, whom I'd known, who had responsible positions. Who had lost their jobs, lost their homes, lost their families. And worse than anything else, lost belief in themselves. They were destroyed men.

One man I had known lived in New Rochelle. Proud of his nice family, his wife and three children. He had been a treasurer in the theater, which housed a play I had managed in 1926. He was very worldly, knew everything—that wonderful kind of knowledge you often find in people of the theater. A completely capable man.

It was in 1931 that I ran into him on the street. After I had passed him, I realized who it was. I turned and ran after him. He had averted his eyes as he went by me. I grabbed hold of him. There was a deadness in his eyes. He just muttered: Good to see you. He didn't want to talk to me. I followed him and made him come in with me and sit down.

He told me that his wife had kicked him out. His children had had such contempt for him 'cause he couldn't pay the rent, he just had to leave, to get out of the house. He lived in perpetual shame. This was, to me, the most cruel thing of the Depression. Almost worse than not having food. Accepting the idea that you were just no good. No matter what you'd been before.

The Depression didn't affect me financially. On the contrary. I was successful almost the moment things crashed. But it did affect me in everything I saw. Making money while all this was going on.

I co-produced a play in October, 1929. It opened at the Bijou Theater. It wasn't a very good play. I stood across the street, alongside the old Astor Hotel, and watched people going into the theater. I wondered what was the matter with them. They looked so down, so silent, sullen. How could they have heard of the play already? It wasn't until the next day, when I got the papers for the reviews, that I realized the stock market crashed. The play closed quickly, but I remember the evening very well.

It wasn't really until well into 1930 that it became visible. The theater, for some reason, kept on going much as it had been. It was a slower descent. Plays were still being produced, great numbers of them, people were working.

Later in the year, I produced and directed *Grand Hotel*. It was surprisingly successful for me, it being my first time as a director. All of a sudden, a man whose pockets had been empty for years, I was making $7,000 a week. Yet the country's slide had begun.

I became very conscious of the effects of the Depression, of the yellowing that seemed to take place on the streets of Broadway, of the stores that were closed, of the shops that had been turned into one or another kind of cheap food places, of shops which had gone bankrupt and were being turned into little gaming parlors with automatic machines.

Broadway was still alive every night, crowded with people as it had always been. But there was a change. Their clothes were shabbier, they stood around more, they walked aimlessly up and down the streets, rather than going somewhere. And those long lines of silent men, accepting the coffee and doughnuts and moving away. . . . It was disturbing to me. Here I was, making money and what did I do about it?

I've always remarked at the ability of people to forget. I think even people who were enveloped in its greatest horrors have forgotten, emotionally forgotten. The memory of pain is extraordinarily evanescent. I wonder if the psychological scars are really visible. I know many people who've lived through it, my contemporaries. I wonder if they remember the suffering and agony and the shame they went through. I really don't know.

When you meet them, does the subject ever come up?

Never, never. I've brought it up sometimes, but I don't find it a subject anybody is interested in. I don't think it's something they want to evade. It's just a bellyache that's passed. They're just not interested in discussing it.

It's fear, I suppose. A man is scared of his job, scared someone might cut in, scared of what happens on the street. The fear in people of great means and in people of small means. Were a Depression to come again, *I* fear we could have a Fascist state.

POSTSCRIPT: *"Every time I go over to Central Park, I walk into the Children's Zoo. This was built during the Depression by WPA workers. It's an absolutely lovely place. I go into the Park often. And I cannot help remembering—look, this came out of the Depression. Because men were out of work, because they were given a way to earn money, good things were created."*

Public Servant—
The City

Elizabeth Wood

*She is Chief of Social Services, Housing Assistance Administration. In
the late Thirties, through the late Forties, she was head of the Chicago
Housing Authority.*

In '33, I'd just been hired as a social worker by the United Charities.
Social work at that time was beginning to get psychiatric. I found this
absolutely obnoxious. I got taken by some of my clients in a way that
made me keenly aware of how stupid were some of our approaches. The
irrelevance of the kind of goodies we were handing out. It was the psychiatric approach. Sit, be passive, and let your client tell you what's
wrong. It was my first contact with poverty. I found out the hard way.

I saw the impact on one family. There were nine children and two
parents living in three rooms. I found them a great, big, sunny apartment, with enough bedrooms for a decent sleeping arrangement. And
a dining room table for the first time. And enough chairs for the first
time. I saw the magic that house performed. The family bloomed. I
learned my first lesson about the meaning of a house. But that wasn't
the whole story. This is my point.

There was a drunken father and a tough little German wife, toothless.
I'll always remember that. The children had every ailment in the book.
The twelve-year-old boy was a truant because he had to wear his sister's

shoes. He was very proud, the only possessor of a toothbrush in the whole family.

I remember the girl I thought was feeble-minded. She changed completely when they moved into the new house. I couldn't quite understand it. Her mother confessed to me that she used some of the food budget to get this little girl a permanent. She was scared to death I was gonna scold her. But that was one of the things that helped this girl out of her condition. She found a job.

In that three-room apartment, when the father came home drunk, he beat up his wife. The girl was right there, next to it. It obviously had an effect on her. In the new place, when the father wanted to beat up his wife, the boys would put him in the back bedroom and lock the door. So there was no more of this savageness near the girl. These things happened just by the virtue of *room*. But there was the quality of the mother, too. She was one of the best social workers I ever knew.

She made the house work its full magic. When the other girl, the sixteen-year-old, started to date, there was a front parlor for her to sit in. There was a plant, there was a sofa. I had kept this room bare. She filled it. The mother had the girl buy a pink electric light bulb, so it looked pretty when she had a date. That's what I call social work. (Laughs.)

In a way, this shows a falsity of the New Deal concept: All you need is a good, sanitary house. The person herself had ideas.

In 1937, the United States Housing Act was passed. The concept was a good one, different from those sterile words. We built quite beautiful projects throughout the country. The standards of the Federal Administration were high. But it never occurred to anybody that the people might make their own decisions about playgrounds, housing design or management policies. So the institutions became more and more institutionalized, while we took in more and more deprived people. In many cases, we tried to pick the nicer of the deprived and avoid the less-nice. We had absolutely no insight . . .

Our legislation is still not phrased in concepts which work today: that sometimes these people have awfully good ideas, better than ours. We're just beginning to learn. Tenants have a right to make their own decisions.

In the early Forties, we ran out of '37 money. By that time, austerity had set in. The new policy seemed to be: Because public housing was for poor people, it ought to look poor. There was a great resentment if it looked nice. That was the beginning of the sterile, barracks-like housing projects.

It had a multiple effect. We housed fewer and fewer people who benefited by the house alone. We found that housing itself was not enough for people who were really defeated. So the rules of the New Deal era aren't good enough today. 'Cause at best we were awfully kind, benevolent Lady Bountifuls. And, boy, that doesn't work these days.

"Project people" was a term of pride back in '37 and '38. Incredible pride. Our problem was preventing the tenants from becoming snobbish about their belongings. I had to get it clear to them that the children across the street had a right to use their playground. There wasn't any other around.

I can remember a young woman who moved into Jane Addams.[1] She got married about the time we planned to build the project. From the day she saw the houses go up, she wanted to move in. She got pregnant and bought new furniture to store in the barn where she was living at the time. When she moved in with her new baby and new furniture, she was the proudest woman in the world.

I remember Mrs. Pacelli. She said, "I never used to talk to my neighbors when I lived in the slums. But here we've all been selected." There was a sense of aristocracy which was very funny. It's quite the opposite today.

There were lots of unsystematized, uninstitutionalized, good native works. After two babies died of whooping cough, a group of women in the project volunteered to find out about preventives. They knocked on all the doors, so that all youngsters under six got whooping cough inoculations. They had so many creative ideas.

This was in spite of us. And we had a perfectly good staff. Nothing wrong with them. We simply had no idea of the independence, the role of citizens. . . .

It remained that way until '49. Then we had to purge. The eviction of high income families, God bless us. The average income for the Addams families was $1,027. When their incomes reached over $1,250, they were evicted. It was a vicious, dirty thing to do. All over the country, I meet people who say: I was evicted from the project and moved into very inferior housing.

[1] One of the first public housing projects in Chicago. It was open for occupancy in the spring of 1938.

Fights over the selection of sites didn't exist in those days. It was a honeymoon, ten years of pure honeymoon. The only limitation on our capacity to produce was our brains. We didn't know how to foster the idea that these people could think for themselves.

By and large, they were two-parent families. Most of them were middle-class oriented, caught in the Depression. A large percentage were WPA families. They were people who were naturally mobile. They sought out a house because it was a good house.

We had a pitiful percentage of Negroes. The sites for the early projects were vacant lands in white areas. It was the official Ickes policy that you did not change the complexion of a neighborhood. Race relations advisers, good people, didn't go any further.

We put twenty-four Negroes on single, segregated stairwells. Then came the turnover in white families, but none among the Negro occupants. We promptly broke up the segregated stairwells and had a steady increase of Negro intake. It was not until the veteran's program in the late Forties that we really adopted an integrated policy.[2]

There followed a descending pattern. The poorest people were heading that way by virtue of relocation—urban renewal. If they didn't know what to do with a family, they'd send them to a project. So there was a crash input of people on welfare and broken families. The feeling of the "project people" changed. It wasn't a question of their right any more. I can still hear the voice of one woman. In a bored tone, she was saying, "I got me a project. If I can't get anything else, I'll move in." At that moment, I knew most clearly our families no longer felt as they used to.

It was no longer a step up. It was a place where you were investigated. Private habits were never investigated in the old days. Because investigators felt they were being rooked by welfare families, the counting began of toothbrushes, birth certificates and sleeping arrangements. The institution of public housing fossilized, stiffened.

If you're the female head of a household and you don't have an identifiable father of all the children, you're really up against it. Welfare has broken up families because of the man-in-the-house rule. It's venal. The damage we've done to human beings is incredible. Today, we don't build homes, we build institutions.

The New Deal was an enormous step. It was a leap forward. The

[2] Miss Wood was subjected to violent attack for insistently pursuing this policy, particularly by local and state politicians.

Government assumed a responsibility toward subsidized housing. But we didn't realize that the house is not enough. There's the person. In ignoring his possibilities, we have a welfare generation. We begot it.

Mick Shufro

He is Public Relations Director of Roosevelt University; he works in a similar capacity for the American Association of Social Workers. In the late Thirties and early Forties, he was Assistant Director of the Chicago Housing Authority.

A MOTHER of nine children was receiving two quarts of milk. Because of a budgetary crisis, she was cut down to one quart. She raised hell at the relief station. She became vituperative. The case worker wrote her up as a psychotic. And sent her to a psychiatrist. Fortunately, he responded as few did at the time. He said: When this woman stops reacting the way she does, let me know. Then she would be abnormal.

At the time of the budgetary cuts, I found out that large dogs at the animal shelter received more per meal than a man on relief. I said so. One of the papers streamered it on the front page. The skeletal budget remained until, suddenly, more money was found.

I couldn't understand this sudden change of heart. Later I learned that shoplifting on State Street had become so great that the merchants petitioned the welfare people to give more monies, so that shoplifting costs would go down. It may have been that if a kid didn't have clothing, his parents shoplifted a pair of pants or a sweater or something of that sort.

I was once director of the Seamen's Division of the Transient Bureau. These men had traveled and were well organized. They never came in to see me alone. It was always a committee. They objected to the rules. I suggested they make up their own rules about people staying there. There were about three hundred people living there at the time. They themselves made up a set of rules that was much stiffer than the Administration's. I wouldn't have made them for Alcatraz. But they made them up, followed them and came through.

The answers they gave to the questionnaires were about eighty percent false. They would tell case workers personal problems that didn't exist. It was deliberate. They were objecting to going through their personal history. They formed a committee. I agreed with them. I said: I don't give a damn about your personal lives. If you're eligible for relief, you're going to get relief.

Many laboring men were able to take relief without losing their self-respect or breaking down. The office worker or the professional very often broke down.

There were all kinds of rumors going on then as now: the Negroes who lived in public housing projects couldn't take care of their property. One day I saw a man in his Sunday clothes, digging in the garden out there. He said, "We have so many visitors watching over us, and telling others how the Negro lives, so I dress up in my best clothes when I'm gardening." You'd see a mother snatch her little children when visitors came around, and they'd come down a few minutes later in absolutely pure white dresses. It was show business and also made its points.

Is there a difference between "relief" then and "welfare" now?

At that time, when we said relief, we meant relief. Everyone then you assumed was an able and willing worker, simply out of work. Today there are people society does not accept as workmen. Never having been given the opportunities, they are *almost* unemployable—"welfare people."

Elsa Ponselle

She is the principal of one of the largest elementary schools in Chicago.

I WAS the youngest one in the family, so I got the college education. My brothers and sisters wanted me to go. They couldn't. It was a step up for us to have one daughter go to college.

I began to teach in December, 1930, and I was paid until June, 1931. When we came back, the city had gone broke. We kept on teaching, of course. I didn't go hungry and had a place to live. My father provided me with enough money to get by. But it was another thing for the men who were married and had children.

441

They began to pay us with warrants, which carried six percent interest. A marvelous investment. But not for the teachers who had to take them for pay. They had to peddle those warrants for what they could get. It was a promise to pay when the city got some money. We didn't think we'd ever get paid, but the businessmen knew better.

There were some stores downtown we will always remember with gratitude. They took those warrants at a hundred percent. Remember the Hub, Lytton's? They were wonderful. Old-timers like us still go there. There are some stores that will not be remembered with any love. They took it with a sixty, seventy-five percent discount. Many teachers were credited with only fifty percent. As time went along, they got it up to ninety. One of my friends bought a grand piano because she got a hundred percent on the warrant. (Laughs.) That was—if I may be forgiven for saying so—a hell of a note.

Finally, with F.D.R. in the White House, somebody went to Washington and we got a federal loan. And that didn't happen without a shove. At the time, the chairman of the Board of Education said we should be happy with what we were getting. We asked him if his wife could live on what we were making. A group got together and organized us. Everybody was heart and soul in the unions those days. Somebody said, "Why not a teachers' union?" And why not?

There were objections, of course: We're not tradespeople, we're not laboring class. We're professionals. As professionals, we're entitled to starve to death quietly and with refinement. Some of us weren't that much interested in being refined and professional. We were much more interested in improving our conditions.

We didn't have sit-ins, of course. That would hurt the children. We determined on one thing: We were not going to hurt the children. We went on teaching, whether we were being paid or not. We kept them apart from it.

We marched down LaSalle Street, we marched down Dearborn, we marched down Michigan Avenue. We marched everywhere. People were appalled. Teachers were supposed to be meek and mild. We were supposed to be the bulwark of the status quo and here we were, joining the revolution. (Laughs.) We were on the side of the great unwashed. How could we do that? I'm really surprised at how many teachers joined the movement, especially the older ones. They marched. It gave the establishment a turn. One of them went to Washington and got the money for us.

The Depression hit other members of my family. My brother, a tailor, like my father, was working one day every three months. He had a wife and two children. We were able to help him out. My sister-in-law came to me one day and said: "You want to hear something really funny? Johnny came home and said he had to bring some canned goods to school for the poor children. Where the hell is he gonna find kids poorer than we are?" We protected the kids from any idea that they were deprived.

Today the kids blithely make $50 and off they go and spend it. As they very properly should. One time, somebody said to me, "What these kids need is to experience a Depression." Two of us, remembering the hard times, screamed at him, "Never! Not in a thousand years!" I don't care how blithe they are in spending money. Nobody should experience a Depression. No young person should.

Do you realize how many people in my generation are not married? Young teachers today, they just naturally get married. All the young men are around. There were young men around when we were young. But they were supporting mothers.

It wasn't that we didn't have a chance. I was going with someone when the Depression hit. We probably would have gotten married. He was a commercial artist and had been doing very well. I remember the night he said, "They just laid off quite a few of the boys." It never occurred to him that he would be next. He was older than most of the others and very sure of himself. This was not the sort of thing that was going to happen to *him*. Suddenly he was laid off. It hit him like a ton of bricks. And he just disappeared.

At our school, we had many Mexican children. When I get violent against big business, I think of those poor little kids. The Mexicans were imported to come up and work on the railroads, and when the work gave out, well, brother, can you spare a dime? They were thrust out, just like that. And they accepted it. I mean, this was the way the world was.

At a time, when it was raining and snowing and the middle-class children were all bundled up, or else kept at home. Our kids came to school every single day, whether they had anything to wear or not. 'Cause it was warm, the classroom was warm.

The Mexican and Negro children were more used to being poor and hungry. The Italian and Greek children and their parents were stunned by it. You hear the saying today: if you really want work, you can get

443

it. My nephew, not so long ago, said to me, referring to the Negroes: Ah, if they want a job, they can get it. I said, "If you ever say that again —I don't care if you're damn near forty years old—I'll slap you! Your father couldn't get a job in the Depression, and he wanted one." Of course, he's forgotten. But, ohhh, I felt all that old rage coming back.

The parents of the children I have today are working, but some of them are very, very poor. During the Depression, when you were poor, you weren't looking around and seeing . . . here's a society in which everybody has something except me. What's wrong with me? What's wrong with my parents, that we don't have these things? By God, I'm gonna get some. I can't blame them. They watch television, and everybody has everything. Why not me?

In the Depression, it wasn't only "not me," it was "not you," too. The rich, then, had an instinct for self-preservation. They didn't flaunt their money, if you remember. They didn't have fancy debutante parties, because it was not the thing to do. They were so God-damned scared they'd have a revolution. They damn near did, too, didn't they? Oooohhh, were they scared! What's more scared than a million dollars?

The Depression was a way of life for me, from the time I was twenty to the time I was thirty. I thought it was going to be forever and ever and ever. That people would always live in fear of losing their jobs. You know, *fear*. And, yet, we had, in a way, a wonderful time. We were young.

Remember? The one great thing was the end of Prohibition. The liquor we drank before was awful. Whoever thought about enjoying a drink? I'm talking about the bootleg. To this day, I can't drink gin, because every time I get a very fine Beefeater martini, all I can remember is that white stuff I drank during Prohibition.

How can you talk about the Depression without talking about F.D.R.? I remember when he was at the Chicago Stadium and all of us ran from school to get there. He came in on his son's arm. We didn't realize that he was really and truly crippled until we saw the braces. He got up there and the place just absolutely went up in smoke. What was tremendous about him was—with all the adoration—his sense of humor. He acted as though he didn't take himself seriously.

And Eleanor. Eleanor. I think she's the greatest thing that ever happened to anybody. I think of the way they talked about her, about her looks, about her voice. I used to get so rabid. Why I didn't have high blood pressure, I don't know.

Not so long ago, one of the parents said to me, "You know, you kind of talk like Eleanor Roosevelt." I said, "You mean her voice?" She said, "Oh, no, your voice isn't like hers." I said, "What do you mean?" She said, "I don't know. You just talk like Eleanor Roosevelt." Wasn't that something?

Sergeant Vincent Murray

A police headquarters on Chicago's South Side.

"I worked for the American Express Company for ten years. In 1933, I was laid off. I was out of work for a year. I went to different aldermen, but there were no jobs to be had. I was recalled by the express company when business picked up a little. . . ."

I JOINED the force in 1935. Five hundred young fellows were sworn in on that particular day. We were saddened when a reporter announced that Will Rogers and Wiley Post were killed in a plane crash in Alaska.

Our starting salary was $2300 a year. We purchased our own uniforms, guns and shirts, et cetera. At that time, there were very few policemen drove automobiles. We'd come to work in a streetcar in uniform. When we'd get to the police station, there'd be fifteen or twenty policemen in uniform on that streetcar. Ninety-five percent of us went to work on streetcars.

I look outside the window there, and to my right, looking west, I see 150 automobiles owned by detectives and owned by uniformed men. What I'm trying to bring out is the difference between 1935, '36, '37, '38 and 1968. Now when I go and ride a bus downtown, I never, never see a uniformed man on a bus. They come here to work in all kinds of cars, Fords, Chevies, Chryslers, you even seen 'em come up in Cadillacs, Mustangs. At that time, we lived within our means. We didn't live over our heads.

These young fellows in the police department today, ninety percent of them are living over their heads. They have cars they can't afford. They have colored televisions they can't afford. And some of 'em are talking about summer houses. And every one of 'em I will say are in

445

debt over their heads. It's impossible on what they're gettin'. If they want to keep up, their wives will have to go out and work. Or else, they moonlight, get extra jobs. At that time, they couldn't get two jobs. They were lucky to have one. Just here in the last month, they have allowed policemen to moonlight by driving taxi cabs.

Today there are twenty squad cars where there used to be two. They probably had fifty foot men around the Loop. Now they might have ten foot men, the rest of them are in squad cars. It was interesting working in the Loop, back then. Every twenty minutes, we were stopped by visitors from out of town. They'd see a policeman in uniform and they inquire about different buildings, different restaurants.

It was at the tail end of the Depression. Around the Loop, you had quite a few employment agencies. And we had an epidemic of con games. When these fellows would come out of this employment agency, this confidence man would walk over and pat him on the shoulder and say, "Pardon me, are you looking for a job?" He'd say, "Yes, I am." "Well," said this fellow, his name was Parsons, "I've got a job for you right now over in the Garland Building. Running an elevator. The job pays $30 a week." Now $30 a week is a lot of money at that time.

So the two of them go over to the Garland Building. This confidence man would take this young fellow on the elevator to the office of the building, and he would tell him to sit in the corner. And he would converse with somebody in the building. He'd walk back and say, "You got the job. You start to work tomorrow. But you need a uniform. The uniform'll cost you $50."

So they'd get in a cab and they would go out to his house, and if this fellow didn't have the $50, he borrowed it from his in-laws or his neighbors. He was so desperate to get that job. So he'd give 'em the $50 and Parsons'd say, "O.K., report tomorrow morning, and I'll have your uniform for you."

The following day, the fellow would go down to the Garland Building and he would go up to the office and he would set there, and he's looking for this fellow, Parsons. Mr. Parsons failed to appear. Then he'd go over and talk to the girl. She'd say, "I don't know any Mr. Parsons."

We had about fifty complaints about this Parsons, who was taking these young fellows. Things got out of hand. The sergeant of the district took about ten young fellows and put them in plain clothes and told them to go around these employment agencies. We had a good description of him.

We found him. About thirty people came in, and all thirty identified him at the show-up. We put that fellow in the penitentiary for five years. That gives you an idea how desperate fellows were to secure work. They'd go for almost anything.

Did you have any encounters with strikers at that time or labor organizers . . . ?

There was nothing wrong with those fellows organizing the CIO. Left wing is a term that was used, where you don't go around with the rank-and-file. They organized the fellows that worked hard for a living up at the stockyards. The American Federation of Labor did nothing for the laborer, nothing.

I can remember when my father worked at the stockyards when I was a little boy. That's fifty years ago. His salary was ten cents an hour. My brother worked up there for the same. He worked ten hours for a dollar a day. If they mentioned unions up there, they'd get fired. American Federation of Labor did nothing for these men. It was during the Depression, the CIO came along.

That's when they started calling 'em left wings and bolsheviks and so forth and so on. Personally I don't think they were any more bolshevik or Communist than I was. They just wanted an honest living, that's all.

If all this happened today, I think the people would take it in their own hands, the way things are going. They're a different breed now. More educated today, more educated.

There was no basic race trouble at that time. The colored stayed by themselves, they never marched into any neighborhoods. People were more or less indifferent to them.

Earl B. Dickerson

President of the Supreme Life Insurance Company. "It is written largely on the lives of Negro people. Now we are seeking to move into the mainstream, due to the fact that competition is coming in from white companies. All this has happened since the 1954 Supreme Court decision."

447

He had been president of the Chicago Urban League, as well as of the National Bar Association, the Cook County Bar Association[3] and the National Lawyers Guild.

From 1939 to 1941, he was a member of the Chicago City Council as alderman from the Second Ward.

"The Depression was like a hurricane. Fortunately these 'Acts of God' are not prejudiced. They kill whites as well as Negroes."

THE SOUTH SIDE was very much as it is now in the ghettos. People standing around on corners. The streets were crowded whether it was Saturday or Monday. People who didn't have carfare to even seek jobs. Hopelessness on their faces, as they sat on stoops. . . . Almost all the Negro companies went out of business. The banks in the community were closed. Though they catered to black depositors, they were operated by whites.

At almost every meeting of the City Council, delegations came down from the South Side, asking for better relief treatment. Many times on the floor of the Council, I argued for more consideration of their needs. The Council was grudging and niggardly in its response. An alderman from a West Side ward[4] accused them of being lazy: "That's why so many of them are on relief," he said.

I replied, "It's like tying a man's hands behind his back, beating him on the head and accusing him of being a coward because he doesn't fight back." During my investigations, I found very few Negroes employed by the city and none by most of the large State Street stores.

The Council was run by Mayor Kelly just as it's now run by Daley. He was a ruthless, domineering figure. It was a one-man show. There were only three aldermen who really challenged him. Paul Douglas was one. John Boyle was another. I was the third.

At first, Kelly was friendly. But when I introduced resolutions challenging the way things were, he changed. I challenged the winking at restrictive covenants that had so much to so with the development of today's ghettos. The School Committee hadn't had a meeting in six years, I discovered. I asked why it was that white students could transfer to other areas at will, but Negro children couldn't. None of my resolutions passed. Kelly didn't approve.

[3] An association of black lawyers.
[4] Popularly known as the "West Side Bloc," celebrated for its close syndicate connections.

Oh yes, once I succeeded. I urged that the traction ordinance include a non-discriminatory provision. At the time, there were no Negro motormen or conductors working the Surface Lines. The pressure was so strong—manpower shortage because of the war—Kelly acceded. Not that he was personally in favor of it. He was never a friend of the Negro people. He rode on Roosevelt's coat tails.

He recounts Mayor Kelly's choosing a relative newcomer to the ranks of the Democratic Party, William A. Dawson, who had been a Republican, as Congressional candidate, over himself in 1942, "because I couldn't take orders."

I have never been to the Council chambers since the day I left. Sometimes I regret those four years. I was denied my full development as a political person. Every door I sought to open for the Negro people was closed. In matters of housing, no success. In employment, no success. In education, no success. All I was able to do was raise the questions and bring them out in the open. . . .

POSTSCRIPT: *"I was appointed by Roosevelt to the first Fair Employment Practices Commission. I served from 1941 to 1943. I remember the hearings in Los Angeles. A big aircraft company, employing twenty thousand, had hired no Negroes. Not until the morning of the hearings did they employ fifteen. I asked the personnel manager in what departments they worked. He replied, 'Custodial.' That means they were sweeping floors.*

"At another company, there were no black bricklayers. The reason given: one or two couldn't work alongside whites. They'd have to get enough to work one side of the building. Since they couldn't find that many, they'd employ none."

Dr. Martin Bickham

THERE WERE MORE than forty thousand unemployed men in town back in 1925. Lumbermen, railroad men, miners . . . they followed the railroads into Chicago.

He was making a study for United Charities, a private welfare agency. His interest was primarily in the unemployed handicapped worker. "There were one-legged men, who had worked the trains. Sawyers, who had lost an arm in training camps. A colony of deaf mutes." They, along with the blacks, were the first displaced.

I saw the Depression coming, as more of these handicapped came into my office. By early 1930, businessmen and social leaders in Chicago had developed the Cook County Relief Administration. They had no thought other than handing out a dole. I knew more was needed for preserving manhood. I developed a plan of work and talked it over with Ed Ryerson, who was chairman of the committee. I was called before them.

I told them about Paris in 1848, how the revolution was forestalled by men being put to work. I told them a revolution was in prospect right here if they didn't give the men a chance to participate in our economy. They accepted my plan.

It was simple. The man was not to earn more than would be required for his family to live. No more than he would be getting on relief, though the pay was union scale. He'd work so many days until the equivalent sum was reached.

Weren't you often asked: "Why would a man work when he'd get the same money on relief?"

The men wanted to work. This was the dominant theme through all the years of the Depression. I very seldom found a man who was willing to accept relief as a process of life. He knew it was debilitating. I'll never forget the morning we opened the office. It was a cold November day, 1930. Thousands of men were lined up for blocks. Many were skilled men and carried their tools with them. In the course of that winter, we put almost ten thousand men to work.

Soon after I opened that office, among the first to see me were the ward committeemen and aldermen. Hinky Dink came and old Bauler, too.[5] I talked to them courteously and asked them what they wanted. They drew out a list. I told them: if these people are on *my* list—or

---

[5] Michael (Hinky Dink) Kenna, alderman of the First Ward for almost half a century, and Matthias (Paddy) Bauler, alderman of the Forty-third Ward, forever and ever, it seemed.

that of any accredited relief agency—they will go to work. Otherwise, they would not. These politicians went out with their tongues in their cheeks. They thought they could get around me. But when they found out, everybody else got the same medicine, they stood up in the City Council and defended my program.

In 1935, when some forces were strenuously attacking the WPA, I developed a reply adopted by Roosevelt and Hopkins: the conservation of human resources. Here is democracy at work, conserving the capacity of breadwinners, conserving family life and the children of the nation. This is a fundamental responsibility of government.

The *Tribune* and some of those birds rode me unmercifully, made fun of me, tried to cry it down. But it captured the imagination of people everywhere. . . .

As I traveled through the state, I'd find crowds of men in the county seats, standing around the hall, idle, gambling or something of the kind. Hungry looking, some of them drinking a little. As the WPA developed, these men disappeared. They would be out on a work project. They began to get wages. We were now away from the relief limit. WPA gave men full wages for full work. If a man worked as a carpenter, he got a carpenter's wage.

There was very little shirking on these jobs. I surveyed them month after month, all over the state. Some of the projects, thought up by committees, may not have been too wise. These were the ones newsmen took digs at—leafraking, as they called it.

In my own neighborhood—I live in a suburb—some of my neighbors would be waiting for me on the porch. Men who had been in business and industry. I found them a number of WPA jobs.

By '31, thousands of Negroes had been laid off. They were the first to go. Scores of them were evicted from their homes in the winter of that year. Their property was sitting out on the walk. That's when the Commies came in, sharp operators from New York. They had parades and organized a riot. The police shot down six or eight Negroes on the street. This flared up the whole community. I spent the next forty-eight hours in the streets down there, trying to quiet things down.

I went down to see Ryerson and the committee of leading businessmen. They were much disturbed. They expected a riot there on Sunday. I said the only way to stop this business is to put these evicted men to

451

work at once. This was on a Saturday. They said, "We don't have the money." I said, "You better get some." By Monday morning, they had the money, and we put three hundred of those men to work in the parks that day. This quieted them. We met the issue. . . .

Evictions, Arrests and Other Running Sores

Mrs. Willye Jeffries

A wisp of a woman: the black of her skin is highlighted by the startling white of her hair. She is seated in her kitchen. From the portable radio, the announcer, in machine-gun tempo, offers the news of the day.

In the adjoining room, on a neatly made bed, a very small boy is curled in sound sleep. He is a neighbor's child.

Now WE had what was known as the Workers Alliance. Local 45, for which I was secretary and treasurer. And we were going into relief stations, sometimes gettin' arrested two, three times a day.

We were fighting for an old lady that had died. And the relief wouldn't give 'em that hundred dollars towards the burial. They didn't want to give you nothing anyway. We got a crowd of about fifty people and went to the station. We gonna stay until we get this hundred dollars for this old lady. We finally succeeded in getting it. But we were two, three days before we could catch up with this man. This man was the head of everything. You see, the police would arrest us then. But when they learned we were fighting for a good cause, then they would let us alone.

There were policemen who felt this way, who would let you alone?

Oh, that guy they used to call Two-Gun Pete.

(Startled) Two-Gun Pete Washington?[1]

That's right. He was one of them. But here at this relief station that day, they had those big patrol vans. You turned that thing bottoms up. Didn't nobody go in. We turned it over. There were a lot of Polish women in this organization, too. They had cayenne pepper, and they threw it in those policemen's eyes, and nobody knew who done it, but they went blind. That cayenne pepper, that red pepper. A lot of the time, the men were knocked down, but they get right up and fight again. The women, they played the biggest roles.

We had, oh a gentleman to die. We went over to the headquarters, and the workers were all working on the first floor then. We had a white lady, weighed about two, three hundred. We called her Ma Kuntz. She looked out. We were marching up and down, you know, picketing the place, because they wouldn't bury this old man. So we just took the corpse over there—not the man, but something resembling the corpse—and just set it in there. Where the workers was. And they all went upstairs. We run them out, just marching around there. We shall not, we shall not be moved. Singing—meaning we shall not be disturbed. When it was lunch time, those workers made up $5 and sent it downstairs and told us to get something to eat.

The police patrol came. Ma Kuntz, she spied them out there well nigh before they got there. She had that old stick, and she's just marching, keeping time with that stick, see? Well, she say, if the patrol should come, now don't nobody get panicky. Just keep on doing what they're doing. So they just come in and they just stood in the door, crossed their legs, kinda stood in the door like that and looked at us. Got back in that patrol and went about their businesses.

But we did get that old man put away. We stayed over two weeks on that first floor. We had blankets, we moved a piano in and we had a big time. We had plenty to eat, 'cause those that weren't picketing saw that we had food every day.

An old time sit-in . . .

Sure, that's what it was. It was a fight, too. But I enjoyed it, I really enjoyed it. I didn't let them think I was powerless, either.

When my husband fell dead, my daughter wasn't two years old. He

[1] Sylvester Washington, a black policeman, celebrated and feared on the South Side. He had a reputation as trigger-happy.

died on the third of September on the job out at the packing . . . and she was two years old on the eighth of November. Well, I had this little girl and I just thought everybody was pushing me around because my husband was gone. And I was very mean. Very mean.

So I moved in a place—the old building is torn down now. The bathrooms and toilets were all on the halls. You could meet the water coming downstairs. It wasn't fit for anybody to live in. I heard about it, and I moved in there to get into a fight. And I got a good fight.

I started organizing those people in there and every time I'd get one leaflet, they'd take 'em down stairs and pile 'em on the landlord's desk. He lived out in Beverly's Hill.[2] He'd come the next morning, with all those leaflets piled up there. Naturally he looked at me. "Miz Jeffries . . ." He was offering me $500 to stop organizing the building. I'd say, "Look, these people I'm organizing are my people and I do not sell them out. Your money is counterfeit."

And, honey, Wilkins[3] had him a paid-off bunch of police officers. They were detectives, plainclothesmen, from Forty-eighth Street.[4] He had a list of every widow woman living in the building, and was on relief. He gave those names to the police officers, and around eleven thirty or twelve o'clock, they'd come in and knock on your door to see if you had a man in there. See? Everywhere they found a man, they had those people on relief cut off.

So on this particular night, when the law knocked on my door, I say, "Who is that?" Me and a fella named Edward Gray was playing a game of cards. We had a drink. We had a pint of liquor settin' on the table, but it wasn't open. He knocked again. He say, "Police officer, open the door." Well, I had a broom handle. I said, "Come on in. You got your goddam key." And that time, he kicked on the door. I threw it open. He run it ag'in. I hit him. I said to my daughter, she was nine years old, "Jean, get out of bed and get down to the next block." The president of the Workers Alliance was on the next block. She went down there and got Tony, and Tony couldn't get here fast enough.

I was having a fight with Malone. Tony said, "O.K., hit him again, Sis." And he stood and held his watch, forty-five seconds, he say, "Hit him again, Sis." I got an old pen knife that I still got in my place that I pick my corns with sometimes. It was lying on the table. When he got

---

[2] Beverly Hills. A middle-class suburb on the Far South Side.
[3] Landlord of the building.
[4] A precinct police station. The busiest in the world, then.

tired of taking those hits over the head, he run under the stick and caught this arm and twisted it. That made me fall against the table. It knocked the knife off. My daughter saw it and run off the bed and run and picked it up. About that time, he just shoved his gun right into her side like that.

So he finally called the patrol. He said, "There's a fighting woman here and can't do nothing with her." I was a big lady. I wasn't skinny like I am now. So here come the police, the patrol, the old black maria. They say, "Gray, you better get out of here. We don't want you." He said to them, "Look, I would be less than gentlemanly to walk out on this woman now. I visited with she and her husband when her husband was livin' and I would be less than a man." He said, "If she gets ninety-nine, I can certainly stand a hundred." O.K., they took us both.

During the time we were waiting to go for trial, we got out a leaflet. Everybody from the South Side that belonged to the Workers Alliance was over at the courtroom that morning. So they messed around that trial all day, talk a little and call us up there.

In the meantime, Malone saw that everything was against him, 'cause he was the intruder. He had no business at my door. He called Gray to come in the hall. So Gray come back and he told me what Malone wanted. He wanted Gray and myself to pay a dollar fine and plead guilty. I said, "Look, I was a free woman when I come in here. And when I walk out I'm gonna be free." I'm not gonna have no record when I got out of here.

Well, the case was called. Wilkins had about fifty people there to appear against us. They were sitting in the back of the courtroom. We went up and the judge say, "Case dismissed." Wilkins and his wife got halfway up there and we were already halfway back. They didn't know what happened. So they all went home.

Wilkins say, "Miz Jeffries, could I take you back to the South Side." I say, "No, thank you. The streetcar runs out there. That's how I got here, that's how I'm going back."

I was doing tenants' work then and, you know, I didn't mind going to court with all those other people. They thought I was a lawyer. (Laughs.)

You see, I had a big, brown briefcase. And after, they commence to holler in court every time I go in court, two and three times a day: "This old lawyer woman!" I got a whole lot of newspapers and tore 'em up and put 'em in that briefcase. (Laughs.) Them were my law books. I had people laughin' about that all the time: "Here comes that old lawyer woman!" Goin' up front, case called . . . and I got my rosary laying there on that thing. The judge had on some, too. And I had a little pocket, here, stick the crucifix down. He thought I was a Catholic like him. (Laughs.) I didn't lose a case.

Well, I went to Washington and came back.[5] It was rainin'. When I got home that morning around eight o'clock, that whole wall was wet. There was no gutter to throw that water off. I had a two-room apartment. I sent for him. So Wilkins comes up. I said, "You see this? You think I can sleep here tonight? You put some gutters up." He said, "Come here." He showed 'em to me layin' out in the yard. I said, "Those gutters have been laying out there for over three weeks. They're no good out there." I said, "Look, I'm not paying any rent until you get those gutters up there." He put the gutters up the next morning.

And I had asked him about enamel paint. He promised me. So he had a cousin that did his painting. He sent him up with cold-water paint. I sent him back: "You can't put that on my walls." He finally come up with the right paint. Painted my two rooms beautiful.

That evening, everybody in the building wanted to see my apartment, it was so pretty. I say, "Look, I'm gonna tie up this whole floor." I tied up the whole second floor. Nobody on this floor paying no rent, 'cause everybody wanted what I wanted, and he didn't give it to 'em. All right. I got everybody's rent. And I wouldn't give it to him. I said, "You're gonna pay your rent when you got the decorations that I got." Some of 'em wanted a bed and some of 'em wanted linoleum and some of 'em wanted chairs and tables.

They got Mrs. Griffin right across from me, they did hers next. I asked her, "Now, you need anything in the apartment?" She said, "I don't need nothing like that." I said, "Then go downstairs and pay your rent." Mrs. Saddler, the next little lady next to me, she had a lot of children. And her husband was dead. I said, "Now what you want in here?" She say, "I need a mattress for my children's bed and I need some chairs and a table." He got it downstairs in the store room, but he won't give it unless you protest for it, see. I say, "Go downstairs and ask for it. But I'm not gonna give you this money unless you get what you want." She went downstairs and got what she wanted. Major[6] up and brought it. As they did the decorating, whatever those people said they wanted, they got it, before he got any rent.

[5] She attended numerous poor people's conventions in the Thirties.
[6] The landlord's building custodian.

So then he proceeded to evict me. I let him evict me. I let the bailiffs come and set me out.

They put your furniture out on the sidewalk . . . ?

Mm-hmm. Yeah, I let 'em come and did that. But we had a committee, see. We had everything arranged. We stayed out there a whole week. That was to excite the neighborhood. To what was happening. I had a very dear friend that lived around that same building. Every morning when I got tired from picketing, I'd go up there and sleep. My little daughter, she slept upstairs every night. So finally he came. "Miz Jeffries," he say, "there's no need for all this." I said, "Sure, there wasn't, but you put me out. So I'm gonna stay here as long as I want. You can't put me off. I'm not on your property, I'm on city property. The block don't belong to you."

It rained, but the men had tarpaulins. Nothing got ruined. We cooked, we had more to eat out there than we had in the house.

A lot of 'em was put out. They'd call and have the bailiffs come and sit them out, and as soon as they'd leave, we would put 'em back where they came out. All we had to do was call Brother Hilton, he's about ninety some years now. Look, such and such a place, there's a family sittin' out there. Everybody passed through the neighborhood, was a member of the Workers Alliance, had one person they would call. When that one person came, he'd have about fifty people with him.

Well, now the landlord'd disconnect that stove and put that piece of pipe away. If it wasn't up the ceiling, they'd take it, and just put the lights off. We had in the organization some men who could do electrical work, see. We'd sneak around through the crowd, and all this nice furniture sittin' on the street, and sometime it snowin'. Find out who own it, see. "If we put it back, would you stay there?" "Yes." "All right, let's go." Take that stuff right on back up there. The men would connect those lights and go to the hardware and get gas pipe, and connect that stove back. Put the furniture back just like you had it, so it don't look like you been out the door.

She moved in and out of several buildings in the area, getting in and out of trouble. She remembered precisely all her old addresses. During the 1936 Campaign, she was assistant to the Democratic precinct captain. She carried every vote in her building for Roosevelt. The landlord was a Republican. "He was gonna put me out because I carried his building

458

Democrat. I said to 'im, 'You shoulda been in that boat.'" As for the other Roosevelt campaigns, "I have swang him every time he got elected."

Nobody had any money. And we formed this organization. We would allow people to pay ten cents a month dues. Then we would give parties and raise money so we could carry on the work. But the majority of people when the war come along, they got ahold to a little money. Then you couldn't tell 'em nothin'. They didn't need you, see. Back in the Thirties, when it was really tough, and nobody was working, we divided whatever we had with each other. Being on relief, I'd get that little piece of check, pay off my rent. They were givin' you then a little surplus food, remember? You'd have to go to the station and pick up some meat and some beans and bread and stuff like that. We'd divide it with our friends.

Now, if they see you ain't got nothing, they ain't thinking about you. They'll throw it in the garbage first. Some of them think they're better than you are. Some of 'em say, "I wouldn't give 'em the time to die."

The same is when we had the picket lines and struggled to get these colored fellas on these streetcars and els. That was a tough struggle, too. But we got 'em on the jobs. Now some of 'em don't know how to treat us. Some of 'em are so nasty when you get on these buses over here. They don't know how they got it. And sometimes I call out and say, "You don't know *how* you got on here. You *got* on here, but you don't know *how* you got on here." There are some of 'em who are sympathetic and will talk about it. I say, well, it was a struggle.

Most of the people from the Thirties are gone in. I'm just around here, me and Drummer Yokum. That's about the only two from the Thirties that I know of.

Harry Hartman

It is somewhere in the County Building. He overflows the swivel chair. Heavy, slightly asthmatic, he's a year or two away from retirement. He's been with the bailiff's office for "thirty-three and a half years"—elsewhere, a few years. He had begun in 1931.

During the Depression, "I was the only guy working in the house at the time. So the windup is they become big shots and I'm still working." But he has had compensations: "It boils down to having a front seat in the theater of life." As court bailiff, he had had in his custody, a sixteen-year-old, who had killed four people on a weekend. During the trial, "he bet me a package of cigarettes, understand, he'd get the chair. And I bet him a package of cigarettes he wouldn't. When the jury come up and found him guilty, he reached back in a nonchalant way back to me and said, 'O.K., give me the cigarettes.' I gave it to him in open court and pictures were taken: KILLER BETS PACKAGE OF CIGARETTES. *You know what I mean, and made a big thing about it." The boy got the chair—"it was quite a shock to him."*

During the Thirties, "I was a personal custodian to the levy bailiff." Writs of replevin and levies were his world, though he occasionally took part in evictions. "Replevins is when somebody buys on a conditional sales contract and doesn't fulfill their contract. Then we come out and take the things back. 'Cause it ain't theirs till the last dollar is paid for. Levy, understand, is to go against the thing—the store, the business—collect your judgment."

WE HAD 'EM every single day. We used to come there with trucks and take the food off the table. The husband would come runnin' out of the house. We'd have to put the food on the floor, take the tables and chairs out. If they were real bad, we'd make arrangements, you understand, to leave a few things there or something. So they could get by. But it was pretty rough there for a lot of people.

Once we went to a house and there were three children. The table seemed to be part of the furniture company's inventory. That and the beds and some other things. The thing that struck us funny was that these people had almost the whole thing paid for, when they went to the furniture company and bought something else. So instead of paying this and making a separate bill, the salesman said, "You take whatever you want and we'll put it on the original bill." They paid for that stuff, and then when they weren't able—when the Depression struck—to pay for the new articles they bought, everything was repossessed.

You know, like radios. You remember at that time, they used to take the radio and put it in a cabinet that would cost $200 or so. The cabinet was the big thing. These people paid off the bedroom set and the dining room set. Next thing they'd want is a nice radio. The radio was put on the bill and boom! everything, the whole inventory, went.

It was a pretty rough deal. But we arranged that we left a lot of things there. On the inventory, we overlooked the beds and some of the other stuff. When we got enough, we said that the mattresses were unsanitary and we weren't gonna take it. If we had our way, we'd see that these people—if the original bill was $500 and they paid $350—we'd figure, well, you could leave a bed for $350 and you could leave a table. Or we'd say the mattress was full of cockroaches. We'd never touch the stuff. I'd just put down: bed missing. I'd ask the guy, "Can you identify that bed as the one sold?" And I'd say to the guy, "Hey, that ain't your bed. Say your brother-in-law's got it, and he gave you this one instead." Or something like that.

I mean, we always had an out. It was a real human aspect. If you really wanted to help somebody, you could. By making it easier for them, you made it easier for yourself. In most cases, people had plenty of warning that if they couldn't pay it, something would have to be done. They were broke and they were holding out as long as they could. But when it came around, a lot of cases they just gave up.

Some of the most pitiful things were when you went into a fine home, where if they were able to sell an oil painting on the wall, it could more than pay their judgment. When you went into factories, where the guy pleaded with you, so he could have his tools, understand, and do his work at home. When you took inventory, if you let him take his stuff, you know, if there was a beef, it'd be bad. But if you let him take what he needed, he didn't care about the rest. 'Cause he'd have bread and butter to go. So you'd use your head in a lot of cases.

It was a question of going in like a *mensch*. There was a rewarding part of it. If you treated that guy good, he appreciated it. And in the long run, we did better than any of the guys that went out on the muscle stuff. When we took inventory, it was our inventory that stood up. I could open a brand new box, say in haberdashery, for shirts. What's to stop me from marking one box "partly full?" All I had to do is take out a shirt and throw it out and I can call it "partly full."

We'd even go out at night to repossess cars in a different way. The attorney would want this or that car, and he'd give you an order to take it. But if we thought the guy was a nice guy and he could get some money up, understand, and he needed the car for his business, we'd tell him to park it half a block away and be sure to get hold of a lawyer, or otherwise we'd tow it in the next time. You see? We did some good.

At that time, they tried all their pullers, the companies, they tried to recover on their own. So they wouldn't have to file in the municipal court. They tried to save that. They had their own pullers. We put a check on them and we took all kinds of phony stars away from them. Chicken Inspector 23, you know. They tried everything. It got so, people were so mad at me—or, you know, anybody to come out. These guys would come out with their fake stars and say they were deputies. Then when we come out, they were ready to shoot us.

One of your greatest guys in town, a fella that's a big banker today, when we went to his home, he met us at the head of the stairs with a rifle. And my boss at the time said, "Yeah, you'll get one of us, but we'll get you, too. Why don't you cool off, and maybe we can discuss this. We don't want this place. We knew you had the money, we knew that. Why don't you get together with the lawyer and work something out? What good would it do if you shot us? We didn't ask to come here." People would get emotionally disturbed.

One time I went to take out a radio and a young girl undressed herself. And she says, "You'll have to leave. I'm in the nude." I said, "You can stay," and we took it out anyhow. All we did was throw her in the bedroom and take the thing out. But we had to have a police squad before the old lady'd let it out. Screamed and hollered and everything else. It was on the second floor and she wanted to throw it downstairs. There were many times we had sofas and divans cut up by a person in a rage.

The only way to gain entrance is if people would open the door for us. Whoever wouldn't let us in, we'd try to get it another way. There are ways, if you want to get it bad enough, you can do it.

I used to work quite a bit at night. We'd go around for the cars and we'd go around for places we couldn't get in in the daytime. We did whatever the job called for.

Remember your feelings when you had to go out on those jobs?

In the beginning, we were worried about it. But after you found out that you could do more good and maybe ease somebody's burden—and at the same time, it was very lucrative as far as you were concerned— why then you just took it in your stride. It was just another job. It wasn't bad.

But we had places where we had to take a guy's truck and take his

462

business away, and he's gone to the drawer and reached for a gun. We'd grab him by the throat, you know what I mean, and muscle and something like that. I don't know if he reached for the gun to kill himself or to scare us or what. Anyway, he went for the drawer and boom! I slammed the door on his hand and my partner got him around the neck. I opened the drawer, and there's a gun there. I said, "Whataya goin' for the gun for?" He said, "I'm going for my keys." (Laughs.) The keys were in his pocket.

We've had guys break down. We've had others that we thought would, and they were the finest of the lot. No problem at all. No matter how much they were burning on the inside.

There were some miserable companies that wanted to salvage *everything*. When we got a writ from them, we didn't want it. But we had to take it. Some of 'em really turned your guts. And there were others, it was a pleasure to know. All in all, we used to look at it and laugh. Take it for whatever it was. If you got so, you knew how to allay hard feelings there, and you knew how to soft soap 'em, you did all right.

Aside from the bed, the table—I suppose the humiliation . . .

We tried to keep it down. That they were sending the stuff back or that they were gonna get new stuff. Frankly, their neighbors were in the same classification as they were. It was things that people knew. It was part of the hardship.

When you saw guys around the house, they'd just stand by . . . ?

Depressed . . . if you came in there and they thought they were failures to their wife and children. But like everything else, they always got over it. Look, people were trying to get by as best they could, and this was our way of getting by. We might as well make it as pleasant as we possibly can. And that's what our boss wanted: less trouble. Because after all, he held a political office and he wanted good will.

The poor people took it easier and were able to much better understand than the people who were in the middle or better classes.

If I walked in a house, say, where they had furniture from Smyth[7] and you come into them . . . first of all on account of being ashamed of never having had things of this type . . . they were the ones who hit hardest of all. They never knew anything like this in their whole career. They'd have maybe a Spanish cabinet, with all the wormwood and that.

---

[7] John M. Smyth Co., one of the better furniture stores in Chicago.

And realize that if they could have sold that, they could have paid their bill what they owed, what the guys were closin' in on 'em for. We had men walk out of the house with tears in their eyes. And it was the woman who took over. The guys couldn't take it. Especially with cars, you know what I mean?

The poor mostly would make the best of it. They knew it was gonna be taken. They knew what they were up against and they knew it was only a matter of time, you know, until somebody took it away. We had less trouble with the poor. Not, I mean, that we enjoyed going against them, 'cause if they were poor, you had to help 'em more than anybody else.

It was a real rough time, but we tried to make it along with a smile. Instead of being a vulture, we tried to be helpful. But they were interesting times.

Did you encounter much resistance in your work?

No. I'd say one in a hundred.

If you'd walk in another room and somebody all of a sudden gets hot and grabs a knife and goes for one . . . I mean this can happen. But you usually get 'em when they start crying, understand. When they start crying, they're already spent. Most of all, it was surprising how they accepted their fate.

What we did then, I don't think we could do today. With the way the people look at the law. And with their action and their feeling, you know what I mean. They wouldn't accept today as they did then. What we did then was different. People still respected the courts and respected the law. They didn't want to revise our laws to satisfy them. (Weary, resigned.) What am I gonna tell you?

Today you get a guy in court, you don't like what the judge says, he calls him a *m f,* you know what I mean? So how can you go in a house, understand, where we had law-abiding citizens like we had in the Thirties? Today we'd possibly run into a lot of trouble. If we started these evictions, we'd move 'em out on the street, they'd move 'em right back in. Whataya gonna do then? Today I think it's different, a different type people.

Before if you wore a badge, it meant something. Today you wear a badge, you better watch out, 'cause somebody'll try to take you to see if they're as good a man as you are. And we're getting older, not younger. (Laughs.)

Today it's tougher for evictions than it was in our day. Today if you evict anybody, you not only have to evict the people, you have to evict about seven or eight organizations that want the people in there. And each can come up with some legal point, why they should remain without giving the landlord any rent. Now I'm not for the landlord. They bled 'em in some of these buildings, I understand. They may be perfectly right. But as far as following the law is concerned, that's something else.

Max R. Naiman

A lawyer. He is sixty-five, though his appearance is that of a short, forty-year-old wrestler.

"I was a restless youth. In 1918, at the tender age of fourteen, I shocked and thrashed grain. I made three treks to the Western states. I worked the harvest fields of the Dakotas, Montana and so on. I used to ride the rods and the blinds. I was a hostler[8] in the freight yards of Idaho. I met the Wobblies. I lived in jungles. They were great educational centers.

"As a farm worker I was victimized. One farmer beat me out of my pay. Where was I gonna find a lawyer to defend me . . . ? I graduated law school in 1932. Out of a class of eighty-five, there was just six that threatened to shove off. The mailman stayed on his job, the bank clerk stayed on his job, the policeman on his job, follow me? But I joined the International Labor Defense.[9] Defending workers. My clients educated me. We spent many hours, waiting to be called. This was the practice of the court, to keep us waiting. . . ."

THERE WERE quite a bit of evictions taking place. As good fortune would have it, the Unemployed Councils developed. They were a bunch of Robin Hoods. They would wait until the bailiff put the furniture out in the street and put it right back where it came from. If there was a padlock in the way, well, then, it was removed, you see? The people were placed back in to the despair of the landlord.

[8] He services engines at the end of a run.
[9] Hereafter referred to as the ILD.

Sometimes these Robin Hoods were so forthright and brazen, they put up a label, stick it on the door: This furniture was moved back by Local 23 of the Unemployed Council.

There was a case where the bailiff and his deputies came to move out a Negro family. The family was a little bit on the alert. They were expecting some legal action, not having obeyed the court's order to get out. The head bailiff shoved his foot in the door and yanked out his pistol to command attention. And also to compel the people to open the door. A struggle developed between the bailiff and the lady of the house. In the course of the struggle, the plank that constitutes the outer edge of the door came off. So the woman picks up the plank and —in the language of the streets—socked him across the wrist and forced him to drop his gun. With the leader of the deputies being thus disabled, they abandoned their attempts to remove the people.

Naturally, warrants were issued for the arrest of this lady and a male companion. It might have been her husband. My clients. It was my practice in those days, trusting very few judges, to always demand a jury trial. It was a long process as against bench trials, where you stand up and give your ditty and it's all over in a matter of minutes. Both my clients were deeply depressed. It's common knowledge when an officer is a victim of bodily harm, of course, a job is done on 'em. There was confusion, the lying that went on. The prosecution's witnesses were thoroughly discredited. The jury found my clients not guilty.

I was hurrying down the corridor to get over to another court. My client had her arm wrapped into mine. She was trying to hold me still for a minute. Finally she stuttered and she says, "Counsel, I loves you so much, I wish I had you in the bushes." (Laughs.) Cases such as those ran into the hundreds. This was my greatest reward. (Laughs.)

Another type of arrest was where clients used to sit at relief stations and wait all day in distress. The distress could be a baby left at home. It could simply be the red tape in getting processed. I had a woman who asked for an increase in the supply of milk for her children. She became very impatient and began to remonstrate. The relief staff could become irritable if the clients attempted to be persuasive. Naturally she was arrested.

She was taken over to the psychopathic hospital. It was a new development in administration tactics at that time. Before it was just straight out-and-out prosecution, subjecting you to fine or imprisonment. This was a new technique: the judge and two psychiatrists, no jury.

The director of Relief, Raymond Hilliard, was well known to me, and I, to him. He apparently took a very hostile attitude toward me. As I went to telephone why the psychiatrist, who was gonna testify on behalf of my client, hadn't yet appeared, I passed by Hilliard and a police officer. He made a very disparaging remark. Provocative. I paid no attention.

Suddenly I was wheeled around on my heels. I find myself face to face with Hilliard. He says to me, "I promised you something. Here it is." And delivered a blow to my face. I was flabbergasted. I backed off. He kept on advancing. I got tangled with my briefcase and my arm in getting my coat off. Somehow I managed to untangle myself before he got much closer. I went over on the counter-offensive. I know a little about the art of fighting. I learned from Jack London that you have to get the first blow and make it decisive. This is from his *Call of the Wild*.

So I advanced with all the energy I could and delivered about two or three blows to this big hulk of a man. He buckled at the knees and down he went. Of course, when you saw him again, he was bleeding profusely. The policeman rushed up and grabs ahold of me. A little, diminutive woman, who was sitting in a car rushed up and she said, "Arrest that man. I saw how that big fellow came behind that little one and hit him." (Laughs.)

He talks to Hilliard, who is now mopping the blood off his face: "Do you want me to arrest him?" Hilliard says no. Then he turns to me as though he wanted to effect reciprocity: "You want to arrest him?" I says no. The little woman persisted: "I'm from Milwaukee and I saw what happened. Arrest that man." Meaning Hilliard.

As I got to the office, lo and behold, I face a gentleman and he says, "I know what happened to Hilliard. He was taken in for emergency aid. I heard you were all beat up." I said, "You got the facts wrong." "Aw," he says, "the city editor sent me to get a picture. Point at your face with your index finger." I says, "I'll give you about ten minutes to get out of here." "Oh," he says, "don't take offense. Give me a fighting pose, then." I says, "This I'll do." The next day, the *Tribune* knighted me "Battling Naiman." (Laughs.)

The ILD would defend anyone engaged in struggle. As far as I know, it did not discriminate concerning one's politics. The police would often refer to them as Communists. I never stopped to ask.

Few people are aware that brutality did not start yesterday. It's a well established way of the past, especially in the Thirties. Some people were holding an open-air meeting in Peoria in the park. The police came around to break it up. They pulled the speakers off the stands and hauled 'em all off to jail. They also grabbed hold of a preacher who protested.

The victims were taken into a large room, say twelve by fifteen. The police made each one run a gauntlet, where they could each take a sock at 'em as they went through. They were put in jail without an opportunity to communicate with anybody. Before the local justice of peace, the whole five of 'em were convicted and sent down to the prison in Vandalia, Illinois. The ILD found out and asked if I would go down and see what it was all about.

In those days, not only were the clients impecunious. Some lawyers were impecunious. I once led a relief organization of three hundred lawyers. I was in a delegation of six that went to Washington. Ultimately, they did set up a project for lawyers. You think it's only workers who were affected by the Depression? (Laughs.) I had very little dough. I was not paid for this activity. The first three or four years of my practice, I had to borrow to live. Occasionally, one would pick up a little case and make a few dollars.

Be that as it may. On this occasion, I ran a writ of habeas corpus—that's a high and holy writ—and got all five of 'em released from custody. Outside the courthouse on this hot July day, we examined our finances, collectively. I must have had about $1.57 in my pocket. The others, of course, had nothing and they were far from home. What could be done with $1.57? We deliberated on the subject.

If one man availed himself of $1.57, there'd be nothing left for the others. We were going to divide and eat to satiety or starve to the extent $1.57 would permit us. We bought a quantity of bread and milk, basic food. (Laughs.) We had our supper in the park, and then we laid to sleep for the night. We formed a ring around a huge tree and each one's head had for a pillow the butt of the fellow in front of him. (Laughs.) The canopy of heaven and the stars above were our blankets. (Laughs.) And our guard was a most beautiful moon.

The police invariably arrested these labor leaders. A little skirmish took place in South Chicago. Three or four people were beaten and sent to the Bridewell Hospital.[10] The police lieutenant pulled out a

---

[10] An adjunct of a Chicago jail at the time.

leaflet that announced a picket line and protest. His lifted his eyes very dramatically and lifted his hands with his palms to the ceiling and said, "Man, is there gonna be trouble!" I didn't press him for what he meant. The next day was the Memorial Day Massacre of 1937.

I handled other matters in the Thirties. Some young men were going to Spain to fight on the Loyalist side. They joined the Lincoln Brigade. A lot of them streamed into my office, to look over their insurance policies, their wills. What lingers in my mind is the caliber of these men. There was this young lawyer. He was an editor for the publishers of legal books, but he wrote briefs on the side for the ILD. In the summer of '36, along that time, I got a card from this fella. Postmarked around the Pyrenees Mountains. He was crossing from France into Spain. The next I hear is that he volunteered to go over the top with hand grenades in his belt to silence a fascist machine-gun nest. The snipers got him.

Virden. A little town in southern Illinois. I stayed in the home of a miner's family. Just because the mine was shut down and he had nothing to pay his rent with, he's thrown out on the street. The furniture of the five defendants. . . .

They had a local council of unemployed. These fellows took the furniture out to the heart of the square and piled it right up against the monument . . . the mattresses and the chairs and the stove. To call attention of how courts, real estate operators and the Main Street boys treated an old pioneer family. This so infuriated the pillars of society that they brought charges of unlawful assembly.

Well, for miles and miles around, long caravans of broken-down Model T Fords, with flat tires and what not, packed the courthouse in support of these arrested miners. Neighbors would come around and visit the house. And share their food with each other. And share their little old rackety cars, going places. The warmth that existed in, let's say, a little joint misery.

Today people are so busy with their cars and with their TVs and so on, that humanism has a little blow to it.

I'm looking forward to Social Security that I may be entitled to. This is one of the programs that always appeared on leaflets raised by people in the struggle for better conditions. There was a slogan among the people: Pass Social Security Legislation. Today thousands of people, when they walk to the mail boxes and pick up their Social Security checks, owe it to these pioneers, who were called every bad name you could think of. . . .

NOTE: *He was the original, after whom Richard Wright created the law-yer, Max, in his novel of the Thirties,* Native Son.

Judge Samuel A. Heller

Retired.

I SAT in the Morals Court for a year or so. One day I had twenty-three defendants, prostitutes. About five or six visitors attended. They were obviously slumming. I said to them: "It's fortunate that we don't have people here to come to revel in the misery of others. I'm delighted that sensitive people of your type are here." (Laughs.)

The girls were all broke, not a penny among them. I thought the visitors were touched. One, the daughter of a former mayor, said, "I want to donate $25 for handkerchiefs, so the girls can wipe away their tears." Handkerchiefs!

In the Thirties, I sat in many police courts. Monday was usually the most crowded day. Most of the drunks were picked up on Saturday night, and kept in jail over Sunday. This police officer was walking up and down with a billy. He hit them in the shins: "Stand up, you're in a courtroom." I said, "Get out of this court and come back without the club." He said, "They've got to respect the court." I said, "Do you? How dare you bring a billy into this courtroom?"

One of the fellows was bloody. He said the police hit him. This same officer said, "He was talking against the Government." I said, "He's not an enemy of the Government. You are. He has a right to his opinion."

Those forty men were terror-stricken, standing in line. I said, "Are you afraid of me? Would you be afraid of me if you saw me on the streets? Please relax." I saw some of them I had discharged scrubbing floors. One was washing an automobile. He said the captain told him to do it. I told the captain to pay this man fifty cents. Since when is he entitled to free labor?

Some men I had already discharged were being lined up against the wall in the back of the room. I discovered that a railroad agent was telling them: If you don't work for us out in Dakota, the judge will send you back to jail. I said, "Get that man." He ran out.

I called the railroad office. "There's a man making an employment agency out of my courtroom. What's his name? I'm issuing a warrant for his arrest." They didn't know, they said. So I threatened to issue a John Doe warrant and arrest whoever is in charge of that office. If it's the president of the company, he'll be arrested.

The man showed up the next day. He said the police and the other judges always let him do it. That's how they got day laborers. They'd send 'em out west for six or eight weeks and let 'em bum their way back.

There was a judge in those days who had fun with drunks. He'd say, "Hold up your hands. Ah, you're playing piano." Some of them had the shakes. I said to him, "My God, what are you doing? These people are scared stiff."

These same judges who had fun with the wretched, oh, did they humble themselves in civil courts! They'd look at the names on the legal briefs. If it was a big firm, oh boy, did they bow! A lot of votes there from the bar association. These same judges, who were so abusive to the poor, were so scared here. You have a chance if the person coming in is as weak as you are—or as strong as you are. There are rights. Everybody's got rights on paper. But they don't mean three cents in actual life.

While sitting in the Landlord and Tenants Court, I had an average of four hundred cases a day. It was packed. People fainted, people cried: Where am I going? I couldn't bluff them and tell them to make an application, there's a job waiting. I was told my predecessor had taken down their names and qualifications. He promised them help. On my first day, I came across thousands of cards in filing cabinets. I told the clerk I was going to examine these files to see how many of these people got jobs. My mistake. Within twenty-four hours, all the files disappeared.

A woman with three children, one in her arms, walked all the way downtown. No carfare, no defense. Oh, they were all desperate and frightened. When I'd come in, they stand up. I would tell them: Will you please sit down, so I can sit down?

These defendants all had five-day notices: if you don't pay rent in five days, suit to dispossess is started. There is no legal defense. Out of a job means nothing, sickness means nothing. I couldn't throw these people out. So I interpreted the law my way: five days was the minimum. No maximum was set. I gave everybody ten days. Of course, I offended the real estate brokers. I made them still more angry by allowing an extra day for each child in the family. Finally, I was giving them thirty days.

About that time, a group of real estate men invited me to lunch. Each was introduced: this one was five thousand tenants, that one, eight thousand. There were about sixty thousand tenants represented—if I may use that word—by these few men. After the meal, the man who had cordially invited me, suddenly became hostile. The others smiled, as though they knew what was coming up. He said, "I'm going to speak straight from the shoulder. Isn't it a fact that judges favor tenants because there are more voters among the tenants than among the landlords?" All of them laughed.

I got up and said, "You didn't speak straight from the shoulder. If you did, you'd have said, 'Are you playing politics in court?' Now I'll *answer* straight from the shoulder. If I were playing politics, I'd play politics with youse guys." I purposely used the vulgar expression. "Because you have long pockets and long memories, and you support those who serve you. Who are these tenants who come into my court? They're destitute, out of jobs, poverty-stricken. When election day comes, one's out looking for a job, another will sell his vote for fifty cents to buy his baby milk, and most will forget it. There's no political reward in helping the poor. But what makes you think the man who sits in judgment between the landlord and the tenant must have the mentality of a renter?

"Someday you'll succeed in intimidating the judge who sits in my place. He'll have the chance of throwing four hundred families out on the streets of the city each day. When a man is hungry and out of a job, and nobody knows it, he can control himself. But when his few pieces of furniture are thrown out into the street, his neighbors know it. He has nothing to lose. A wise man comes along and says, 'Idiots, why don't you organize? Quit paying rent. When you get the five-day notice, ask for a jury trial.' "

One of the real estate boys said to me, absolutely astonished, "Can *they* ask for a *jury* trial?" So I said to this brilliant man, "What makes you think the right of trial by jury is limited to rent collectors?

"With a jury trial, you can hardly try one—at most, two—cases a day. At the rate of two thousand cases a week, in four months you'd have 32,000 people asking for jury trials. If they closed every court in this state, you still wouldn't have enough judges to try your case. And then you'd wish there were a man like Heller, who had the courage to tell you: Why don't you mind your own business and let him mind his business?"

One of them said, "I admire your candor, but you're not doing yourself any good." He was right. When I ran for office, the real estate organizations sent out thousands of letters: I have no respect for private property. They defeated me. They keep score. The poor are so busy trying to survive from one day to the next, they haven't the time or energy to keep score.

There was a man running against me, who said you can evict people without notice, if it's done peacefully. We agreed to have a public debate. He didn't show up. In the election—in the very neighborhood where many of the tenants live—he got thousands of votes and I got hundreds.

During those hard times, I learned a good lesson. A good deal of the misery that the poor suffer—and ignorance—is due to the fact that they're not organized. They're isolated, brainwashed.

I could have remained on the bench until I died. If I could have degraded myself . . . just go along. I couldn't do it. But I was on the bench for twenty-one years—and that, to me, is a miracle.

A Young Man From Detroit and Two Girl Companions

He is twenty-four and does collection work for a bank. "I call people who are slightly behind on their bills. I feel sorry for a lot of them, but it's my job. . . .

"The salesmen are robbers. They quote a person one figure and when it comes time to sign the contract, they give a different figure. They don't tell the people the interest rates they're paying on some of these loans. The people we deal with are not very educated . . . honest, hardworking people. Many of them colored. And poor whites."

The two girls—one, twenty, the other nineteen—work in the same bank as the young man . . . "in check credit. You can continually borrow and make monthly payments on it. It can go on for years and years. . . ."

The Young Man's Story

ONE OF THE GENTLEMEN at work was telling me he wanted to take his daughter to a hamburger drive-in. She said: I don't want to be seen with you. It seems like it's not "in" to be seen at a drive-in with your parents. You're some kind of kook. You never saw this during the Depression, 'cause they went through everything, all for one and one for all, within a family.

I think a Depression now might even solve this problem of civil rights. It would be man for man. I don't think there'd be as much prejudice. If you're going to be standing in a bread line, whether you're white or black, and someone of the other skin will give you a piece of bread, you're not gonna turn it down. This might solve the whole problem.

I think some people would really go insane. My family has told me of people who had really gone crazy during the Depression of '29. The financial losses they took. I think history would repeat itself all over. A lot of people, who invest a lot of money, who are used to living on fifty, sixty thousand, they might just go crazy, not having that much. He wouldn't know what to do. Psychologically, his mind couldn't take being a second-class average Mr. Joe, after being on top for so long.

I try to put away something. I have it either in investments or a savings account. Then if I want something, I know the money is there. I bought a suit one time on credit, and after I paid the suit off, I tore up the credit card. Another thing: my generation, we're so clothes-conscious. But I betcha they're worrying about how they're gonna pay that next charge when it comes up.

Does your job disturb you, at times . . . ?

No, 'cause I feel it's bread in my mouth and I've got a job to do. The only thing that bothers me is when a nice guy—we have to garnish his wages, 'cause that's the only way we're gonna get that money. He's got to realize when he signs a home improvement contract, he signs this note—he has this obligation. It's not me. I didn't put the knife in their back. I'm just doing a job.

The First Girl's Story

To ME, the Depression's a story told. Just like World War II. To me, it means nothing, except I'd hate to experience it. I'm not used to low-class living.

474

What kind of living are you used to?

Middle-class. (Laughs.) I'm on my own now, and it's rough. (Laughs.)

What do you think would happen if a Depression came today?

If I could get hold of a pill, that would end everything. And everyone I really cared for, I wish they'd do the same thing. I'd be afraid to experience it. I just couldn't take it. I couldn't see having my family starve, I really couldn't.

You've never experienced want yourself . . . ?

Yes, I want a lot of things right now.

By want I mean need. Have you ever experienced going without?

I was afraid of my father. Getting a pair of shoes or something like that, it was left up to me. When I baby-sat, I used my own money because I didn't want to ask my father for too much. But I never starved. I've never really been hungry.

When you see people on welfare, what are your thoughts?

I feel sorry for them and I don't. Their husbands or themselves can go out and get work. I know there are so many jobs to be had by them. The Welfare Department should be cleaned up. All the good money that's going to waste.

One of my girl friends, she works at this steel company. She was this secretary there. A lot of colored fellas worked there. This one she was telling me about: he'd work for six months or eight months, he'd quit. First, he'd get thrown in jail and then he'd call up his wife so that she could get aid from the state. That's what really gets me. I can't really see my good tax money going to waste. And I haven't been paying it that long, but I will be.

I just want one happy life, that's it. And have a family and a nice little home, car, just to be comfortable. A housewife.

The Second Girl's Story

I'm middle-class, happy, middle-class. My father works in a sausage company, he delivers meat. My mother is working in a die-cast company.

475

DEPRESSION, it means loneliness. It was just a time when everything was very lonely and depressing. Everybody was like individual, fighting to keep their family alive. My mom, when she was young, went through it. So now she tries to give me everything, because I don't have to go through it.

My father's family had it real good. There were four guys in the family. Each one had their own car in the middle of the Depression. They had brand new cars. They had a nice home. All my mom keeps telling me is how hard she had it and how easy my father had it.

If it happened today, I don't think the country'd be able to stick together like they did in the first one. I think the whole place would just fall apart. And America'd be completely ruined. Everybody seems to be just out for themselves. You gotta get a bigger car than your neighbor. Your daughter has to be dressed better than your neighbor's daughter. Where back then it seemed like everybody tried to help each other, now it's hard to get a relative to help you. Really. Why should I help him? I could have a bigger car and show that I'm much better. Because today everybody's all to themselves.

Like when I lived in Jacksonville, Florida. I was six or seven. A false alarm went off—they blew the alarm to take shelter for fallout. In case there's an air raid. Well, it went off. We were in school at the time. Everyone was going nuts. People were running around. They didn't care what happened to the kids. They were all to themselves.

They were all running out into the street. There were so many cars, you couldn't even get across the street. People wouldn't let you in their cars, if you wanted to get in. There were mothers running, and their kids were following behind them screaming.

It was so terrible, these people. You could tell they didn't care. Some people thought the Russians were coming. And the teacher said: Everybody, get under your desks. Other teachers were running around: What are we gonna do with the kids? And then it seemed like the teachers just disappeared.

Outside was terrible. Cars were packed. Women were running with children, and maybe four men in one car, and yet they wouldn't open the cars to let the women with the kids in. They weren't even going two miles an hour. There were so many people, nobody could get by. Yet nobody would help anybody else.

It's probably gotten worse now. If anything ever happens—like you say, a Depression—probably the whole country would be overrun by

Communists or it'll be nothing . . . unless everybody gets together and fights for everybody, not just themself.

I feel sorry for most people on welfare today, I really do. But it's something I don't like to talk about because when I think of things that depress me, I'd rather just block it out of my mind and say, well, I'll think about it tomorrow. There are rotten ones, and you just don't want to take the time to think about the poor ones.

I consider myself rotten in those ways. Because I think about these people who are really starving, right now, living in shacks—and yet I'd go completely out of my mind, so I'll think about it tomorrow. I don't want to think about it now. There's a lot of people who don't even take the time to think at all.

Honor and
Humiliation

Eileen Barth

In 1933, she graduated from a university, where she majored in social service administration. Immediately, she was engaged as a case worker for the county.

I WAS TWENTY-ONE when I started and very inexperienced. My studies at school didn't prepare me for this. How could I cope with this problem? We were still studying about immigrant families. Not about mass unemployment. The school just hadn't kept up with the times. We made terrible blunders. I'm sure I did.

There was a terrible dependence on the case worker. What did they feel about a young girl as their boss? Whom they had to depend on for food, a pitiful bare minimum? There was always the fear of possibly saying the wrong thing to her. The case worker represented the Agency. We seemed powerful because we were their only source of income. Actually, there was little we could do.

I had a terrible guilt feeling. I was living rather well sharing a nice apartment with two other girls. My top pay was $135 a month, which made me well off. Yet there were constant layoffs. I always felt that if I lost my job, I might go on relief, too. So I never really had a sense of security myself.

I think most case workers felt as I did. Though there were quite a few who were self-righteous. They felt some of the people weren't looking hard enough for work. Or they were loafers. They believed some of the stuff that came out in the newspapers. Even then. They sometimes made it very difficult for the clients. There was a lot of hypocrisy and sham.

I worked with both whites and blacks. One could say the blacks were more accustomed to poverty. But they still said, "I wouldn't come here if I had work." There was a lot of waiting around the relief offices. Where they came to pick up their food orders. These places were mostly old warehouses, very dismal. That was another thing, dispiriting. Sitting around and waiting, waiting, waiting. . . .

The case worker was often the object of their anger. Where else could they give vent to their feelings? So they took it out on us. They didn't know the cause of their problems. Of course, there were tensions. At one time, my job was to cover the entire city. I often worked at night. I found myself in very strange neighborhoods at all hours. I took it as a matter of course. Yet I knew when these people felt put upon. . . .

In 1934, a case worker was killed by her client, while sitting in the chair at his home. A youngish white man living with his mother. The story is: she had promised him a job. CWA was coming in. He was so overwhelmed by his joblessness he became maddened to the point where he shot her. He dragged his mother to the district office. He killed the supervisor, a clerical worker and then killed his mother and himself.

We were all frightened. Bulletins were issued to all the offices: case workers could take a moratorium on visits. We weren't told we *must not* visit. So I decided I'd go anyway. I was young and felt the clients needed me. (Laughs softly.) If this were to happen now, would I go? I don't know.

I remember, for a time after that, peering into the window, before I rang the bell. I guess I was pretty scared. One family said to me it was terrible, but some case workers deserve to be killed. He looked at me and smiled, "But not you, Miss Barth." (Laughs.)

I'll never forget one of the first families I visited. The father was a railroad man who had lost his job. I was told by my supervisor that I really had to *see* the poverty. If the family needed clothing, I was to investigate how much clothing they had at hand. So I looked into this man's closet—(pauses, it becomes difficult)—he was a tall, gray-haired man, though not terribly old. He let me look in the closet—he was so insulted. (She weeps angrily.) He said, "Why are you doing this?" I remember his

479

feeling of humiliation . . . this terrible humiliation. (She can't continue. After a pause, she resumes.) He said, "I really haven't anything to hide, but if you really must look into it. . . ." I could see he was very proud. He was so deeply humiliated. And I was, too. . . .

Ward James

He is seventy-three. He teaches at a fashionable private school for boys, out East. He was born in Wisconsin; attended school there.

BEFORE THE CRASH, I was with a small publishing house in New York. I was in charge of all the production and did most of the copy. It was a good job. The company was growing. It looked like a permanent situation. I was feeling rather secure.

I realized that people weren't secure in the publishing business. There was no tenure. We didn't have any union. That was the first move I made, organizing the Book and Magazine Union in New York.[1] A lot of white collar people at the time felt unions were not for them. They were above it.

Until 1935, I had my job with this publishing house. They insisted I take a month vacation without pay and a few other things, but it wasn't really too distressing. It became tougher and tougher.

I was fired. No reasons given. I think my work with the union had a good deal to do with it, although I couldn't prove it. What hurt was that I'd gotten pretty good in writing technical books for boys. I had three published. By now, with things getting tight, no publisher wanted any book that wouldn't be a best seller.

I was out of work for six months. I was losing my contacts as well as my energy. I kept going from one publishing house to another. I never got past the telephone operator. It was just wasted time. One of the

[1] "I was also engaged at that time in organizing the Consumers Union. Our idea was to help people of what we now call the inner city to buy more intelligently. Advertising was even less regulated than it is today. Merchants were on the make. Now, Consumers Union, still a worthwhile organization, serves the middle class well. But I'd like to think some day it will get into the ghettos and do some real work."

worst things was occupying your time, sensibly. You'd go to the library. You took a magazine to the room and sat and read. I didn't have a radio. I tried to do some writing and found I couldn't concentrate. The day was long. There was nothing to do evenings. I was going around in circles, it was terrifying. So I just vegetated.

With some people I knew, there was a coldness, shunning: I'd rather not see you just now. Maybe *I'll* lose my job next week. On the other hand, I made some very close friends, who were merely acquaintances before. If I needed $5 for room rent or something, it was available.

I had a very good friend who cashed in his bonus bonds to pay his rent. I had no bed, so he let me sleep there. (Laughs.) I remember getting down to my last pair of pants, which looked awful. One of my other friends had just got a job and had an extra pair of pants that fit me, so I inherited them. (Laughs.)

I went to apply for unemployment insurance, which had just been put into effect. I went three weeks in succession. It still hadn't come through. Then I discovered the catch. At that time, anybody who earned more than $3,000 a year was not paid unemployment insurance unless his employer had O.K.'ed it. It could be withheld. My employer exercised his option of not O.K.'ing it. He exercised his vindictive privilege. I don't think that's the law any more.

I finally went on relief. It's an experience I don't want anybody to go through. It comes as close to crucifixion as. . . . You sit in an auditorium and are given a number. The interview was utterly ridiculous and mortifying. In the middle of mine, a more dramatic guy than I dived from the second floor stairway, head first, to demonstrate he was gonna get on relief even if he had to go to the hospital to do it.

There were questions like: Who are your friends? Where have you been living? Where's your family? I had sent my wife and child to her folks in Ohio, where they could live more simply. Why should anybody give you money? Why should anybody give you a place to sleep? What sort of friends? This went on for half an hour. I got angry and said, "Do you happen to know what a friend is?" He changed his attitude very shortly. I did get certified some time later. I think they paid $9 a month.

I came away feeling I didn't have any business living any more. I was imposing on somebody, a great society or something like that.

That ended with a telegram from Chicago, from the Illinois Writers Project. I had edited a book for the director, who knew my work. He needed a top editor to do final editorial work on the books being published, particularly the Illinois Guide. I felt we really produced something.

This was the regional office, so I worked on Guide books for four or five other states. The *Tribune* said it cost two million and wasn't worth it. No matter, they were really quite good.

The first day I went on the Project, I was frightened as much as I'd ever been in my life. My confidence had been almost destroyed in New York. I didn't know a single person here. But I found there was a great spirit of cooperation, friendliness. I discovered quickly my talents were of use.

Had been in Chicago about a month or two. I remember I wanted to buy a suit on credit. I was told nobody on the WPA could get credit in any store in Chicago. It was some years later before I could establish credit of any kind.

I bought an inexpensive radio, an Emerson. My son, David, who was four or five, dictated letters to his mother to be sent to his grandmother: "We have a radio. We bought it all ourselves. Nobody gave us it all." Apparently, he had resented that he and his mother had been living rent-free in Ohio. And she may have been getting clothes from her sister. Yeah, there was an impact even on the very young.

Do you recall the sentiments of people during the depths of the Depression?

There was a feeling that we were on the verge of a bloody revolution, up until the time of the New Deal. Many people, among them, intellectuals, without knowing what else to do, worked with the Communist Party. The Communists naturally exploited this. It began to change with the New Deal and pretty much came to an end with the Russian-German pact.

I remember a very sinking feeling during the time of the Bank Holiday. I walked down to the corner to buy a paper, giving the man a fifty-cents coin. He flipped it up in the air and said, "This is no good." And he threw it in the middle of the street. (Laughs.) Some took the Holiday as a huge joke. Others had hysteria, like this newsboy: there isn't any money, there isn't anything. Most people took it calmly. It couldn't get much worse—and something was being *done*.

Everyone was emotionally affected. We developed a fear of the future which was very difficult to overcome. Even though I eventually went into some fairly good jobs, there was still this constant dread: everything would be cut out from under you and you wouldn't know what to do. It would be even harder, because you were older. . . .

Before the Depression, one felt he could get a job even if something happened to this one. There were always jobs available. And, of course, there were always those, even during the Depression: If you wanted to work, you could really get it. Nonsense.

I suspect, even now, I'm a little bit nervous about every job I take and wonder how long it's going to last—and what I'm going to do to cause it to disappear.

I feel anything can happen. There's a little fear in me that it might happen again. It does distort your outlook and your feeling. Lost time and lost faith. . . .

Ben Isaacs

It is a house, with garden and patio, in a middle-class suburb on the outskirts of Chicago.

I WAS IN BUSINESS for myself, selling clothing on credit, house to house. And collecting by the week. Up to that time, people were buying very good and paying very good. But they start to speculate, and I felt it. My business was dropping from the beginning of 1928. They were mostly middle-class people. They weren't too rich, and they weren't too poor.

All of a sudden, in the afternoon, October, 1929 . . . I was going on my business and I heard the newspaper boys calling, running all around the streets and giving news and news: stock market crashed, stock market crashed. It came out just like lightning.

I remember vividly. I was on my route, going to see my customer. It didn't affect me much at the time. I wasn't speculating in the market. Of course, I had invested some money in some property and some gold bonds, they used to call it. Because I have more confidence in the gold bonds than the stock market. Because I know the stock market goes up and down. But the gold bond, I was told from the banks, is just like gold. Never lose its value. Later we found to our sorrow that was fake.

They turned out to be nothing. Those banks, they'd take the people's money that they were saving, they would loan it out a mortgage on the property. The property was worth $100,000, they would sell $200,000 gold bonds on that property. The banks.

I have suspicions the bankers knew. They were doing it for their own personal gain. If it wasn't for the Crash, this fake would probably keep going on. Lotta these banks closed down overnight.

We lost everything. It was the time I would collect four, five hundred dollars a week. After that, I couldn't collect fifteen, ten dollars a week. I was going around trying to collect enough money to keep my family going. It was impossible. Very few people could pay you. Maybe a dollar if they would feel sorry for you or what.

We tried to struggle along living day by day. Then I couldn't pay the rent. I had a little car, but I couldn't pay no license for it. I left it parked against the court. I sold it for $15 in order to buy some food for the family. I had three little children. It was a time when I didn't even have money to buy a pack of cigarettes, and I was a smoker. I didn't have a nickel in my pocket.

Finally people started to talk me into going into the relief. They had open soup kitchens. Al Capone, he had open soup kitchens somewhere downtown, where people were standing in line. And you had to go two blocks, stand there, around the corner, to get a bowl of soup.

Lotta people committed suicide, pushed themselves out of buildings and killed themselves, 'cause they couldn't face the disgrace. Finally, the same thing with me.

I was so downcasted that I couldn't think of anything. Where can I go? What to face? Age that I can't get no job. I have no trade, except selling is my trade, that's all. I went around trying to find a job as a salesman. They wouldn't hire me on account of my age. I was just like dried up. Every door was closed on me, every avenue. Even when I was putting my hand on gold, it would turn into dust. It looked like bad luck had set its hand on my shoulder. Whatever I tried, I would fail. Even my money.

I had two hundred dollar in my pocket. I was going to buy a taxi. You had to have your own car to drive a taxi, those days. The man said: You have to buy your car from us. Checker Cab Company. So I took the two hundred dollar to the office, to make a down payment on the taxi. I took the money out—he said the kind of car we haven't got, maybe next week. So I left the office, I don't know what happened. The two hundred dollar went away, just like that. I called back: Did you find any money on the table? He said no, no money.

Things were going so bad with me, I couldn't think straight. Ordinarily, I won't lose any money. But that time, I was worrying about my family, about this and that. I was walking the street just like the easy person, but I didn't know whether I was coming or going.

I didn't want to go on relief. Believe me, when I was forced to go to the office of the relief, the tears were running out of my eyes. I couldn't bear myself to take money from anybody for nothing. If it wasn't for those kids—I tell you the truth—many a time it came to my mind to go commit suicide. Than go ask for relief. But somebody has to take care of those kids. . . .

I went to the relief and they, after a lotta red tape and investigation, they gave me $45 a month. Out of that $45 we had to pay rent, we had to buy food and clothing for the children. So how long can that $45 go? I was paying $30 on the rent. I went and find another a cheaper flat, stove heat, for $15 a month. I'm telling you, today a dog wouldn't live in that type of a place. Such a dirty, filthy, dark place.

I couldn't buy maybe once a week a couple of pounds of meat that was for Saturday. The rest of the days, we had to live on a half a pound of baloney. I would spend a quarter for half a pound of baloney. It was too cold for the kids, too unhealthy. I found a six-room apartment for $25 a month. It was supposed to be steam heat and hot water. Right after we move in there, they couldn't find no hot water. It wasn't warm enough for anybody to take a bath. We had to heat water on the stove. Maybe the landlord was having trouble with the boiler. But it was nothing like that. The landlord had abandoned the building. About two months later, all of a sudden—no water. The city closed it for the nonpayment of the water bill.

My wife used to carry two pails of water from the next-door neighbors and bring it up for us to wash the kids and to flush the toilet with it, and then wash our hands and face with it, or make tea or something, with that two pails of water. We lived without water for almost two months.

Wherever I went to get a job, I couldn't get no job. I went around selling razor blades and shoe laces. There was a day I would go over all the streets and come home with fifty cents, making a sale. That kept going until 1940, practically. 1939 the war started. Things start to get a little better. My wife found a job in a restaurant for $20 a week. Right away, I sent a letter to the relief people: I don't think I would need their help any more. I was disgusted with relief, so ashamed. I couldn't face it any more.

485

My next-door neighbor found me a job in the factory where he was working. That time I was around fifty. The man said, "We can't use you." They wouldn't hire nobody over forty-five. Two weeks later, this same man said, "Go tell Bill (the name of the foreman) I sent you. He'll hire you." They hire me. They give me sixty cents an hour. Twenty-year-old boys, they were paying seventy, seventy-five cents an hour. They were shortage of hand, that's why they hire me.

I read in the paper that some place they're paying a good salary, dollar an hour. I took the street car to go look for that job. On the way . . . I don't know what happened . . . something, like kicked me in the head. I said: I'm going back to my old business. People are now doing good, people's working in the war factory. So I got off the street car and I came into the store I was dealing with before.

I told them I was gonna go back to my old business. They laughed at me: What are you gonna sell? You can't find no merchandise. I said: Whatever you people are selling, I'll do the same thing. All this time that I was working, skimping, and my wife was working, I had saved $400. So I invested that $400 and start to go back into business.

Thank goodness, things changed. I came back. I came back. It was the end of 1944. If I had stayed in the factory I would probably still be on relief. Lotta people, even my wife, they told me don't go. We have only a few hundred dollar saved, you're gonna throw it out into the street. I said I'm not going back in the factory.

So for you the hard times were—

1928 to 1944. I was realizing that many and many other people are in the same boat. That gave me a little encouragement. I was looking at these people, waiting in line to get their relief, and I said, My God, I am not the only one. And those were wealthy people . . . they had failed. But still my heart won't tick. Because I always prayed in my heart that I should never depend on anybody for support. When that time came, it hurted me. I couldn't take it.

Shame? You tellin' me? I would go stand on that relief line, I would look this way and that way and see if there's nobody around that knows me. I would bend my head low so nobody would recognize me. The only scar it left on me is my pride, my pride.

How about your friends and neighbors?

They were the same thing, the same thing. A lot of them are well-to-do now and have much more money than I have. But in those days, we were all on relief and they were going around selling razor blades and shoe laces.

We were going to each other's. That was the only way we could drown our sorrow. We were all living within a block of each other. We'd come to each other's house and sit and talk and josh around and try to make a little cheerfulness.

Today we live far away from the rest of our friends. Depression days, that time, we were all poor. After things got better and people became richer and everyone had their own property at different neighborhoods, we fall apart from each other.

Howard Worthington

I DON'T KNOW how I survived. I was working with a bond house on La-Salle Street. We were specializing in foreign securities. I was so grateful we were not mixed up in the stock market. Thank goodness, it wasn't going to affect me. The next thing I know, we failed. The head of the company disappeared with $7 million worth of assets.

Oh gosh, a friend of mine was making $25,000 a year. They cut him to $5,000. He walked right over the Board of Trade Building, the top, and jumped. I wasn't even makin' five at the time. (Laughs.)

I don't think I should have been in the investment business. It was pressure from my wife. A man in that business has to know lots of people with money. I was never an opportunist. I like people because they're people. They could be broke.

I got a job with the Cook County Board of Public Welfare. I had to eat. I earned $95 a month—I was going to say a week. (Laughs.) My boss was as nice a colored woman as you ever met in your life. I had a title—I keep saying it. I don't know whether it was true or not. I was Director of Occupational Assistance and Self Help. There was no status working for Illinois Emergency Relief. My wife felt it a great deal more than I did. She dolled it up. She used that title among her friends. I really enjoyed some of the experiences, I really did.

I have to pay tribute to my wife. She managed an apartment building in Evanston. We got a six-room apartment free. I also picked up gadgets that I bought for fifty cents and sold for a dollar. It bought my lunch, paid my carfare. I drove some of my friends nuts. Every time I got a new gadget, I was in to sell it to 'em. They had jobs.

There was a fellow invented something called Bergenize. It was beautiful to demonstrate. You'd dip your hands in a can of it. It was colorless. Then you'd dip your hands in the dirtiest grease, wash it off with cold water, and they'd be as clean as could be.

I had six cans of Bergenize. Before I went out to sell, I'd dip my hands in this stuff. I walked into a garage and went to the grease pit. I dipped my hands into it, walked over to the faucet and turned the water on. My hands got dirtier and dirtier and dirtier. (Laughs.) You see, I had washed my hands back home and forgot to put the stuff back on. I can still remember the garageman looking at me and shaking his head. I panicked and walked out. (Laughs.)

"My dad was sales manager for a leading coffee house. He was over sixty-five and still earning an excellent salary. This was in the early Thirties. Jesus, I remember this as though it were yesterday. My mother was playing the piano, I was playing the mandolin, my brother and sister were singing. The doorbell rang. A special delivery for my dad. He was fired. After thirty-eight years with the company. Just like that. A cloud over the whole festive. . . .

"Dad opened an employment agency for salesmen. He had been president of the Sales Managers' Association. He had a lot of friends. But he never made it. A salesman would come in, suit not pressed, needed a haircut. My dad would give the guy two bucks. The guy'd get the job and my dad never collected his fee. (Laughs.) He died in 1936."

I think I drank more than I should have. It was a release. I didn't lose my job because of it. But . . . my wife's mother lived with us. She wasn't a member of the WCTU[2] but she was close. She considered it a weakness on my part that I wasn't able to withstand all the tensions without some release. In the afternoon, I had a few drinks. I had to time it so I didn't get home until after she was in bed. (Laughs.)

My wife did such a good job of managing that Evanston building, the bank moved us to a four-room flat on the South Side. A hell of a neighborhood. She had rented all but our own apartment, so the bank said:

---

[2] Women's Christian Temperance Union; headquarters, Evanston.

Out. They got $150 for it. This was the reward for doing a good job.

We had four generations living in that four room. My son, my wife, her mother and her mother's mother. Grandma was delightful, but trouble! Margaret and I slept under the table.

Oh, I tell you. . . . If I only had the guts and knowledge I could have done so much better. I would have gone into something that I felt. . . .

When I got out of school in 1921, we had kind of a depression in '21. (Laughs.) While at the University, I managed the *Illinois Agriculturalist*. I think my place was with *Prairie Farmer* or something of that nature. But I happened to get into the investment business. If I had gone into agriculture. . . .

POSTSCRIPT: *"I'll never forget that Depression Easter Sunday. Our son was four years old. I bought ten or fifteen cents' worth of eggs. You didn't get too many eggs for that. But we were down. Margaret said, 'Why he'll find those in five minutes.' I had a couple in the piano and all around. Tommy got his little Easter basket, and as he would find the eggs, I'd steal 'em out of the basket and re-hide them. The kid had more fun that Easter than he ever had. He hunted Easter eggs for three hours and he never knew the difference. (Laughs.)*

"My son is now thirty-nine years old. And I bore him to death every Easter with the story. He never even noticed his bag full of Easter eggs never got any fuller. . . ."

Stanley Kell

It is an all-white, middle-class neighborhood on Chicago's Northwest Side. "The majority of homes here are around from $17,000 to $24,-000." He heads the organization dedicated to the proposition of keeping blacks out. "My white Christian neighbors? They agree with me about the integration problem. But they think I'm too strong, too active."

His is a one-family dwelling on the corner. Among the appliances within, aside from a 25-inch color TV set, are a stereo set, a Hammond organ and a grandfather's clock.

It is after supper. His wife is at a neighborhood meeting: tonight's subject—the school busing crisis. Their two small boys, in the manner of small boys, are running around the house, excitedly, laughing. . . . He is forty-two years old.

IT'S A LONG WAY from Maxwell Street,[3] I'll tell ya. Where I had to dig for a loaf of bread. If I told my children exactly what a kid had to do in them days to get something to eat in his stomach in order to live. . . .

The first thing that hits me about the Depression is my dad. His business—he's coming up from downstairs. We're living above the machine shop that my dad owned. He was in the cap business, making caps for milk bottles. I remember him coming up the stairs and saying: "Well, the business is gone. We're broke. And the banks have no money."

And my mother being a European woman of Polish ancestry, and knowing how to make ends meet, I remember her for many, many weeks, pots of soup. And the main ingredient was that loaf of bread. I had been used to going for bread. But from now on, it was a daily venture. In them days, we used to wear knickers. This daily venture was always full of peril.

I think it was only a nickel a loaf. I had to take that nickel and make sure I got to that Maxwell Street. There was a long viaduct, and you had to be sure you ducked through there to save that nickel. Coming back with that bread was full of danger, too. There was always somebody waitin' to grab it off ya. Poor kids, too. No doubt they were hungry. Negro kids. I was such a good runner, later I got to be a track man.

The reason I fight probably as I do, I remember my dad organizing a committee of depositors for closed banks. And passing out handbills is one of the things I remember. For many a month and many a year, he held meetings. He did a pretty good job on this, 'cause I remember him saying you got two cents on the dollar back, that would be quite a windfall. He often wondered how he'd pay his mortgage off. The few cents he was able to get out was enough to pay the mortgage on the house.

He had to sell the machinery for so much on the dollar in order to pay off his debts. He never did owe anybody. When he went bankrupt, everybody got paid off on whatever he owed. Not like you read today, in today's paper, a guy owes six, eight million dollars and they laugh it off.

---

[3] Chicago's open market area; gradually disappearing as expressways converge upon it.

In them days it was some kind of scandal if you owed somebody any money.

I remember my first bank account. I carried a sign during the Depression. In Chicago, there was a great day in them days, was May Day. And it wasn't Communistically affiliated. In Chicago, May Day was the day for everybody to express themselves. Whether they were a bum, he could get in line of the parade. Or a big fraternity alliance.

My dad was president of the depositors of the closed Polish banks. I'll never forget the sign I carried: I AM A BOY. YOU HAVE TAKEN MY MONEY. DOES MONEY MEAN AS MUCH TO YOU AS IT DOES TO ME IN YOUR BANK? IF YOU NEED THIS MONEY, TAKE THE KEYS TO THIS BANK, THROW 'EM IN THE LAKE AND STAY IN JAIL. The man in jail at the time was the banker. He is buried in St. Adalbert's—he committed suicide. I'm tryin' to think of his name, 'cause he was a great legend behind closed banks.

If you'd say a thing like that: it's Communist. Well, it isn't Communist. I remember the unions being organized in them days. And little splotches of factory environment that was dissatisfied would march in these parades. Certain factions would assemble on May Day: WESTERN ELECTRIC EMPLOYEES: ORGANIZE FOR BETTER BENEFITS. DON'T JOIN THE COMPANY UNION. That was a bad word.

As a kid, I remember picking up ten milk bottles for a penny in the junk yard to get that penny. And with these pennies, I was able to accumulate enough pennies to buy a bag of marbles. I used to get a hundred marbles for a dime. That was ten marbles for a penny. Then I'd sell 'em five marbles for a penny. Which made me a penny. Even then, I was trying to accumulate money by buying something and selling it. And to this day, it seems to instill itself upon me as I'm always buying and selling. It seems to get in your blood, it seems you seem to get like Jewish. I'm doin' the same thing with my kids now. I'm trying to instill that they can buy something, sell for a profit, put the profit away, take the next and reinvest it. The Depression taught me this.

I say we shouldn't go through another, it was so horrible. I feel for some of these people today that feel that we owe them a living that perhaps this is what we need. But then I go back and say: well, if it happens to them, where will we . . . to try to say to my children you'll have to go through Depression. Or that loaf of bread that's so easy getting now, that they'd have to go get it like I had to chase somewhere. And who would give it to 'em for a nickel?

My mother used to go with me down Maxwell Street. I can still see the mess of people walking back and forth, and barkers trying to get you into the doors and gypsy women trying to tell your fortune. Even now that I know about prostitution, I can just imagine they used to operate on that street in them days, winkin' at ya. Women on the corner winkin'. What was she winkin' about? In them days, you didn't know what she was winkin' about. Today you'd know.

And oh, how could I forget the booze, the beer-running days. I used to go to Sacred Heart Church. The man that used to distill the booze and beer used to hide it in the basement of the church. Revenue officers would never believe that the church was the sanctity for the beer. I remember going down in the basement of the church, the beer smell was there. I'd say: what are all these barrels of beer doing here? And good Father Healy, he used to be quite a little devil with all that beer down there. I think he survived because he used to hold the beer down there. If the revenue agents ever knew that the churches were the sanctity for beer runners! Joe Fusco—he was investigated several years ago for his tie-in with Capone and all that—Joe Fusco was a great supporter of the Sacred Heart Church. Of course, Sacred Heart Church was a great supporter of Joe Fusco, too.

Beer, there was a Depression, but they still had their beer. I don't remember anyone being alcoholic or get out of hand like they do today. I own a liquor store. How'd I ever get in the liquor business? I don't drink, I don't smoke, I love children. And people in Chicago hate me. They think I'm a bigot and a racist.

You try to show your children respect, and you try to show your children authority, but there's always gonna be in this world somebody that thinks they're better than the law. Today it's the breakdown of law and order today causing all this turmoil that we're having today. I don't think it would be allowed in them days to let it get out of hand, where you can spit at an officer or hit him or dare him to touch you. You woulda been smashed. Why, you didn't even talk to 'em, you were thrun in. It never happened to me, but I can still see some of the older folks that something happened, they were thrun in the old paddy wagon. I remember crawling in the alley of the old Scotland Yard station to see the men behind the bars. By looking at those people behind the bars that I gained respect for law and order.

That's another thing. I don't ever remember saying to my parents: I don't want to do my homework. The work was there, you had to do it as part of your survival. Bred into you as part of your characteristic. The Polish people are famous for the belt. I remember my dad saying: go stand in the corner and kneel on some rice, that'll teach ya. I remember many a time saying: Gee, dad, I can't learn this. Well, get in that corner and kneel on that rice.

In them days you knew the parents were authority. You knew if you behaved anywhere, there was a lickin' in store for you. A good solid whack. To this day I still carry a belt.[4] I can say to myself: what's good for me, what helped me to learn, and I've never been arrested for disobedience—these kids today, why are they getting away with murder, talking back with their elders? When I have kids standing in front of me: Who do you think you are, telling me not to do this? Who are you to say I can't break this? I'd like to take a poke at 'em or take a belt and give 'em a couple of good whacks. Then they say: We'll sue ya. In them days the father was the boss.

I remember running up the streetcar and meeting the father. Also I remember not running up to meet him because I had it coming for something I done wrong. What I did wrong, I can't recollect today.

Did you ever feel scared of your father when he wasn't working? When he felt low?

Oh, yeah. After all, he's lost his bank account, he's worked hard, he's a foreigner, he can't speak English, in fact he had to change his name in order to get a job. He was discriminated. I suppose he blamed a lot of things on this happening, on Hoover. I suppose he would take it out on the kids. But a kid could sense there was something wrong, and he'd stay away from the issue.

The people that were in the adjoining flat, they had to go on relief. They were Lithuanians and were very wonderful people, too, with their culture. They survived the Depression on potato bread, with gravy and soup.

Bones, beef bones, and there was a big hunk of meat besides. The beef bone, the celery, the cabbage, the beets or onions and tomato, all thrun in that pot. And what a fragrance! Today you don't smell them fragrances. And loaves of bread. How can you forget the loaves of bread? They musta been about ten pounds and about three feet in length. These are the reflections that I treasure.

---

[4] Though he carried the belt, during the conversation, his little boys ran under and around him, delightedly, unafraid.

I do remember this family getting for relief purposes prunes, which they used to make prune pudding. I remember raisins being in the diet of reliefers.

In them days, you didn't get it like today, $400, $500 because they have three kids. In them days you got a bag of groceries and this was it. You learned how to eat and make it last. Everybody learned how to prepare. If she didn't know, she'd give it to somebody who knew how. And they divided between themselves. I don't remember anybody ever being hungry.

As hard as it was, my mother was always able to put away two cents, five cents, ten cents, to make sure we worked ourselves out of that community. It was a good community, but they had their mind to progress farther.

Here I'm talkin' about the hard life I had, here's a guy comes through tellin' 'em, well, we have to integrate, everybody's gonna live equal. Oh no, not after the way I worked like I did, nobody's gonna live equal. You start off rough, if you come rough into Chicago. You don't start in equal with me. You go on the bottom rung and start climbing up. The Negro has got to learn. God put us in this world just to fight our way forward, up the ladder or down the ladder. Whether we're black, white or green.

Suppose a Depression came to America again?

Chaos, chaos. I just dread. I don't talk about it. Never be able to live. I'd be able to live. My house is almost paid off and the taxes are high. You wouldn't believe you're sitting on $900 a year taxes. Thank goodness I know how to make a buck. But if things keep on the way they are, and making me a Nazi between my neighbors and my Negroes, I won't have no business.[5]

If a Depression hits, what would happen? It would be a civil war. There'd be murder, greed, there would be manifestation of such magnitude as has never been seen in this world. Money means nothing, it's hunger. To get whatever another person has, I'll take it away from 'em. If somebody doesn't have it, they'll do everything to get it.

Was there a different attitude among people in the old days?

Yes. If anybody knew how to make something to keep or last longer—they traded recipes, they traded clothes—they'd give hints and there was no what they call keeping up with the Joneses. If the lady across the

[5] The majority of patrons at his liquor store are black.

street got color TV, I got a color TV. I'm against it. A lady down the street got an organ, you have got to get an organ.

You have a Hammond organ. . . .

Yeah, I know. See, everything is because somebody else has got it, you gotta have it. We gotta keep up with the Joneses.

POSTSCRIPT: *Before the conversation ended, he was asked one last question:*

Are you . . . do you have a conflict within you . . . ?

"Yes I do. I have a conflict inside of me. It hurts that I have to say to a Negro I can't accept you as a neighbor because of the area. In front of my club, I took it upon myself to speak for open housing. And the people booed me. I did such a terrific job for open housing that they threw books at me and everything. When the vote came out, it was my hand only for open housing. I'm not really against integration, but the membership says to me: we're going to be against integration. My club having four hundred people has made me president. That puts me in charge of their opinion. They tell me they can't live with a Negro, and I believe it.

"By coincidence, today, I'm talking to a most charming little Negro girl. You'd want her for a neighbor. But you can't. It's fantastic, a shame. It's gotta come out of your mouth the opposite of what you feel inside. Isn't that crazy?"

Horace Cayton

Sociologist; co-author (with St. Clair Drake) of Black Metropolis.

He had come to Chicago from Seattle, where his father was editor of a Negro newspaper, and he himself had served as a deputy sheriff. His grandfather, Hiram Revels, was the first black Senator from Mississippi, following Reconstruction.

I'LL TELL YOU how naïve I was. This was along 1930, 1931. When I first got to Chicago, I came into the Union Station, got into a taxi cab

495

and told the driver, "Take me to the best Negro hotel." He turned around and looked at me like I was a fool. He took me to the only hotel he knew. It was a whorehouse. I was never so hurt in my life. I don't know what I imagined. Something, oh, fancy, like the Ritz. Only it wasn't the Ritz.

I had a romantic notion about the black belt, the cabarets, the jazz—that was there, too. When we rolled out Michigan Boulevard and cut over to South Parkway, it was exciting. I walked around the streets, day and night, just like I did in Paris. It was a fantastic world. I met wealthy Negroes, but I knew nothing of the masses.

I was eating lunch on the South Side. I saw a group of Negroes marching by, marching by twos together, and silent. Not loud and boisterous. These people had a destination, had a purpose. These people were on a mission. They were going someplace. You felt the tension.

I still had my dessert to eat, but I was curious. I got in the back and marched along. I was dressed better than they were, but they showed no animosity toward me. I said to the chap next to me, "Where we going?" He said, "We just gonna put some people back in the building. They were evicted."

It was a ramshackle building. A shanty, really. A solid crowd of black had formed and they were talking great . . . what Robert E. Park[6] called an "indignation meeting." They used to have these indignation meetings down South, where Negroes just let off steam because they couldn't contain themselves, from some injustice that had been done. They'd lock the doors and have an indignation meeting and curse out white people. Here was action.

They moved out from the church just rags of covers, broken down bedsteads and a chiffonier back into the house. Then they had a spiritual meeting. The weather was below zero at the time. We stood there and heard the sirens. Police cars. Everyone grew tense. A frail, old black woman waved her hand and said, "Stand tight. Don't move." They started to sing: ". . . Like a tree that's standing in the water, we shall not be moved. . . ." Then they sang another wonderful song, "Give Me That Old Time Religion." (He sings a phrase, ending with ". . . It's good enough for me.") They added Communist words: "It's good enough for Brother Stalin, and it's good enough for me." And they had other verses, like: "It's good enough for Father Lenin, and it's good enough for me."

---

[6] Professor of Sociology at the University of Chicago; mentor of Horace Cayton.

While they were singing, the tension was felt in the crowd. The sirens were there like a Greek chorus, coming from all directions. Somebody said, "It's the Red Squad." The old woman said, "Stand fast." But they came through like Gangbusters, with clubs swinging. They pulled the old woman off, but in the general confusion, she disappeared in the crowd.

I didn't run because I was so taken up with this great drama. I had never really felt the Depression and what it had done to human beings till then. I don't know why I wasn't clubbed. I was on the outside and I was better dressed.[7]

Truth is, the Communists made very little inroads with the Negro people. The Communists embraced many of the causes, but the black people didn't take them seriously. For example, the Party would have a float in the Bud Billiken parade down South Parkway.[8] But they really didn't penetrate. They raised issues that Negroes were interested in and they learned a lot from the Communists. They accepted help from anybody. Why shouldn't they? They'd be damn fools if they didn't.

One of the reasons the Communists flopped is they didn't know how to deal with the Negro church. The church was the first Negro institution, preceding even the family in stability. Even in slavery where there was really no family tie, the first organization was the church. The Communists came in flat-footed with this vulgar Marxist thing. I was lucky I didn't join. Now I say that, 'cause at my age, I don't give a damn what I join. Hell, I mean, let them drop dead, the bunch of them.

The church played a role in the black community during the Depression . . . ?

Adam Clayton Powell's Abyssinian Baptist Church, his dad had, had led that church and got a great deal of strength from it. Father Divine epitomized that whole period. He was the essence of it. Father Divine was God in a brass bed.

One time in New York, I was in the Village. There was a little fish and clam juice restaurant. A pretty little white girl worked there. She said, "I was born in Father Divine's Heaven." She was ten or twelve before she found out Father Divine wasn't God. She was white as snow.

---

[7] His impressions of this incident appeared as an article that year in *The Nation.*

[8] An annual parade on the South Side, sponsored by the Chicago *Defender.* It was a feature for children. Merchants and social clubs of the area would have floats.

She was from Crumb Elbow, that was his community. All his churches were called Heavens. He would buy hotels, and they'd be Heavens. He fed more people during the Depression than anybody.

That indignation meeting in Chicago shocked me to my depths. The grimness of hunger and no place to sleep, of cold, of people actually freezing to death.[9]

I remember the original lie-in. Negroes were out of work, after promise after promise after promise. One day a group of them lay down in front of the streetcar tracks. They all had white conductors and white motormen. They couldn't come through. Mayor Kelly tried to make a deal with them. They were going to lay down and stop the God damn traffic from running through. They would erect a wall of human beings, a black wall. They hoped for jobs. They didn't really hope for and didn't get platform jobs. But there were people digging ditches for the utilities, just common labor. And Negroes weren't on there. So they said, "We'll just shut off the damn thing. It can't work and we're starving and these gangs of workers doing most of the menial work were white. Right in the black community.[10]

Do you remember the attitude of the black community then in contrast to today's . . . ?

In spite of the Depression, there was hope. Great hope, even though the people suffered. To be without money is a disgrace in America today. The middle class looks upon welfare Negroes as morally corrupt because they haven't worked. But in the Depression, there were so many whites who were on relief. So the Negro would look, and he wouldn't

[9] "Mrs. Mary Eggleston's apartment at 1449 E. 65th Street is without heat in Saturday's near-zero temperatures because the building's owner hadn't connected a furnace. . . . For warmth, Mrs. Eggleston and her four children wear sweaters and overcoats and huddle around a kitchen range. . . . There used to be five children, but 14 year old Nadine died Monday. She had sickle anemia and her mother thinks her death was hastened by the cold . . . 'the doctor told me to keep her warm. . . .'" (Chicago *Daily News,* January 25, 1969)

[10] "They were laying that track from Fifty-first and South Park to Cottage Grove and none of the colored boys was workin'. And some of 'em said, 'What the hell are we gonna do?' So one of the fellas said, 'Follow me.' So they fell in line right there on Fifty-first Street, and that gang of men walked up to them fellas that were working and take the shovels away from them. And told 'em to get the hell outa there. They'd taken them jobs, they been workin' on the surface lines ever since . . ." (Clyde Fulton, an eighty-five-year-old black man, recalling the early Thirties)

see any great difference. Oh, there was a difference: a disproportion of Negroes on labor than on skilled jobs in WPA. But if Negroes were on relief, so were whites: we're gonna have a better day. That was the feeling. That hope is gone. It's crystal hard now. It's hatred and disillusion.

What was the black people's attitude toward Roosevelt?

Oh yeah, that was something. He broke the tradition. My father told me: "The Republicans are the ship. All else is the sea." Frederick Douglass said that. They didn't go for Roosevelt much in '32. But the WPA came along and Roosevelt came to be a god. It was really great. You worked, you got a paycheck and you had some dignity. Even when a man raked leaves, he got paid, he had some dignity. All the songs they used to have about WPA:

> I went to the poll line and voted
> And I know I voted the right way
> So I'm askin' you, Mr. President
> Don't take away this W P and A.

They had a lot of verses. We used to sing them:

> Oh, I'm for you, Mr. President
> I'm for you all the way
> You can take away the alphabet
> But don't take away this WPA.

When they got on WPA, you know what they'd mostly do. First, they'd buy some clothes. And tried to get a little better place to live. The third thing was to get your teeth fixed. When you're poor, you let your teeth go. Especially, the child. If she's got a rotten or snaggle tooth and that tooth may ache, dulled by aspirin or something or whiskey. Then they'd pull them out. They'd get their teeth fixed. WPA. . . .

There was some humanity then. We don't have humanity today. No, God damn it, these bastards, they're not going to do right, as sure as I'm sitting here, they're not gonna do right. I've withdrawn. I feel like I felt when I was in France and Germany in 1935. We're heading, driven like figures toward a tragedy. I see nothing to do. It's futile.

NOTE: *At the time of this conversation, he was working on a biography of Richard Wright.*

W. L. Gleason

He is eighty years old; lives by himself in Minneapolis. He types out a diary—"daily happenings just for the hell of it, to keep boredom from my door."

WELL, I went through that Depression, which took place during the good years of my life. The good physical years, the best mental years. But they were years which made a lot of bums out of good people.

In 1922, I bought a lot and, with my lily-white hands, I built a summer cottage on it. In the same year, I bought a Ford touring car. In the same year, I bought a modern six-room house for six thousand bucks. And in the same year, my wife bought a four-hundred-buck piano.

Damned if I didn't pay it all off, every penny. And then give the whole damn thing away as a divorce penalty, along with barrels and barrels of interest at six and a half percent.

However, when my thoughts run back over the years, as they often do in my dreams, both day and night, one incident, event, happening, never fails to come in for a review. . . .

My oldest boy, Bob, managed to hook onto a job, cutting lawn down on the lake shore. There was no power for the lawn mower, other than legs, arms and lungs. Bob used all of them. In order to spend the two bits, which he was to get for the job (twenty-five cents to you, $00.25 to the bank).

The old gal who owned the place was in the money. Bob completed the job in record time, and knocked on the door to collect his two bits. The old gal opened the door and exclaimed, "Oh, but you didn't trim the trees." She closed the door. Bob took off down the road, and never, never did come back for his two bits.

And the hell of it is that all these many, many years, it sticks out in my mind like a damn sore thumb. I suppose it will be growing like a cancer through all the days I have left. There were so many things happened during the Great Depression. There were some nice things happened, there were worse ones. Like three major strikes, which touched closely on my friends. So why in the billy hell has this happening taken the limelight for me over all the others?

Strive and Succeed

> This was Luke Larkin, the son of a carpenter's widow. . . . He had a pleasant expression, and a bright, resolute look, a warm heart, and a clear intellect, and was probably in spite of his poverty, the most popular boy in Groveton.
>
> He has struggled upward from a boyhood of privation and self-denial into a youth and manhood of prosperity and honor. There has been some luck about it, I admit, but after all he is indebted for most of his good fortune to his own good qualities.
>
> —*Struggling Upward* by Horatio Alger, Jr.

Harry Norgard

A free-lance commercial artist.

IN 1933, I lost my job. It was the year of the Century of Progress. It came as a shock. 'Cause one day the man tells me I'm set for life, and the next day he tells me I'm all through. "We have to tighten our belts."

I went out to free lance, find my own accounts. Within two months, I was making half again what I left. This was in the heart of the Depression. I always felt deeply in my heart, you could always sell something if you offer the buyer something better than he's getting.

It didn't matter to me whether there was a Depression or not. Bemoaning your fate gets you nowhere. I knew wherever you make an effort, you make headway.

It's true a great many people lost their shirts. In many ways, it was their own fault. There were millions of people buying stock, being hot shots. It stands to reason when people engage in a business they know nothing about, they're gonna get hurt.

One man I know made a killing in the market—on paper. "I'm gonna have a house on Sheridan Road, I'm gonna have a Packard, I'm gonna have a chauffeur, I'm gonna have everything." Hoggish. He used to take his children to see four or five apartment buildings: ". . . this one is for you, that one is for you, this other is for you." He was gonna leave his children a big legacy. He had no business calling it his property. His equity in each of them was so small, they were topped by first, second and third mortgages. The man was up to his eyebrows in debt on each one. His dominoes fell, one on top of the other.

People with real money didn't get hurt during the Depression. Because they were able to take advantage of the distressed property. Buying them up. The people who got hurt were people who had no business doing what they were doing in the first place. They were lambs in a den of wolves.

I was prudent. I always liked to feel liquid. I knew where I could lay my hand on a dollar whenever I needed it. The Bank Holiday didn't even touch me.

Some people were victims of circumstance. It was no fault of their own. Many people did their best to find something to do. I heard of a former banker who became a caddy at the golf club he had at one time been a member of. There were people with a great deal of spunk, who wouldn't frighten easily.

Someone once said to me: The worst thing that can happen to a man is to have a good job. Because when you have a good job, you're in a safe, secure, snug harbor. People will stay where it's nice and warm and cozy. A man really does better for himself if he's thrown to the wolves, so to speak.

Our greatest successes in business were made by illiterate men. They couldn't speak the language. They couldn't write. They made no appearance you could be proud of. From sheer necessity, they had to go into business for themselves. They had to roll up their sleeves and go out. If they became junk men, they opened a junk shop. Then they were dealing in scrap metal. Before you know it, they were steel tycoons.

The Depression *made* a lot of people. I know one man who found himself out of work. He began thinking and thinking. He wrote sixteen letters to manufacturers and explained he could offer them a service at no cost. Three or four of them wrote back. In a few short years, he became an extremely wealthy man. He gave them something they needed, even though at the time they didn't know they needed it.

Al Capone operated a soup kitchen. People would line up a half a block long. He was becoming kind of a Robin Hood in that era. He would go to ball games, people would get up and cheer him. They didn't regard him as an underworld character. They thought of him as a sport. He was spreading good cheer among the poor. Things like that were happening everywhere.

They don't give you medals for money. But they don't give you medals for being poor, either.

Roosevelt was to the people like the Holy Father was to the Catholics. At first, I felt pretty much the way everyone else did. Later on, it became apparent to me he was selling the country down the river to the big unions.

The consequence: when the first sit-down strike happened in Detroit —I happen to know some people who lived through it—these strikers tore the place apart inside. They tore up the pipes, they broke the windows, they ripped the machinery out, they did hundreds of thousands of dollars damages.

You heard this from . . . ?

People who saw it, people who sat it. And they weren't even punished for a thing like that. I'm sure if General Motors had sent in a squad of goons to wreck the headquarters of the United Automobile Workers, something would have been done about it. Unionists got special treatment all along the line.

I think a great deal of this was encouraged by Socialist agitators. I never marched up and down the street to help myself. It never occurred to me to blame anybody but myself for what was happening to me. It would be the last thought to enter my mind.

As for the WPA, a picture comes to my mind of men leaning on shovels, as I'm driving through Outer Drive. I've seen photographs of these people, sitting on curbs and smoking cigarettes.

So today a man will do the least he can for the most he can get. In the Depression, those who acted that way never lasted very long. In those days, you could pick up an employee any hour on the hour, just open up the window and yell and somebody would come in for a job. Those who retained their job had the fear of God put in 'em. One thought was uppermost in their minds: I got to do as good a job as I can or else I'm gonna get canned. I firmly believe the only way you can get most people to do a job is to put the fear of God into 'em.

Do you think another Depression might be good for us?

No, I wouldn't say that. What I do say is we are not all deserving the sympathy some of these bleeding hearts have for the people. A great deal of their misery is self-inflicted. These people are constantly looking for assistance. What would happen if we all had this attitude?

General Robert E. Wood

In the library of his Lake Forest home, he is watching a television baseball game. At eighty-nine, "I have three bosses—my wife, my secretary and my nurse. It's terrible." (Laughs.)

"MacArthur and I were great friends. We were cadets at the Point together. We were in the same class. When he formed the Rainbow Division, he offered me a colonelcy in it. I was transferred to Pershing's general staff and became Quartermaster General of the army."

He had left Montgomery Ward, a mail-order house, in 1924 and came to Sears, Roebuck as a vice president.

I ALWAYS ASSOCIATED the Depression with one of the best things I ever did for Sears, Roebuck. I founded All-State Insurance in '31, which was the depth of the Depression. It proved an enormous success. Now its earnings are in the neighborhood of ninety million a year. All-State started out pretty slow. But it never lost money, even in '31.

It was a mail-order business. I transferred it into a chain store as well as mail order. Pass goods over the counter instead of through the mail. I gradually converted it from mail order serving the rural people exclusively to a chain store in the cities. That's what made me president. In 1928. The same year as Hoover, who was a friend of mine.

With the Crash, you became aware of trouble because your sales absolutely disappeared. Business didn't drop off gradually. It took a plunge, just like that. Of course, it hit me as well as everybody else. But I felt sure things would come back.

I voted for Roosevelt in '32. Yeah. That surprise you? I thought it was time for a change. While I was a Republican, I voted for Roosevelt. I've forgotten just when I became disenchanted with Franklin D. It was sometime during his Administration. I liked him, couldn't help liking him. I was one of the few men in so-called Big Biz that voted for him and supported him. He was very kind to me. He offered me several appointments. Had me down to Washington several times. But he did oversell the truth, you know. He'd shift from one thing to another. I lost confidence in him.

Did the Wagner Act affect you in any way, the emergence of the CIO?

Not with Sears. We've never had a strike. We had no organization. Sears was one of the first firms in the United States that shared the profits with employees. We've always had peaceful labor relations. For over fifty years, we never had a strike. We're not unionized. But we never lifted a finger. We told employees they could join a union if they wanted to: if you want to join, go ahead and join it. But they never figured it brought them anything.

Things began to pick up around '34 and '35. It was '36 before they began to pick up strong. '32 was bad, '33 was bad, '31 was the worst of all. We cut, including myself. I started with a salary cut. We had to cut or we'd have perished.

We had to lay off thousands of people. It was terrible. I used to go through the halls of the building and these little girls, they were all terrified. I remember one Italian girl I called in. She had a family of ten, father, mother and eight children. She was the only one working. It was terrible. But we had to lay 'em off. I could see how frightened to death they were.

The Depression ended in '33. But it didn't begin to recover on a big scale until '36.

Some people say it didn't end until the war.

Oh, that's ridiculous. You began to pick up in '36. It wasn't big but it was all right.

Were there friends of yours who suffered?

Neighbors and friends. Not my college friends because I went to West Point and all my classmates were in the army. They were immune at that time. It was a good place to be. (Laughs.)

I was very fortunate. While I had no capital of my own, I had a very good salary. I didn't have to shut down, so to speak. (Laughs.) No, I didn't have to cut down on servants or anything like that.

I always felt the Depression was temporary. You couldn't stop this country. I founded All-State in the darkest period, didn't I?

POSTSCRIPT: *"I was an isolationist, you know. I still think it was a mistake for us to have gone into the war. We've got an empire here, and we've got two great undeveloped continents, North and South America. Why should we get mixed up in the affairs of Europe which is an old-time continent? We've got unlimited room to expand, and why we should get mixed up in an old, tired Europe, I couldn't see."*

A. A. Fraser

For thirty years, he looked over the books of a lumber company. At last, he became an officer and a member of its board.

WE HAD SAWMILLS in Arkansas, Mississippi and South Carolina. The money was flowing in so fast, we didn't know what to do with it. But that year, '28, we liquidated these holdings. There wasn't any more timber to cut. We left in Arkansas 45,000 acres of stump.

We bought it at $1, $1.50 a thousand. But we figured by the time it ran out, it was worth $5 a thousand. So when a million feet went through the mill, you could deduct $5 million from your income tax return. Depletion allowance. You see, when the stump is left, that's the end of the capital. Like oil and coal.

Was an attempt made to replant?

No, not in those states. We had houses to liquidate and a railroad and a big store. These towns belonged to the company. You should have seen our offices, beautiful. Like old plantation mansions. Our money was made with cheap wages. A dollar a day. Mostly Negroes. We sold it en bloc to speculators.

People would fight for those jobs. A case of supply and demand. Why didn't we pay more? That was the going wage. You had to make money. You see, without money, we would never have been able to build those mills. We were capitalists. It was free enterprise. We employed a lot of men, so you certainly can't blame us.

What did these people do when the homes were sold?

What did who do?

The people who lived there.

Oh. Some of them got jobs with other companies. Some of them lost their jobs. That was a tragedy.

Then I realized my life-long ambition to be on the board of directors of several companies. First thing I know, I'm sixty-eight and in good health. So I quit. I finally made it to the Gold Coast. So I just follow my own investments. Got rid of all the cats and dogs. I only buy blue chip stocks. All I do is study stocks and give advice to widows, who live in my building. They stop me in the lobby every day: "What's good today?" I give 'em free advice.

Tom Sutton

A lawyer, with offices in a suburb, west of Chicago. His wife, a physician, shares the quarters.

He heads Operation Crescent, an organization of white property owners:

"The wealthy have a place to run. My people are caught in a trap. They're lower middle class, the forgotten ones. Every member on our board is a former liberal. Our best ideas come from the skilled laborers. They have the pulse of the people. They feel abandoned by their priests and their schools. They are hurting, hurting, hurting. . . . They have no place to go but themselves. They don't hate Negroes. They may prefer

whites, but that doesn't mean they hate Negroes. And nobody really wants to admit hate. . . ."

THE REASON a man works is not because he enjoys work. The only reason any of us work is because if we don't work, we don't eat. To think that any man may sit in society and say: I don't wanna. O.K., if you want to starve, starve. He'll work. Believe me, he'll work.

Those who went through the Depression have a little more pride in their possessions, have a little more pride in the *amount* of possessions they have. They know that it was a fortunate person in the Thirties who have as much as they have today. They're much more money conscious.

Money is important to people, especially children of the Depression. You can see when they come into the office here, they're trying to see: Am I a wealthy or am I a poor lawyer? If I'm poor, they don't have that much confidence. They're sort of happy that they're shaking hands with some of the wealthy.

I hate people to know how much money I have. I would never want to admit it if I was broke. I would never want to admit I was a millionaire. One thing the Depression did was to make us secretive. It was ours. During the Depression, nobody would admit that they were broke. My friends who went through the Depression with me, I'll never know how much money they have, because they won't talk about it. Whether they're broke or wealthy.

In the Depression, you didn't want to admit you had problems, that you were suffering. This is mine. If I don't have the money, that's my problem, not your problem. If I did have money, that's not your affair. I don't know if our family was particularly secretive. . . .

The last Depression was blamed on the lack of regulation. This Depression which is coming will be blamed on too much regulation. The way we'll try to get out of it is to truly go back to a free system of exchange. Whether that'll work, I don't know.

People blamed Hoover for the Depression. He had no control over it. If the Depression hits now, they'll blame the Government. You always have one danger when you blame Government: disturbances tend to create chaos. Chaos will create a demand for a strong man. A strong man will be most repressive. The greater the Depression, the greater the chaos.

I don't think we're basically a revolutionary country. We have too large a middle class. The middle class tends to be apathetic. An apathetic middle class gives stability to a system. They never get carried away strongly, one way or the other. Maybe we'll have riots, maybe we'll have shootings. Maybe we'll have uprisings as the farmers did in Iowa. But you won't have revolution.

I remember standing in my father's office in the Reaper Block,[1] watching a march on City Hall. I was seven or eight. I remember his comment about red flags and revolution. He said, "The poor devils are just looking for bread." They weren't out to harm anyone. All they were marching for was food. I thought: Why were they looking for food? There were plenty of stores.

There was always talk in the house about the financial crisis. I remember listening to Father Coughlin about money changers in the temple. I lived in a Protestant neighborhood. It seemed there were more Protestants listening to Father Coughlin than there were Catholics. My father listened to him. He was like everybody else: anybody that had a solution, they'd grab onto it.

But he was a liberal and a Democrat and a strong supporter of Roosevelt. One of my favorite pastimes, during the campaign, was sitting across the front room, watching him repeat after Roosevelt as Roosevelt talked. You know, telling off the other side. Since most of his brothers-in-law were conservative Republicans, he enjoyed that particularly.

I went along with him. I can remember writing a term paper in high school: "The Need for a Planned Economy." I take it out and read it once in a while, just to see how foolish youth can be. How could anyone take that seriously?

The income tax changed me. I was making some money. It burned me up thinking now I had to file it with the Government. It was the fact that I had to sit down and report to somebody what I made. I had to keep records. And I'm so tired of keeping records.

I'm a happy-go-lucky Irish type. As long as I've got enough money to pay rent next month, I'm happy. I don't like to sit down: Did I make a big fortune or did I lose a deal? How much did I pay the secretary? How much did I pay for the cabs? Half the time when I had arguments with Internal Revenue, I don't keep track of those things. We have to be bookkeepers: ten cents for the cab tip, twenty-five cents for a meal, what have you. We're building the bookkeeper type. The New Deal and all those agencies contributed to this. . . .

---

[1] An office building in the Loop, since torn down. Many lawyers had their quarters there.

Of course, we had social problems thrown in with the Depression. We had the beginning of the liberal movement in which Communists were in the forefront. They made use of labor with strikes, sit-ins, the many problems we had at that time. A free economy would have straightened out these problems.

Looking back, many individuals would have been hurt, etc. But as a result of the programs, many more are now hurt than would have been hurt at the time. In an attempt to alleviate a temporary situation, they've created a monstrosity.

Many of the people I knew in law school, children of the Depression, talked about how they had to quit school for help. The father who had been a doctor took a janitor's job. They would do anything rather than take public money. Then it was just the thought that you couldn't take someone else's money. It was a matter of pride. Now I have some of that left over. . . .

POSTSCRIPT: *"And there's the added feature: I am somewhat of a snob. My children are going to know some of the best of society. Not the best, necessarily. Though money is an indication. They're going to know the best who are working a little harder, applying themselves with greater effort, and will be going further. We work a great deal for our children. It's nice to think there are wonderful ditchdiggers in the world, but that's for somebody else's daughter."*

Emma Tiller

In the mid-Thirties, she found herself "on my own, and the world was sorta new to me. I wasn't no longer where I had to take orders. I'm grown, I can do as I please, go where I want to, come back when I want to. . . ."

I TRAINED my own self to cook. I always been a listener and a long memory. I could listen to one of Betty Crocker's whole programs and memorize for years afterwards. Cook it. I never doubted myself in nobody's kitchen. Which always means I had a job. You felt this independent because you knew they needed you. That's why I studied to be a good cook.

If it was an ordinarily rich family, you had the whole house under your control. So I ordered the food and I cooked somethin' and it didn't turn out the way I want it, I dumped it out and cooked somethin' else. 'Cause I'm tryin' to learn how to be a good cook. Rich people could afford me. 'Cause when you make mistakes, if I got money, I ain't gonna cry about you wasted sugar, you wasted this, you wasted that. I quit those jobs.

In 1937, I was workin' for a very wealthy family in Wichita Falls. Her husband was a doctor. She told me she was going to have forty people for lawn dinner, ate outdoors. When you work for them rich people in the South, you don't go and buy no frozen peas and beans and rolls. Uh-uh, you cook them rolls, you shells them peas, you string them beans. . . .

She was supposed to get some caterers in to serve this food, because this food has got to be cooked in the kitchen and served outside. I kept askin' her: Has she seen the caterer mans? No, she said, she'd get 'em. So this week came and I asked her again. The dinner was to be Tuesday. No, but she'd get 'em.

So I said to myself: This woman intends to make me serve this meal from this stove, after cookin' for forty people. And you serve it in courses, yeah. So I said: Mm-hmmm, I better start plannin' what I'm gonna do with her now. Another thing I didn't like about her, she was a very stingy person. I was gettin' kinda bored with this house anyway. And gettin' more independent, too. Remember, I was a pretty good cook by now. She'd have this habit . . . when I get through work, I want my money, and I don't want to have to ask you for it or wait two hours, while you fool around. Give me my money. I tell 'em: give it to me while I'm livin'.

Every week when I get through workin' she would go and get in bed. She would lay there and pretend she was sleepin'. I come in. (Utters a mock sigh.) Oh, go in there, Emma. I think my purse is in there. And when I get back with that purse, she'd be dozed off again. And you gotta stand there and call her gently: here is your purse.

So I knew she wasn't gonna get anybody to help me. So that Monday, week before, we had to start the gatherin' of vegetables. She says, "We'll start orderin' the stuff Monday." They always say "we" when they mean "you." So Monday we brought about a bushel and a half of green beans, washed 'em, packing 'em away. She ordered about three hundred pounds of ice, 'cause the refrigerator couldn't hold it all. Then she was gonna serve peaches with cream on 'em. I opened all the peach cans and poured 'em in crocks and then put that down in ice.

She recounts, in loving detail, the other foods to be prepared: the caviar and a variety of other hors d'oeuvres; the nature of exotic condiments; the scores of capons, . . . "all the fancy dishes, all the little extra things. . . . I fixed up special puddings and salads. . . ."

This you also has to serve. This is before dinner, along with the drinks. They is the whiskiest folks you ever saw. *Then* you serve this hot dinner. Imagine anybody putting all this work on one human being.

I know I'm gonna leave. But since she has been so nasty, I'm gonna put her into a real doozy. She got forty people, doctors, teachers, oil mens, that all hadda be big shots. Some of 'em comin' from New York. Mm-hmm this here is real nice.

So I works up until Saturday. All the food is prepared for the Monday cookin' for the Tuesday servin'. That Saturday, I had to wake her up again, that sleep: give me my money. I said to myself: Sister, if you knew what I had on my mind, you wouldn't lay down.

That Sunday, I was supposed to go back at eleven and fix their lunch. I got my money and I didn't see no point to it, because I'm not goin' back there. With all this food stacked up, corn cut off the cob, big tub and half full of that . . .

She did call Sunday the lady next door: Was I sick? I didn't answer. She didn't worry much. She know *I had to be there* on Monday. That Monday, I went visitin'. I'm a week advance on my rent and I got about $6 in my pocket. I'm rich. I was supposed to be on the job at eight o'clock. I didn't get out of bed till nine. I decided I'd lounge around till the last of the week. A good cook is always in demand.

So on Monday she calls the lady where I rented from, where I had servant quarter in the back. You see, when I'm workin' for a family like that, I always rent some place else. Because when you lose your job, you don't lose your house.

So eleven o'clock, I come back from visitin'. This other white lady said, "That woman you work for says you had all the food fixed up out there and she's got forty rich people that is comin' there for dinner Tuesday, and you left and didn't say nothin' about it. Is you sick?"

"No, ma'am, I'm not sick."

"How come you didn't go to work?"

I said, "Didn't I pay you your rent Saturday?"

"Yes, you did."

"When the time comes you don't get your rent, that's the time you says somethin' to me. But when I work, whether I work or don't work is none of your business. That woman been knowin' for six weeks she was gonna have forty people there. She thinks she's gonna make me do all that work for that same $7. Not on your life."

She was to pay you $7 for that day?

Seven bucks a week, honey. So this landlady says, "My, my, my, you should be ashamed of yourself." I said, "I'm not ashamed. I done enough work for that woman. I have to wake her up every time it come time for her to pay me, she go to sleep. If that woman had died, her husband woulda said he didn't owe me. I don't like anybody sleepin' on my money." And I said, "And where would *you* be without Rosalie?" Rosalie used to do all *her* slave work. That shut 'er up.

How did the lawn party go?

I had it all figured out, don't think I haven't thought of every bit of it. I could see them big pot-gut doctors and their wives with all their fancy dresses and all, comin' into her house, and sittin' up there with her eyes full of tears. . . .

If you was stupid enough to let 'em get away with it, they'll give you an extra dollar or two. And she figure on some of these people givin' you a little tip—and that was gonna be your pay. You got your tongue hangin' out. . . .

That was my awakenin'. I felt good. I think all Negroes have this feelin', when they feel secure enough they can hold up their heads like mens and womens. It's like that old sayin': as long as you got your hand in the lion's mouth, you have to be easy till you get it out. Well, I got my hand out. . . .

W. Clement Stone

"The attainment of one goal should be the springboard to another higher and more noble effort." Signed—W. A. Ward. "Optimism is the faith that leads to achievement." Signed—Helen Keller. "Smile, be happy, keep smiling."

There are numerous such inspirational messages in the corridors and elevators of the Combined Insurance Company of America Building. Happy, fox-trotty string music is heard through the halls, a soft background.

Behind a huge desk, sits the ebullient president. He has a pencil-thin mustache ("in those days, movie stars, Ronald Colman, John Gilbert and others did it"); he wears a wide bow tie ("it's an indication of an extrovert, someone with a high energy level, someone who has drive, who gets things done"); he smokes long, thick Cuban cigars ("when we had our Castro troubles, I bought up the equivalent of three warehouses"). He offers me a couple. "When you take the label off, you'll see it's '59." His laugh is unique; it has a five-note rise. He happily concedes these phenomena are carefully planned. It's a matter of image.

He is a celebrated philanthropist and was listed in Fortune *as one of America's new centi-millionaires. His companies employ at least four thousand, with sales representatives in many other countries. Some are welfare states, where he sells "supplementary coverage."*

"I started selling newspapers at the age of six on the South Side of Chicago. I found if I tried to sell at a busy corner, the larger kids would beat me up. So I found out that if I'd go in a restaurant, and even if the owner would push me out a few times, sooner or later I'd sell my pile of papers. Actually, that's what started me on cold canvassing—calling on people unannounced."

MANY OF US learned in the Depression how to turn a disadvantage into an advantage. First of all, we have what is known as PMA, positive mental attitude. It's based on the premise that God is always a good God, that with every adversity there's a seed of greater benefit.

During the Depression, there were tremendous advantages to a sales manager. A man was willing to accept any kind of job. All I needed to do was to take a man out and show him how to make twenty, thirty, forty dollars a day, and I had a salesman. We—I use the editorial we—know how to make supermen out of ordinary men.

Would you mind expanding on this?

Rrrrrright!

(He presents me with several books: Success Through A Positive Mental Attitude, The Success System That Never Fails *and* Think and Grow Rich. *He refers to the last: "That's the greatest book that came out of the Depression. In 1937. By Napoleon Hill. That book motivated more people to success than any book you can buy by a living author.")*

Actually, in the Depression years, many men who were successful in the Twenties became has-beens. They had a negative mental attitude. They were men making $30,000 a year and didn't have the courage to start at the bottom and work up. Others realized opportunities were unlimited, if they were willing to think and willing to pay the price. A person doesn't have to be poor. Anyone in the United States could acquire great wealth today.

I said to myself: Why shouldn't I earn in a day what others earn in a week? Why shouldn't I earn in a week, what others earn in a month? Why shouldn't I earn in a month, what others earn in a year? How can I do it? The answer was simple. Work scientifically.

First of all, I'd always thank God for my blessings. Then I'd use a very simple prayer: Please, God, help me sell. Please, God, help me sell. Please, God, help me sell. Please, God, help me sell. Please, God, help me sell. This did many things, the mystic power of prayer. It got me keyed up. I threw all the energy I had into it. Immediately afterward, I'd unwind and relax.

Do you recall any sad moments during those hard days . . . ?

I don't believe in sadness. I believe if you have a problem, that's good. When I'd have a poor day, I would try to figure out what's wrong with me. Maybe I needed more rest or go see a movie. The next day would be a rrrecoooord day!

515

When the Depression hit, I had over a thousand licensed salesmen in the United States. I soon found out they weren't selling. So I traveled the country and wound up with 235. I trained these men. And we sold more insurance than in the boom days when we had a thousand men.

Here, he discusses the self-motivator: self commands, affirmation. "You say fifty or a hundred times in the morning, fifty or a hundred times at night, for, say, ten days, until it affects the self-conscious mind: 'Success is achieved by those who try.' Or, 'Where there's nothing to lose by trying and a great deal to gain, by all means try.' Or, 'Do it now.' Or, 'Do the right thing because it is right.' "

My man'd go into a place, he might be nervous. So we'd have him talk loudly, talk rapidly, emphasize certain words, hesitate where there's a period or a comma, a smile in his voice, and when he talked for a long time, he'd use modulation. It worked a hundred times out of a hundred.

In the Thirties, I sold accident insurance. Cold canvas. Unannounced, I'd call on banks, stores, offices, during business hours. And sell the manager and get permission to sell in the establishment.

First of all, you'd need a good introduction, so they'll listen. I've used one continuously since, because it works: "I believe this will interest you also." *You* is a very important word. At that point, if I'd hesitate, he might say, "What have you got?" "Well, since you asked me, I'll tell ya." Ordinarily, I wouldn't wait. I just go in about the time the prospect gets a little nervous and wants to get away. I'd release tension by using humor.

If you don't see anything funny about your standard joke, you'd laugh at yourself for telling it. (Laughs in a five-note ascending scale.) Right! I'd say, "If you're hurt—we even pay if your feelings are hurt, how's that?" (Laughs.)

Of course, I used the directional force of the eyes and my fountain pen, so the individual looked at what I'm pointing to. Thus, he concentrates through the sense of sight and the sense of hearing. If you had an objection, it wouldn't occur to you in that short span of time. You have a nervous system, I know how to tap it.

You'd have to have an effective close. If you wanted the person to say yes, you'd ask an affirmative question: "You see what I mean?" Now you just shook your head yes, whether you understood me or not. Why? Because I made it easy for you. If I want a no, it's very easy. Make a negative statement. Now you don't have accident insurance, do you? Be frank. . . .

No, no, I haven't. No.

You see? I made it easy for you to say no. That eliminated a lot of argument. So it was a matter of a one-two-three sale. I made 122 sales in one day in the Depression. Since then, we've had men who've done much better. If I wanted to sell you an accident insurance policy, it would never occur to me that you wouldn't buy. There's no reason why you shouldn't.

(Quickly) So, during the Depression, you'd call on the top man. . . .

The reason I'd call on the head of a company, you find a man who has worked his way up from the bottom is much more generous than one who hasn't. What I really wanted was his permission, and I made it easy for him to give it to me. If he didn't take the policy, I'd say: (enthusiastically) "Well, thanks just the same. I'll see you again next year!" Then, as I would leave, I'd say, "Oh, by the way, would it be all right to see the others? If they're not too busy, I'll show it to them. If they want it, all right. If not, all right." I'd be on my way out and the answer would always be yes. Because it's a reflex action.

I would certainly not be in the sight of the president too frequently. I'd go from department to department. If it were an office, I'd go from desk to desk.

Unannounced?

I wouldn't even tell 'em my name. Every man, every woman, every child needs protection. In a Depression, they need it more than any other time. If a person had enough money for a ton of coal, it was more advantageous for him to have a half a ton of coal and my policy than just a ton of coal without the policy. The system worked.

I was a student of the human mind and would get keyed up. If I wanted to sell you an accident insurance policy, you're sold. Give me one of your liabilities, and I'll turn it into an asset.

It's the Depression, I have three children, my wife is ill, the company is failing, I'm afraid they'll lay me off. . . .

The first thing to do is pray for guidance. Then engage in thinking time. You condition your mind to determine what you want. Figure out

517

the logical way to achieve it. Don't worry about the thousand reasons you shouldn't achieve it. All you need is one good reason why you should. If you had PMA, a positive mental attitude, you'd do more than that for which you are paid, so the firm couldn't afford to let you go. Instead they'd push you up. This is in the Depression, right?

Right. Now you come up to me. You're gonna sell me. I'm really worried, I say to you: "I'd love to buy your insurance, but I'm so frantic, I just can't—"

The response is so simple: "That's exactly why you need it." I'd close in on you. If you didn't have money, that wouldn't bother me. I'd say, "You can go next door and borrow it." And if you wanted it badly enough, you would. Why not?

As a student of the human mind, what you'd do is push the right buttons. If someone would say, "I don't believe in insurance," you'd go along with them: "I'll be truthful with you, I don't think you'll have an accident. If I did, in fairness to my company, I wouldn't sell you a policy." You'd hesitate. Then he'd say, "You can't tell." I'd say, "You're right." And I'd show him the policy and sell 'im.

All this time, with bread lines, apple sellers, people on relief, crisis, you just went along. . . .

Rrrright! Because of mental attitude, the power every human being possesses—the human mind.

In those days, it was very easy to do what others were afraid to do. There might be ten salesmen ahead of me and ten salesmen behind me and it was very interesting. They might be trying to sell insurance. But with my PMA, I sold. Whether they sold or not, I never took the time to find out.

Ray Wax

He is a stockbroker, living in a middle-class suburb, just outside New York City. It is a recent endeavor. Previously, he had been a builder and a real estate broker.

*Though his words come easily, he feels he has little of worth to re-
count. He is restless, a fever possesses him. . . .*

My OLD MAN in 1928 had a million dollars in cash. Between the market,
the races and the numbers racket, he lost everything. Going to the
horses, sitting in a box for almost four years, with the touts who were
supposed to pick the winners for him . . . he went through a million.
In '31, my old man gave me $5: "Here, take care of the house."

It took me twenty years to figure out what happened. I always figured
there was some kind of logic I didn't understand. Maybe it was some
kind of lack in me. 'Cause I was brought up in a middle-class family:
all the privileges, the house with the servant—all of a sudden, one day
it's all gone. Now I had to find out who the hell I was.

Here I am being thrown into some kind of goddam pot and I had to
learn how to live. Really, without Horatio Alger I wouldn't have made it.
I really believed there was room for you in this society, that there was
work, that you could overcome adversity.

One day I started out looking for a job. Within three hours, I found
one as a shipping clerk. $10 a week, of which I gave six home. I became
a good shipping clerk. I worked alone. My world was the four walls of
the shipping room.

I had no illusion about getting an education. I didn't have the drive,
didn't know what I wanted to be. I began to feel I was peripheral. I
didn't fit into a world where people spent four years in a institution and
came out with a guaranteed job or point of view. Or became a doctor or
dentist.

I used to ride the New York subways and look at the chalk board at
employment agencies. In the street, there'd be hundreds of men looking
at these boards. I did chance jobs.

One day on the subway, I picked up a paper and it said: "Experienced Florist Wanted." The date on the paper was the day before, but I
figured the hell with it, I'll try.

I showed up at Everybody's Florist, that's what it was called. I saw a
gang of men in front of Everybody's Florist and I said, "Are they hiring
anybody?" And a guy said, "No, they hired everybody yesterday." Another guy said, "Look kid, they don't know who the hell they hired. Just
get in the crowd." So I got in the crowd. As we moved through the door,
he said, "What's your name?" I said, "Ray." He said, "We didn't hire
you." And I said, "Yes, you did hire me." He said, "You're full of shit."

I said, "So help me God, you really did hire me." He said, "All right," and he gave me a batch of flowers.

Roses and carnations, three cents for this and five cents for that. These guys were buying the glut of the New York flower market. They had the concession to put men out on any station of the IRT system, for which they gave a cut to the IRT. This is the way I became a flower vendor.

In the early Thirties, guys made a living by buying a batch of flowers and working for themselves. The IRT bull would come along and chase them. But if they worked for Everybody's Florist, they had a set spot. These guys would say: Look, you poor bastards, don't go hustling for yourself. Come in with us and you'll be able to make a living.

Here I am selling flowers, and they don't look bad. You can put up a little sign: Thirty-five cents for a dozen roses, fifty cents for a dozen carnations. The only place you can set up is where the turnstiles are. You try to find yourself a little living room and you're up against the wall, up against the tile. All these people, hundreds and thousands pouring out of the subway, and there I am looking like some sort of sick dog making a chance sale.

I think the first day maybe I sold $8. My pay working for Everybody's Florist was $2 a day. Later when I became top drawer, my top pay was like $3.

How'd you get to be top drawer?

I grew up on Horatio Alger. I remember reading every Horatio Alger. I was really bit in the ass. I really believed that if you ran out and stopped the horses, you married the boss's daughter. So help me God. And if you get a fucking job and worked harder than anybody else and they saw the gleam in your eye, they somehow recognized that you had it. There were all these other guys struggling behind you, but somehow you were sitting at the desk and you were calling the orders. It was only right. It was the way the world was made, it was the way it was supposed to happen.

The next day I brought 'em back the money I got, the $8. And the guy said, "You fucking little bum, is this all the money you brought? Look, you little bastard, you gotta do better."

At first, with the roar of the train, up against the wall, with your box on the floor, they wouldn't see you. So I put up a stand: a board with the stuff at eye level, at a height where every one could see it. And I found out that if I began to open my mouth and hollered a little, I did better. "Here y'are, getcha roses here!" I'll always remember the peonies: "Get your peeeooonies here!"

It used to get so cold down there. I used to wear two pairs of pants. No relief. If you had to pee . . . I used to time the trains so I could get into the fuckin' pissoir and unbutton two flies so I could pee before the next train came in. It was a joke trying to get through two pair of pants to get to your pecker and pee and get back out in time for the next train.

In the worst hour of the Depression, if you were aggressive, if you wanted to scrounge, if you believed in Horatio Alger, you could survive. If you were on your own, you could stumble through, wearing a monkey suit or finding an off-beat job. For me, people that worked all day and went home to their families, they were fags. They were the ones who could come up behind me when I was working and put their hand on my ass. Respectable men going home to their wives and children: Drive you back? Won't you let me come back later and drive you back? I wanted to sell the son of a bitch flowers, so I wouldn't put him down completely.

Every day I took back more money and took out more flowers. By the time I came in after the third or fourth day, they were kinda glad to see me. I worked for Everybody's Florist for twenty-three days without a break. In the course of those twenty-three days, something happened to me.

Wherever I worked, I made more money than anybody else. In my ignorance, I thought I was a better hustler than anybody else. The reason I made more money than any of the other guys was that they stole. I used to work and bring them all the money, for a lousy $2 a day. But these other guys, the hustlers, were making a lot of money and every day, depending on what their gross take was, stole a proportionate amount of money. They didn't steal it. Clipping, they called it. They clipped a few bucks.

After I worked there ten, twelve days, I said to the three thugs who ran Everybody's Florist: I want to tell you how to run this business. I began to tell them their checkout stinks, half their flowers come back, they don't know what the hell they're buying. Right out of Horatio Alger. I'm twenty years old and they're listening. O.K., but there's one thing wrong. The transom's open.

I walk out the door, two guys grab me by the throat. They put me up against the wall and they say, "Listen, you little son of a bitch, when you work here, you work like everyone else. If you're gonna work here and sell flowers, you're gonna steal. And then you'll make a living." From then on, I never make less than $75, $100 a week and a hundred and a quarter. I became one of their top men.

I could clip ten, fourteen, twenty dollars on a good day. I'd have to hustle $100, $150 in flowers. And that was a lot of hustling 'cause they were selling roses at three cents apiece and 'mums at, big deal, five cents apiece. To live in that atmosphere, you had to play their game. Eventually, I became one of the boys.

When you'd come in at ten o'clock or whatever, Tommy or Harry would say, "You little bastard, how did you do today?" I'd say, "Gee, Harry, I had a good day. I did $40." "That stinks," he'd say. Then, "Have a drink." And toss a bottle of booze over to you. I hadn't eaten all day and that goddam subway, between trains I'd run up and grab a sandwich and be right down. Now they push the bottle in your face and you take a slug because you got to prove you're one of the boys.

And they'd say, "You wanna get laid? We got a hooker downstairs. Three ways for a half a dollar." I'd walk down the goddam stairs and sure enough there'd be a black broad on the table and some guy banging away at her and her hollering and moaning and slightly drunk. . . . What are you gonna do? This is the world I lived in. At least twice a week, there'd be a broad in the basement. There'd be booze on the table. Somehow you had to survive. I never went down in the basement.

Under the Brooklyn Bridge, you'd find the guy with a pink cat sittin' on top of a fire hydrant. He's the pimp. He'll say, "Wait a minute. There's another guy that wants to go up. I'll take you both up." You go through a locked door and you'd be trooping up and through another locked door and you'd come out into a kitchen. You'd come into an apartment which was made up of a hot stove—heating douche water—and a round wooden table, where there'd be an old Italian man, sitting there, looking down. . . . This was a Luciano house, a syndicate house. I guess the cops got paid off.

Myself, when I would come in I'd look down, sit down, not look at the other men. And you didn't know what would come out. There would be two girls, a little beat around the edges. If you went in a room, you made it quick with the girl. It was the best thing you could do for the girls. She'd say, "Honey, you were great, don't worry about it. You'll be around when these old bastards won't be able to get it up." The girl was good for forty, fifty men a day. I came back to the house often. This was a dollar house in the Thirties.

I've been to a few houses later in life, in Europe, but I've never gone through a locked door or up some stairs without me being back in Sand Street . . . following Louie up the stairs with my heart beating, to break into a room with a couple of old men sitting around a wooden table, looking down.

The whorehouses on Sand Street were the only thing that saved my sanity. I had no relationship to the rest of the world.

I lived in a world completely alone. The only thing that sustained me during that period: I continued to read, I continued to hustle. I had a vague sense of myself. Every guy had a gun or a knife except me. I carried a book, so they called me the professor. But finally I began to forget English. Everything reduced to four-letter words.

Also the money I made was slowly being eaten up by my family. I used to keep the cash I stole in *The History of the Jews in Poland*. I used to come home and find a note from my old man: Dear boy, took twenty. Signed, Pop. At the end of that year, I had $150 for all my effort. I left them a note saying I was going to Baltimore for a week. I never came back. I felt I had paid my debt in the subways.

His Baltimore experiences involved "Textile U," a huge shipping room, where the employer urged long working hours on the promise of his "finding a place in the firm," where colleagues put him wise to the way of things; setting up lending libraries in drugstores. . . . "I liked handling books," meeting radicals, intellectuals, students at Johns Hopkins. . . . It was the time of the Oxford Pledge and the movement against Fascism; his temptation to go to Spain as a member of the Lincoln Brigade. . . . "I was an ideal recruit, alone, on the run, searching for something"; a serious affair with a schoolteacher, running away. . . . "This is part of the Depression. You lived in a fear of responsibility for another person. You backed off when someone got close."

New Orleans, Corpus Christi, Houston, Port Isabel, down the Gulf to Mexico. "The Richard Halliburton dream, I had that one, too. There was a great world of adventure. If you believe in Horatio Alger and Richard Halliburton, you believe something will work out."

The Depression ended for me about '37. There seemed to be more work available. You weren't feeling guilty if you drove through the streets with a car. I moved into the middle classes, a little unhappy. . . .

Where I lived in this suburb, there's so much hostility. They feel the welfare people are getting a ride on their back, playing a game. During the Depression, you felt they had a right. . . . Oh, they were crazy for Roosevelt, my neighbors. They'll even tell you why. He was a good man to them because he saved the economy.

The young people growing up in that hour, they were not afraid of the society, they weren't threatened by it. They had great hope. They felt somehow they would overcome it. Today the young people are in rebellion, but they're frustrated. They haven't the illusions we had. . . .

I was born out of the Depression. I gave up my illusions. No more Horatio Alger. I had a few bad hours, a few bad years. But I found excitement. It was an awakening.

Epilogue

Reed

THE RAFT

He is from an upper middle-class suburb of Chicago, attends college and has worked during the summer months. He is nineteen.

CHESTER AND I planned to go down the Mississippi on a raft. Prompted, of course, by Mark Twain. We'd build ourselves a raft, start at Joliet and go down to New Orleans. My father thought I was joking. He said I couldn't go. I called Chester and told him to come over.

As the conversation started, it was good-humored. When my father saw we were serious, tears began to well up in his eyes, and he got a lump in his throat.

He started saying he had dreams when he was young, wanted to do the same sort of things. He was young during the Depression. To put himself through school at Amherst—and all the time very emotional about it—he'd gone with no money and had little to eat. That he and my mother had to scrimp during the early years of their marriage. I had an opportunity which he never had.

What struck me as rather strange was his saying: if I saved some money this year, maybe next summer I could go to Europe. Which is something, he said, he'd always wanted to do. While he was talking about the Depression, he was almost on the verge of crying.

Why would he agree to a European trip and not to the other one?

I think the Mississippi trip was just not his idea of fun. He saw it as a hardship. It might just be that he'd like to tell his friends that his son is off to Europe. He wouldn't want to tell his friends that his son is on the Mississippi River on a raft.

How often has he brought up this subject—the Depression?

Oh, very rarely. It was a surprising thing. And never before in such terms, never as emotionally. He said, "Why, now, Reed!" As if I'd done something very wrong. Very seldom have I been addressed in that tone of voice, as if I had committed some serious insult to him.

CHESTER: *What struck me was his talking about dreams. Dreams was his word. We didn't talk about this as our dream. "You boys have dreams. I had dreams, my wife and I have dreams we haven't accomplished." Our Mississippi thing didn't strike him as the right kind of dream to have somehow.*

I've noticed recently they've been concerned with status more than I thought they were before. He would like to send himself to Europe. I don't know what to make of it all. It was a side of my father which I'd never seen before. Something we touched off, innocently enough, which just got out of control. I was amazed and a little embarrassed. He reacted as though I was making some decision in my life which was contrary to everything he ever wanted for me. It was just a trip down the Mississippi.

He said: Too often you look at our generation and say we did nothing. We did an awful lot of things.

CHESTER: *We didn't start talking about the Depression. We were talking about a raft. He started talking about the Depression.*

He kept on saying: You people don't seem to realize what we did. You seem to disregard the American tradition. We countered by saying that, of course, this raft trip was exactly in the American tradition. More so than going to Europe, I think. He said: Although America is messed up, it's better than we found it, and I don't want you to forget this. Too often you look upon our generation and say we did nothing. We did an awful lot of things.

(Musing.) It wasn't as if it was a memory, but an open wound. He talked about the Depression as if it had just happened yesterday. We touched a nerve.

You know, his ship's come in. He doesn't want to see our raft go out.

Virginia Durr

A TOUCH OF RUE

Wetumpka, Alabama. It is an old family house on the outskirts of Montgomery. A creek runs by. . . . She and her husband, Clifford, are of an old Alabamian lineage. During Franklin Roosevelt's Administration, he was a member of the Federal Communications Commission. She had been a pioneer in the battle to abolish the poll tax.

OH, NO, the Depression was not a romantic time. It was a time of terrible suffering. The contradictions were so obvious that it didn't take a very bright person to realize something was terribly wrong.

Have you ever seen a child with rickets? Shaking as with palsy. No proteins, no milk. And the companies pouring milk into gutters. People with nothing to wear, and they were plowing up cotton. People with nothing to eat, and they killed the pigs. If that wasn't the craziest system in the world, could you imagine anything more idiotic? This was just insane.

And people blamed themselves, not the system. They felt they had been at fault: . . . "if we hadn't bought that old radio" . . . "if we hadn't bought that old secondhand car." Among the things that horrified me were the preachers—the fundamentalists. They would tell the people they suffered because of their sins. And the people believed it. God was punishing them. Their children were starving because of their sins.

527

People who were independent, who thought they were masters and mistresses of their lives, were all of a sudden dependent on others. Relatives or relief. People of pride went into shock and sanitoriums. My mother was one.

Up to this time, I had been a conformist, a Southern snob. I actually thought the only people who amounted to anything were the very small group which I belonged to. The fact that my family wasn't as well off as those of the girls I went with—I was vice president of the Junior League —made me value even more the idea of being well-born. . . .

What I learned during the Depression changed all that. I saw a blinding light like Saul on the road to Damascus. (Laughs.) It was the first time I had seen the other side of the tracks. The rickets, the pellagra—it shook me up. I saw the world as it really was.

She shamed, cajoled and persuaded the dairy company into opening milk dispensaries. When they sought to back down, she convinced them that "if these people got a taste of milk, they might get in the habit of buying it—when they got jobs."

When the steel companies closed down in Birmingham, thousands were thrown out of work. She was acquainted with some of the executives; she argued with them: "You feed the mules who work in your mines. Why don't you feed the people? You're responsible."

The young today are just play-acting in courting poverty. It's all right to wear jeans and eat hamburgers. But it's entirely different from not having any hamburgers to eat and no jeans to wear. A great many of these kids—white kids—seem to have somebody in the background they can always go to. I admire their spirit, because they have a strong sense of social justice. But they themselves have not been deprived. They haven't experienced the terror. They have never seen a baby in the cradle crying of hunger. . . .

I think the reason for the gap between the black militants and the young white radicals is that the black kids are much more conscious of the thin edge of poverty. And how soon you can be reduced to living on relief. What you *know* and what you *feel* are very different. Terror is something you *feel*. When there is no paycheck coming in—the absolute, stark terror.

What frightens me is that these kids are like sheep being led to slaughter. They are romantic and they are young. I have a great deal more faith in movements that start from necessity—people trying to change things because of their own deprivation. We felt that in the labor surge of the Thirties. The people who worked hardest to organize were the ones in the shops and in the mills.

The Depression affected people in two different ways. The great majority reacted by thinking money is the most important thing in the world. Get yours. And get it for your children. Nothing else matters. Not having that stark terror come at you again. . . .

And there was a small number of people who felt the whole system was lousy. You have to change it. The kids come along and they want to change it, too. But they don't seem to know what to put in its place. I'm not so sure I know, either. I do think it has to be responsive to people's needs. And it has to be done by democratic means, if possible. Whether it's possible or not—the power of money is such today, I just don't know. Some of the kids call me a relic of the Thirties. Well, I am.

THE END
